Colonels in Blue—U.S. Colored
Troops, U.S. Armed Forces,
Staff Officers and Special Units

ALSO BY ROGER D. HUNT AND FROM MCFARLAND

*Colonels in Blue—Missouri and the Western States and Territories:
A Civil War Biographical Dictionary* (2019)

*Colonels in Blue—Illinois, Iowa, Minnesota and Wisconsin:
A Civil War Biographical Dictionary* (2017)

*Colonels in Blue—Indiana, Kentucky and Tennessee:
A Civil War Biographical Dictionary* (2014)

*Colonels in Blue—Michigan, Ohio and West Virginia:
A Civil War Biographical Dictionary* (2011)

Colonels in Blue—U.S. Colored Troops, U.S. Armed Forces, Staff Officers and Special Units

A Civil War Biographical Dictionary

ROGER D. HUNT

McFarland & Company, Inc., Publishers
Jefferson, North Carolina

LIBRARY OF CONGRESS CATALOGUING-IN-PUBLICATION DATA

Names: Hunt, Roger D., author.
Title: Colonels in blue. U.S. colored troops, U.S. armed forces, staff officers and special units / Roger D. Hunt.
Description: Jefferson, North Carolina : McFarland & Company, Inc., Publishers, 2022 | "A Civil War biographical dictionary." | Includes bibliographical references and index.
Identifiers: LCCN 2022023404 | ISBN 9781476686196 (paperback : acid free paper) ♾
ISBN 9781476644622 (ebook)
Subjects: LCSH: United States—History—Civil War, 1861-1865—Biography—Dictionaries. | United States—Armed Forces—Officers—Biography—Dictionaries. | United States—History—Civil War, 1861-1865—Registers—Dictionaries. | BISAC: HISTORY / Military / United States | BIOGRAPHY & AUTOBIOGRAPHY / Reference
Classification: LCC E467 .H896 2022 | DDC 973.7/41—dc23/eng/20220517
LC record available at https://lccn.loc.gov/2022023404

BRITISH LIBRARY CATALOGUING DATA ARE AVAILABLE

ISBN (print) 978-1-4766-8619-6
ISBN (ebook) 978-1-4766-4462-2

© 2022 Roger D. Hunt. All rights reserved

No part of this book may be reproduced or transmitted in any form or by any means, electronic or mechanical, including photocopying or recording, or by any information storage and retrieval system, without permission in writing from the publisher.

On the cover: *left to right* William Emery Merrill (Henry Ulke, 278 Pennsylvania Avenue, Washington, DC; author's photograph); Nathan W. Daniels (author's photograph); Charles Rivers Ellet (author's photograph)

Printed in the United States of America

McFarland & Company, Inc., Publishers
Box 611, Jefferson, North Carolina 28640
www.mcfarlandpub.com

In Memory of Henry Deeks
Civil War Photo Historian and Mentor
(1946–2019)

Henry Deeks

Table of Contents

Acknowledgments	ix
Introduction	1
U.S. Colored Troops	3
Regiments	3
Biographies	11
U.S. Armed Forces	123
Regiments	123
Biographies	127
U.S. Marine Corps	150
Biographies	150
U.S. Sharpshooters	154
Regiments	154
Biographies	154
U.S. Veteran Volunteers	157
Regiments	157
Biographies	158
U.S. Volunteers	168
Regiments	168
Biographies	168
Veteran Reserve Corps	171
Regiments	171
Biographies	172
Aides-de-Camp	180
Biographies	180
Quartermasters	213
Biographies	213

Commissaries of Subsistence 241
    Biographies 241
Miscellaneous Organizations 248
    Biographies 249

Bibliography 283
Index 305

Acknowledgments

Although I appreciate the contributions of all of the individuals in the following list, I want to mention a few individuals whose contributions to this volume have been especially noteworthy. Everitt Bowles, Rick Carlile, the late Henry Deeks, Craig Johnson, Steve Meadow, Jim Quinlan (The Excelsior Brigade), and Larry Strayer have always been helpful in providing elusive photographs and valuable information. Ron Coddington has always been especially active in supporting my efforts. Roberta Fairburn and Jan Perone have been especially helpful in supporting my research activities at the Abraham Lincoln Presidential Library. Randy Hackenburg, the late Dr. Richard Sommers and the late Michael J. Winey have provided ready access to the unparalleled photo archives of the U.S. Army Military History Institute during the past 40 years. Alan Aimone has been equally hospitable in providing access to the outstanding collections at the U.S. Military Academy Library.

Jill M. Abraham, National Archives, Washington, D.C.
Alan C. Aimone, U.S. Military Academy Library, West Point, NY
Michael Albanese, Kendall, NY
Terese Austin, William L. Clements Library, Ann Arbor, MI
Gil Barrett, New Bern, NC
Richard A. Baumgartner, Huntington, WV
Randy Beck, St. Charles, MO
Bruce P. Bonfield, Naples, FL
Jaime Ellyn Bourassa, Missouri Historical Society, St. Louis, MO
Everitt Bowles, Woodstock, GA
Mike Brackin, Winterville, NC
Timothy R. Brookes, East Liverpool, OH
Rick Brown, Leesburg, VA
Paul J. Brzozowski, Fairfield, CT
Tom Buffenbarger, U.S. Army Heritage & Education Center, Carlisle, PA
David L. Callihan, Harrisburg, PA
Richard F. Carlile, Dayton, OH
Allen Cebula, Mooresville, IN
Ronald S. Coddington, Arlington, VA
Sherrie Colbert, Iowa Gold Star Military Museum, Johnston, IA
Henry Deeks, Ashburnham, MA
Dennis Edelin, National Archives, Washington, D.C.
Elizabeth E. Engel, State Historical Society of Missouri, Columbia, MO
Jerry Everts, Lambertville, MI
Roberta Fairburn, Abraham Lincoln Presidential Library, Springfield, IL
Anne Healy Field, Washington, D.C.
Perry M. Frohne, Oshkosh, WI
Sarah Galligan, New Hampshire Historical Society, Concord, NH
William A. Gladstone, West Palm Beach, FL
Lauren Gray, Kansas State Historical Society, Topeka, KS
Jay A. Graybeal, U.S. Army Heritage & Education Center, Carlisle, PA
John P. Gurnish, Mogadore, OH
Randy Hackenburg, Boiling Springs, PA
Michael Hammerson, London, England
Thomas Harris, New York, NY
Heidi Heller, Minnesota Historical Society, St. Paul, MN
Ann Ruyle Hoffstetter, Staunton, IL
Michael A. Hogle, Okemos, MI

Acknowledgments

Lisa Horsley, Abraham Lincoln Presidential Library, Springfield, IL
Russell P. Horton, Wisconsin Veterans Museum, Madison, WI
Craig T. Johnson, New Freedom, PA
Wayne Jorgenson, Eden Prairie, MN
Alan Jutzi, The Huntington Library, San Marino, CA
Dennis M. Keesee, Westerville, OH
Frank D. Korun, Ijamsville, MD
Michael Kraus, Pittsburgh, PA
John W. Kuhl, Pittstown, NJ
Mary Beth Linné, National Archives, Washington, D.C.
Louise LoBello, Franklin & Marshall College, Lancaster, PA
Robert F. MacAvoy, Clark, NJ
Vann R. Martin, Kingston, TN
Julie Mayle, Rutherford B. Hayes Presidential Library, Fremont, OH
Michael J. McAfee, Newburgh, NY
Cliff McCarthy, Stone House Museum, Belchertown, MA
Edward McGuire, New York State Library, Albany, NY
Marcus S. McLemore, Poland, OH
Sarah T. McNeive, Topeka, KS
Steven J. Meadow, Midland, MI
Mike Medhurst, Oak Brook, IL
Tom Molocea, North Lima, OH
Jim Mundie, Kenner, LA
Michael Musick, Harpers Ferry, WV
Olaf, Berkeley, CA
Ronn Palm, Kittanning, PA
Gloria and Jon Payne, Harpers Ferry, IA
Jan Perone, Abraham Lincoln Presidential Library, Springfield, IL
Nicholas P. Picerno, Bridgewater, VA
Becki Plunkett, State Historical Society of Iowa, Des Moines, IA
Brad and Donna Pruden, Marietta, GA
Jim Quinlan, Alexandria, VA
David L. Richards, Gettysburg, PA
Jeffrey I. Richman, Brooklyn, NY
Jim Rivest, Sun Prairie, WI
Stephen B. Rogers, Ithaca, NY
Paul Russinoff, Baltimore, MD
Steve Saathoff, Franklin Grove, IL
Tom Schmidt, Sharlot Hall Museum, Prescott, AZ
Alan J. Sessarego, Gettysburg, PA
John Sickles, Merrillville, IN
Elena Smith, California State Library, Sacramento, CA
Dr. Richard J. Sommers, Carlisle, PA
Marc and Beth Storch, DeForest, WI
Larry M. Strayer, Urbana, OH
Karl E. Sundstrom, North Riverside, IL
David W. Taylor, Sylvania, OH
Ann Toplovich, Tennessee Historical Society, Nashville, TN
Ken C. Turner, Ellwood City, PA
Michael W. Waskul, Ypsilanti, MI
Michael J. Winey, Mechanicsburg, PA
Richard A. Wolfe, Bridgeport, WV
Robert J. Younger, Dayton, OH
Buck Zaidel, Cromwell, CT
Ray Zielin, Orland Park, IL
Dave Zullo, Lake Monticello, VA

I am also indebted to the staffs of the following libraries for their capable assistance:

Abraham Lincoln Presidential Library & Museum, Springfield, IL
California State Library, Sacramento, CA
Chicago History Museum, Chicago, IL
Civil War Library & Museum, Philadelphia, PA
Colorado Historical Society, Denver, CO
Connecticut State Library, Hartford, CT
Family History Library, Salt Lake City, UT
Franklin & Marshall College, Lancaster, PA
The Huntington Library, San Marino, CA
Indiana Historical Society, Indianapolis, IN
Indiana State Library, Indianapolis, IN
Iowa Gold Star Military Museum, Johnston, IA
Kansas State Historical Society, Topeka, KS
Library of Congress, Washington, D.C.
Milwaukee Public Library, Milwaukee, WI
Minnesota Historical Society, St. Paul, MN
Missouri Historical Society, St. Louis, MO
National Archives, Washington, D.C.
National Society Daughters of the American Revolution, Washington, D.C.
New England Historic Genealogical Society, Boston, MA
New Hampshire Historical Society, Concord, NH

Acknowledgments

New York Genealogical and Biographical Society, New York, NY
The New-York Historical Society, New York, NY
New York State Library, Albany, NY
Oakland Public Library, Oakland, CA
Ohio Genealogical Society, Mansfield, OH
Ohio Historical Society, Columbus, OH
Oregon Historical Society, Portland, OR
Rutherford B. Hayes Presidential Center, Fremont, OH
San Diego Public Library, San Diego, CA
Schaffer Library, Union College, Schenectady, NY
Sharlot Hall Museum, Prescott, AZ
Spokane Public Library, Spokane, WA
State Historical Society of Iowa, Des Moines, IA
State Historical Society of Iowa, Iowa City, IA
State Historical Society of Missouri, Columbia, MO
Stone House Museum, Belchertown, MA
Tacoma Public Library, Tacoma, WA
Tennessee Historical Society, Nashville, TN
Tennessee State Library and Archives, Nashville, TN
U.S. Army Heritage & Education Center, Carlisle, PA
U.S. Military Academy Library, West Point, NY
Washington State Historical Society, Tacoma, WA
Western Reserve Historical Society, Cleveland, OH
William L. Clements Library, University of Michigan, Ann Arbor, MI
Wisconsin Historical Society, Madison, WI
Wisconsin Veterans Museum, Madison, WI

Introduction

At the beginning of the Civil War the Regular Army of the United States numbered only 1,098 officers and 15,304 enlisted men. Faced with this shortage of manpower in suppressing the escalating rebellion, President Abraham Lincoln issued a call for 75,000 militia for three months' service on April 15, 1861, and then a call for 500,000 volunteers for three years of service on July 22, 1861. These calls for troops and others issued later in the war specified that the various state governors would appoint the commanding officers of the regiments raised in their states.

Patriotic fervor throughout the Northern states resulted in spirited competition to complete the organization of regiments to meet the state quotas. In most cases the prospective commanders of these regiments were prominent citizens whose military background (if any) consisted of service in a local militia organization. In general the early war Union army colonels were known more for their patriotic enthusiasm than for their military competence. Many of them were more successful in convincing their fellow townsmen to enlist than they were in actually leading them into battle. Fortunately for the Union cause, the colonels who stayed in the service eventually acquired the necessary military skills or were replaced by subordinates who proved their capabilities on the field of battle.

This book is the eighth in a series of books containing photographs and biographical sketches of that diverse group of motivated citizens who attained the rank of colonel in the Union army, but failed to win promotion to brigadier general or brevet brigadier general. This volume presents the colonels of the U.S. Colored Troops, the U.S. Armed Forces, and also Special Military Units, such as the U.S. Veteran Volunteers, the U.S. Volunteers, the Veteran Reserve Corps and miscellaneous organizations. Also included are the Union Army Staff Officers who attained the rank of colonel. Preceding the photographs and biographical sketches for each category is a breakdown of all the colonels in that category, with the name of each colonel being followed by the dates of his service. Included in this breakdown are the colonels who were promoted beyond the rank of colonel, with their final rank shown. Those indicated as attaining the rank of brigadier general are covered in the book *Generals in Blue*, by Ezra J. Warner, while those attaining the rank of brevet brigadier general are covered in the book *Brevet Brigadier Generals in Blue*, by Roger D. Hunt and Jack R. Brown.

Some explanatory notes are necessary concerning the content of the biographical sketches:

  1. The date associated with each rank may be the date when the colonel was commissioned or appointed or the date when he was mustered at that rank.

Introduction

Generally, the date of muster was used whenever available. The reader should be aware that these dates were often adjusted or corrected by the War Department during and after the war, so that any hope of providing totally consistent dates is virtually impossible.

2. When the word "Colonel" is italicized, this indicates that the colonel was commissioned as colonel but never mustered as such.

3. The following abbreviations are used in the text:

AAG	Assistant Adjutant General
ACM	Assistant Commissary of Musters
ACP	Appointment, Commission, and Personal
ADC	Aide-de-Camp
AGO	Adjutant General's Office
AIG	Assistant Inspector General
aka	also known as
AQM	Assistant Quartermaster
BG	Brigadier General
Brig.	Brigadier
Bvt.	Brevet
Capt.	Captain
CB	Commission Branch
Co.	County or Company
Col.	Colonel
CSA	Confederate States Army
DOW	Died of Wounds
EMM	Enrolled Missouri Militia
GAR	Grand Army of the Republic
Gen.	General
GSW	Gun Shot Wound
KIA	Killed in Action
Lt.	Lieutenant
MOLLUS	Military Order of the Loyal Legion of the United States
NHDVS	National Home for Disabled Volunteer Soldiers
RQM	Regimental Quartermaster
Twp.	Township
U.S.	United States
USA	United States Army
USAHEC	United States Army Heritage & Education Center
USCT	United States Colored Troops
USMA	United States Military Academy
USMC	United States Marine Corps
USV	United States Volunteers
Vol.	Volume
VRC	Veteran Reserve Corps
VS	Volunteer Service

U.S. Colored Troops

Regiments

1st Cavalry
Jeptha Garrard   Dec. 7, 1863   Resigned April 25, 1865,
                                                Bvt. Brig. Gen., USV

2nd Cavalry
George W. Cole   Dec. 10, 1863   Mustered out Feb. 12, 1866,
                                                Bvt. Brig. Gen., USV

3rd Cavalry
Embury D. Osband   Oct. 10, 1863   Resigned June 24, 1865,
                                                Bvt. Brig. Gen., USV

4th Cavalry
James Grant Wilson   Sept. 14, 1863   Resigned June 16, 1865,
                                                Bvt. Brig. Gen., USV

5th Cavalry
James S. Brisbin   March 1, 1864   Promoted Brig. Gen., USV,
                                                May 1, 1865

Louis H. Carpenter   Nov. 2, 1865   Mustered out March 16, 1866
6th Cavalry
James F. Wade   Sept. 19, 1864   Mustered out April 15, 1866,
                                                Bvt. Brig. Gen., USV

1st Heavy Artillery
John A. Shannon   Nov. 4, 1864   Resigned May 13, 1865
John E. McGowan   Sept. 5, 1865   Mustered out March 31, 1866,
                                                Bvt. Brig. Gen., USV

3rd Heavy Artillery (originally 1st TN Heavy Artillery of African Descent)
Ignatz G. Kappner   Sept. 4, 1863   Mustered out April 30, 1866
4th Heavy Artillery (originally 2nd TN Heavy Artillery of African Descent)
Charles H. Adams   May 27, 1863   Revoked Jan. 26, 1864
James N. McArthur   May 8, 1864   Resigned Dec. 2, 1865
5th Heavy Artillery (originally 1st MS Heavy Artillery of African Descent)
Herman Lieb   Aug. 7, 1863   Mustered out May 20, 1866,
                                                Bvt. Brig. Gen., USV

6th Heavy Artillery (originally 2nd MS Heavy Artillery of African Descent)
Bernard G. Farrar   Jan. 21, 1864   Resigned May 8, 1865,
                                                Bvt. Brig. Gen., USV

Hubert A. McCaleb   Sept. 26, 1865   Mustered out May 13, 1866
7th Heavy Artillery (designation of regiment changed to 11th Infantry, Jan. 23, 1865)
William D. Turner   April 22, 1864   Mustered out Jan. 12, 1866
8th Heavy Artillery
Henry W. Barry   April 28, 1864   Mustered out Feb. 10, 1866,
                                                Bvt. Brig. Gen., USV

9th Heavy Artillery (regiment failed to complete organization)

10th Heavy Artillery (originally 1st Heavy Artillery, Corps d'Afrique)
Charles A. Hartwell　　　　　Oct. 1, 1865　　　　　Mustered out Feb. 22, 1867,
　　　　　　　　　　　　　　　　　　　　　　　　　　　Bvt. Brig. Gen., USV

11th Heavy Artillery (originally 14th RI Heavy Artillery)
Jay Hale Sypher　　　　　　　Aug. 11, 1864　　　　Mustered out Oct. 2, 1865,
　　　　　　　　　　　　　　　　　　　　　　　　　　　Bvt. Brig. Gen., USV

12th Heavy Artillery
Norman S. Andrews　　　　　July 25, 1864　　　　　Mustered out April 24, 1866

13th Heavy Artillery
John D. Abry　　　　　　　　July 22, 1864　　　　　Revoked Oct. 7, 1864
Jacob T. Foster　　　　　　　June 23, 1865　　　　　Mustered out Nov. 18, 1865

14th Heavy Artillery (regiment not entitled to a colonel since it never attained full strength)

1st Infantry
John H. Holman　　　　　　May 22, 1863　　　　　Mustered out Sept. 29, 1865,
　　　　　　　　　　　　　　　　　　　　　　　　　　　Bvt. Brig. Gen., USV

2nd Infantry
Stark Fellows　　　　　　　　Feb. 16, 1864　　　　　Died May 23, 1864
Benjamin R. Townsend　　　July 20, 1864　　　　　Mustered out Jan. 5, 1866

3rd Infantry
Benjamin C. Tilghman　　　July 28, 1863　　　　　Resigned May 16, 1865,
　　　　　　　　　　　　　　　　　　　　　　　　　　　Bvt. Brig. Gen., USV
Frederick W. Bardwell　　　Sept. 9, 1865　　　　　Mustered out Oct. 31, 1865

4th Infantry
Samuel A. Duncan　　　　　Sept. 16, 1863　　　　　Mustered out May 4, 1866,
　　　　　　　　　　　　　　　　　　　　　　　　　　　Bvt. Brig. Gen., USV

5th Infantry
Lewis McCoy　　　　　　　　Oct. 27, 1863　　　　　Declined
James W. Conine　　　　　　Nov. 20, 1863　　　　　Discharged Sept. 13, 1864
Giles W. Shurtleff　　　　　　Sept. 29, 1864　　　　Resigned June 12, 1865,
　　　　　　　　　　　　　　　　　　　　　　　　　　　Bvt. Brig. Gen., USV
John B. Cook　　　　　　　　Sept. 26, 1865　　　　Mustered out Oct. 8, 1865

6th Infantry
John W. Ames　　　　　　　Sept. 28, 1863　　　　　Mustered out Sept. 20, 1865,
　　　　　　　　　　　　　　　　　　　　　　　　　　　Bvt. Brig. Gen., USV

7th Infantry
James Shaw, Jr.　　　　　　　Nov. 18, 1863　　　　　Mustered out Oct. 13, 1866,
　　　　　　　　　　　　　　　　　　　　　　　　　　　Bvt. Brig. Gen., USV

8th Infantry
Charles W. Fribley　　　　　Nov. 24, 1863　　　　　KIA Feb. 20, 1864
Samuel C. Armstrong　　　　Nov. 3, 1864　　　　　Mustered out Nov. 10, 1865,
　　　　　　　　　　　　　　　　　　　　　　　　　　　Bvt. Brig. Gen., USV

9th Infantry
Thomas Bayley　　　　　　　Dec. 28, 1863　　　　　Mustered out Jan. 4, 1867

10th Infantry
John A. Nelson　　　　　　　Oct. 6, 1863　　　　　　Discharged March 15, 1864
Elias Wright　　　　　　　　Aug. 15, 1864　　　　　Resigned June 17, 1865,
　　　　　　　　　　　　　　　　　　　　　　　　　　　Bvt. Brig. Gen., USV

11th Infantry (designation of regiment changed from 7th Heavy Artillery, Jan. 23, 1865)
William D. Turner　　　　　April 22, 1864　　　　　Mustered out Jan. 12, 1866

12th Infantry
Charles R. Thompson　　　　Aug. 17, 1863　　　　　Mustered out Jan. 16, 1866,
　　　　　　　　　　　　　　　　　　　　　　　　　　　Bvt. Brig. Gen., USV

13th Infantry
John A. Hottenstein　　　　　Oct. 30, 1863　　　　　Mustered out Jan. 10, 1866

14th Infantry
James Trimble   Nov. 17, 1863   Revoked
Thomas J. Morgan   Jan. 1, 1864   Resigned Aug. 15, 1865,
                                                       Bvt. Brig. Gen., USV
Henry C. Corbin   Sept. 23, 1865   Mustered out March 26, 1866,
                                                       Bvt. Brig. Gen., USV
15th Infantry
Thomas J. Downey   March 11, 1864   Dismissed Dec. 6, 1864
William Inness   March 2, 1865   Mustered out April 7, 1866
16th Infantry
William B. Gaw   Feb. 13, 1864   Mustered out April 30, 1866
17th Infantry
William R. Shafter   April 19, 1864   Mustered out April 25, 1866,
                                                       Bvt. Brig. Gen., USV
18th Infantry
Augustus O. Millington   Oct. 25, 1864   Cashiered June 2, 1865
19th Infantry
Henry G. Thomas   Jan. 16, 1864   Promoted Brig. Gen., USV,
                                                       Nov. 30, 1864
Joseph G. Perkins   March 1, 1865   Mustered out Jan. 15, 1867
20th Infantry
Nelson B. Bartram   Jan. 20, 1864   Mustered out Oct. 7, 1865
21st Infantry
Milton S. Littlefield   April 1, 1863   Mustered out April 25, 1866,
                                                       Bvt. Brig. Gen., USV
22nd Infantry
Joseph B. Kiddoo   Jan. 6, 1864   Mustered out Jan. 28, 1867,
                                                       Bvt. Brig. Gen, USV
23rd Infantry
Cleaveland J. Campbell   July 15, 1864   DOW June 13, 1865,
                                                       Bvt. Brig. Gen., USV
24th Infantry
Orlando Brown   June 19, 1865   Mustered out Aug. 28, 1868,
                                                       Bvt. Brig. Gen., USV
25th Infantry
Gustavus A. Scroggs   March 4, 1864   Resigned July 6, 1864
Frederick L. Hitchcock   Nov. 16, 1864   Mustered out Dec. 6, 1865
26th Infantry
William Silliman   Feb. 8, 1864   DOW Dec. 17, 1864
William B. Guernsey   May 30, 1865   Mustered out Aug. 28, 1865
27th Infantry
Albert M. Blackman   Sept. 1, 1864   Resigned May 16, 1865,
                                                       Bvt. Brig. Gen., USV
28th Infantry
Charles S. Russell   Aug. 27, 1864   Mustered out Nov. 8, 1865,
                                                       Bvt. Brig. Gen., USV
29th Infantry
Clark E.K. Royce   Jan. 1, 1865   Mustered out Nov. 6, 1865
30th Infantry
Delevan Bates   March 23, 1864   Mustered out Dec. 10, 1865,
                                                       Bvt. Brig. Gen., USV
31st Infantry
Henry C. Ward   Nov. 6, 1864   Mustered out Nov. 7, 1865,
                                                       Bvt. Brig. Gen., USV
32nd Infantry
George W. Baird   March 18, 1864   Mustered out Aug. 22, 1865

33rd Infantry (originally 1 SC Infantry of African Descent)
Thomas W. Higginson	Nov. 10, 1862	Resigned Oct. 27, 1864
William T. Bennett	Dec. 18, 1864	Mustered out March 10, 1866, Bvt. Brig. Gen. USV

34th Infantry
James Montgomery	March 5, 1863	Resigned Sept. 23, 1864
William W. Marple	Jan. 26, 1865	Mustered out Feb. 28, 1866, Bvt. Brig. Gen., USV

35th Infantry (originally 1st NC Infantry of African Descent)
James C. Beecher	June 9, 1863	Mustered out June 1, 1866, Bvt. Brig. Gen., USV

36th Infantry (originally 2nd NC Infantry of African Descent)
Alonzo G. Draper	Aug. 1, 1863	Died Sept. 3, 1865, Bvt. Brig. Gen., USV

37th Infantry (originally 3rd NC Infantry of African Descent)
Nathan Goff, Jr.	Oct. 25, 1864	Discharged June 4, 1867, Bvt. Brig. Gen., USV

38th Infantry
Henry T. Noyes	Sept. 28, 1864	Resigned Dec. 10, 1864
Robert M. Hall	Dec. 31, 1864	Mustered out Jan. 25, 1867, Bvt. Brig. Gen., USV

39th Infantry
Ozora P. Stearns	April 28, 1864	Mustered out Dec. 4, 1865

40th Infantry
Frederick W. Lister	July 12, 1865	Mustered out April 25, 1866, Bvt. Brig. Gen., USV

41st Infantry
Llewellyn F. Haskell	Nov. 1, 1864	Mustered out Sept. 30, 1865, Bvt. Brig. Gen., USV

42nd Infantry
William W. Wright	March 2, 1864	Declined

43rd Infantry
Stephen B. Yeoman	July 8, 1864	Mustered out Oct. 20, 1865, Bvt. Brig. Gen., USV

44th Infantry
Lewis Johnson	Sept. 16, 1864	Mustered out April 30, 1866, Bvt. Brig. Gen., USV

45th Infantry
Ulysses Doubleday	Oct. 8, 1864	Discharged Sept. 12, 1865, Bvt. Brig. Gen., USV

46th Infantry (originally 1st AR Infantry of African Descent)
William F. Wood	May 1, 1863	Resigned Aug. 8, 1864
Julian E. Bryant	Sept. 12, 1864	Died May 14, 1865
Eliphalet Whittlesey	June 14, 1865	Mustered out Jan. 1, 1868, Bvt. Brig. Gen., USV

47th Infantry (originally 8th LA Infantry of African Descent)
Hiram Scofield	May 5, 1863	Mustered out Jan. 5, 1866, Bvt. Brig. Gen., USV

48th Infantry (originally 10th LA Infantry of African Descent)
John G. Klinck	April 12, 1863	Declined
Frederick M. Crandal	Aug. 8, 1863	Mustered out Jan. 4, 1866, Bvt. Brig. Gen., USV

49th Infantry (originally 11th LA Infantry of African Descent)
Nathaniel McCalla	April 23, 1863	Declined
Edwin W. Chamberlain	May 7, 1863	Resigned Sept. 26, 1863
Van E. Young	Oct. 8, 1863	Mustered out June 14, 1866

U.S. Colored Troops

50th Infantry (originally 12th LA Infantry of African Descent)
Charles A. Gilchrist | July 27, 1863 | Mustered out June 9, 1866, Bvt. Brig. Gen., USV

51st Infantry (originally 1st MS Infantry of African Descent)
Isaac F. Shepard | May 9, 1863 | Promoted Brig. Gen., USV, Oct. 27, 1863

Alonzo Watson Webber | March 15, 1864 | Mustered out June 16, 1866, Bvt. Brig. Gen., USV

52nd Infantry (originally 2nd MS Infantry of African Descent)
George M. Ziegler | Aug. 2, 1863 | Mustered out May 5, 1866, Bvt. Brig. Gen., USV

53rd Infantry (originally 3rd MS Infantry of African Descent)
Richard H. Ballinger | May 19, 1863 | Resigned March 11, 1864
Orlando C. Risdon | March 24, 1864 | Mustered out June 6, 1866, Bvt. Brig. Gen., USV

54th Infantry (originally 2nd AR Infantry of African Descent)
Charles S. Sheley | May 21, 1863 | Discharged Jan. 23, 1864
John E. Cone | March 26, 1864 | Resigned Feb. 22, 1865

55th Infantry (originally 1st AL Infantry of African Descent)
James M. Alexander | June 11, 1863 | Dismissed April 27, 1864
James M. Irvin | June 18, 1864 | Resigned March 16, 1865
Nelson B. Bartram | Nov. 17, 1865 | Mustered out Dec. 31, 1865

56th Infantry (originally 3rd AR Infantry of African Descent)
John Guylee | Sept. 29, 1863 | Resigned March 11, 1864
William S. Brooks | April 9, 1864 | KIA July 26, 1864
Charles Bentzoni | Jan. 29, 1865 | Mustered out Sept. 15, 1866

57th Infantry (originally 4th AR Infantry of African Descent)
Thomas D. Seawell | Aug. 10, 1863 | Resigned May 10, 1864, Bvt. Brig. Gen., USV

Andrew B. Morrison | May 23, 1864 | Resigned Oct. 22, 1864
Paul Harwood | Jan. 9, 1865 | Mustered out Oct. 19, 1866

58th Infantry (originally 6th MS Infantry of African Descent)
Absalom S. Smith | Aug. 31, 1863 | Dismissed Jan. 18, 1864
Simon M. Preston | March 25, 1864 | Mustered out April 30, 1866, Bvt. Brig. Gen., USV

59th Infantry (originally 1st TN Infantry of African Descent)
Edward Bouton | June 28, 1863 | Mustered out Jan. 31, 1866, Bvt. Brig. Gen., USV

60th Infantry (originally 1st IA Infantry of African Descent)
John G. Hudson | Nov. 30, 1863 | Mustered out Oct. 15, 1865, Bvt. Brig. Gen., USV

61st Infantry (originally 2nd TN Infantry of African Descent)
Frank A. Kendrick | Aug. 27, 1863 | Died March 31, 1865
John Foley | July 18, 1865 | Mustered out Dec. 30, 1865

62nd Infantry (originally 1st MO Infantry of African Descent)
Theodore H. Barrett | Dec. 29, 1863 | Mustered out Jan. 19, 1866, Bvt. Brig. Gen., USV

63rd Infantry (originally 9th LA Infantry of African Descent)
John Eaton, Jr. | Oct. 10, 1863 | Discharged Dec. 18, 1865, Bvt. Brig. Gen., USV

64th Infantry (originally 7th LA Infantry of African Descent)
Samuel Thomas | Jan. 1, 1864 | Mustered out Jan. 5, 1867, Bvt. Brig. Gen., USV

65th Infantry (originally 2nd MO Infantry of African Descent)
DeWitt C. Brown | April 2, 1864 | Resigned Nov. 1, 1864
Alonzo J. Edgerton | July 12, 1865 | Mustered out Jan. 8, 1867, Bvt. Brig. Gen., USV

66th Infantry (originally 4th MS Infantry of African Descent)
William T. Frohock	Jan. 13, 1864	Resigned Sept. 20, 1864, Bvt. Brig. Gen., USV
Michael W. Smith	Feb. 8, 1865	Mustered out March 20, 1866

67th Infantry (originally 3rd MO Infantry of African Descent)
Alonzo J. Edgerton	Feb. 15, 1864	To 65th Infantry, July 12, 1865

68th Infantry (originally 4th MO Infantry of African Descent)
Joseph Blackburn Jones	June 27, 1864	Resigned Oct. 13, 1865, Bvt. Brig. Gen., USV

69th Infantry
Lucien B. Eaton	April 24, 1865	Resigned May 18, 1865

70th Infantry
James T. Organ	April 1, 1864	Discharged Nov. 7, 1864
Willard C. Earle	Nov. 9, 1864	Resigned Oct. 23, 1865

71st Infantry
Willard C. Earle	March 29, 1864	To 70th Infantry, Nov. 9, 1864

72nd Infantry
Alexander Duncan	Oct. 27, 1864	Mustered out July 21, 1865

73rd Infantry (originally 1st LA Native Guards)
Spencer H. Stafford	Sept. 27, 1862	Discharged Sept. 15, 1863
Chauncey J. Bassett	Nov. 2, 1863	DOW May 8, 1864
Samuel M. Quincy	May 29, 1864	To 96th Infantry, Sept. 27, 1865

74th Infantry (originally 2nd LA Native Guards)
Nathan W. Daniels	Oct. 12, 1862	Dismissed Aug. 11, 1863
William M. Grosvenor	Nov. 2, 1863	Dismissed May 28, 1864
Ernest W. Holmstedt	June 19, 1864	Mustered out Nov. 14, 1865

75th Infantry (originally 3rd LA Native Guards)
John A. Nelson	Nov. 26, 1862	Resigned Aug. 14, 1863
Henry W. Fuller	Nov. 23, 1863	Mustered out Nov. 25, 1865, Bvt. Brig. Gen., USV

76th Infantry (originally 4th LA Native Guards)
Charles W. Drew	April 8, 1863	Resigned Aug. 19, 1865, Bvt. Brig. Gen., USV

77th Infantry (originally 5th Infantry, Corps d'Afrique)
Charles A. Hartwell	Dec. 8, 1863	To 10th Heavy Artillery, Oct. 1, 1865

78th Infantry (originally 6th Infantry, Corps d'Afrique)
Alban B. Botsford	March 2, 1863	Resigned Sept. 22, 1863
Samuel B. Jones	Dec. 10, 1863	Mustered out Aug. 17, 1865, Bvt. Brig. Gen., USV
Charles L. Norton	Aug. 26, 1865	Mustered out Jan. 6, 1866

79th (Old) Infantry (originally 7th Infantry, Corps d'Afrique)
Henry G. Thomas	March 20, 1863	Resigned June 5, 1863, Brig. Gen., USV
James C. Clark	June 5, 1863	Died Sept. 5, 1864

79th (New) Infantry (originally 1st KS Infantry of African Descent)
James M. Williams	May 2, 1863	Mustered out Oct. 1, 1865, Bvt. Brig. Gen., USV

80th Infantry (originally 8th Infantry, Corps d'Afrique)
Cyrus Hamlin	Feb. 12, 1863	Promoted Brig. Gen., USV, Dec. 3, 1864
William S. Mudgett	March 7, 1865	Mustered out March 1, 1867, Bvt. Brig. Gen., USV

81st Infantry (originally 9th Infantry, Corps d'Afrique)
John F. Appleton　　　　　　June 25, 1863　　　　　　Resigned July 29, 1864,
　　　　　　　　　　　　　　　　　　　　　　　　　　　　Bvt. Brig. Gen., USV

Edward Martindale　　　　　Aug. 6, 1864　　　　　　　Resigned Aug. 7, 1865
Charles B. Gaskill　　　　　　Sept. 1, 1865　　　　　　　Resigned Dec. 31, 1865
Samuel M. Quincy　　　　　　Jan. 22, 1866　　　　　　　Mustered out Nov. 30, 1866,
　　　　　　　　　　　　　　　　　　　　　　　　　　　　Bvt. Brig. Gen., USV

82nd Infantry (originally 10th Infantry, Corps d'Afrique)
Ladislas L. Zulavsky　　　　　Nov. 1, 1863　　　　　　　Mustered out Sept. 10, 1866

83rd (Old) Infantry (originally 11th Infantry, Corps d'Afrique)
Albert Stickney　　　　　　　Aug. 27, 1863　　　　　　　Declined
Homer B. Sprague　　　　　　Nov. 11, 1863　　　　　　　Declined
Edward Martindale　　　　　Feb. 1, 1864　　　　　　　　To 81st Infantry,
　　　　　　　　　　　　　　　　　　　　　　　　　　　　Aug. 6, 1864

83rd (New) Infantry (originally 2nd KS Infantry of African Descent)
Samuel J. Crawford　　　　　Nov. 1, 1863　　　　　　　Resigned Nov. 7, 1864,
　　　　　　　　　　　　　　　　　　　　　　　　　　　　Bvt. Brig. Gen., USV

84th Infantry (originally 12th Infantry, Corps d'Afrique)
William H. Dickey　　　　　　Oct. 16, 1863　　　　　　　Mustered out March 14, 1866,
　　　　　　　　　　　　　　　　　　　　　　　　　　　　Bvt. Brig. Gen., USV

85th Infantry (regiment not entitled to a colonel since it never attained full strength)

86th Infantry (originally 14th Infantry, Corps d'Afrique)
Mardon Wilson Plumly　　　Sept. 7, 1863　　　　　　　Resigned Aug. 8, 1864

87th (Old) Infantry (originally 16th Infantry, Corps d'Afrique)
Matthew C. Kempsey　　　　Oct. 17, 1863　　　　　　　Resigned July 6, 1864

87th (New) Infantry (regiment not entitled to a colonel since it never
　　attained full strength)

88th (Old) Infantry (originally 17th Infantry, Corps d'Afrique)
Luther Goodrich　　　　　　Oct. 16, 1863　　　　　　　Resigned May 25, 1864

88th (New) Infantry
Edmund R. Wiley, Jr.　　　　Aug. 10, 1865　　　　　　　To 3rd Heavy Artillery,
　　　　　　　　　　　　　　　　　　　　　　　　　　　　Jan. 4, 1866

89th Infantry (originally 18th Infantry, Corps d'Afrique)
John B. Weber　　　　　　　　Nov. 7, 1863　　　　　　　Resigned June 20, 1864

90th Infantry (originally 19th Infantry, Corps d' Afrique)
Charles E. Bostwick　　　　　Oct. 5, 1863　　　　　　　Mustered out Aug. 29, 1864

91st Infantry (originally 20th Infantry, Corps d' Afrique)
Eliot Bridgman　　　　　　　Oct. 15, 1863　　　　　　　Mustered out Aug. 15, 1864

92nd Infantry (originally 22nd Infantry, Corps d'Afrique)
Henry N. Frisbie　　　　　　　Oct. 24, 1863　　　　　　　Mustered out Dec. 31, 1865
,　　　　　　　　　　　　　　　　　　　　　　　　　　　Bvt. Brig. Gen., USV

93rd Infantry (originally 25th Infantry, Corps d'Afrique)
Simon Jones　　　　　　　　　Sept. 19, 1863　　　　　　Discharged July 10, 1865

94th Infantry (regiment failed to complete its organization)

95th Infantry (originally 1st Engineers, Corps d'Afrique)
Justin Hodge　　　　　　　　April 10, 1863　　　　　　　Resigned July 6, 1864

96th Infantry (originally 2nd Engineers, Corps d'Afrique)
John C. Cobb　　　　　　　　Aug. 17, 1863　　　　　　　Resigned July 18, 1865
Samuel M. Quincy　　　　　　Sept. 27, 1865　　　　　　To 81st Infantry,
　　　　　　　　　　　　　　　　　　　　　　　　　　　　Jan. 22, 1866

97th Infantry (originally 3rd Engineers, Corps d'Afrique)
George D. Robinson　　　　　Sept. 12, 1863　　　　　　Mustered out April 6, 1866,
　　　　　　　　　　　　　　　　　　　　　　　　　　　　Bvt. Brig. Gen., USV

98th Infantry (originally 4th Engineers, Corps d' Afrique)
Charles L. Norton　　　　　　March 3, 1864　　　　　　To 78th Infantry,
　　　　　　　　　　　　　　　　　　　　　　　　　　　　Aug. 26, 1865

99th Infantry (originally 15th Infantry, Corps d' Afrique)
George H. Hanks   Sept. 3, 1863   Dismissed April 7, 1865
100th Infantry
Reuben D. Mussey   June 14, 1864   Mustered out Dec. 26, 1865,
                                                          Bvt. Brig. Gen., USV

101st Infantry
Robert W. Barnard   Nov. 1, 1864   Mustered out Jan. 21, 1866
102nd Infantry (originally 1st MI Colored Infantry)
Henry Barns   Sept. 25, 1863   Resigned April 12, 1864
Henry L. Chipman   April 15, 1864   Mustered out Sept. 30, 1865,
                                                          Bvt. Brig. Gen., USV

103rd Infantry
Stewart L. Woodford   March 6, 1865   Resigned Aug. 23, 1865,
                                                          Bvt. Brig. Gen., USV

104th Infantry
Douglas Frazar   March 27, 1865   Mustered out March 5, 1866,
                                                          Bvt. Brig. Gen., USV

105th Infantry (regiment failed to complete its organization)
106th Infantry (regiment not entitled to a colonel since it never attained full strength)
107th Infantry
William H. Revere, Jr.   July 11, 1864   Died Sept. 20, 1865,
                                                          Bvt. Brig. Gen., USV

108th Infantry
John S. Bishop   Sept. 19, 1865   Mustered out March 21, 1866
109th Infantry
Orion A. Bartholomew   June 25, 1864   Mustered out March 9, 1866,
                                                          Bvt. Brig. Gen., USV

110th Infantry (originally 2nd AL Infantry of African Descent)
Wallace Campbell   Dec. 26, 1863   Resigned May 6, 1865
111th Infantry (originally 3rd AL Infantry of African Descent)
William H. Lathrop   April 22, 1864   KIA Sept. 25, 1864
Joel A. Dewey   April 29, 1865   Promoted Brig. Gen., USV,
                                                          Nov. 20, 1865

112th Infantry (regiment not entitled to a colonel since it never attained full strength)
113th (Old) Infantry (regiment not entitled to a colonel since it never attained full strength)
113th (New) Infantry
Lauriston W. Whipple   April 1, 1865   Mustered out April 9, 1866
114th Infantry
Thomas D. Sedgewick   July 3, 1864   Mustered out April 2, 1867
115th Infantry
Robert H. Earnest   Oct. 16, 1864   Resigned Nov. 6, 1865
116th Infantry
William W. Woodward   July 15, 1864   Mustered out Dec. 15, 1865
117th Infantry
Lewis G. Brown   July 22, 1864   Mustered out Aug. 10, 1867,
                                                          Bvt. Brig. Gen., USV

118th Infantry
John C. Moon   Dec. 1, 1864   Mustered out Feb. 6, 1866,
                                                          Bvt. Brig. Gen., USV

119th Infantry
Charles G. Bartlett   May 10, 1865   Mustered out April 27, 1866,
                                                          Bvt. Brig. Gen., USV

120th Infantry *(regiment not entitled to a colonel since it never attained full strength)*

121st Infantry
Hubert A. McCaleb	March 10, 1865	Discharged June 30, 1865

122nd Infantry
James Hamilton Davidson	Dec. 14, 1864	Mustered out Jan. 17, 1866

123rd Infantry
Samuel A. Porter	Oct. 13, 1864	Mustered out Oct. 16, 1865, Bvt. Brig. Gen., USV

124th Infantry
Andrew W. Brazee	Nov. 26, 1864	Declined
Frederick H. Bierbower	May 15, 1865	Mustered out Oct. 24, 1865

125th Infantry
Charles D. Armstrong	Jan. 23, 1865	Resigned April 9, 1866
William R. Gerhart	April 20, 1866	Mustered out Dec. 20, 1867

126th Infantry *(regiment failed to complete its organization)*

127th Infantry
Benjamin F. Tracy	Sept. 10, 1864	Discharged June 13, 1865, Bvt. Brig. Gen., USV

128th Infantry
Charles H. Howard	April 6, 1865	Mustered out Oct. 10, 1866, Bvt. Brig. Gen., USV

135th Infantry
John E. Gurley	March 28, 1865	Mustered out Oct. 23, 1865

136th Infantry
Richard Root	July 15, 1865	Mustered out Jan. 4, 1866

137th Infantry
Martin R. Archer	April 8, 1865	Mustered out Jan. 15, 1866

138th Infantry
Frederick W. Benteen	July 1, 1865	Mustered out Jan. 6, 1866

Biographies

John David Abry

2 Lieutenant, Engineers, Western Department, July 31, 1861. 1 Lieutenant, Assistant Topographical Engineer, Staff of Brig. Gen. John M. Schofield, District of Missouri, March 1, 1862. Resigned Aug. 31, 1862. Appointed Colonel, 13 U.S. Colored Heavy Artillery, July 22, 1864. Appointment revoked, Oct. 7, 1864, with officers of his regiment accusing him of "conduct unbecoming an officer and a gentleman in pretending to enlist a colored woman as laundress and associating with her in a familiar manner disgraceful to his position; in associating and drinking in grog shops with the lowest class of citizens and private soldiers; and in appearing in the streets in a very ungentlemanly and undignified manner."

Born: 1820? France
Died: Oct. 2, 1894 East St. Louis, IL
Occupation: Civil engineer and architect
Miscellaneous: Resided East St. Louis, St. Clair Co., IL
Buried: St. Peter's Cemetery, East St. Louis, IL (no longer in existence)
References: Letters Received, Colored Troops Branch, Adjutant General's Office, File P46(CT)1865, National Archives. Correspondence Concerning Fremont's Appointments, 1861–64 (RG 94, Entry 164), National Archives. Pension File,

National Archives. Obituary, *East St. Louis Journal*, Oct. 3, 1894. Obituary, *St. Louis Republic*, Oct. 4, 1894. Obituary, *St. Louis Globe-Democrat*, Oct. 4, 1894.

Charles Henry Adams

Captain, Co. B, 10 IL Infantry (3 months), April 29, 1861. Major, 10 IL Infantry, May 3, 1861. Lieutenant Colonel, 10 IL Infantry, May 27, 1861. Honorably mustered out, July 29, 1861. Commissioned as Colonel, 45 IL Infantry, Sept. 9, 1861, but did not accept commission. Lieutenant Colonel, 1 IL Light Artillery, Oct. 23, 1861. Shell wound both legs, Corinth, MS, April 25, 1862. Appointed Colonel, 2 TN Heavy Artillery of African Descent (later 4 U.S. Colored Heavy Artillery), May 27, 1863. Appointment as colonel revoked, Jan. 26, 1864, supposedly "at his own request," but Major Gen. Stephen A. Hurlbut, in forwarding the revocation order, commented, "Mr. Adams has been found to be totally unfit for the position, and the necessities of the case demanded this step." Chief of Artillery, Reserve Artillery, Army of the Tennessee, Sept. 1864. Honorably mustered out as Lieutenant Colonel, 1 IL Light Artillery, Nov. 2, 1864. Battle honors: Shiloh, Corinth.

Born: April 24, 1836 Newbury, VT

Died: Oct. 28, 1906 Winthrop Beach, MA

Occupation: Farmer before war. Stock broker, insurance agent, U.S. Pension Bureau inspector, and U.S. War Department clerk after war.

Miscellaneous: Resided Jacksonville, Morgan Co., IL, before war; Chicago, IL, 1865–81; and Washington, D.C., 1881–1906

Buried: Arlington National Cemetery, Arlington, VA (Section 3, Lot 1565)

References: Pension File and Military Service File, National Archives. Letters Received, Volunteer Service Branch, Adjutant General's Office, File K457(VS)1862, National Archives. Andrew N. Adams, editor. *A Genealogical History of Robert Adams of Newbury, Mass., and His Descendants, 1635–1900.* Rutland, VT, 1900. Ephraim A. Wilson. *Memoirs of the War.* Cleveland, OH, 1893.

James Madison Alexander

Chaplain, Birge's 1 Regiment of Sharpshooters, Sept. 17, 1861. Designation of regiment changed to Western Sharpshooters, 14 MO Infantry, April 4, 1862. Designation of regiment changed to 66 IL Infantry, Nov. 20, 1862. Honorably mustered out, June 10, 1863. Colonel, 1 AL Infantry of African Descent, June 11, 1863. Commanded Post of Corinth (MS), District of Corinth, 16 Army Corps, Department of the Tennessee, Sept. 1863. Commanded 1 Colored Brigade, District of Memphis, 16 Army Corps, Department of the Tennessee, Feb. 1864. Designation of regiment changed to 55 U.S. Colored Infantry, March 11, 1864. On the recommendation of his immediate commanding general (Chetlain) and of the Major General commanding the 16 Army Corps (Hurlbut), he was dismissed April 27, 1864, for "embezzlement, conduct to the prejudice of good order and military discipline, conduct unbecoming an officer and a gentleman, disobedience of orders, neglect of duty, incompetency, and false muster," upon charges preferred by Adjutant George Haskin, who was himself dismissed a month later. He appealed his dismissal to President Lincoln, arguing that all evidence in his favor had been excluded, but

James Madison Alexander (Armstead & White, Artists, Corinth, MS; Richard F. Carlile Collection).

James Madison Alexander (author's photograph).

Lincoln denied his appeal, July 9, 1864, upon the recommendation of Provost Marshal General Joseph Holt, who concluded that "the interests of the service will not be promoted by his resumption of command as colonel of the regiment," noting that "the accused by reason of infirmities of temper and lack of prudence is not a suitable person to exercise command."

Born: Aug. 13, 1825 Rockingham Co., VA

Died: 1870? Disappeared on a business trip through New Orleans, LA, to Mobile, AL. Later reported killed in a street riot in New Orleans, LA.

Education: Graduated Hanover (IN) College, 1851. Attended Presbyterian Theological Seminary of the North-West, Chicago, IL.

Occupation: Presbyterian clergyman

Miscellaneous: Resided Paris, Edgar Co., IL

Buried: Place of burial unknown

References: Pension File and Military Service File, National Archives. Letters Received, Colored Troops Branch, Adjutant General's Office, File A15(CT)1863, National archives.

Norman S. Andrews

1 Lieutenant, Battery F, 1 MI Light Artillery, Dec. 30, 1861. Colonel, 12 U.S. Colored Heavy Artillery, July 25, 1864. Chief of Artillery, Staff of Brig. Gen. Stephen G. Burbridge, Military District of Kentucky, Jan.–March 1865. Commanded 1 Brigade, 2 Division, Department of Kentucky, June–Aug. 1865. Commanded 2 Division,

Department of Kentucky, Aug.–Sept. 1865. Honorably mustered out, April 24, 1866. Battle honors: Richmond, Morgan's Raid into Kentucky.

Born: Nov. 24, 1824 Monroe Co., NY
Died: May 5, 1882 Three Rivers, MI
Occupation: Civil engineer and surveyor
Offices/Honors: St. Joseph County Surveyor, 1854–62 and 1874–78. U.S. Marshal, Eastern District of Michigan, 1867–69.
Miscellaneous: Resided Three Rivers, St. Joseph Co., MI
Buried: Riverside Cemetery, Three Rivers, MI (Section X, Block 1, Lot 6)
References: *Portrait and Biographical Album of St. Joseph County, Michigan.* Chicago, IL, 1889. Obituary, *Three Rivers Tribune*, May 12, 1882. Pension File and Military Service File, National Archives. Letters Received, Colored Troops Branch, Adjutant General's Office, File A238(CT)1864, National Archives. *History of St. Joseph County, Michigan.* Philadelphia, PA, 1877.

Norman S. Andrews (Smith's Excelsior Gallery, Cor. 4th & Jefferson Sts., Louisville, KY; author's photograph).

Martin Robert Archer

Sergeant, Co. H, 3 OH Cavalry, Sept. 17, 1861. 1 Sergeant, Co. H, 3 OH Cavalry, Oct. 10, 1861. 1 Lieutenant, Co. H, 3 OH Cavalry, Nov. 13, 1862. Captain, Co. G, 3 OH Cavalry, June 8, 1863. Major, 3 OH Cavalry, Dec. 2, 1864. Honorably mustered out, April 7, 1865. Colonel, 137 U.S. Colored Infantry, April 8, 1865. Commanded Post of Macon (GA), District of Columbus, Department of Georgia, Aug. 1865. Honorably mustered out, Jan. 15, 1866. Battle honors: Wilson's Raid.

Born: May 10, 1835 New York
Died: Dec. 1, 1878 Gainesville, GA
Occupation: Farmer
Offices/Honors: Postmaster, Gainesville, GA, 1873–78
Miscellaneous: Resided Wauseon,

Norman S. Andrews (USAHEC [RG98S-CWP Albums Box 2/3.13]).

Fulton Co., OH; Dahlonega, Lumpkin Co., GA; and Gainesville, Hall Co., GA, after 1871

Buried: Alta Vista Cemetery, Gainesville, GA (Block 2, Lot 27)

References: Pension File and Military Service File, National Archives. Letters Received, Colored Troops Branch, Adjutant General's Office, File A358(CT)1865, National Archives. Thomas Crofts, compiler. *History of the Service of the Third Ohio Veteran Volunteer Cavalry in the War for the Preservation of the Union from 1861–1865.* Toledo, OH, 1910.

Charles Dorsey Armstrong

1 Lieutenant, Co. D, 2 KY Cavalry, Dec. 1, 1861. Acting ADC, Staff of Brig. Gen. Lovell H. Rousseau, 4 Brigade, 2 Division, Army of the Ohio, Feb.–June 1862. Acting ADC, Staff of Major Gen. Lovell H. Rousseau, 1 Division, Centre, 14 Army Corps, Army of the Cumberland, Nov.–Dec. 1862. Captain, Co. D, 2 KY Cavalry, Dec. 19, 1862. Acting AQM, Staff of Colonel Thomas B. Fairleigh, Post of Louisville (KY), District of Kentucky, Department of the Ohio, May–Nov. 1864. Honorably mustered out, Nov. 24, 1864. Colonel, 125 U.S. Colored Infantry, Jan. 23, 1865. Commanded Post of Cairo (IL), Department of the Ohio, Dec. 1865–Jan. 1866. Suffering from "an obstinate and protracted spell of intermittent fever" and desiring to continue care for an invalid sister, he resigned April 9, 1866, upon learning of the expected transfer of his regiment to New Mexico. Battle honors: Stone's River.

Born: June 16, 1837 Jefferson Co., KY

Died: Nov. 1, 1934 Jeffersonville, IN

Education: Attended Hanover (IN) College. Graduated Georgetown (KY) College, 1857.

Occupation: Lawyer and school teacher

Miscellaneous: Resided Louisville, Jefferson Co., KY; and Jeffersonville, Clark Co., IN

Buried: Walnut Ridge Cemetery, Jeffersonville, IN (Section O, Lot 9)

References: Pension File and Military Service File, National Archives. Obituary, *Jeffersonville Evening News*, Nov. 2, 1934. Letters Received, Colored Troops Branch, Adjutant General's Office, Files A32(CT)1865 and O20(CT)1866, National Archives. Russell K. Brown, "The Last Civil War Volunteers: The 125th U.S. Colored Infantry in New Mexico, 1866–1867," *Army History*, No. 92 (Summer 2014).

George William Baird

Private, 1 Independent Battery, CT Light Artillery, Aug. 25, 1862. Private, Co. H, 13 Regiment, Veteran Reserve Corps, Dec. 19, 1863. Colonel, 32 U.S. Colored

George William Baird (Bundy & Williams, 314 & 326 Chapel St., New Haven, CT; courtesy The Excelsior Brigade).

George William Baird (J. E. McClees, Artist, 910 Chestnut Street, Philadelphia, PA; courtesy Henry Deeks).

Infantry, March 18, 1864. Commanded District of Hilton Head, Department of the South, Sept. 1864. Commanded Post of Beaufort (SC), District of Port Royal, Department of the South, May–June 1865. Commanded Post of Hilton Head (SC), District of Port Royal, Department of South Carolina, July 1865. Honorably mustered out, Aug. 22, 1865. Battle honors: Honey Hill.

Born: Dec. 13, 1839 Milford, CT

Died: Nov. 28, 1906 Asheville, NC

Education: Graduated Yale University, New Haven, CT, 1863

Occupation: Regular Army (Brig. Gen., Deputy Paymaster General, retired Feb. 20, 1903)

Offices/Honors: Medal of Honor, Bear Paw Mountain, MT, Sept. 30, 1877, "Most distinguished gallantry in action with the Nez Perce Indians."

Miscellaneous: Resided Milford, New Haven Co., CT

Buried: Milford Cemetery, Milford, CT (Section G)

References: Obituary Circular, Whole No. 914, New York MOLLUS. Pension File and Military Service File, National Archives. Letters Received, Colored Troops Branch, Adjutant General's Office, Files W131(CT)1864 and W178(CT)1864, National Archives. Herbert W. Beecher. *History of the First Light Battery Connecticut Volunteers, 1861–1865.* New York City, NY, 1901. *A History of the Class of 1863, Yale College, Being the Fourth of Those Printed by Order of the Class.* New Haven, CT, 1905. Obituary, *New York Times,* Nov. 30, 1906. Obituary, *Hartford Courant,* Nov. 29, 1906. Walter F. Beyer and Oscar F. Keydel, editors. *Deeds of Valor: How America's Heroes Won the Medal of Honor.* Detroit, MI, 1903.

Richard Henry Ballinger

1 Sergeant, Co. A, 3 IL Cavalry, Aug. 21, 1861. 2 Lieutenant, Co. A, 3 IL Cavalry, Feb. 6, 1862. Captain, Co. A, 3 IL Cavalry, Sept. 12, 1862. Colonel, 3 MS Infantry of African Descent (later 53 U.S. Colored Infantry), May 19, 1863. Resigned March 11, 1864, due to "matters of a personal and private nature." Citing "charges of an aggravated character on file at this headquarters," Brig. Gen. Isaac F. Shepard recommended acceptance of the resignation and commented further, "In my opinion the good of the service demands that this officer vacate his commission, which a more competent man should fill." Battle honors: Pea Ridge, Chickasaw Bluffs, Arkansas Post, Vicksburg Campaign.

Born: Feb. 7, 1833 Barbourville, KY

Died: July 23, 1906 Seattle, WA

Education: Studied law in law office of Abraham Lincoln and William H. Herndon

Richard Henry Ballinger (Abraham Lincoln Presidential Library & Museum).

Occupation: Lawyer, livestock farmer, and newspaper editor

Offices/Honors: Postmaster, Virden, IL, 1869–72

Miscellaneous: Resided Chatham, Sangamon Co., IL; and Boonesboro, Boone Co., IA, before war. Resided Nilwood, Macoupin Co., IL, 1861–69; Virden, Macoupin Co., IL, 1869–73; Larned, Pawnee Co., KS, 1873–84; Kankakee, Kankakee Co., IL, 1884–90. Port Angeles, Clallam Co., WA; Port Townsend, Jefferson Co., WA; and Seattle, King Co., WA, 1896–1906.

Buried: Lake View Cemetery, Seattle, WA (Lot 31)

References: Obituary, *Seattle Daily Times*, July 23, 1906. Obituary circular, Whole No. 142, Washington MOLLUS. *The United States Biographical Dictionary.* Kansas Volume. Chicago and Kansas City, 1879. Alfred T. Andreas. *History of the State of Kansas.* Chicago, IL, 1883. Pension File and Military Service File, National Archives. Letters Received, Volunteer Service Branch, Adjutant General's Office, File B2075(VS)1862, National Archives.

Frederic William Bardwell

Private, Co. F, 2 OH Infantry (3 months), April 29, 1861. Absent at muster out, July 31, 1861. 2 Lieutenant, 10 Independent Battery, OH Light Artillery, Nov. 20, 1861. 1 Lieutenant, 10 Independent Battery, OH Light Artillery, Jan. 9, 1862. Resigned March 3, 1863, since "I find myself incompetent to perform the duties of that position." Major, 3 U.S. Colored Infantry, July 24, 1863. Chief of Artillery, District of Florida, Department of the South, Sept. 1864–June 1865. Lieutenant Colonel, 3 U.S. Colored Infantry, June 29, 1865. Chief of Artillery and Judge Advocate, Military District of East Florida, Department of Florida, July–Sept. 1865. Colonel, 3 U.S. Colored Infantry, Sept. 9, 1865. Honorably mustered out, Oct. 31, 1865.

Born: March 13, 1832 Belchertown, MA

Died: Aug. 17, 1878 Lawrence, KS

Education: Graduated Lawrence Scientific School, Harvard University, Cambridge, MA, 1856

Occupation: Civil engineer and college professor

Offices/Honors: Professor of Mathematics and Astronomy, Antioch College, Yellow Springs, OH, before war. Professor of Mathematics and Engineering, University of Kansas, Lawrence, KS, 1869-78.

Miscellaneous: Resided Yellow Springs, Greene Co., OH, before war; Washington, D.C.; and Lawrence, Douglas Co., KS, 1869–78

Buried: Oak Hill Cemetery, Lawrence, KS (Old Section 5, Lot 56)

References: Obituary, *Lawrence*

Frederick William Bardwell (author's photograph).

Standard, Aug. 23, 1878. Obituary, *Lawrence Daily Journal,* Aug. 18, 1878. Portia Chamberlain, editor. *Bardwell/Bordwell Descendants.* Book 2. Los Altos, CA, 1974. Military Service File, National Archives. Letters Received, Colored Troops Branch, Adjutant General's Office, Files B80(CT)1863 and F199(CT)1865, National Archives. Wilson Sterling, editor. *Quarter-Centennial History of the University of Kansas, 1866–1891.* Topeka, KS, 1891.

Robert William Barnard

1 Lieutenant, 19 U.S. Infantry, May 14, 1861. Captain, 19 U.S. Infantry, July 16, 1863. Superintendent of Contrabands, Department of the Cumberland, June 1864–June 1865. Colonel, 101 U.S. Colored Infantry, Nov. 1, 1864. Honorably mustered out of volunteer service, Jan. 21, 1866. Bvt. Major, USA, Sept. 1, 1864, for gallant and meritorious services during the Atlanta Campaign. Bvt. Lieutenant Colonel, USA, March 13, 1865, for gallant and meritorious services during the war. Battle honors: Atlanta Campaign (Buzzard Roost, Resaca).

Born: Sept. 11, 1827 Washington, D.C.
Died: July 21, 1870 Baton Rouge, LA
Occupation: Regular Army (Captain, 19 U.S. Infantry, died July 21, 1870)
Miscellaneous: Resided Washington, D.C.
Buried: Oak Hill Cemetery, Washington, D.C. (Lot 9 East, unmarked)

References: Pension File and Military Service File, National Archives. Letters received, Commission Branch, Adjutant General's Office, File B518(CB)1870, National Archives. Obituary, *Washington Evening Star,* July 23, 1870. Robert Barnard

Robert William Barnard (J.H. Van Stavoren, 53 College St., Nashville, TN; author's photograph).

Robert William Barnard (Philp & Solomons' Metropolitan Gallery, 332 Pennsylvania Avenue, Washington, D.C.; author's photograph).

Robert William Barnard (with Officers of the 101st U.S. Colored Troops, seated left to right, Adjutant Thomas V. Nichols, Lt. Col. Henry G. Davis, Col. Barnard, Capt. Lycurgus Grim, 1st Lt. William Gable, 1st Lt. Huntington C. Jessup, and standing left to right, Capt. Frank M. Crawford, 1st Lt. William H. Brown, RQM George N. Jenkins, 1st Lt. William W. Pringle, 2nd Lt. Ferdinand A. Wilde, 1st Lt. Henry Campbell) (William A. Gladstone Collection).

Family Papers, 1658–1917 (MS 541), Historical Society of Washington, D.C. Letters Received, Colored Troops Branch, Adjutant General's Office, File K8(CT)1864, National Archives.

Henry Barns

Colonel, 1 MI Colored Infantry, Sept. 25, 1863. Having no qualifications or desire for service in the field, he resigned April 12, 1864. Designation of regiment changed to 102 U.S. Colored Infantry, May 23, 1864.
    Born: Aug. 13, 1815 Appledore, Kent County, England
    Died: July 21, 1871 Detroit, MI (committed suicide by gun shot)
    Occupation: Printer and journalist
    Offices/Honors: Michigan Senate, 1859–61. Postmaster, Detroit, MI, 1866–67.
    Miscellaneous: Resided Detroit, MI
    Buried: Elmwood Cemetery, Detroit, MI (Section A, Lot 194)
    References: "Henry Barns. The True Story of the Founder of the Detroit Tribune," *Detroit News-Tribune*, Jan. 6, 1901. Obituary, *Detroit Advertiser and Tribune*, July 22, 1871. Obituary, *Detroit Free Press*, July 22, 1871. Military Service File, National Archives. Letters Received, Colored Troops Branch, Adjutant General's Office, Files

B131(CT)1863, B187(CT)1863, B29(CT)1864, B407(CT)1864, and W993(CT)1864, National Archives. Norman McRae. *Negroes in Michigan During the Civil War.* Lansing, MI, 1966. *Michigan Biographies.* Lansing, MI, 1924. *Michigan: A Centennial History of the State and Its People.* Vol. 5. Chicago, IL, 1939.

Nelson Burr Bartram

Captain, Co. B, 17 NY Infantry, May 22, 1861. Major, 17 NY Infantry, Nov. 1, 1861. Lieutenant Colonel, 17 NY Infantry, May 10, 1862. Acting ADC and Chief of Staff, Staff of Brig. Gen. Daniel Butterfield, 3 Brigade, 1 Division, 5 Army Corps, Army of Virginia, Aug.–Sept. 1862. Acting AIG and Chief of Staff, Staff of Brig. Gen. Daniel Butterfield, 5 Army Corps, Center Grand Division, Army of the Potomac, Nov.–Dec. 1862. Honorably mustered out, June 2, 1863. *Lieutenant Colonel,* 15 NY Cavalry, July 11, 1863. Resigned Sept. 10, 1863. Lieutenant Colonel, 8 U.S. Colored Infantry, Oct. 31, 1863. Honorably mustered out, Jan. 19, 1864. Colonel, 20 U.S. Colored Infantry, Jan. 20, 1864. Commanded District of Carrollton (LA), Defenses of New Orleans, Department of the Gulf, May–Aug. 1864. Honorably mustered out, Oct. 7, 1865. Colonel, 55 U.S. Colored Infantry, Nov. 17, 1865. Honorably mustered out, Dec. 31, 1865. Battle honors: Peninsular Campaign (Yorktown, Hanover Court House, Seven Days Battles), 2nd Bull Run, Antietam, Fredericksburg, Chancellorsville.

Born: Feb. 7, 1835 Westport, CT

Died: Dec. 25, 1886 New York City, NY

Occupation: School teacher before war. U.S. Custom House officer after war.

Offices/Honors: Deputy Collector of the Port of New York, 1883–86

Nelson Burr Bartram (Massachusetts MOLLUS Collection, USAHEC [Vol. 72, p 3557]).

Nelson Burr Bartram (Whitney's Metropolitan Photograph Gallery, 585 Broadway, New York; author's photograph).

Miscellaneous: Resided Port Chester, Westchester Co., NY; and White Plains, Westchester Co., NY

Buried: Rural Cemetery, White Plains, NY

References: Obituary, *New York Times*, Dec. 27, 1886. Pension File and Military Service File, National Archives. Letters Received, Colored Troops Branch, Adjutant General's Office, File B273(CT)1863, National Archives. Carlton E. Sanford. *Thomas Sanford, the Emigrant to New England: Ancestry, Life and Descendants, 1634–1910.* Rutland, VT, 1911. "Wiley Sword's War Letters Series," *Blue & Gray Magazine*, Vol. 24, Issue 3 (Fall 2007). J. Thomas Scharf. *History of Westchester County, New York.* Philadelphia, PA, 1886. *Banquet Given by the Members of the Union League Club of 1863 and 1864, to Commemorate the Departure for the Seat of War of the Twentieth Regiment of United States Colored Troops Raised by the Club.* New York City, NY, 1886.

Nelson Burr Bartram (Whitney & Paradise, Photographers, 585 Broadway, New York, late of Brady's New York & Washington Galleries; Richard F. Carlile Collection).

Chauncey J. Bassett

Captain, Co. G, 6 MI Infantry, Aug. 20, 1861. Major, 1 LA Native Guards, Sept. 27, 1862. Lieutenant Colonel, 1 LA Native Guards, March 5, 1863. Designation of regiment changed to 1 Infantry, Corps d'Afrique, June 6, 1863. Commanded 1 Brigade, 1 Division, Corps d'Afrique, Department of the Gulf, Sept. 1863–Jan. 1864. Colonel, 1 Infantry, Corps d'Afrique, Nov. 2, 1863. Designation of regiment changed to 73 U.S. Colored Infantry, April 4, 1864. GSW breast, during capture of U.S. Steamer, *City Belle*, near Cheneyville, LA, May 3, 1864. Battle honors: Baton Rouge, Port Hudson Campaign, Red River Campaign.

Born: Aug. 7, 1830 Lee, MA

Died: May 8, 1864 DOW Cheneyville, LA

Occupation: Carpenter and master mechanic

Miscellaneous: Resided Lee, Berkshire Co., MA; and Allegan, Allegan Co., MI

Buried: Fairmount Cemetery, Lee, MA

References: Pension File and Military Service File, National Archives. Letters Received, Colored Troops Branch, Adjutant General's Office, File B239(CT)1864, National Archives. Stuart Murray. *A Time of War: A Northern Chronicle of the Civil War.* Lee, MA, 2001. James G. Hollandsworth, Jr. *The Louisiana Native Guards: The*

Chauncey J. Bassett (A. I. Blauvelt, Photographer, Port Hudson, LA; author's photograph).

Black Military Experience During the Civil War. Baton Rouge, LA, 1995. David C. Edmonds. *The Guns of Port Hudson: The Investment, Siege and Reduction.* Lafayette, LA, 1984. Joseph T. Wilson. *The Black Phalanx: A History of the Negro Soldiers of the United States in the Wars of 1775–1812, 1861–65.* Hartford, CT, 1888.

Thomas Bayley

Colonel, 9 U.S. Colored Infantry, Dec. 28, 1863. Commanded Bayley's Brigade, Hilton Head District, Department of the South, April–May 1864. Commanded 2 Brigade, 1 Division, 25 Army Corps, Department of Virginia, Feb.–March 1865. Commanded 2 Brigade, 1 Division, 25 Army Corps, Department of Texas, Sept.–Oct. 1865. Commanded 1 Brigade, 1 Division, 25 Army Corps, Department of Texas, Oct.–Dec. 1865. Sub-Assistant Commissioner, Bureau of Refugees, Freedmen and Abandoned Lands, Marshall TX, Dec. 1865–Nov. 1866. Honorably mustered out, Jan. 4, 1867.

Born: April 10, 1827 Boston, MA

Died: Nov. 17, 1919 St. Louis, MO

Occupation: Lawyer and Notary Public

Miscellaneous: Resided Decatur, Macon Co., IL; Belleville, St. Clair Co., IL; and St. Louis, MO

Buried: Jefferson Barracks National Cemetery, St. Louis, MO (Section OPS2, Grave 2111B)

References: *The United States Biographical Dictionary and Portrait Gallery of Eminent and Self-Made Men.* Illinois Volume. Chicago, Cincinnati, and New York, 1876. Pension File and Military Service File, National Archives. Letters Received, Colored Troops Branch, Adjutant General's Office, File B424(CT)1863, National Archives. *History of the Ninth U.S.C. Troops from Its Organization Till Muster Out.* Philadelphia, PA, 1866. Death notice, *St. Louis Post-Dispatch*, Nov. 18, 1919. Death notice, *St. Louis Globe-Democrat*, Nov. 18, 1919.

Thomas Bayley (Massachusetts MOLLUS Collection, USAHEC [Vol. 109, p. 5641]).

Thomas Bayley (Randy Beck Collection).

Frederick William Benteen

1 Lieutenant, Co. C, Bowen's Battalion, MO Cavalry, Sept. 1, 1861. Captain, Co. C, Bowen's Battalion, MO Cavalry, Oct. 1, 1861. Captain, Co. C, 9 MO Cavalry, Oct. 1, 1862. Regiment consolidated with 10 MO Cavalry, Dec. 4, 1862. Major, 10 MO Cavalry, Dec. 19, 1862. Lieutenant Colonel, 10 MO Cavalry, Feb. 27, 1864. Commanded 4 Brigade, Provisional Cavalry Division, Army of the Border, Oct.–Nov. 1864. Honorably mustered out, June 30, 1865. Colonel, 138 U.S. Colored Infantry, July 1, 1865. Honorably mustered out, Jan. 6, 1866. Battle honors: Pea Ridge, King's Creek, Iuka, Meridian Expedition, Price's Missouri Expedition (Big Blue, Mine Creek), Wilson's Raid (Columbus).

Born: Aug. 24, 1834 Petersburg, VA

Died: June 22, 1898 Atlanta, GA

Occupation: Regular Army (Captain, 7 U.S. Cavalry, July 28, 1866; Major, 9 U.S. Cavalry, Dec. 17, 1882; retired July 7, 1888)

Offices/Honors: Bvt. Major, USA, March 2, 1867, for gallant and meritorious services in the battle of the Osage. Bvt. Lieutenant Colonel, USA, March 2, 1867, for gallant and meritorious services in the charge on Columbus, GA. Bvt. Colonel, USA, Aug. 13, 1868, for gallant and meritorious conduct in an engagement with hostile Indians on the Saline River, KS, 13 August 1868. Bvt. Brigadier General, USA, Feb. 27, 1890, for gallant services in action against Indians on the Little Big Horn, MT, 25 and 26 June 1876, and in action against Indians at Canyon Creek, MT, 13 September 1877.

Frederick William Benteen (Massachusetts MOLLUS Collection, USAHEC [Vol. 118, p. 6072]).

Frederick William Benteen (post-war) (*Companions of the Military Order of the Loyal Legion of the United States.* Second Edition, New York City, NY, 1901).

Miscellaneous: Resided St. Louis, MO; and Atlanta, GA

Buried: Arlington National Cemetery, Arlington, VA (Section 3, Lot 1351)

References: Charles K. Mills. *Harvest of Barren Regrets: The Army Career of Frederick William Benteen, 1834–98.* Glendale, CA, 1985. James B. Klokner. *The Officer Corps of Custer's Seventh Cavalry, 1866–1876.* Atglen, PA, 2007. Obituary, *Atlanta Constitution,* June 22 and 23, 1898. Dan L. Thrapp. *Encyclopedia of Frontier Biography.* Glendale, CA, 1988. Military Service File, National Archives. Letters Received, Colored Troops Branch, Adjutant General's Office, File B654(CT)1865, National Archives. Robert M. Utley, editor. *Life in Custer's Cavalry: Diaries and Letters of Albert and Jennie Barnitz, 1867–1868.* New Haven, CT, 1977. Kenneth Hammer. *Men With Custer: Biographies of the 7th Cavalry, 25 June 1876.* Fort Collins, CO, 1972. Obituary Circular, Whole No. 408, Ohio MOLLUS. Len Eagleburger. *The Fighting 10th: The History of the 10th Missouri Cavalry, U.S.* Bloomington, IN, 2004. Lumir F. Buresh. *October 25th and the Battle of Mine Creek.* Kansas City, MO, 1977.

Charles Bentzoni

2 Lieutenant, 11 U.S. Infantry, Nov. 27, 1861. 1 Lieutenant, 11 U.S. Infantry, March 17, 1862. Colonel, 56 U.S. Colored Infantry, Jan. 29, 1865. Commanded District of Eastern Arkansas, Department of Arkansas, April 1865 and June–August 1865. Commanded St. Francis River District, Department of Arkansas, Jan.–March 1866. Commanded Post of Helena (AR), Department of Arkansas, March–July 1866. Honorably mustered out, Sept. 15, 1866. Bvt. Captain, USA, Sept. 30, 1864, for gallant and meritorious services in the battle of Poplar Spring Church, VA. Bvt. Major and Bvt. Lieutenant Colonel, USA, March 13, 1865, for gallant and meritorious services during the war. Battle honors: Richmond Campaign (Poplar Spring Church).

Born: Oct. 11, 1830 Breslau, Silesia, Prussia

Died: Oct. 8, 1907 Los Angeles, CA

Other Wars: Served in British Army during Crimean War

Occupation: U.S. Army enlisted man (1 Sergeant, 11 U.S. Infantry) and clerk before war. Regular Army (Major, 1 U.S. Infantry, retired Oct. 11, 1894)

Miscellaneous: Resided San Francisco, CA; and Los Angeles, CA, after retirement

Buried: Hollywood Forever Cemetery, Hollywood, CA (Section 19, Lot 3)

Charles Bentzoni (The National Archives [BA-106]).

Charles Bentzoni (post-war) (*Album Portraits of Companions of the Commandery, State of Illinois MOLLUS.* Chicago, IL, 1892).

References: James M. Guinn. *Historical and Biographical Record of Southern California.* Chicago, IL, 1902. Obituary, *Los Angeles Times,* Oct. 9, 1907. Obituary Circular, Whole No. 874, California MOLLUS. Martin W. Ofele. *German-Speaking Officers in the U.S. Colored Troops, 1863–1867.* Gainesville, FL, 2004. Pension File and Military Service File, National Archives. Letters Received, Colored Troops Branch, Adjutant General's Office, Files B631(CT)1864 and W968(CT)1864, National Archives. Mitchell Yockelson, "Their Memory Will Not Perish: Commemorating the 56th United States Colored Troops," *Gateway Heritage,* Vol. 22, No. 3 (Winter 2001–02). James W. Erwin, "The Teacher, the Preacher and the Prussian: Officers of the 56th United States Colored Infantry," http://www.jameswerwin.com/the-t.html.

Frederick Huber Bierbower

Captain, Co. A, 40 KY Infantry, Aug. 18, 1863. Major, 40 KY Infantry, March 5, 1864. Acting Judge Advocate, Staff of Brig. Gen. Stephen G. Burbridge, Military District of Kentucky, July 1864–Feb. 1865. Honorably mustered out, Feb. 24, 1865. Colonel, 124 U.S. Colored Infantry, May 15, 1865. Commanded Post of Camp Nelson (KY), 1 Division, Department of Kentucky, May–Sept. 1865. Honorably mustered out, Oct. 24, 1865. Battle honors: Morgan's Raid into Kentucky (Cynthiana).

Born: Sept. 12, 1833 Chambersburg, PA

Died: Nov. 24, 1910 Maysville, KY

Occupation: Acting Master's Mate, USN, 1853–56. Lawyer and U.S. Internal Revenue official after war.

Miscellaneous: Resided Maysville, Mason Co., KY. Well known as a bibliophile and antiquarian.

Buried: Maysville Cemetery, Maysville, KY (Section 4, Lot 94)

References: Temple Bodley. *History of Kentucky: The Blue Grass State.* Chicago and Louisville, 1928. E. Polk Johnson. *A History of Kentucky and Kentuckians.* Chicago and New York, 1912. Obituary, *Maysville Daily Public Ledger,* Nov. 25, 1910. Obituary, *Louisville Courier-Journal,* Nov. 26, 1910. Pension File and Military Service File, National Archives. Letters Received, Volunteer Service Branch, Adjutant General's Office, File B3203(VS)1864, National Archives. Richard D. Sears. *Camp Nelson, Kentucky: A Civil War History.* Lexington, KY, 2002. James C. Bierbower and Charles W. Beerbower, compilers. *House of Bierbauer: Two Hundred Years of Family History, 1742–1942.* New Wilmington, PA, 1942.

John Soast Bishop

Major, 32 IL Infantry, Nov. 20, 1861. Resigned Dec. 6, 1861. Sergeant, Co. A, 68 IL Infantry, May 27, 1862. 1 Lieutenant, Adjutant, 68 IL Infantry, June 20, 1862. Honorably mustered out, Sept. 26, 1862. Captain, Co. H, 107 IN Minute Men, July 14, 1863. Honorably mustered out, July 18, 1863. Lieutenant Colonel, 108 U.S. Colored

John Soast Bishop (Cook & Newberry, Photographers, Rock Island, IL; courtesy Henry Deeks).

Infantry, July 1, 1864. Commanded Post of Munfordville (KY), District of Kentucky, Aug.–Sept. 1864. Colonel, 108 U.S. Colored Infantry, Sept. 19, 1865. Commanded Columbus Sub-district, Northern District of Mississippi, Department of Mississippi, Sept. 1865. Honorably mustered out, March 21, 1866.

Born: March 23, 1834 Philadelphia, PA

Died: Jan. 23, 1915 Philadelphia, PA

Education: Attended Philadelphia (PA) Central High School

Occupation: Bookseller before war. Regular Army (Captain, 13 U.S. Infantry, retired March 23, 1898).

Miscellaneous: Resided Jacksonville, Morgan Co., IL; Indianapolis, Marion Co., IN; and Philadelphia, PA

Buried: Arlington National Cemetery, Arlington, VA (Section 3, Lot 2039)

John Soast Bishop (post-war) (*A Biographical Album of Prominent Pennsylvanians. First Series.* **Philadelphia, PA, 1888**).

References: *A Biographical Album of Prominent Pennsylvanians.* First Series. Philadelphia, PA, 1888. Charles Morris, editor. *Makers of Philadelphia.* Philadelphia, PA, 1894. Obituary, *Philadelphia Evening Public Ledger,* Jan. 26, 1915. Pension File and Military Service File, National Archives. Theodore M. Banta. *A Frisian Family: The Banta Genealogy, Descendants of Epke Jacobse, Who Came from Friesland, Netherlands, to New Amsterdam, February 1659.* New York City, NY, 1893.

Charles Edward Bostwick

Private, Co. B, 7 NY National Guard, May 25, 1862. Captain, Co. B, 128 NY Infantry, Aug. 18, 1862. Major, 1 Engineers, Corps d'Afrique (later 95 U.S. Colored Infantry), May 23, 1863. Colonel, 19 Infantry, Corps d'Afrique, Oct. 5, 1863. Designation of regiment changed to 90 U.S. Colored Infantry, April 4, 1864. Commanded Engineer Brigade, Department of the Gulf, June–July 1864. Honorably mustered out, Aug. 29, 1864.

Born: July 2, 1835 Pine Plains, Dutchess Co., NY

Died: Nov. 30, 1919 Minneapolis, MN

Occupation: Merchant before war. U.S. Quartermaster Department clerk and insurance agent after war.

Miscellaneous: Resided Amenia, Dutchess Co., NY, to 1867; St. Paul, Ramsey Co., MN, 1867–70; and Duluth, St. Louis Co., MN, after 1870

Buried: Forest Hill Cemetery, Duluth, MN (Section I, Block 4, Lot 7)

References: *Commemorative Biographical Record of the Upper Lake Region.*

Chicago, IL, 1905. Obituary, *Duluth Herald,* Dec. 1, 1919. Obituary, *Duluth News Tribune,* Dec. 1, 1919. Obituary, *Minneapolis Morning Tribune,* Dec. 1, 1919. Pension File and Military Service File, National Archives. Letters Received, Colored Troops Branch, Adjutant General's Office, File B1040(CT)1864, National Archives. Henry A. Bostwick, compiler. *Genealogy of the Bostwick Family in America: The Descendants of Arthur Bostwick of Stratford, Conn.* Hudson, NY, 1901. David H. Hanaburgh. *History of the One Hundred and Twenty-Eighth Regiment, New York Volunteers in the Late Civil War.* Poughkeepsie, NY, 1894.

Alban Bates Botsford

Captain, Co. G, 78 NY Infantry, March 24, 1862. Colonel, 6 Infantry, Corps d'Afrique (later 78 U.S. Colored Infantry), March 2, 1863. Resigned Sept. 22, 1863, since "I have some property that has been confiscated by the Rebels, and as it is now within our lines, I can save it."

Born: Sept. 1, 1823 Arcade, NY

Died: March 17, 1895 Grand Rapids, MI

Education: Graduated Cincinnati (OH) Eclectic Medical Institute, 1850. Graduated Cleveland (OH) Homeopathic Medical College, 1874.

Occupation: Physician and dentist

Miscellaneous: Resided Albion, Orleans Co., NY, to 1858; Franklin, St. Mary Parish, LA, 1858-61; Albion, Orleans Co., NY, 1865–74; and Grand Rapids, Kent Co., MI, after 1874

Buried: Oak Hill Cemetery, Grand Rapids, MI (Section I, Lot 34)

References: Albert Baxter. *History of the City of Grand Rapids, Michigan.* New York and Grand Rapids, 1891. Obituary, *Grand Rapids Evening Press,* March 18, 1895. *Botsford Family Genealogy: The Line of Joseph, 1.1.12; Youngest Son of Elnathan, 1.1; Grandson of Henry, 1.* Baltimore, MD, 1983. Pension File and Military Service File, National Archives. Wilson A. Smith and Wesley A. Dunn, editors, *The Medical Current,* Vol. 11, No. 6 (June 1895). Isaac S. Signor, editor. *Landmarks of Orleans County, New York.* Syracuse, NY, 1894.

Andrew W. Brazee

1 Lieutenant, Co. H, 49 NY Infantry, Sept. 9, 1861. Captain, Co. H, 49 NY Infantry, March 30, 1862. Judge Advocate, Staff of Brig. Gen. Albion P. Howe, 2 Division, 6 Army Corps, Army of the Potomac, May–July 1863. Provost Marshal, Staff of Brig. Gen. Albion P. Howe (and others), 2 Division, 6 Army Corps, Army of the Potomac, Nov. 1863–Aug. 1864. Major, 49 NY Infantry, Aug. 4, 1864. Provost Marshal, Staff of Brig. Gen. George W. Getty, 2 Division, 6 Army Corps, Army of the Shenandoah, Aug.–Sept. 1864. Honorably mustered out, Oct. 18, 1864. *Colonel,* 124 U.S. Colored Infantry, Nov. 26, 1864 (Declined). Battle honors: Rappahannock Station.

Born: Dec. 17, 1826 Royalton, Niagara Co., NY

Died: Sept. 1, 1891 Denver, CO

Education: Attended Wilson (NY) Collegiate Institute

Occupation: Lawyer

Offices/Honors: District Attorney, Niagara Co., NY, 1856–59. Brig. Gen., New

York State National Guard, 1867–70. Associate Justice, Colorado Territory Supreme Court, 1875–76.

Miscellaneous: Resided Lockport, Niagara Co., NY, to 1875; and Denver, Arapahoe Co., CO, after 1875.

Buried: Fairmount Cemetery, Denver, CO (Block 5, Lot 62)

References: *History of the City of Denver, Arapahoe County, and Colorado.* Chicago, IL, 1880. Obituary, *Rocky Mountain News,* Sept. 2, 1891. Pension File, National Archives. Letters Received, Colored Troops Branch, Adjutant General's Office, File B1280(CT)1864, National Archives. Frederick D. Bidwell, compiler. *History of the Forty-Ninth New York Volunteers.* Albany, NY, 1916. John Y. Simon, editor. *The Papers of Ulysses S. Grant.* Vol. 26: 1875. Carbondale, IL, 2003.

Eliot Bridgman

Captain, Co. F, 31 MA Infantry, Feb. 19, 1862. Commanded Post of Fort Pike (LA), Defenses of New Orleans, Department of the Gulf, Dec. 1862–Aug. 1863. Colonel, 20 Infantry, Corps d'Afrique, Oct. 15, 1863. Commanded Post of Fort Pike (LA), Defenses of New Orleans, Department of the Gulf, March–July 1864. Designation of regiment changed to 91 U.S. Colored Infantry, April 4, 1864. Honorably mustered out, Aug. 15, 1864, upon consolidation of regiment with 74 U.S. Colored Infantry. Superintendent, U.S. Military Railroad, from Little Rock to Duvall's Bluff, AR, Jan.–June 1865.

Born: May 7, 1830, Belchertown, Hampshire Co., MA

Died: April 22, 1906, Tacoma, WA

Occupation: Butcher and farmer to 1878; and lumber dealer and miller after 1878

Miscellaneous: Resided Belchertown, Hampshire Co., MA, to 1878; Sauk Centre, Stearns Co., MN; Little Falls, Morrison Co., MN; Seattle, King Co., WA; Minneapolis, Hennepin Co., MN; and Tacoma, Pierce Co., WA, 1902–06

Buried: Greenwood Cemetery, Sauk Centre, MN

References: *History of the Upper Mississippi Valley.* Minneapolis, MN, 1881. Obituary, *Sauk Centre Herald,* May 3, 1906. Obituary, *Little Falls Herald,* May 4, 1906. Pension File and Military Service File, National Archives. Letters Received, Volunteer Service Branch, Adjutant General's Office, File B516(VS)1869, National Archives. Burt N. Bridgman and Joseph C. Bridgman, compilers. *Genealogy of the Bridgman Family: Descendants of James Bridgman, 1636–1894.* Hyde Park, MA, 1894. Warren Upham and Rose B. Dunlap, compilers. *Collections of the Minnesota*

Eliot Bridgman (courtesy Belchertown Historical Association).

Historical Society, Volume 14. Minnesota Biographies, 1655–1912. St. Paul, MN, 1912. Obituary, *Tacoma Daily Ledger,* April 23, 1906.

William Sanford Brooks

Private, Co. F, 1 IA Infantry, May 14, 1861. Honorably mustered out, Aug. 21, 1861. 2 Lieutenant, Co. D, 19 IA Infantry, Aug. 20, 1862. GSW left thigh, Prairie Grove, AR, Dec. 7, 1862. Captain, Co. D, 19 IA Infantry, March 28, 1863. Lieutenant Colonel, 3 AR Infantry of African Descent, Sept. 21, 1863. Designation of regiment changed to 56 U.S. Colored Infantry, March 11, 1864. Colonel, 56 U.S. Colored Infantry, April 9, 1864. GSW left lung, Wallace's Ferry, AR, July 26, 1864. Battle honors: Wilson's Creek, Prairie Grove, Vicksburg Campaign, Wallace's Ferry.

Born: Sept. 4, 1839 Hamilton Twp., Butler Co., OH

Died: July 26, 1864 KIA Wallace's Ferry, AR

Occupation: Farmer

Miscellaneous: Resided Locust Grove Twp., Jefferson Co., IA

Buried: Brooks Cemetery, Locust Grove Twp., Jefferson Co., IA

References: Iowa DAR, Log Cabin Chapter. Jefferson County Records, 1960–1961. Military Service File, National Archives. Letters Received, Colored Troops Branch, Adjutant General's Office, Files B534(CT)1864 and W968(CT)1864, National Archives. *History of Jefferson County, Iowa.* Chicago, IL, 1879. J. Irvine Dungan. *History of the Nineteenth Regiment Iowa Volunteer Infantry.* Davenport, IA, 1865. Mitchell Yockelson, "Their Memory Will Not Perish: Commemorating the 56th United States Colored Troops," *Gateway Heritage,* Vol. 22, No. 3 (Winter 2001–02). James W. Erwin, "The Teacher, the Preacher and the Prussian: Officers of the 56th United States Colored Infantry," http://www.jameswerwin.com/the-t.html.

William Sanford Brooks (author's photograph).

DeWitt Clinton Brown

Captain, Co. C, 26 MO Infantry, Nov. 26, 1861. Resigned April 25, 1863, "laboring under excessive nervous irritability and great mental depression, depending partly on indigestion, but more on some real or fancied injustice received at the hands of his commanding officer." Colonel, 65 U.S. Colored Infantry, April 2, 1864. Resigned Nov. 1, 1864, "suffering from chronic dyspepsia of six months standing and follicular inflammation of the larynx, the last becoming very much aggravated by the active use of his voice." Brig. Gen. Daniel Ullmann forwarded the resignation with the endorsement, "The Surgeon's certificate in this case is not sufficient, but, as this officer is habitually inefficient, the acceptance of his resignation is recommended." Battle honors: Iuka, Corinth.

Born: April 17, 1832, Centerville, OH

Died: Feb. 23, 1875 Dayton, OH

Education: Graduated Brown University, Providence, RI, 1853

Occupation: School teacher and lawyer

Offices/Honors: Sub-Assistant Commissioner, Texas Bureau of Refugees, Freedmen, and Abandoned Lands, 1867–68. Louisiana House of Representatives, 1870–72.

Miscellaneous: Resided Cincinnati, OH; Dayton, Montgomery Co., OH; and Ascension Parish, LA. Unsuccessful applicant for U.S. Military Academy appointment.

Buried: Woodland Cemetery, Dayton, OH (Section 65, Lot 807)

References: Obituary, *Dayton Daily Journal*, Feb. 24, 1875. "Funeral of Col. DeWitt C. Brown," *Dayton Daily Journal*, Feb. 26, 1875. Military Service File, National Archives. Letters Received, Volunteer Service Branch, Adjutant General's Office, File K291(VS)1862, National Archives. William L. Richter, "'The Revolver Rules the Day!': Colonel DeWitt C. Brown and the Freedmen's Bureau in Paris, Texas, 1867–1868," *Southwestern Historical Quarterly*, Vol. 93, No. 3 (January 1990). Paul E. Steiner. *Medical History of a Civil War Regiment: Disease in the Sixty-Fifth United States Colored Infantry*. Clayton, MO, 1977. Benjamin D. Dean. *Recollections of the 26th Missouri Infantry in the War for the Union*. Lamar, MO, 1892. U.S. Military Academy Cadet Application Papers, 1805–1866, File No. 31, 1851, National Archives. *Historical Catalogue of Brown University, 1764–1904*. Providence, RI, 1905.

Julian Edward Bryant

2 Lieutenant, Co. E, 33 IL Infantry, Sept. 2, 1861. 1 Lieutenant, Co. E, 33 IL Infantry, June 18, 1862. Acting ADC, Staff of Brig. Gen. Charles E. Hovey, 2 Brigade, 1 Division, 15 Army Corps, Army of the Tennessee, Dec. 1862–April 1863. Major, 1 MS Infantry of African Descent, July 28, 1863. Designation of regiment changed to 51 U.S. Colored Infantry. March 11, 1864. Lieutenant Colonel, 51 U.S. Colored Infantry, March 16, 1864. Colonel, 46 U.S. Colored Infantry, Sept. 12, 1864. Commanded Post of Milliken's Bend (LA), District of Vicksburg, Department of the Tennessee, Sept.–Oct. 1864. Battle honors: Bayou Cache, Chickasaw Bluffs, Arkansas Post, Milliken's Bend.

Born: Nov. 9, 1836 Princeton, IL

Julian Edward Bryant (author's photograph).

Julian Edward Bryant (James Barnet, editor. *The Martyrs and Heroes of Illinois in the Great Rebellion.* Second Edition. Chicago, IL, 1866).

Julian Edward Bryant (photographed by Joe H. Scibird, Corner Center & Jefferson Streets., Bloomington, Illinois; author's photograph).

Died: May 14, 1865 Brazos Santiago, TX (accidentally drowned while bathing in the Gulf of Mexico)

Occupation: Artist and teacher of drawing, Illinois State Normal University, Bloomington, IL

Miscellaneous: Resided Princeton, Bureau Co., IL. Nephew of noted poet William Cullen Bryant.

Buried: Oakland Cemetery, Princeton, IL

References: Donald M. Murray and Robert M. Rodney, "Colonel Julian E. Bryant: Champion of the Negro Soldier," *Journal of the Illinois State Historical Society*, Vol. 56, No. 2 (Summer 1963). James Barnet, editor. *The Martyrs and Heroes of Illinois in the Great Rebellion.* Second Edition. Chicago, IL, 1866. Obituary, *Bureau County Republican*, June 1, 1865. Karen Berfield, "Julian Bryant: Martyr for Equality," *Civil War Times Illustrated*, Vol. 22, Issue 2 (April 1983). Henry C. Bradsby, editor. *History of Bureau County, Illinois.* Chicago, IL, 1885. Military Service File, National Archives. Letters Received, Colored Troops Branch, Adjutant General's Office, File B13(CT)1863, National Archives. Virgil G. Way, compiler. *History of the Thirty-Third Regiment Illinois Veteran Volunteer Infantry in the Civil War.* Gibson City, IL, 1902.

Wallace Campbell

1 Lieutenant, Co. F, 12 IL Infantry (3 months), May 2, 1861. Honorably mustered out, Aug. 1, 1861. Captain, Co. F, 12 IL Infantry (3 years), Aug. 3, 1861. Colonel, 2 AL Infantry of African Descent, Dec. 26, 1863. Designation of regiment changed to

Wallace Campbell (Hesler, Artist, No. 113 Lake Street, Chicago, IL; author's photograph).

Wallace Campbell (L.M. Strayer Collection).

110 U.S. Colored Infantry, June 25, 1864. Commanded Colored Troops, Left Wing, 16 Army Corps, Department of the Tennessee, April–Aug 1864. Commanded Post of Athens (AL), District of Northern Alabama, Department of the Cumberland, Aug.–Sept. 1864. Surrendered Post of Athens, AL, and taken prisoner, Sept. 24, 1864. Exchanged Dec. 6, 1864. Despite widespread condemnation of his conduct in surrendering Athens and despite his request for a court of inquiry, no further action was taken in his case. He resigned May 6, 1865, since "The regiment is at present unarmed and broken into detachments doing duty as Pioneers in 2nd Division, 15th Army Corps." Battle honors: Fort Donelson, Shiloh, Forrest's Raid into Northern Alabama and Middle Tennessee (Athens).

Born: 1838? Galena, IL

Died: Feb. 10, 1893 Wheaton, IL

Education: Attended Western Military Institute, University of Nashville (TN), 1856–57

Occupation: Bookkeeper before war. Maltster after war.

Miscellaneous: Resided Galena, Jo Daviess Co., IL, before war; Chicago, IL; and Wheaton, DuPage Co., IL, after war. Son of Colonel George W. Campbell (Commissary of Subsistence).

Buried: Graceland Cemetery, Chicago, IL (Section B, Lot 350)

References: Pension File and Military Service File, National Archives. William A. Dobak. *Freedom by the Sword: The U.S. Colored Troops, 1862–1867.* Washington, D.C., 2011. "Funeral of Col. Wallace Campbell," *Chicago Daily Tribune,* Feb. 14, 1893. Death Notice, *Chicago Daily Tribune,* Feb. 12, 1893. *The History of Jo Daviess County, Illinois.* Chicago, IL, 1878.

Louis Henry Carpenter

Private, Co. C, 6 U.S. Cavalry, Nov. 1, 1861. 2 Lieutenant, 6 U.S. Cavalry, July 17, 1862. Acting ADC, Staff of Major Gen. Philip H. Sheridan, Cavalry Corps, Army of the Potomac, May–Sept. 1864. 1 Lieutenant, 6 U.S. Cavalry, Sept. 28, 1864. Lieutenant Colonel, 5 U.S. Colored Cavalry, Oct. 1, 1864. Commanded Post of Camp Nelson (KY), 1 Division, Department of Kentucky, March–April 1865. Commanded Post of Covington (KY), 1 Division, Department of Kentucky, April–May 1865. Colonel, 5 U.S. Colored Cavalry, Nov. 2, 1865. Honorably mustered out of volunteer service, March 16, 1866. Bvt. 1 Lieutenant, USA, July 3, 1863, for gallant and meritorious services in the battle of Gettysburg, PA. Bvt. Captain, USA, Sept. 19, 1864, for gallant and meritorious services in the battle of Winchester, VA. Bvt. Major and Bvt. Lieutenant Colonel, USA, March 13, 1865, for gallant and meritorious services during the war. Bvt. Colonel, USV, Sept. 28, 1865, for meritorious services during the war. Battle honors: Fredericksburg, Beverly Ford, Gettysburg Campaign (Fairfield), Wilderness, Spotsylvania, Yellow Tavern, Trevilian Station, Winchester, Fisher's Hill, Marion, Saltville.

Born: Feb. 11, 1839 Glassboro, NJ

Died: Jan. 21, 1916 Philadelphia, PA

Education: Graduated Philadelphia (PA) Central High School, 1856. Attended University of Pennsylvania, Philadelphia, PA.

Other Wars: Brig. Gen., USV, Spanish American War

Occupation: Regular Army (Brig. Gen., retired Oct. 19, 1899)

Offices/Honors: Medal of Honor, Indian Campaigns, Kansas and Colorado, Sept.–Oct. 1868. "Was gallant and meritorious throughout the campaign, especially in the combat of October 15 and in the forced march on September 23, 24 and 25 to the relief of Forsyth's Scouts, who were known to be in danger of annihilation by largely superior forces of Indians."

Miscellaneous: Resided Philadelphia, PA

Buried: Trinity Episcopal Church New Cemetery, Swedesboro, NJ

References: St. Clair A. Mulholland. *Military Order Congress Medal of Honor Legion of the United States.* Philadelphia, PA, 1905. William H. Powell and Edward Shippen, editors. *Officers of the Army and Navy (Regular) Who Served in the Civil War.* Philadelphia, PA, 1892. Edward Carpenter and Louis Henry Carpenter, compilers. *Samuel Carpenter and His Descendants.* Philadelphia,

Louis Henry Carpenter (Stowe's Photographic Gallery, McDowell's Block, Corner 4th & Green Sts., Louisville, KY; courtesy Henry Deeks).

Louis Henry Carpenter (H.D. Stowe, 212 Fourth Street, Between Main & Market, Louisville, KY; author's photograph).

Louis Henry Carpenter (post-war) (USAHEC [RG641S-MOL-PA11.27]).

PA, 1912. Letters Received, Colored Troops Branch, Adjutant General's Office, File C653(CT)1865, National Archives. Military Service File, National Archives. William H. Carter. *From Yorktown to Santiago with the Sixth U.S. Cavalry.* Baltimore, MD, 1900. George Lang, Raymond L. Collins, and Gerard F. White, compilers. *Medal of Honor Recipients, 1863–1994.* New York City, NY, 1995. Richard D. Sears. *Camp Nelson, Kentucky: A Civil War History.* Lexington, KY, 2002. Obituary, *Washington Evening Star,* Jan. 21, 1916.

Edwin W. Chamberlain

Major, 1 IA Cavalry, June 13, 1861. Reacting to the hostility of Colonel Fitz-Henry Warren and the scorn of regimental officers, who told him that his "continuance in the office of Major is utterly at variance with the peace, harmony and usefulness of the regiment," he resigned April 4, 1863, "not willing longer to submit to such degrading and insulting treatment." *Colonel,* 11 LA Infantry of African Descent (later 49 U.S. Colored Infantry), May 7, 1863. Dismissed Sept. 16, 1863, for "cowardice in front of the enemy in the engagement at Milliken's Bend, LA." Dismissal revoked and resignation accepted, Sept. 26, 1863. Battle honors: Milliken's Bend.

Born: 1832? Alton, NH

Died: March 23, 1882, Chicago, IL

Occupation: Insurance agent

Miscellaneous: Resided Burlington, Des Moines Co., IA; St. Louis, MO; and Chicago, IL

Buried: Graceland Cemetery, Chicago, IL (Section R, Lot 42)

References: Obituary, *Chicago Daily Tribune,* March 28, 1882. Military Service File, National Archives. Letters Received, Volunteer Service Branch, Adjutant General's Office, File R466(VS)1862, National Archives. Letters Received, Colored Troops Branch, Adjutant General's Office, File C42(CT)1863, National Archives. William A. Dobak. *Freedom by the Sword: The U.S. Colored Troops, 1862–1867.* Washington, D.C., 2011. Cyrus Sears. *The Battle of Milliken's Bend and Some Reflections Concerning the Colored Troops, the Debt We Owe Them, and How We Paid It.* Columbus, OH, 1909. John Wearmouth, editor. *The Cornwell Chronicles: Tales of an American Life on the Erie Canal, Building Chicago, in the Volunteer Civil War Western Army, on the Farm, in a Country Store.* Bowie, MD, 1998. Charles H. Lothrop. *A History of the First Regiment Iowa Cavalry Veteran Volunteers.* Lyons, IA, 1890.

Edwin W. Chamberlain (Whipple, 297 Washington St., Boston, MA; Abraham Lincoln Presidential Library & Museum).

James Cushman Clark

Captain, Co. H, 7 NY Cavalry, Nov. 6, 1861. Honorably mustered out, March 31, 1862. Captain, AAG, USV, May 12, 1862. AAG, Staff of Brig. Gen. Truman Seymour, 3 Division, 5 Army Corps, Army of the Potomac (and later 1 Brigade, 3 Division, 3 Army Corps, Army of Virginia). Resigned Dec. 3, 1862. Lieutenant Colonel, 7 Infantry, Corps d'Afrique, Feb. 25, 1863. Colonel, 7 Infantry, Corps d'Afrique, June 5, 1863. Commanded 2 Brigade, 2 Division, Corps d'Afrique, Department of the Gulf, March–July 1864. Designation of regiment changed to 79 (Old) U.S. Colored Infantry, April 4, 1864. Battle honors: Peninsular Campaign (Mechanicsville, Gaines' Mill, New Market Cross Roads), 2nd Bull Run, Port Hudson.

Born: Dec. 7, 1814 Wynantskill, Rensselaer Co., NY
Died: Sept. 5, 1864 Troy, NY (inflammation of the stomach)
Occupation: Merchant (confectionery and fancy goods)
Miscellaneous: Resided Troy, Rensselaer Co., NY
Buried: Oakwood Cemetery, Troy, NY (Section F, Lot 131)

References: Obituary, *Troy Daily Times,* Sept. 6, 1864. Obituary, *Troy Daily Whig,* Sept. 6, 1864. Pension File and Military Service File, National Archives. Letters Received, Colored Troops Branch, Adjutant General's Office, File C22(CT)1864, National Archives. Letters Received, Adjutant General's Office,

James Cushman Clark (USAHEC [RG 526S-NYSAG.2371]).

Files C490(AGO)1862, C1160(AGO) 1862, and C1289(AGO)1862, National Archives.

James Cushman Clark (Brooks & Blauvelt, Photographers, Port Hudson, LA; Massachusetts MOLLUS Collection, USAHEC [Vol. 109, p 5645L]).

John Clifford Cobb

1 Lieutenant, Co. H, 4 ME Infantry, June 15, 1861. Resigned Sept. 27, 1861. 1 Lieutenant, Co. D, 15 ME Infantry, Dec. 10, 1861. Colonel, 2 Engineers, Corps d'Afrique, Aug. 17, 1863. Commanded Post of Matagorda Island (TX), 13 Army Corps, Department of the Gulf, Jan. 1864. Commanded Provisional Brigade, 1 Division, 13 Army Corps, Department of the Gulf, March–June 1864. Designation of regiment changed to 96 U.S. Colored Infantry, April 4, 1864. Commanded 1 Brigade, 3 Division, U.S. Colored Troops, Department of the Gulf, Oct. 1864–Feb. 1865. Commanded Engineer Brigade, Military Division of West Mississippi, May 1865. Resigned July 18, 1865, since "I find my private affairs require my personal attention, and it is a duty which I owe to myself and family to leave the service." Battle honors: 1st Bull Run, Fort Gaines and Fort Morgan, Mobile Campaign.

Born: March 3, 1837, Westbrook, ME
Died: April 2, 1910, Portland, ME
Occupation: Lawyer
Offices/Honors: Maine House of Representatives, 1871
Miscellaneous: Resided Rockland, Knox Co., ME, before war; Windham, Cumberland Co., ME, 1865–72; and Portland, Cumberland Co., ME, after 1872
Buried: Evergreen Cemetery, Portland, ME (Section R, Lot 717)
References: *Biographical Review Cumberland County, Maine.* Boston, MA,

John Clifford Cobb (courtesy Henry Deeks).

John Clifford Cobb (Moses & Piffet, 93 Camp Street, New Orleans, LA; courtesy Wayne Jorgenson).

1896. Obituary Circular, Whole No. 279, Maine MOLLUS. Samuel T. Dole. *Windham in the Past.* Auburn, ME, 1916. Pension File and Military Service File, National Archives. Letters Received, Colored Troops Branch, Adjutant General's Office, File C116(CT)1866, National Archives. John C. Cobb, "One Year of My More Than Three Years' Service with the Army of the Gulf," *War Papers Read Before the Commandery of the State of Maine MOLLUS.* Vol. 3. Portland, ME, 1908.

John E. Cone

Civilian drillmaster with 25 IL Infantry in Jefferson City, MO, in Sept. 1861. Civilian drillmaster with 107 IL Infantry in Elizabethtown, KY, in Oct. 1862. Colonel, 54 U.S. Colored Infantry, March 26, 1864. "The circumstances of my family requiring my presence at home and attention to business," he resigned Feb. 22, 1865, giving as additional reasons, "to promote the efficiency of my regiment and the good of the service by surrendering the command to a more efficient officer, and to promote harmony and cooperation among the officers of the regiment."

Born: Nov. 25, 1827 Cortland Co., NY
Died: Jan. 8, 1885 Homer, IL
Occupation: Lawyer
Miscellaneous: Resided Chicago, IL (1860); Tomah, Monroe Co., WI (1870); Urbana, Champaign Co., IL (1880); and Homer, Champaign Co., IL
Buried: Old Homer Cemetery, Homer, IL
References: William Whitney Cone, compiler. *Some Account of the Cone Family in America, Principally of the Descendants of Daniel Cone, Who Settled in*

Haddam, Connecticut, in 1662. Topeka, KS, 1903. *History of Champaign County, Illinois.* Philadelphia, PA, 1878. Obituary, *Champaign Daily Gazette,* Jan. 13, 1885. Pension File and Military Service File, National Archives. Letters Received, Colored Troops Branch, Adjutant General's Office, File C220(CT)1864, National Archives. Letters Received, Volunteer Service Branch, Adjutant General's Office, File C112(VS)1861, National Archives. Letters Received, Adjutant General's Office, File C1245(AGO)1861, National Archives. A. Fred Kaufman, "The Fifty-Fourth U.S. Colored Infantry: The Forgotten Regiment," *Ozark Historical Review,* Vol. 16, No.1 (Spring 1987).

James William Conine

2 Lieutenant, Co. E, 1 KY Infantry, May 10, 1861. 1 Lieutenant, Adjutant, 1 KY Infantry, June 28, 1861. Acting ADC, Staff of Brig. Gen. Jacob D. Cox, Nov. 1861–Oct. 1863. Co. E, 1 KY Infantry, was detached as Simmonds' Independent Battery, KY Light Artillery, Jan. 1862. 1 Lieutenant, Simmonds' Independent Battery, KY Light Artillery, March 30, 1862. Colonel, 5 U.S. Colored Infantry, Nov. 20, 1863. Honorably discharged "on account of physical disability, from wounds received in action," Sept. 13, 1864. Battle honors: South Mountain, Antietam, Morgan's Ohio Raid, Petersburg (June 15–18, 1864).

Born: Dec. 13, 1836 New Haven, CT

Died: Oct. 26, 1895 Apalachicola, FL

Occupation: Carriage maker before war. Railroad worker and prison guard after war.

Miscellaneous: Resided Lexington, Fayette Co., KY (1860); Middleport, Meigs Co., OH; Columbus, Franklin Co., OH (1870); Lafayette, Tippecanoe Co., IN; and Apalachicola, Franklin Co., FL

Buried: Magnolia Cemetery, Apalachicola, FL (Block 34, Lot 10, Grave A)

John E. Cone (E.R. Gard's Photographic Art Palace, 102 Lake St., Chicago, IL; courtesy Henry Deeks).

James William Conine (courtesy Dennis M. Keesee).

References: Pension File and Military Service File, National Archives. Letters Received, Colored Troops Branch, Adjutant General's Office, File C322(CT)1863, National Archives. Versalle F. Washington. *Eagles on Their Buttons: A Black Infantry Regiment in the Civil War*. Columbia, MO, 1999.

John Benajah Cook

1 Sergeant, Co. K, 1 ME Infantry (3 months), May 3, 1861. Honorably mustered out, Aug. 5, 1861. 2 Lieutenant, Co. K, 7 ME Infantry, Aug. 21, 1861. 1 Lieutenant, Co. K, 7 ME Infantry, Dec. 25, 1861. Captain, Co. I, 7 ME Infantry, Jan. 24, 1862. GSW right leg, Antietam, MD, Sept. 17, 1862. Major, 22 U.S. Colored Infantry, Jan. 1, 1864. GSW right side and right arm, Fort Harrison, VA, Sept. 30, 1864. Lieutenant Colonel, 5 U.S. Colored Infantry, Oct. 21, 1864. Honorably discharged, April 13, 1865, "on account of physical disability from wounds received in action." Restored to his command, May 8, 1865, having provided satisfactory evidence that he is physically fit to perform service in the field. Colonel, 5 U.S. Colored Infantry, Sept. 26, 1865. Honorably mustered out, Oct. 8, 1865. Battle honors: Yorktown, Antietam, Petersburg (June 15, 1864), New Market Heights, Fort Harrison.

James William Conine (Hoag & Quick's Art Palace, No. 100 4th St., opp. Post Office, Cincinnati, Ohio; courtesy Timothy R. Brookes).

Born: Dec. 30, 1839 Willimantic, CT

Died: Oct. 15, 1892 Chicago, IL

Occupation: Weaver and cotton mill overseer before war. Grain merchant and dealer in agricultural implements after war.

Offices/Honors: North Carolina Senate, 1868–70. Commander, Iowa Department, GAR, 1883–84.

Miscellaneous: Resided Lewiston, Androscoggin Co., ME; Johnston Co., NC, 1867–71; and Carroll, Carroll Co., IA, after 1871

Buried: Carroll City Cemetery, Carroll, IA (Lot 37)

References: Pension File and Military Service File, National Archives. Obituary, *Carroll Sentinel,* Oct. 17–18, 1892. *History of Western Iowa: Its Settlement and Growth.* Sioux City, IA, 1882. "The Senate of North Carolina," *Raleigh Daily Standard,* Dec. 18, 1868. Obituary, *Waterloo Courier,* Oct. 26, 1892. Letters Received, Volunteer Service Branch, Adjutant General's Office, File C1218(VS)1864, National Archives. Versalle F. Washington. *Eagles on Their Buttons: A Black Infantry Regiment in the Civil War.* Columbia, MO, 1999. Letters Received, Commission Branch, Adjutant General's Office, File C1451(CB)1866, National Archives. Letters Received, Colored Troops Branch, Adjutant General's Office, File A357(CT)1865, National Archives. Paul Maclean. *History of Carroll County, Iowa.* Chicago, IL, 1912.

John Benajah Cook (author's photograph).

Nathan W. Daniels

1 Lieutenant, Co. H, 13 OH Infantry, May 10, 1862. Honorably mustered out, July 13, 1862. Colonel, 2 LA Native Guards, Oct. 12, 1862. Commanded Post of Ship Island (MS), Department of the Gulf, Jan.–April 1863. Designation of regiment changed to 2 Infantry, Corps d'Afrique (later 74 U.S. Colored Infantry), June 6, 1863. Dismissed Aug. 11, 1863, "for conduct unbecoming an officer and a gentleman, in grossly insulting an officer of the Navy, while in company with a lady." Judge Advocate General Joseph Holt declined, July 18, 1867, to take action on his appeal for revocation of his dismissal, describing Daniels as "a disgrace to the service ... in view of the circumstances of the gross misconduct upon which his dismissal was based." Battle honors: Pascagoula.

Nathan W. Daniels (author's photograph).

Born: May 10, 1835, Syracuse, NY

Died: Oct. 2, 1867 New Orleans, LA (yellow fever)

Occupation: Lawyer

Offices/Honors: Appointed U.S. Collector of Internal Revenue, 2 District of Louisiana, June 24, 1865, "but owing to his radical sentiments, his friends deserted him, and refused the necessary bonds to enable him to enter upon the duties of the office."

Miscellaneous: Resided Waterville, Lucas Co., OH,

Nathan W. Daniels (right, and friend) (Alexander Gardner, Galleries 511 Seventh Street and 332 Pennsylvania Avenue, Washington, DC; courtesy Olaf).

Nathan W. Daniels (left, and friend) (Library of Congress [Nathan W. Daniels Diary and Scrapbook]).

before war; Washington, D.C.; Pointe Coupee Parish, LA; and New Orleans, LA, after war. His second wife was Cora L.V. Hatch, a famous psychic medium and leader of Spiritualism.

Buried: Lafayette Cemetery No. 1, New Orleans, LA (Square 2, Tomb 292, unmarked)

References: Clare P. Weaver, editor. *Thank God My Regiment an African One: The Civil War Diary of Colonel Nathan W. Daniels.* Baton Rouge, LA, 1998. "Nathan W. Daniels Diary and Scrapbook," https://www.loc.gov/collections/nathan-w-daniels-diary-and-scrapbook/. Clark Waggoner, editor. *History of the City of Toledo and Lucas County, Ohio.* New York and Toledo, 1888. Letters Received, Colored Troops Branch, Adjutant General's Office, Files D103(CT)1863 and G27(CT)1863, National Archives. Military Service File, National Archives. James G. Hollandsworth, Jr. *The Louisiana Native Guards: The Black Military Experience During the Civil War.* Baton Rouge, LA, 1995. William A. Dobak. *Freedom by the Sword: The U.S. Colored Troops, 1862–1867.* Washington, D.C., 2011.

James Hamilton Davidson

1 Lieutenant, Co. B, 14 KY Infantry, Oct. 10, 1861. Captain, Co. B, 14 KY Infantry, June 6, 1862. Resigned June 17, 1863. Major, 49 KY Infantry, Dec. 23, 1863. Colonel, 122 U.S. Colored Infantry, Dec. 14, 1864. Commanded Military Prison and Post, Newport News, VA, April–May 1865. Commanded 2 Brigade, 3 Division, 25 Army Corps, District of the Rio Grande, Department of Texas, Oct. 1865. Honorably mustered out, Jan. 17, 1866. Battle honors: Middle Creek, Operations at Cumberland Gap (Tazewell).

Born: Jan. 25, 1839 Burlington, OH

Died: Dec. 1, 1925 Chicago, IL

Education: Graduated Ohio Wesleyan University, Delaware, OH, 1861

Occupation: Lawyer and real estate agent

Miscellaneous: Resided Burlington, Lawrence Co., OH, before war; St. Paul, Ramsey Co., MN; and Chicago, IL, after war

Buried: Oakland Cemetery, St. Paul, MN (Block 51, Lot 3)

References: Earnest H. Davidson, "The Life of Colonel James H. Davidson," www.minnesotalegalhistoryproject.org/assets/Col.%20James%20Davidson.pdf. Christopher C. Andrews, editor. *History of St. Paul, Minnesota.* Syracuse, NY, 1890. Nelson W. Evans. *A History of Scioto County, Ohio, Together*

James Hamilton Davidson (post-war, 1889) (Zimmerman & Whitstruck; Minnesota Historical Society [por 14342 r3]).

with A Pioneer Record of Southern Ohio. Portsmouth, OH, 1903. Elizabeth D. Harbaugh. *The Davidson Genealogy.* Ironton, OH, 1948. Almira L. White. *Genealogy of the Descendants of John White of Wenham and Lancaster, Massachusetts, 1638–1900.* Haverhill, MA, 1900. Pension File and Military Service File, National Archives. Letters Received, Volunteer Service Branch, Adjutant General's Office, File D378(VS)1864, National Archives. Letters Received, Commission Branch, Adjutant General's Office, File D581(CB)1865, National Archives.

Thomas Jefferson Downey

1 Lieutenant, Co. B, 113 OH Infantry, Oct. 10, 1862. Captain, Co. D, 113 OH Infantry, Jan. 14, 1863. Colonel, 15 U.S. Colored Infantry, March 11, 1864. Commanded Post of Springfield (TN), District of Tennessee, Department of the Cumberland, Aug.–Dec. 1864. Dismissed Dec. 6, 1864, for complicity with a New York recruiting agent in procuring fraudulent credits for his New York district by representing certain men recruited for the regiment in Tennessee as being recruited for his district.

Born: Oct. 20, 1828 Canton, OH
Died: March 31, 1869 Nelsonville, OH
Occupation: Presbyterian clergyman
Miscellaneous: Resided Reynoldsburg, Franklin Co., OH; Tiffin, Seneca Co., OH; and Nelsonville, York Twp., Athens Co., OH
Buried: Fort Street Cemetery, Nelsonville, OH
References: Military Service File, National Archives. "Nelsonville Church Re-Dedicated," *Athens Sunday Messenger*, Oct. 17, 1926. Obituary, *Wyandot County Republican*, April 15, 1869. Obituary, *Jackson Standard*, April 8, 1869. "An Episode of the Late War," *Lebanon Courier*, Oct. 31, 1872. Francis M. McAdams. *Every-Day Soldier Life, or A History of the One Hundred and Thirteenth Ohio Volunteer Infantry.* Columbus, OH, 1884. Court-martial Case

James Hamilton Davidson (post-war) (Christopher C. Andrews, editor. *History of St. Paul, Minnesota.* Syracuse, NY, 1890).

Thomas Jefferson Downey (Charles A. Saylor, Reading, PA; courtesy Ann Ruyle Hoffstetter).

Files, 1809–1894, File LL-3193, National Archives. Letters Received, Volunteer Service Branch, Adjutant General's Office, File A265(VS)1865, National Archives. Letters Received, Colored Troops Branch, Adjutant General's Office, File M40(CT)1865, National Archives. www.ancestry.com.

Alexander Duncan

Sergeant, Co. B, 11 OH Infantry (3 months), April 26, 1861. Honorably mustered out, June 20, 1861. 1 Sergeant, Co. B, 11 OH Infantry (3 years), June 20, 1861. Captain, Co. B, 11 OH Infantry, Oct. 9, 1861. Honorably mustered out, June 21, 1864. Colonel, 72 U.S. Colored Infantry, Oct. 27, 1864. Commanded Post of Covington and Newport (KY), 1 Division, Department of Kentucky, March–April 1865 and June 1865. Honorably mustered out, July 21, 1865. Lieutenant Colonel, 125 U.S. Colored Infantry, July 22, 1865. Commanded Post of Cairo (IL), Department of the Ohio, Jan.–April 1866. Commanded Post of Fort Selden (NM), District of New Mexico, Department of the Missouri, Aug.–Nov. 1866. Commanded Post of Fort Bayard (NM), District of New Mexico, Department of the Missouri, Nov. 1866–Aug. 1867. Honorably mustered out, Dec. 20, 1867.

Born: May 12, 1834, PA

Died: May 25, 1890, Oakland, CA

Occupation: Boat captain before war. Salesman and bookkeeper after war.

Miscellaneous: Resided Piqua, Miami Co., OH, before war; San Francisco, CA; and Oakland, Alameda Co., CA, after war

Buried: Mountain View Cemetery, Oakland, CA (GAR Plot, Section 3, Grave 22)

References: Pension File and Military Service File, National Archives.

Thomas Jefferson Downey (post-war) (courtesy Ann Ruyle Hoffstetter).

Alexander Duncan (courtesy The Excelsior Brigade).

Obituary, *San Francisco Chronicle*, May 26, 1890. Obituary, *Oakland Evening Tribune*, May 26, 1890. Letters Received, Colored Troops Branch, Adjutant General's Office, Files D360(CT)1864 and O20(CT)1866, National Archives. Letters Received, Commission Branch, Adjutant General's Office, File D836(CB)1866, National Archives. Russell K. Brown, "The Last Civil War Volunteers: The 125th U.S. Colored Infantry in New Mexico, 1866–1867," *Army History*, No. 92 (Summer 2014). Joshua H. Horton and Solomon Teverbaugh, compilers. *A History of the Eleventh Regiment, (Ohio Volunteer Infantry)*. Dayton, OH, 1866.

Willard Chauncey Earle

Captain, Co. B, 12 IA Infantry, Nov. 25, 1861. Taken prisoner, Shiloh, TN, April 6, 1862. Confined Madison, GA; and Richmond, VA. Paroled Oct. 12, 1862. *Colonel*, 71 U.S. Colored Infantry, March 29, 1864. Regiment consolidated with 70 U.S. Colored Infantry, Nov. 8, 1864. Colonel, 70 U.S. Colored Infantry, Nov. 9, 1864. Commanded Sub-District of Vidalia (LA), District of Natchez, Department of Mississippi, March 1865. Commanded Post of Rodney (MS), District of Natchez, Department of Mississippi, April–May 1865. Tendered his resignation, July 11, 1865, since "the war is over, and my private business demands my attention." Sentenced by court martial, Aug. 25, 1865, to be suspended from command for thirty days, with loss of rank and pay, for "Failing to receipt for private property taken from a citizen." Although Brig. Gen. John W. Davidson recommended his dismissal from the service, Judge Advocate General Joseph Holt concluded that "the evidence affords good reasons for believing that [Davidson] must have been influenced by a singular misapprehension of the facts of the case." His resignation was finally accepted, Oct. 23, 1865. Battle honors: Fort Donelson, Shiloh, Jackson, Vicksburg Campaign.

Born: Oct. 7, 1833 Honesdale, PA

Died: Feb. 10, 1920 St. Petersburg, FL

Education: Attended Rush Medical College, Chicago, IL. Graduated Jefferson Medical College, Philadelphia, PA, 1867.

Occupation: Lumber manufacturer and miller before war. Physician and merchant after war.

Offices/Honors: Iowa House of Representatives, 1882–84 and 1907–09. Iowa Senate, 1886–88.

Miscellaneous: Resided Waukon, Allamakee Co., IA

Buried: Oakland Cemetery, Waukon, IA (Lot 139)

Willard Chauncey Earle (post-war) (State Historical Society of Iowa, Des Moines).

References: Ellery M. Hancock.

Willard Chauncey Earle (post-war) (Huffman and Barnard, Waukon, IA; courtesy Gloria and Jon Payne).

Past and Present of Allamakee County, Iowa: A Record of Settlement, Organization, Progress and Achievement. Chicago, IL, 1913. *A Memorial and Biographical Record of Iowa.* Chicago, IL, 1896. Benjamin F. Gue. *Biographies and Portraits of the Progressive Men of Iowa.* Des Moines, IA, 1899. Obituary, *Waukon Standard,* Feb. 18, 1920. W. E. Alexander. *History of Winneshiek and Allamakee Counties, Iowa.* Sioux City, IA, 1882. Pension File and Military Service File, National Archives. Letters Received, Colored Troops Branch, Adjutant General's Office, File E74(CT)1864, National Archives. Court-martial Case Files, 1809–1894, File MM-2902, National Archives. David W. Reed. *Campaigns and Battles of the Twelfth Regiment Iowa Veteran Volunteer Infantry from Organization, September 1861, to Muster-Out, January 20, 1866.* Evanston, IL, 1903. Pliny Earle, compiler. *Ralph Earle and His Descendants.* Worcester, MA, 1888.

Robert Helm Earnest

2 Lieutenant, Co. F, 26 KY Infantry, Jan. 3, 1862. 1 Lieutenant, Co. F, 26 KY Infantry, April 10, 1862. Captain, Co. F, 26 KY Infantry, June 22, 1862. Captain, Co. B, 26 KY Infantry, April 1, 1864. Colonel, 115 U.S. Colored Infantry, Oct. 16, 1864. Commanded Post of Paris (KY), Military District of Kentucky, Department of the Ohio, Dec. 1864. Resigned Nov. 6, 1865, due to "the illness of my family and the embarrassed condition of my pecuniary affairs." Battle honors: Shiloh.

Born: Feb. 16, 1833 Franklin, KY

Died: March 10, 1916 McAlester, OK

Occupation: School teacher and law student before war. Lawyer after war.

Offices/Honors: County Judge, Fort Bend Co., TX, 1886–88. United States Commissioner, McAlester, OK, 1891–93 and 1907–15.

Miscellaneous: Resided Franklin, Simpson Co., KY, to 1872; Richmond, Fort Bend Co., TX, 1872–91; and McAlester, Pittsburg Co., OK, after 1891

Buried: Oak Hill Cemetery, McAlester, OK (Section 25)

References: Luther B. Hill. *A History of the State of Oklahoma.* Chicago and New York, 1909.

Robert Helm Earnest (Wm. Bryan, Photographer, Russellville, KY; author's photograph).

Obituary, *Tulsa Daily World*, March 12, 1916. Pension File and Military Service File, National Archives. Letters Received, Colored Troops Branch, Adjutant General's Office, File E114(CT)1864, National Archives. Clarence R. Wharton. *History of Fort Bend County*. Houston, TX, 1950.

Lucien Bonaparte Eaton

2 Lieutenant, Co. I, 65 OH Infantry, Oct. 5, 1861. 1 Lieutenant, Co. I, 65 OH Infantry, Nov. 22, 1861. Captain, Co. I, 65 OH Infantry, Jan. 1, 1863. Acting AIG, Staff of Colonel Charles G. Harker, 3 Brigade, 1 Division, 21 Army Corps, Army of the Cumberland, March–Oct. 1863. Acting AIG, Staff of Colonel Charles G. Harker, 3 Brigade, 2 Division, 4 Army Corps, Army of the Cumberland, Oct.–Dec. 1863. *Lieutenant Colonel*, 69 U.S. Colored Infantry, March 17, 1865. *Colonel*, 69 U.S. Colored Infantry, April 24, 1865. Resigned May 18, 1865, "the war being over and my services no longer required." Battle honors: Perryville, Stone's River, Chickamauga, Missionary Ridge, Atlanta Campaign.

Born: March 8, 1837, Sutton, NH

Died: May 24, 1915, Memphis, TN

Education: Attended Phillips Academy, Andover, MA. Graduated Dartmouth College, Hanover, NH, 1859.

Lucien Bonaparte Eaton (John Cadwallader, 107 Summit Street, Toledo, OH; Eaton-Shirley Family Papers (1790–1939), William L. Clements Library, University of Michigan).

Lucien Bonaparte Eaton (J.P. Vail, Palmyra, NY; Eaton-Shirley Family Papers [1790–1939], William L. Clements Library, University of Michigan).

Occupation: School teacher before war. Newspaper editor and lawyer after war.

Offices/Honors: U.S. Marshal, Western District of Tennessee, 1870–77. Tennessee House of Representatives, 1881–83.

Miscellaneous: Resided Cleveland, Cuyahoga Co., OH, before war; Memphis, Shelby Co., TN, after war. Brother of Bvt. Brig. Gen. John Eaton, Jr.

Buried: Woodland Cemetery, Dayton, OH (Section 43, Lot 1008)

References: Nellie Zada Rice Molyneux, compiler. *History Genealogical and Biographical of the Eaton Families.* Syracuse, NY, 1911. O.F. Vedder. *History of the City of Memphis and Shelby County, Tennessee.* Syracuse, NY, 1888. Eaton-Shirley Family Papers (1790–1939), William L. Clements Library, University of Michigan. *History of Tennessee* from *the Earliest Time to the Present, Together with an Historical and a Biographical Sketch of the County of Shelby and the City of Memphis.* Nashville, TN, 1887. Walter J. Fraser, Jr., "Lucien Bonaparte Eaton: Politics and the Memphis Post, 1867–1869," *West Tennessee Historical Society Papers,* Vol. 20 (1966). Robert M. McBride and Dan M. Robison. *Biographical Directory of the Tennessee General Assembly.* Vol. 2, 1861–1901. Nashville, TN, 1979. George T. Chapman. *Sketches of the Alumni of Dartmouth College.* Cambridge, MA, 1867. Letters Received, Colored Troops Branch, Adjutant General's Office, File E71(CT)1864, National Archives. Pension File and Military Service File, National Archives. Wilbur F. Hinman. *The Story of the Sherman Brigade.* Alliance, OH, 1897.

Stark Fellows

1 Lieutenant, Co. D, 14 NH Infantry, Sept. 23, 1862. Lieutenant Colonel, 2 U.S. Colored Infantry, Aug. 19, 1863. Colonel, 2 U.S. Colored Infantry, Feb. 16, 1864. Battle honors: Tampa.

Born: April 15, 1840, Sandown, NH

Died: May 23, 1864, Key West, FL (yellow fever)

Education: Attended Thetford (VT) Academy. Graduated Dartmouth College, Hanover, NH, 1862.

Occupation: Student

Miscellaneous: Resided Sandown, Rockingham Co., NH; and Weare, Hillsborough Co., NH

Buried: Barrancas National Cemetery, Pensacola, FL (Section 16, Grave 1). Cenotaph in Center Cemetery, Sandown, NH.

References: Obituary, *Exeter News-Letter and Rockingham Advertiser,* June 13, 1864. Richard Holmes. *A View from Meeting House Hill: A History of Sandown, New Hampshire.* Portsmouth, NH, 1988. Horace

Stark Fellows (Massachusetts MOLLUS Collection, USAHEC [Vol. 126, p. 6470L]).

S. Cummings. *Dartmouth College. Sketches of the Class of 1862.* Washington, DC, 1884. *Biographical Review (Volume XXI) Containing Life Sketches of Leading Citizens of Strafford and Belknap Counties, New Hampshire.* Boston, MA, 1897. Military Service File, National Archives. Francis H. Buffum. *A Memorial of the Great Rebellion: Being a History of the Fourteenth Regiment New Hampshire Volunteers, Covering Its Three Years of Service, with Original Sketches of Army Life, 1862–1865.* Boston, MA, 1882. Letters Received, Colored Troops Branch, Adjutant General's Office, File C39(CT)1863, National Archives. George T. Chapman. *Sketches of the Alumni of Dartmouth College.* Cambridge, MA, 1867.

John Foley

1 Lieutenant, Co. H, 62 IL Infantry, April 10, 1862. Captain, Co. H, 62 IL Infantry, Sept. 23, 1862. Lieutenant Colonel, 2 West TN Infantry of African Descent, June 30, 1863. Designation of regiment changed to 61 U.S. Colored Infantry, March 11, 1864. Chief of Outposts, Staff of Brig. Gen. James C. Veatch, Post and Defenses of Memphis (TN), District of West Tennessee, Department of Mississippi, Dec. 1864. *Colonel,* 61 U.S. Colored Infantry, July 18, 1865. Honorably mustered out, Dec. 30, 1865. Battle honors: Operations against the Memphis and Charleston Railroad in West Tennessee (Wolf River Bridge), Expedition from La Grange, TN, to Tupelo, MS (Tupelo), Forrest's Raid into Northern Alabama and Middle Tennessee (Eastport).

Born: Nov. 13, 1829 Clark Co., OH

Died: April 27, 1883, Bloomington, IL

Occupation: Farmer and stock raiser

Miscellaneous: Resided Monticello, Piatt Co., IL, to 1870; and Quincy, Greenwood Co., KS, after 1870

Buried: Toronto Cemetery, Toronto, Woodson Co., KS

References: Obituary, *Toronto Topic,* May 4, 1883. Obituary, *Eureka Herald,* May 3, 1883. Military Service File, National Archives. Letters Received, Colored Troops Branch, Adjutant General's Office, File F215(CT)1865, National Archives. www.findagrave.com. www.ancestry.com.

Jacob Thomas Foster

Captain, 1 Independent Battery, WI Light Artillery, Sept. 29, 1861. Chief of Artillery, Staff of Brig. Gen. George W. Morgan, 7 Division, Army of the Ohio, April–June 1862. Chief of Artillery, Staff of Brig. Gen. George W. Morgan, Cumberland Division, District of Western Virginia, Department of the Ohio, Sept.–Oct. 1862. Chief of Artillery, Staff of Brig. Gen. Peter J. Osterhaus, 9 Division, 13 Army Corps, Army of the Tennessee, Jan.–July 1863. Shell wound, left shoulder, Big Black River Bridge, MS, May 17, 1863. Chief of Artillery, Staff of Major Gen. Edward O.C. Ord, 13 Army Corps, Department of the Gulf, Sept. 1863–Jan. 1864. Chief of Artillery, Staff of Major Gen. Nathaniel P. Banks, Department of the Gulf, Sept. 1864. Honorably mustered out, Oct. 13, 1864. Lieutenant Colonel, 1 WI Heavy Artillery, Dec. 24, 1864. Commanded Post of Smithland (KY), District of Western Kentucky, Department of Kentucky, March–May 1865. Colonel, 13 U.S. Colored Heavy Artillery, June 23, 1865. Honorably mustered out, Nov. 18, 1865. Battle honors: Cumberland Gap Campaign,

Chickasaw Bluffs, Arkansas Post, Big Black River Bridge, Vicksburg Campaign, Red River Campaign.

Born: June 23, 1827, Mentz, Cayuga Co., NY

Died: Dec. 31, 1906 Chicago, IL

Education: Attended Auburn (NY) Academy

Occupation: Civil engineer and bank cashier before war. Civil engineer and surveyor after war.

Miscellaneous: Resided La Crosse, La Crosse Co., WI, before war; and Chicago, IL, after war

Buried: Oakwoods Cemetery, Chicago, IL (Section H, Division 1, Lot 166)

References: Alfred T. Andreas. *History of Chicago from the Earliest Period to the Present Time.* Chicago, IL, 1884. Frederick Clifton Pierce. *Foster Genealogy, Being the Record of the Posterity of Reginald Foster, an Early Inhabitant of Ipswich, in New England.* Chicago, IL, 1899. Obituary, *Chicago Inter Ocean,* Jan. 1, 1907. Obituary, *La Crosse Tribune,* Jan. 2, 1907. Dan Webster and Don C. Cameron. *History of the First Wisconsin Battery Light Artillery.* Washington, D.C., 1907. Pension File and Military Service File, National Archives. Letters Received, Colored Troops Branch, Adjutant General's Office, File F239(CT)1864, National Archives. Benjamin F. Bryant, editor. *Memoirs of La Crosse County.* Madison, WI, 1907. *History of La Crosse County, Wisconsin.* Chicago, IL, 1881.

Jacob Thomas Foster (Dan Webster and Don C. Cameron. *History of the First Wisconsin Battery Light Artillery.* Washington, D.C., 1907).

Jacob Thomas Foster (Carpenter & Mullen, Magnolia Gallery, Lexington, KY; author's photograph).

Charles Wesley Fribley

Private, Co. A, 11 PA Infantry (3 months), April 24, 1861. Honorably mustered out, July 31, 1861. 1 Sergeant, Co. F, 84 PA Infantry, Oct. 24, 1861. 2 Lieutenant, Co. F, 84 PA Infantry, May 19, 1862. *1 Lieutenant, Adjutant,* 84 PA Infantry, July 17, 1862. Captain, Co. F, 84 PA Infantry, Oct. 1, 1862. Acting AAG, Staff of Colonel Samuel M. Bowman, 2 Brigade, 3 Division, 3 Army Corps, Army of the Potomac, March–June 1863. Colonel, 8 U.S. Colored Infantry, Nov. 24, 1863. GSW heart,

Charles Wesley Fribley (O.H. Willard's New Galleries. 1206 Chestnut Street, Philadelphia, PA; author's photograph).

Charles Wesley Fribley (R.W. Addis, Photographer, 308 Penna. Avenue, Washington, D.C.; courtesy David L. Richards).

Olustee, FL, Feb. 20, 1864. Battle honors: Falling Waters, Kernstown, Cedar Mountain, 2nd Bull Run, Fredericksburg, Chancellorsville, Olustee.

Born: Sept. 25, 1835 Loyalsock Twp., Lycoming Co., PA

Died: Feb. 20, 1864 KIA Olustee, FL

Education: Attended Dickinson Seminary, Williamsport, PA

Occupation: School teacher

Miscellaneous: Resided Muncy, Lycoming Co., PA

Buried: Olustee, FL (body never recovered)

Charles Wesley Fribley (Massachusetts MOLLUS Collection, USAHEC [Vol. 109, p. 5635]).

References: David L. Richards. *"Recollections of Col. Charles W. Fribley,"* From the October 25, 1870 and November 1, 1870, Issues of the Muncy Luminary. Gettysburg, PA, 1994. Henry C. Moyer, "Col. Charles W. Fribley," *The Now and Then*, Vol. 2, No. 11 (March–April 1890). David L. Richards.

Priceless Treasures: A History of the Muncy Soldiers' Memorial and the Patriots It Commemorates. Muncy, PA, 2001. Obituary, *Philadelphia Inquirer,* March 22, 1864. Obituary, *Sunbury American,* March 5, 1864. Pension File and Military Service File, National Archives. Letters Received, Colored Troops Branch, Adjutant General's Office, File F105(CT)1863, National Archives.

Charles Byron Gaskill

Private, Co. A, 44 NY Infantry, Aug. 30, 1861. 2 Lieutenant, Co. K, 44 NY Infantry, Dec. 23, 1861. 1 Lieutenant, Co. K, 44 NY Infantry, May 14, 1862. GSW right thigh, Gaines' Mill, VA, June 27, 1862. Taken prisoner, Gaines' Mill, VA, June 27, 1862. Confined Richmond, VA. Exchanged August 27, 1862. Resigned Dec. 18, 1862, since "my wound is yet partially unhealed, and is such as to render the performance of my duties impossible." Captain, Co. I, 6 Infantry, Corps d'Afrique (later 78 U.S. Colored Infantry), March 27, 1863. Acting AAG, 2 Brigade, 2 Division, Corps d'Afrique, Department of the Gulf, Sept. 1863–March 1864. Major, 81 U.S. Colored Infantry, April 8, 1864. Acting AAG, Staff of Brig. Gen. George L. Andrews, Corps d'Afrique, Department of the Gulf, April–July 1864. Lieutenant Colonel, 81 U.S. Colored Infantry, Sept. 28, 1864. Colonel, 81 U.S. Colored Infantry, Sept. 1, 1865. Resigned Dec. 31, 1865, due to "personal interests which are of such a character as to hazard my entire future both socially and pecuniarily." Bvt. Major, USA, March 2, 1867, for gallant and meritorious services at the battle of Gaines' Mill, VA. Bvt. Lieutenant Colonel, USA, March 2, 1867, for gallant and meritorious services at the battle of Fredericksburg, VA. Battle honors: Yorktown, Hanover Court House, Gaines' Mill, Fredericksburg.

Born: Nov. 28, 1841 Porter, Niagara Co., NY

Died: Oct. 8, 1919 Niagara Falls, NY

Other Wars: Spanish-American War (Captain of the Port of Ponce, Puerto Rico)

Occupation: Printer before war. Regular Army (Captain, 25 U.S. Infantry, honorably discharged Dec. 1, 1870). A leader in the commercial development of Niagara Falls, building a flour mill and a pulp mill and organizing the Niagara Falls Power Company.

Charles Byron Gaskill (Massachusetts MOLLUS Collection, USAHEC [Vol. 114, p. 5891L]).

Miscellaneous: Resided Niagara Falls, Niagara Co., NY
Buried: Oakwood Cemetery, Niagara Falls, NY
References: Edward T. Williams. *Niagara County, New York: A Concise Record of Her Progress and People, 1821–1921.* Chicago, IL, 1921. Obituary, *Niagara Falls Gazette,* Oct. 8, 1919. Edward T. Williams. *Official Record of the Niagara Falls Memorial Commission, In Succession to the William B. Rankine Memorial Commission.* Niagara Falls, NY, 1924. Obituary, *Buffalo Evening Times,* Oct. 8, 1919. Pension File and Military Service File, National Archives. Letters Received, Colored Troops Branch, Adjutant General's Office, File G243(CT)1865, National Archives. Letters Received, Commission Branch, Adjutant General's Office, File G691(CB)1866, National Archives. Eugene A. Nash. *A History of the Forty-Fourth Regiment New York Volunteer Infantry.* Chicago, IL, 1911. I. Richard Reed. *One Hundred Years Ago Today: Niagara County in the Civil War As Reported in the Pages of the Niagara Falls Gazette.* Lockport, NY, 1966.

William Burr Gaw

2 Lieutenant, Volunteer Topographical Engineer, Staff of Major Gen. John C. Fremont, Western Department, Sept. 30, 1861. Acting ADC, Staff of Brig. Gen. Schuyler Hamilton, 2 Division, Army of the Mississippi, March–May 1862. *Captain,* Volunteer Topographical Engineer, April 6, 1862. Assistant Engineer, Staff of Major Gen. William S. Rosecrans, Army of the Mississippi, June–Oct. 1862. Assistant Engineer, Staff of Major Gen. James B. McPherson, 17 Army Corps, Army of the Tennessee, Nov. 1862–June 1863. Chief Topographical Engineer, Staff of Major Gen. George H. Thomas, 14 Army Corps, Army of the Cumberland, June–Dec. 1863. Colonel, 16 U.S. Colored Infantry, Feb. 13, 1864. Commanded Post of Chattanooga (TN), District of East Tennessee, Department of the Cumberland, July 1865–April 1866. Honorably mustered out, April 30, 1866. Battle honors: New Madrid, Point Pleasant, Island No. 10, Fort Pillow, Siege of

William Burr Gaw (on Lookout Mountain, 1865) (Massachusetts MOLLUS Collection, USAHEC [Vol. 65, p. 3217]).

Corinth, Iuka, Corinth, Operations on the Mississippi Central Railroad (Coffeeville), Vicksburg Campaign, Chickamauga, Chattanooga Campaign (Missionary Ridge).

Born: 1830? OH

Died: Jan. 7, 1890 Washington, D.C.

Occupation: Civil engineer

Miscellaneous: Resided Castalia, Erie Co., OH, to 1870; Minneapolis, Hennepin Co., MN (1880); Miles City, Custer Co., MT, 1881–85; and Girard, Crawford Co., KS, after 1885

Buried: Arlington National Cemetery, Arlington, VA (Section 13, Grave 13716)

References: Obituary, *Cincinnati Commercial Gazette,* Jan. 27, 1890. Obituary, *Sandusky Daily Register,* Jan. 31, 1890. Obituary, *Girard Herald,* Jan. 18, 1890. Obituary, *Hutchinson Weekly World,* Jan. 16, 1890. Obituary, *Daily Yellowstone Journal,* Jan. 14, 1890. Pension File and Military Service File, National Archives. Letters Received, Colored Troops Branch, Adjutant General's Office, File G240(CT)1864, National Archives. Letters Received, Commission Branch, Adjutant General's Office, Files G737(CB)1865, G838(CB)1865, and T356(CB)1866, National Archives. www.ancestry.com.

William Rickenbaugh Gerhart

2 Lieutenant, Co. E, 6 PA Militia, Sept. 15, 1862. Discharged Sept. 28, 1862. 1 Sergeant, Independent Battery I, PA Light Artillery (6 months), July 2, 1863. 2 Lieutenant, Independent Battery I, PA Light Artillery, Aug. 26, 1863. Honorably mustered out, Jan. 7, 1864. Major, 121 U.S. Colored Infantry, Aug. 17, 1864. Major, 125 U.S. Colored Infantry, July 1, 1865. Colonel, 125 U.S. Colored Infantry, April 20, 1866. Commanded Post of Fort Bliss (TX), District of New Mexico, Department of the Missouri, July–Sept. 1866. Commanded Post of Fort Craig (NM), District of New Mexico, Department of the Missouri, Sept. 1866–Sept. 1867. Honorably mustered out, Dec. 20, 1867.

Born: Jan. 10, 1844 Gettysburg, PA

Died: Aug. 6, 1906 Lancaster, PA

Education: Graduated Franklin and Marshall College, Lancaster, PA, 1863

Occupation: Student before war. Civil engineer and patent solicitor after war.

Miscellaneous: Resided Lancaster, Lancaster Co., PA

Buried: Greenwood Cemetery, Lancaster, PA (Mifflin Section, Lot 1266)

References: *Portrait and Biographical Record of Lancaster County, Pennsylvania.* Chicago, IL, 1894. *Franklin and*

William Rickenbaugh Gerhart (courtesy Archives and Special Collections, Franklin and Marshall College, Lancaster, PA).

Marshall College Obituary Record. Nos. 12–13 (Vol. 2-Parts 8–9). Lancaster, PA, 1909. Obituary, *Lancaster New Era,* Aug. 7, 1906. Ross G. Gerhart. *The Johann Peter and Elisabeth (Schmidt) Gerhart Family of Earlington, Franconia Township, Montgomery County, Pennsylvania, 1739–1989.* Baltimore, MD, 1990. Obituary, *Reading Daily Times,* Aug. 8, 1906. Pension File and Military Service File, National Archives. Letters Received, Colored Troops Branch, Adjutant General's Office, File G255(CT)1864, National Archives. Letters Received, Commission Branch, Adjutant General's Office, File G691(CB)1865, National Archives. Russell K. Brown, "The Last Civil War Volunteers: The 125th U.S. Colored Infantry in New Mexico, 1866–1867," *Army History,* No. 92 (Summer 2014).

Luther Goodrich

Captain, Co. E, 75 NY Infantry, Sept. 17, 1861. Provost Marshal, Post of Baton Rouge (LA), Department of the Gulf, Jan.–Oct. 1863. Colonel, 17 Infantry, Corps d'Afrique, Oct. 16, 1863. Commanded 2 Brigade, 2 Division, Corps d'Afrique, Department of the Gulf, Jan.–March 1864. Designation of regiment changed to 88 U.S. Colored Infantry (Old), April 4, 1864. Resigned May 25, 1864, since "I have two sons and a nephew of my own family who have been in the service from the beginning of the war, and have a wife and their children at home who need my care at this time." Private, Co. B, 2 U.S. Veteran Volunteer Infantry, March 7, 1865. Honorably discharged, June 25, 1865. Battle honors: Labadieville.

Born: July 9, 1815 Auburn, NY
Died: Dec. 4, 1865 Auburn, NY
Occupation: Farmer and Auburn State Prison keeper
Miscellaneous: Resided Auburn, Cayuga Co., NY
Buried: Fort Hill Cemetery, Auburn, NY (Consecration Dell, Lot 21)
References: Pension File and Military Service File, National Archives. Lafayette W. Case, editor. *The Goodrich Family in America: A Genealogy of the Descendants of John and William Goodrich of Wethersfield, Conn., Richard Goodrich of Guilford, Conn., and*

Luther Goodrich (A.I. Blauvelt, Photographer, Port Hudson, LA; author's photograph).

William Goodridge of Watertown, Mass. Chicago, IL, 1889. Henry Hall and James Hall. *Cayuga in the Field: A Record of the 19th New York Volunteers, All the Batteries of the 3rd New York Artillery, and 75th New York Volunteers.* Auburn, NY, 1873.

William Mason Grosvenor

1 Lieutenant, Adjutant, 13 CT Infantry, Feb. 18, 1862. Captain, Co. I, 13 CT Infantry, Feb. 15, 1863. GSW left arm, Port Hudson, MS, June 14, 1863. Colonel, 2 Infantry, Corps d'Afrique, Nov. 2, 1863. Designation of regiment changed to 74 U.S. Colored Infantry, April 6, 1864. Found guilty of two specifications of keeping in his quarters a woman, not his wife, he was dismissed, May 28, 1864, by General Court Martial for "conduct unbecoming an officer and a gentleman." Explaining that in one instance the woman was his brother's wife, accompanied by her husband and their daughter, and in the other instance the woman was "a lady of respectable family," accompanied by her young brother, he appealed to President Lincoln for a revocation of the order for his dismissal. President Lincoln did not revoke his dismissal, but he did remove, Aug. 3, 1864, his disability to reenter the service "on the ground that the sentence appears not to be sustained by the evidence." Battle honors: Georgia Landing, Irish Bend, Port Hudson.

Born: April 24, 1835, Ashfield, MA
Died: July 20, 1900, Englewood, NJ
Education: Attended Yale University, New Haven, CT
Occupation: Newspaper editor and journalist
Miscellaneous: Resided New Haven, CT, to 1866; St. Louis, MO, 1866–75; New York City, NY; and Englewood, Bergen Co., NJ
Buried: Evergreen Cemetery, New Haven, CT (Maple Avenue, Lot 784, unmarked)
References: Allen Johnson and Dumas Malone, editors. *Dictionary of American Biography.* New York City, NY, 1964. *The National Cyclopaedia of American Biography.* Vol. 20. New York City, NY, 1929. Obituary, *New York Tribune,* July 21, 1900. Obituary, *New York Times,* July 21, 1900. Obituary, *New Haven Register,* July 21, 1900. Pension File and Military Service File, National Archives. Court-martial Case Files, 1809–1894, File NN-1887, National Archives. Letters Received, Colored Troops Branch, Adjutant General's Office, File R40(CT)1866, National Archives. James G. Hollandsworth, Jr. *The Louisiana Native Guards: The Black Military Experience During the Civil*

William Mason Grosvenor (post-war, 1866) (State Historical Society of Missouri, Photograph Collection [Missouri Press Portraits, P1196, 010349]).

War. Baton Rouge, LA, 1995. Homer B. Sprague. *History of the 13th Infantry Regiment of Connecticut Volunteers during the Great Rebellion.* Hartford, CT, 1867.

William Bellamy Guernsey

Captain, Co. E, 89 NY Infantry, Oct. 31, 1861. Resigned July 16, 1862, "forced to this action by the urgency of my private affairs." Lieutenant Colonel, 26 U.S. Colored Infantry, Jan. 30, 1864. Commanded Second Separate Brigade, Department of the South, Feb.–May 1865. Colonel, 26 U.S. Colored Infantry, May 30, 1865. Honorably mustered out, Aug. 28, 1865. Battle honors: Johns' Island.

Born: Nov. 28, 1828 Norwich, NY
Died: July 20, 1898 Norwich, NY
Education: Attended Rensselaer Polytechnic Institute, Troy, NY
Occupation: Lawyer and inventor
Miscellaneous: Resided Norwich, Chenango Co., NY; New York City, NY; and Jersey City, Hudson Co., NJ. Patented a number of railway and electrical appliances, among the latter being an alarm system for protecting banks and private dwellings.
Buried: Mount Hope Cemetery, Norwich, NY (Section 3, Lots 1–3)
References: Obituary, *Chenango Semi-Weekly Telegraph,* July 23, 1898. *Book of Biographies: Biographical Sketches of Leading Citizens of Chenango County, New York.* Buffalo, NY, 1898. Eva G. Card and Howard A. Guernsey, compilers. *The Garnsey-Guernsey Genealogy.* Urbana, IL, 1963. Pension File and Military Service File, National Archives. Letters Received, Volunteer Service Branch, Adjutant General's Office, File D411(VS)1862, National Archives. "26th USCT's Other Commanding Officer," www.correctionhistory.org/html/chronicl/cw-usct/26th-usct-on-parade.html.

William Bellamy Guernsey (Bogardus, Photographer, 363 Broadway, New York; author's photograph).

John Edgar Gurley

Captain, Co. C, 33 WI Infantry, Oct. 18, 1862. Picket Officer, Staff of Brig. Gen. Walter Q. Gresham, Brig. Gen. Giles A. Smith, and Brig. Gen. William W. Belknap, 4 Division, 17 Army Corps, Army of the Tennessee, May 1864–March 1865. Colonel, 135 U.S. Colored Infantry, March 28, 1865. Honorably mustered out, Oct. 23, 1865. Battle honors: Vicksburg Campaign, Jackson, Atlanta Campaign (Atlanta).

Born: April 24, 1838, Ontario, Canada

Died: April 2, 1869, Sandwich, IL

Education: Attended Lombard College, Galesburg, IL

Occupation: Lawyer

Miscellaneous: Resided Shullsburg, Lafayette Co., WI, before war; and Platteville, Grant Co., WI, after war

Buried: Pine Mound Cemetery, near Sandwich, LaSalle Co., IL

References: Albert E. Gurley. *The History and Genealogy of the Gurley Family.* Hartford, CT, 1897. Obituary, *Chicago Tribune,* May 1, 1869. Pension File and Military Service File, National Archives. Letters Received, Colored Troops Branch, Adjutant General's Office, File G163(CT)1865, National Archives. *Biographical and Historical Record of Ringgold and Decatur Counties, Iowa.* Chicago, IL, 1887. Beulah Folkedahl, "The Reorganized Church of Jesus Christ of Latter Day Saints in Southwestern Wisconsin," *Wisconsin Magazine of History,* Vol. 36, No. 2 (Winter 1952–53). *History of Lafayette County, Wisconsin.* Chicago, IL, 1881. "A War Relic: E.H. Gurley Receives a Memento of the Rebellion," *Ukiah Republican Press,* Jan. 25, 1901.

John Edgar Gurley (Z. P. McMillen, Photographer, No. 25 Main Street, Galesburg, IL; Craig T. Johnson Collection).

John Guylee

1 Lieutenant, Co. A, 4 IA Cavalry, Nov. 23, 1861. Acting ADC and Acting AQM, Staff of Major Gen. Samuel R. Curtis, Department of the Missouri, May 1862–Aug. 1863. Colonel, 3 AR Infantry of African Descent (later 56 U.S. Colored Infantry), Sept. 29, 1863. Resigned March 11, 1864, "in consequence of failing health."

Born: Jan. 1, 1815 Loughborough, Leicestershire, England

Died: May 8, 1885, Mount Pleasant, IA

Occupation: Tailor and Methodist clergyman before war. Methodist clergyman and agent for American Bible Society after war.

Miscellaneous: Resided Keokuk, Lee Co., IA; and Sidney, Fremont Co., IA, before war; Mount Pleasant, Henry Co., IA, after war

Buried: Forest Home Cemetery, Mount Pleasant, IA (Section 6, Lot 50)

References: Obituary, *Mount Pleasant Journal,* May 14, 1885. Pension File and Military Service File, National Archives. Letters Received, Colored Troops Branch, Adjutant General's Office, File G24(CT)1863, National Archives. Letters Received, Commission Branch, Adjutant General's Office, File G524(CB)1863, National

John Guylee (State Historical Society of Iowa, Des Moines).

John Guylee (Hoelke & Benecke, Photographers, S.E. Cor. 4th St. & Market Sts., St. Louis, MO; author's photograph).

Archives. William Forse Scott. *The Story of a Cavalry Regiment: The Career of the Fourth Iowa Veteran Volunteers from Kansas to Georgia, 1861–1865.* New York City, NY, 1893. William Forse Scott. *Roster of the Fourth Iowa Cavalry Veteran Volunteers, 1861–1865.* New York City, NY, 1902. Mitchell Yockelson, "Their Memory Will Not Perish: Commemorating the 56th United States Colored Troops," *Gateway Heritage*, Vol. 22, No. 3 (Winter 2001–02). James W. Erwin, "The Teacher, the Preacher and the Prussian: Officers of the 56th United States Colored Infantry," http://www.jameswerwin.com/the-t.html.

George H. Hanks

2 Lieutenant, Co. H, 12 CT Infantry, Jan. 1, 1862. 1 Lieutenant, Co. H, 12 CT Infantry, June 27, 1862. Superintendent of Negro Labor, Department of the Gulf, Feb. 1863–Sept. 1864. Commissioner of Enrollment, Department of the Gulf, Aug. 1863–Sept. 1864. Colonel, 15 Infantry, Corps d'Afrique, Sept. 3, 1863. Designation of regiment changed to 5 Engineers, Corps d'Afrique, Feb. 10, 1864. Designation of regiment changed to 99 U.S. Colored Infantry, April 4, 1864. Although acquitted by court martial in Dec. 1864 of the charge of accepting a bribe from a plantation owner for the use of Negro laborers in his charge, he was dismissed April 7, 1865, for "having fraudulently and in violation of the trust reposed in him, accepted money by way of gratification, and in consideration of the services of certain Negro laborers under his charge," upon rejection of the verdict by Major Gen. Stephen A. Hurlbut, who commented, "It appears that Colonel Hanks did receive from J.A. Albrecht

George H. Hanks (M.H. Kimball, Photographer, 477 Broadway, New York; author's photograph).

one-hundred-fifty dollars, which the witness calls a present, but which was in reality to pay him for sending Negroes to Albrecht." In a letter to President Andrew Johnson, May 11, 1865, Hanks protested, "I have been unjustly and illegally dismissed the military service after three and a half years of constant and arduous duty." The office of the Judge Advocate General, upon review of the case, concluded, June 17, 1865, "In view of his general good character, his declared innocence of all other charges and specifications against him, and of the fact that he is shown to have discharged the only one of his employees believed to have accepted a corrupt reward for his service, his denial is entitled to some consideration, but until he shall more fully and satisfactorily explain the circumstances attending the deposit and final disposition of that money, this office would not feel warranted in making a positive recommendation that the order of dismissal in this case be revoked."

Born: 1830? Saratoga Springs, NY

Died: Oct. 23, 1871 Fort Scott, KS (committed suicide by poison)

Occupation: Merchant dealing in lamps and illuminating materials before war. Adams Express agent after war.

Miscellaneous: Resided Hartford, Hartford Co., CT; Brownsville, Cameron Co., TX; and Fort Scott, Bourbon Co.., KS. His wife Emily, son Charles, and daughter Alice, all died in 1866, within two months of each other.

Buried: Fort Scott National Cemetery, Fort Scott, KS (Section 3, Grave 251)

References: Obituary, *Fort Scott Daily Monitor*, Oct. 24–25, 1871. Military Service File, National Archives. Letters Received, Colored Troops Branch, Adjutant General's Office, File J36(CT)1865, National Archives. Court-martial Case Files, 1809–1894, File MM-1573, National Archives. www.findagrave.com.

Paul Harwood

Private, Co. E, 8 NY State Militia (3 months), April 25, 1861. Honorably mustered out, Aug. 2, 1861. 2 Lieutenant, Co. E, 1 CT Heavy Artillery, April 11, 1862. Taken prisoner, Gaines' Mill, VA, June 27, 1862. Exchanged Aug. 27, 1862. 1 Lieutenant, Co. A, 1 CT Heavy Artillery, Dec. 11, 1863. Major, 57 U.S. Colored Infantry, June 9, 1864. Acting AAG, Staff of Colonel Alexander Cummings, Superintendent of Colored Enlistments, Department of Arkansas, Aug.–Dec. 1864. Colonel, 57 U.S. Colored Infantry, Jan. 9, 1865. Commanded Post of Fort Smith (AR), Frontier District, Department of Arkansas, Feb.–April 1866. Commanded Post of Fort Stanton (NM), District of New Mexico, Department of the Missouri, Sept. 1866. Honorably mustered out, Oct. 19, 1866. Battle honors: First Bull Run, Peninsular Campaign (Yorktown, Gaines' Mill).

Born: May 28, 1841 Philadelphia, PA

Died: Aug. 7, 1899 New York City, NY

Occupation: Regular Army (Captain, 20 U.S. Infantry, retired April 20, 1891)

Miscellaneous: Resided Philadelphia, PA; New Haven, New Haven Co., CT: and East Orange, Essex Co., NJ

Buried: Woodlands Cemetery, Philadelphia, PA (Section I, Lots 281–283)

References: Obituary, *Philadelphia Public Ledger*, Aug. 11, 1899. Obituary, *Army and Navy Journal*, Aug. 12, 1899. Obituary, *New York Times*, Aug. 8, 1899. Obituary, *New York Tribune*, Aug. 8, 1899. Pension File and Military Service File, National

Archives. William H. Powell. *Powell's Records of Living Officers of the United States Army.* Philadelphia, PA, 1890. Letters Received, Colored Troops Branch, Adjutant General's Office, Files H373(CT)1864, M774(CT)1864, A60(CT)1865, and H294(CT)1865, National Archives. Letters Received, Appointment, Commission and Personal Branch, Adjutant General's Office, File 5968(ACP)1880, National Archives. Letters Received, Commission Branch, Adjutant General's Office, File H1415(CB)1866, National Archives. George H. Shirk, "The Lost Colonel," *Chronicles of Oklahoma,* Vol. 35, No. 2 (Summer 1957). John C. Taylor and Samuel P. Hatfield, compilers. *History of the First Connecticut Artillery and of the Siege Trains of the Armies Operating Against Richmond, 1862–1865.* Hartford, CT, 1893.

Thomas Wentworth Higginson

Captain, Co. C, 51 MA Infantry, Sept. 25, 1862. Colonel, 1 SC Infantry of African Descent, Nov. 10, 1862. Contused wound left side, Willstown Bluff, SC, July 10, 1863. Designation of regiment changed to 33 U.S. Colored Infantry, Feb. 8, 1864. "Suffering from prostration consequent upon chronic diarrhea and gunshot wound in left side received while in the line of his duty," he resigned Oct. 27, 1864. Battle honors: Jacksonville, Willstown Bluff.

Born: Dec. 22, 1823 Cambridge, MA

Died: May 9, 1911 Cambridge, MA

Education: Graduated Harvard University, Cambridge, MA, 1841. Graduated Harvard Theological School, 1847.

Occupation: Clergyman, reformer and author

Offices/Honors: Massachusetts House of Representatives, 1880–81

Miscellaneous: Resided Cambridge, Middlesex Co., MA; and Newport, Newport Co., RI, 1865–78

Buried: Cambridge Cemetery, Cambridge, MA (Prospect Avenue, Lot 1207D)

References: Allen Johnson and Dumas Malone, editors. *Dictionary of American Biography.* New York City, NY, 1964. Mary Thacher Higginson. *Thomas Wentworth Higginson: The Story of His Life.* Boston, MA, 1914. Obituary, *Boston Globe,* May 10, 1911. Thomas W. Higginson. *Cheerful Yesterdays.* Boston, MA, 1900. Thomas W. Higginson. *Army Life in a Black Regiment: A New Edition with Notes and a Supplementary Chapter.* Boston, MA, 1900. Thomas W. Higginson. *Descendants of the Reverend Francis*

Thomas Wentworth Higginson (courtesy Henry Deeks).

Thomas Wentworth Higginson (courtesy Henry Deeks).

Thomas Wentworth Higginson (J. W. Black, 173 Washington St., Boston, MA; courtesy Henry Deeks).

Higginson. N.p., 1910. Edmund J. Cleveland and Horace G. Cleveland, compilers. *The Genealogy of the Cleveland and Cleaveland Families.* Hartford, CT, 1899. Military Service File, National Archives. Bennie J. McRae, Jr., Curtis M. Miller, and Cheryl Trowbridge-Miller. *Nineteenth Century Freedom Fighters: The 1st South Carolina Volunteers.* Charleston, SC, 2007.

Frederick Lyman Hitchcock

1 Lieutenant, Adjutant, 132 PA Infantry, Aug. 22, 1862. Shell wound left side of head and GSW right leg, Fredericksburg, VA, Dec. 13, 1862. Major, 132 PA Infantry, Jan. 24, 1863. Honorably mustered out, May 24, 1863. Lieutenant Colonel, 25 U.S. Colored Infantry, Jan. 20, 1864. Acting AIG, Staff of Brig. Gen. Alexander Asboth, District of West Florida, Department of the Gulf, June–Oct. 1864. Colonel, 25 U.S. Colored Infantry, Nov. 16, 1864. Honorably mustered out, Dec. 6, 1865. Battle honors: South Mountain, Antietam, Fredericksburg, Chancellorsville.

Born: April 18, 1837 Waterbury, CT
Died: Oct. 9, 1924 Scranton, PA
Occupation: Lawyer, real estate agent and fire insurance agent
Offices/Honors: Colonel, 13 Regiment, PA National Guard, 1883–88
Miscellaneous: Resided Scranton, Lackawanna Co., PA
Buried: Dunmore Cemetery, Scranton, PA
References: Frederick L. Hitchcock. *History of Scranton and Its People.* New York City, NY, 1914. Obituary, *Scranton Times*, Oct. 9, 1924. Obituary, *Scranton Republican*, Oct. 10, 1924. Joseph Anderson, editor. *The Town and City of Waterbury, Connecticut, from the Aboriginal Period to the Year Eighteen Hundred and Ninety-Five.*

New Haven, CT, 1896. Pension File and Military Service File, National Archives. Letters Received, Colored Troops Branch, Adjutant General's Office, File H37(CT)1864, National Archives. Frederick L. Hitchcock. *War From the Inside: The Story of the 132nd Regiment Pennsylvania Volunteer Infantry in the War for the Suppression of the Rebellion, 1862–1863*. Philadelphia, PA, 1904. Mary L. Hitchcock, compiler. *The Genealogy of the Hitchcock Family Who Are Descended from Matthias Hitchcock of East Haven, Conn., and Luke Hitchcock of Wethersfield, Conn.* Amherst, MA, 1894.

Justin Hodge

1 Lieutenant, RQM, 1 CT Infantry (3 months), April 23, 1861. Discharged May 28, 1861. Acting AQM, Staff of Colonel Erasmus D. Keyes, 1 Brigade, 1 Division, Department of Northeastern Virginia, June–July 1861. Captain, AQM, USV, Aug. 5, 1861. AQM, Staff of Brig. Gen. Christopher C. Augur, Dec. 1861–March 1863. Colonel, 1 Engineers, Corps d'Afrique, April 10, 1863. Commanded Post of Brazos Santiago (TX), 13 Army Corps, Department of the Gulf, Nov. 1863–July 1864. Designation of regiment changed to 95 U.S. Colored Infantry, April 4, 1864. Due to the reduced strength of his regiment (419 men), he resigned colonel's commission, July 6, 1864, to return to quartermaster duties. Chief Quartermaster, 6 Army Corps, Army of the Shenandoah, Oct. 1864–Jan. 1865. AQM, Staff of Major Gen. Henry W. Slocum, Left Wing, Army of Georgia, Feb.–April 1865. Honorably mustered out, Oct. 13, 1866. Battle honors: First Bull Run, Cedar Mountain, Port Hudson, Shenandoah Valley Campaign, Campaign of the Carolinas.

Frederick Lyman Hitchcock (Wenderoth, Taylor & Brown, 912–914 Chestnut Street, Philadelphia, PA; USAHEC [RG98S-CWP13.43]).

Born: April 21, 1815 Roxbury, CT
Died: Oct. 24, 1900 Riverton, CT
Other Wars: Mexican War (1 Lieutenant, RQM, 9 U.S. Infantry)
Occupation: Stonecutter and marble dealer
Offices/Honors: Adjutant General of Connecticut, 1855. Connecticut House of Representatives, 1884.
Miscellaneous: Resided Riverton, Litchfield Co., CT
Buried: Riverton Cemetery, Barkhamsted, CT (unmarked)
References: Barbara Jean Mathews. *Philo Hodge (1756–1842) of Roxbury,*

Connecticut. Baltimore, MD, 1992. Obituary, *Winsted Herald,* Oct. 31, 1900. Obituary, *Connecticut Western News,* Nov. 1, 1900. Obituary, *Hartford Courant,* Oct. 26, 1900. Military Service File, National Archives. Letters Received, Commission Branch, Adjutant General's Office, File H65(CB)1864, National Archives. William Wallace Lee, compiler. *A Catalogue of Barkhamsted Men Who Served in the Various Wars, 1775 to 1865.* Meriden, CT, 1897. Orlando John Hodge, compiler. *Hodge Genealogy from the First of the Name in This Country to the Present Time.* Boston, MA, 1900. *History of Litchfield County, Connecticut, With Illustrations and Biographical Sketches of the Prominent Men and Pioneers.* Philadelphia, PA, 1881.

Justin Hodge (McPherson & Oliver, No. 132 Canal Street, New Orleans, LA; author's photograph).

Ernest W. Holmstedt

Major, 41 NY Infantry, June 6, 1861. Lieutenant Colonel, 41 NY Infantry, Sept. 6, 1861. Resigned April 21, 1863, "as a proposal has been made to me to enter in another regiment." Lieutenant Colonel, 4 Infantry, Corps d'Afrique, Feb. 29, 1864. Designation of regiment changed to 76 U.S. Colored Infantry, April 4, 1864. Colonel, 74 U.S. Colored Infantry, June 19, 1864. Commanded Post of Ship Island (MS), Department of the Gulf, Aug. 1864–Oct. 1865. Honorably mustered out, Nov. 14, 1865. Battle honors: Cross Keys, Groveton, Second Bull Run.

Born: 1829? Sweden

Died: Oct. 10, 1867 New Orleans, LA (yellow fever)

Other Wars: Mexican War (Private, Co. H, Colonel Hughes' Regiment, DC and MD Volunteers)

Occupation: Engaged in "agency business for planters, laborers, and emigrants" after war

Miscellaneous: Resided New York before war; and New Orleans, LA, after war

Buried: Girod Street Cemetery, New Orleans, LA (closed 1957)

Ernest W. Holmstedt (courtesy Henry Deeks).

References: Nels Hokanson. *Swedish Immigrants in Lincoln's Time.* New York and London, 1942. Military Service File, National Archives. Ella Lonn. *Foreigners in the Union Army and Navy.* Baton Rouge, LA, 1951. Letters Received, Colored Troops Branch, Adjutant General's Office, Files G455(CT)1865 and L325(CT)1865, National Archives. David G. Martin. *Carl Bornemann's Regiment: The Forty-First New York Infantry (DeKalb Regiment) in the Civil War.* Hightstown, NJ, 1987. David C. Rankin, editor. *Diary of a Christian Soldier: Rufus Kinsley and the Civil War.* Cambridge, UK, 2004. Death notice, *New Orleans Daily Picayune,* Oct. 12, 1867. "Col. Ernest Holmstedt, Gravier Street," *New Orleans Times,* Dec. 21, 1865. "De Kalb Regiment United States Volunteers," *New York Herald,* June 17, 1861.

John A. Hottenstein

Captain, Co. H, 42 IL Infantry, Aug. 31, 1861. Major, 42 IL Infantry, Sept. 27, 1862. Lieutenant Colonel, 42 IL Infantry, Jan. 1, 1863. Colonel, 13 U.S. Colored Infantry, Oct. 30, 1863. Sentenced by court-martial, June 20, 1864, to be dismissed the service on "grave and infamous charges," he was released from arrest and returned to duty when the sentence was disapproved upon referral of the case to the Judge Advocate General. Commanded Post of Johnsonville (TN), District of Tennessee, Department of the Cumberland, Sept. 1864. Commanded 2 Colored Brigade, Provisional Detachment (District of the Etowah), Department of the Cumberland, Nov.–Dec. 1864. Accepted surrender of all Confederate officers and soldiers in Department of Western Kentucky, May 4, 1865. Honorably mustered out, Jan. 10, 1866. Battle honors: Island No. 10, Siege of Corinth, Stone's River, Chickamauga, Nashville.

Born: Nov. 9, 1835 Lenawee Co., MI

Died: March 11, 1880, Pueblo, CO

Occupation: Regular Army (Sergeant, 3 U.S. Infantry) before war. Farmer after war.

Miscellaneous: Resided Kankakee, Kankakee Co., IL, before war; and Humboldt, Allen Co., KS, after war

John A. Hottenstein (Allen Cebula Collection).

Buried: Mount Hope Cemetery, Humboldt, KS (Addition 1, Block A, Lot 4)

References: Obituary, *Humboldt Union*, March 20, 1880. Pension File and Military Service File, National Archives. Letters Received, Volunteer Service Branch, Adjutant General's Office, File H1293(VS)1863, National Archives. Obituary, *Colorado Daily Chieftain*, March 13, 1880. Court-martial Case Files, 1809–1894, File NN-2114, National Archives. L. Wallace Duncan and Charles F. Scott, editors. *History of Allen and Woodson Counties, Kansas.* Iola, KS, 1901.

William Inness

1 Lieutenant, Co. C, 19 IL Infantry, June 17, 1861. Taken prisoner, Winchester, TN, June 16, 1862. Confined at Madison, GA. Paroled Oct. 12, 1862. Captain, Co. C, 19 IL Infantry, Sept. 7, 1862. Major, 13 U.S. Colored Infantry, Oct. 26, 1863. Assistant Commissioner for the Organization of Colored Troops, Nashville, TN, Oct. 1864–March 1865. Colonel, 15 U.S. Colored Infantry, March 2, 1865. Acting Commissioner for the Organization of Colored Troops, Nashville, TN, March–June 1865. Commanded Post of Nashville (TN), Military Division of the Tennessee, Jan. 1866. Honorably mustered out, April 7, 1866. Battle honors: Stone's River, Chickamauga.

Born: 1838 Sutherlandshire, Scotland
Died: Feb. 4, 1911 Wichita, KS

William Inness (Bogardus, Photographer, 363 Broadway, New York; Allen Cebula Collection).

William Inness (S.M. Fassett, Chicago, IL; courtesy Missouri Historical Society, St. Louis [P0084–0548]).

Occupation: Hatter, fur merchant, and foundry superintendent to 1876; and dry goods merchant after 1876

Miscellaneous: Resided Chicago, IL; and Wichita, Sedgwick Co., KS, 1876–1911

Buried: Maple Grove Cemetery, Wichita, KS (Section A, Lot 39)

References: Obituary, *Wichita Beacon*, Feb. 6, 1911. Obituary, *Wichita Daily Eagle*, Feb. 5, 1911. Pension File and Military Service File, National Archives. Letters Received, Colored Troops Branch, Adjutant General's Office, File I16(CT)1865, National Archives.

William Inness (Massachusetts MOLLUS Collection, USAHEC [Vol. 54, p. 2699]).

James Meikle Irvin

Captain, Co. I, 7 IA Infantry, Aug. 2, 1861. Acting AIG, Staff of Brig. Gen. Grenville M. Dodge, District of Corinth, 16 Army Corps, Army of the Tennessee, Dec. 1862–March 1863. Acting AIG, Staff of Brig. Gen. Grenville M. Dodge, 2 Division, 16 Army Corps, Army of the Tennessee,

James Meikle Irvin (author's photograph).

James Meikle Irvin (courtesy a private collection).

March–May 1863. Lieutenant Colonel, 1 AL Infantry of African Descent, May 18, 1863. Designation of regiment changed to 55 U.S. Colored Infantry, March 11, 1864. Colonel, 55 U.S. Colored Infantry, June 18, 1864. Resigned March 16, 1865, "on account of physical disability from chronic diarrhea." Battle honors: Belmont, Fort Henry, Fort Donelson, Shiloh, Iuka, Corinth.

Born: July 1, 1821, New Castle, Lawrence Co., PA

Died: March 10, 1900, Pasadena, CA

Occupation: Farmer and commission merchant before war. Store clerk after war.

Miscellaneous: Resided Eddyville, Wapello Co., IA, before war; Kent, Portage Co., OH, 1865–92; and Pasadena, Los Angeles Co., CA, after 1892

Buried: Mountain View Cemetery, Altadena, CA (Mountain Meadows Section, Lot 1686)

James Meikle Irvin (author's photograph).

References: Obituary, *Los Angeles Times*, March 11, 1900. Pension File and Military Service File, National Archives. Letters Received, Volunteer Service Branch, Adjutant General's Office, File W962(VS)1862, National Archives. Henry I. Smith. *History of the Seventh Iowa Veteran Volunteer Infantry During the Civil War.* Mason City, IA, 1903. www.ancestry.com.

Simon Jones

Colonel, 25 Infantry, Corps d'Afrique, Sept. 19, 1863. Designation of regiment changed to 93 U.S. Colored Infantry, April 4, 1864. Commanded 2 Brigade, 3 Division, Corps d'Afrique, Department of the Gulf, Oct.–Dec. 1864. Commanded Post of Brashear City (LA), District of La Fourche, Southern Division of Louisiana, Department of the Gulf, Feb.–April 1865. Commanded District of Carrollton (LA), Southern Division of Louisiana, Department of the Gulf, May 1865. Reported as incompetent by a Board of Examination, he was honorably discharged, July 10, 1865, his regiment having been broken up, June 23, 1865, on account of its bad condition and the ignorance and incompetency of a greater part of its officers.

Born: 1833? Marion Co., MS
Died: Nov. 11, 1882 New Orleans, LA
Education: Attended Aranama College, Goliad, TX
Occupation: Agent in the Quartermaster's Department, Department of the Gulf, before entering service. Lawyer after war.
Offices/Honors: U.S. Register of Public Lands, New Orleans, LA, 1866. Unsuccessful candidate for the U.S. House of Representatives in the contested Louisiana elections of 1868. Deputy Collector of U.S. Internal Revenue, 1875–76.
Miscellaneous: Resided Corpus Christi, Nueces Co., TX, before war; New Orleans, LA, 1865–68 and 1881–82; Jackson, Hinds Co., MS, 1868–75; and Enterprise, Clarke Co., MS, 1875–81
Buried: Probably St. Louis Cemetery No. 3, New Orleans, LA, where his widow, Mary O. (Gueringer) Jones, was buried in Sept. 1912.
References: Pension File and Military Service File, National Archives. "Colonel Simon Jones," *New Orleans Republican*, March 24, 1868. Letters Received, Colored Troops Branch, Adjutant General's Office, File J116(CT)1865, National Archives. Death Notice, *New Orleans Daily Picayune*, Nov. 12, 1882. William A. Dobak. *Freedom by the Sword: The U.S. Colored Troops, 1862–1867.* Washington, D.C., 2011.

Ignatz G. Kappner

Private, Co. E, 7 NY State Militia, April 26, 1861. Honorably mustered out, June 3, 1861. Appointed 1 Lieutenant, Engineer Corps, by Major Gen. John C. Fremont, July 30, 1861. Retained on duty on the staff of Major Gen. Henry W. Halleck after Fremont's Engineer Corps was disbanded. Attached to the staff of Major Gen. William T. Sherman in June 1862 and engaged in the erection of field fortifications. 1 Lieutenant, Co. B, Engineer Regiment of the West, March 26, 1863. Honorably mustered out May 29, 1863. Colonel, 1 TN Heavy Artillery of African Descent, Sept. 4, 1863. Commanded Fort Pickering (TN), District of Memphis (later District of West Tennessee), 16 Army Corps, Department of the Tennessee, Oct. 1863–Nov. 1864. Designation of regiment changed to 2 U.S. Colored Heavy Artillery, March 11, 1864. Designation of regiment changed to 3 U.S. Colored Heavy Artillery, April 26, 1864. Commanded Fort Pickering (TN), District of West Tennessee, Department of Mississippi, Dec.

Ignatz G. Kappner (author's photograph).

1864–April 1865. Commanded Fort Pickering (TN), District of West Tennessee, Department of the Cumberland, April–June 1865. Commanded 2 Infantry Brigade, District of West Tennessee, Department of Tennessee, July–Sept. 1865. Commanded 3 Brigade, Department of Tennessee, Sept. 1865. Honorably mustered out, April 30, 1866. Battle honors: Attack on Memphis.

Born: Feb. 4, 1827 Agram, Austria

Died: Oct. 20, 1891 St. Louis, MO

Occupation: Engaged in the banking business. Business manager, *St. Louis Post-Dispatch*, 1885-91.

Offices/Honors: City Treasurer, St. Joseph, MO, 1870–73. Director of St. Joseph Bridge Building Co., 1871.

Miscellaneous: Resided New York City, NY, before war; St. Joseph, Buchanan Co., MO, 1867–76; and St. Louis, MO, after 1876

Buried: Mount Mora Cemetery, St. Joseph, MO (Section C, Block 5, Lot 1, unmarked)

Ignatz G. Kappner (courtesy Missouri Historical Society, St. Louis [P0233–2559]).

References: Obituary Circular, Whole No. 82, Missouri MOLLUS. Obituary, *St. Louis Post-Dispatch*, Oct. 20, 1891. Obituary, *St. Joseph Herald*, Oct.25, 1891. Stephen Beszedits, "Ignatz Kappner: A Hungarian Officer in the United States Colored Troops during the Civil War," *Vasvary Collection Newsletter*, (2015, No. 2). Istvan Kornel Vida. *Hungarian Émigrés in the American Civil War: A History and Biographical Dictionary*. Jefferson, NC, 2012. Martin W. Ofele. *German-Speaking Officers in the U.S. Colored Troops, 1863–1867*. Gainesville, FL, 2004. *The History of Buchanan County, Missouri*. St. Joseph, MO, 1881. Military Service File, National Archives. Letters Received, Colored Troops Branch, Adjutant General's Office, File K3(CT)1863, National Archives. William A. Neal. *An Illustrated History of the Missouri Engineer and the 25th Infantry Regiments*. Chicago, IL, 1889.

Matthew Chapman Kempsey

Chaplain, 176 NY Infantry, Dec. 18, 1862. Colonel, 16 Infantry, Corps d'Afrique, Oct. 17, 1863. Tried by Court-Martial, Dec. 21, 1863, for cohabiting with a colored woman, drunkenness, and inattention to his duties, he was sentenced to a forfeiture of two months' pay and public reprimand. Reported by Major Gen. Francis J. Herron, March 9, 1864, as "entirely unfitted for his command and of such habits of life as are unbecoming to an officer and degrading the high position he holds," he was brought before a Board of Examination, which found him "disqualified for the position of colonel" and recommended that he resign. Designation of regiment changed to 87 U.S. Colored Infantry, April 4, 1864. His resignation was accepted, July 6, 1864, "for the good of the service."

Born: April 8, 1832 Ireland

Died: Jan. 22, 1895 Cedar Rapids, IA

Education: Graduated Madison (now Colgate) University, Hamilton, NY, 1860. Attended Hamilton (NY) Theological Seminary.

Occupation: Baptist clergyman and in later years merchant dealing in millinery and notions and life insurance agent

Miscellaneous: Resided Hamilton, Madison Co., NY; and Jersey City, Hudson Co., NJ, before war; Monticello, Jones Co., IA (1870); Batavia, Kane Co., IL, 1873–75; Anamosa, Jones Co., IA (1880), and Cedar Rapids, Linn Co., IA, after war

Buried: Riverside Cemetery, Anamosa, IA

References: Obituary, *Anamosa Eureka*, Jan. 24, 1895. Obituary, *Anamosa Journal*, Jan. 24, 1895. Pension File and Military Service File, National Archives. Court-martial Case Files, 1809–1894, File LL-1648, National Archives. *The History of Jones County, Iowa*. Chicago, IL, 1879. www.ancestry.com.

Frank Asbury Kendrick

Captain, Co. E, 2 IA Cavalry, Sept. 4, 1861. Major, 2 IA Cavalry, Nov. 1, 1862. Colonel, 2 West TN Infantry of African Descent, Aug. 27, 1863. Designation of regiment changed to 61 U.S. Colored Infantry, March 11, 1864. GSW head, Memphis, TN, Aug. 21, 1864. Commanded 1 Brigade, U.S. Colored Troops, District of West Tennessee, Department of Mississippi, Dec. 1864–Jan. 1865. Commanded 2 Brigade, Post and Defenses of Memphis, District of West Tennessee,

Frank Asbury Kendrick (E.H. McKenney, No. 1 Washington Block, Biddeford, ME; author's photograph).

Department of Mississippi, Jan.–Feb. 1865. Commanded 1 Brigade, District of Morganza (LA), Northern Division of Louisiana, Department of the Gulf, March 1865. Battle honors: Siege of Corinth, Iuka, Operations on Mississippi Central Railroad (Coffeeville), Operations against the Memphis and Charleston Railroad in West Tennessee (Wolf River Bridge), Expedition from La Grange, TN, to Tupelo, MS (Tupelo), Attack on Memphis, Forrest's Raid into Northern Alabama and Middle Tennessee.

Born: Sept. 12, 1834 Saco, ME

Died: March 31, 1865 New Orleans, LA (typho-malarial fever)

Occupation: Livery stable keeper

Miscellaneous: Resided Saco, York Co., ME; and Davenport, Scott Co., IA

Buried: Laurel Hill Cemetery, Saco, ME

References: Obituary, *Daily Davenport Democrat*, April 13, 1865. Obituary, *Davenport Daily Gazette*, April 13, 1865. Obituary, *Portland Daily Press*, April 17, 1865. Pension File and Military Service File, National Archives. Letters Received, Colored Troops Branch, Adjutant General's Office, File K16(CT)1864, National Archives. Lyman B. Pierce. *History of the Second Iowa Cavalry.* Burlington, IA, 1865. William A. Dobak. *Freedom by the Sword: The U.S. Colored Troops, 1862–1867.* Washington, D.C., 2011.

John Graham Klinck

Captain, AQM, USV, Aug. 3, 1861. Chief Quartermaster, Staff of Brig. Gen. Thomas J. McKean (and Brig. Gen. Thomas W. Sherman), 6 Division, Army of West Tennessee, April–May 1862. Chief Quartermaster, Staff of Brig. Gen. James B. McPherson, Right Wing, 13 Army Corps, Department of the Tennessee, Nov.–Dec. 1862. Chief Quartermaster, Staff of Major Gen. James B. McPherson, 17 Army Corps, Department of the Tennessee, Dec. 1862–April 1863. *Colonel,* 10 LA Infantry of African Descent (later 48 U.S. Colored Infantry), April 12, 1863 (Declined). Superintendent of Land and Water Transportation, Military Division of West Mississippi, May–June 1864. Honorably mustered out, July 28, 1865.

Born: Aug. 7, 1820 Peterboro, NY

Died: Dec. 5, 1873 Brighton, NY

Occupation: Farmer before war. Engaged in auction and commission business after war.

Miscellaneous: Resided Richfield, Lucas Co., OH, before war; and Brighton, Monroe Co., NY, after war

Buried: Mount Hope Cemetery, Rochester, NY (Section L, Lot 76)

References: Obituary, *Rochester*

John Graham Klinck (courtesy Everitt Bowles).

Democrat and Chronicle, Dec. 6, 1873. "Our Lake Providence Correspondence," *New York Herald*, April 23, 1863. "A Great Gathering of Negroes—Incipient Movements Toward Their Organization into Regiments—A Biographical Sketch of Colonel John G. Klinck," *Philadelphia Inquirer*, April 25, 1863. "Col. John G. Klinck and the Colored Regiments," *Cazenovia Republican*, May 13, 1863. Carded Records Relating to Staff Officers, National Archives. Letters Received, Adjutant General's Office, File K225(AGO)1861, National Archives.

William Hopkins Lathrop

1 Lieutenant, Co. G, 39 OH Infantry, Aug. 2, 1861. Captain, Co. G, 39 OH Infantry, Dec. 28, 1861. Acting AAG, Staff of Colonel John W. Fuller, 1 Brigade, 2 Division, Army of the Mississippi, April–Oct. 1862. Major, 39 OH Infantry, Oct. 2, 1862. Colonel, 3 AL Infantry of African Descent, April 22, 1864. Designation of regiment changed to 111 U.S. Colored Infantry, June 25, 1864. GSW Sulphur Branch Trestle, AL, Sept. 25, 1864. Battle honors: Corinth, Forrest's Raid into Northern Alabama and Middle Tennessee (Sulphur Branch Trestle).

Born: May 4, 1833 Sherburne, NY

Died: Sept. 25, 1864 KIA Sulphur Branch Trestle, AL

Education: Graduated Hamilton College, Clinton, NY, 1853. Attended Cincinnati (OH) Law School.

Occupation: Lawyer

Miscellaneous: Resided Cincinnati, OH

Buried: Spring Grove Cemetery, Cincinnati, OH (Section 46, Lot 30)

References: Elijah B. Huntington. *A Genealogical Memoir of the Lo-Lathrop Family in this Country.* Ridgefield, CT, 1884. "The Funeral of Colonel Lathrop," *Cincinnati Commercial Tribune*, March 14, 1865. Pension File and Military Service File, National Archives. Letters Received, Colored Troops Branch, Adjutant General's

John Graham Klinck (Powelson, Photographer, 58 State St., Rochester, NY; author's photograph).

William Hopkins Lathrop (L.M. Strayer Collection).

Office, File L198(CT)1864, National Archives. Charles H. Smith. *The History of Fuller's Ohio Brigade, 1861–1865.* Cleveland, OH, 1909. *Catalogue of the Officers and Students of Hamilton College, with Societies, 1865–66.* Clinton, NY, 1866. H. Seger Slifer, editor. *Catalogue of Chi Psi Fraternity, 1841–1932.* Ann Arbor, MI, 1929. www.findagrave.com.

Edward Martindale

Captain, Commissary of Subsistence, USV, Sept. 19, 1861. Chief Commissary, Staff of Brig. Gen. John W. Davidson and Colonel William H. Irwin, 3 Brigade, 2

Edward Martindale (Brady, Washington; author's photograph).

Division, 6 Army Corps, Army of the Potomac, April–Sept. 1862. Lieutenant Colonel, 26 NJ Infantry, Jan. 6, 1863. Honorably mustered out, June 27, 1863. Colonel, 11 Infantry, Corps d'Afrique, Feb. 1, 1864. Designation of regiment changed to 83 U.S. Colored Infantry, April 4, 1864. Resignation as Captain accepted, May 2, 1864. Colonel, 81 U.S. Colored Infantry, Aug. 6, 1864. Commanded Provisional Brigade, 18 Army Corps, Army of the James, Oct.–Dec. 1864. Commanded 2 Brigade, 3 Division, 25 Army Corps, Army of the James, Dec. 1864. Commanded 3 Brigade, 2 Division, 25 Army Corps, Army of the James, Jan.–March 1865. Judge Advocate, Staff of Brig. Gen. George H. Gordon, Eastern District of Virginia, Department of Virginia, Army of the James, March–May 1865. Commanded Post of Petersburg (VA), District of the Nottoway, Department of Virginia, Army of the James, May–June 1865. Resigned Aug. 7, 1865, since "it is of the utmost importance to my private interests that I may be permitted to retire from the service." Battle honors: Peninsular Campaign (Yorktown, Williamsburg, Mechanicsville, Gaines' Mill, Savage Station, White Oak Swamp, Malvern Hill), Antietam, Fredericksburg, Chancellorsville.

Born: Feb. 4, 1817 Sandy Hill (now Hudson Falls), NY

Died: July 14, 1904 San Diego, CA

Education: Graduated Union College, Schenectady, NY, 1836

Occupation: Lawyer

Miscellaneous: Resided New Providence, Essex Co., NJ; and Summit, Union Co., NJ, before war; New York City, NY; and Brooklyn, NY, 1865–83; Des Moines, Polk Co., IA, 1883–99; and San Diego, San Diego Co., CA, 1899–1904. Brother of Brig. Gen. John H. Martindale. One of the founders of the Psi Upsilon fraternity.

Buried: Kingsbury Cemetery, Kingsbury, Washington Co., NY

References: *Portrait and Biographical Album of Polk County, Iowa.* Chicago, IL, 1890. *A Memorial and Biographical Record of Iowa.* Chicago, IL, 1896. Obituary Circular, Whole No. 769, California MOLLUS. Obituary, *Des Moines Register and Leader,* July 28, 1904. Obituary, *San Diego Union,* July 16, 1904. Alan A. Siegel. *For the Glory of the Union: Myth, Reality, and the Media in Civil War New Jersey.* Rutherford, NJ, 1984. Military Service File, National Archives. Letters Received, Colored Troops Branch, Adjutant General's Office, File M31(CT)1864, National Archives. Henry C. Johnson, editor. *Tenth General Catalogue of the Psi Upsilon Fraternity.* Bethlehem, PA, 1888.

James Neilson McArthur

Sergeant Major, 12 IL Infantry (3 months), May 3, 1861. 1 Lieutenant, Co. G, 12 IL Infantry (3 years), Aug. 1, 1861. Acting ADC, Staff of Brig. Gen. John McArthur, 1 Brigade, 6 Division, Army of the Tennessee, May–Oct. 1862. Captain, Co. G, 12 IL Infantry, Oct. 5, 1862. Colonel, 4 U.S. Colored Heavy Artillery, May 8, 1864. Commanded Post of Columbus (KY), District of Western Kentucky, Department of the Ohio, Aug.–Dec. 1864. Commanded Post of Columbus (KY), District of West Tennessee, Department of Mississippi, Dec. 1864–Feb. 1865. Commanded Post of Henderson (KY), District of Western Kentucky, Department of Kentucky, April–July 1865. Commanded District of Western Kentucky, and also 2 Brigade, 1 Division, Department of Kentucky, Aug.–Oct. 1865. Suffering from remittent fever accompanied by congestion of the lungs, he resigned, Dec. 2, 1865, due to "the impaired state of my

James Neilson McArthur (L.M. Strayer Collection).

James Neilson McArthur (A. Hesler, Artist, No. 113 Lake Street, Chicago, IL; courtesy Michael Hammerson).

James Neilson McArthur (seated center, with Brig. Gen. John McArthur, standing left, and Major George Pomutz [15 Iowa Infantry], standing right) (courtesy Michael Hammerson).

health." Battle honors: Fort Henry, Fort Donelson, Shiloh, Siege of Corinth, Iuka, Corinth.

Born: July 27, 1839 Erskine, Renfrewshire, Scotland

Died: Oct. 11, 1914 Buffalo, NY

Occupation: Machinist and mechanical engineer before war. Clerk, bookkeeper, and Deputy Collector of U.S. Internal Revenue after war.

Miscellaneous: Resided Chicago, IL; and Buffalo, Erie Co., NY, after 1867. Brother of Brig. Gen. John McArthur.

Buried: Forest Lawn Cemetery, Buffalo, NY (Section D, Lot 151)

References: Obituary, *Buffalo Evening News*, Oct. 12, 1914. *The Union Army*. New York Edition. Vol. 8. Madison, WI, 1908. Obituary, *Buffalo Commercial*, Oct. 12, 1914. Obituary, *Buffalo Enquirer*, Oct. 12, 1914. Pension File and Military Service File, National Archives. Letters Received, Colored Troops Branch, Adjutant General's Office, File M464(CT)1864, National Archives. www.ancestry.com.

Hubert Anville McCaleb

Sergeant, Co. I, 11 IL Infantry, Sept. 4, 1861. GSW head, thigh, and foot, Fort Donelson, TN, Feb. 15, 1862. 2 Lieutenant, Co. I, 11 IL Infantry, March 24, 1863. 1 Lieutenant, Co. I, 11 IL Infantry, July 10, 1863. Lieutenant Colonel, 2 MS Heavy Artillery of African Descent, Nov. 8, 1863. Designation of regiment changed to 5 U.S. Colored Heavy Artillery, March 11, 1864. Designation of regiment changed to 6 U.S. Colored Heavy artillery, April 26, 1864. Commanded Post of Vidalia (LA), District of Vicksburg, Department of the Tennessee, May–Oct. 1864. Colonel, 121 U.S. Colored Infantry, March 10, 1865. The regiment failing to complete organization, he was honorably discharged, June 30, 1865. Lieutenant Colonel, 6 U.S. Colored Heavy Artillery, July 1, 1865. Colonel, 6 U.S. Colored Heavy Artillery, Sept. 26, 1865. Commanded Post of Natchez (MS), Department of Mississippi, Feb.–March 1866. Honorably mustered out, May 13, 1866. Battle honors: Fort Donelson, Vicksburg Campaign, Vidalia.

Hubert Anville McCaleb (Bowman & Rawson, Photographic Artists, and Dealers in Photographic Albums, Gilt Frames, &c, Peru, IL; Frank D. Korun Collection).

Born: Feb. 10, 1838 Magnolia, Putnam Co., IL

Died: March 24, 1878 Humboldt, KS (committed suicide)

Occupation: Farmer before war. Ice merchant and county court clerk after war.

Hubert Anville McCaleb (Bowman & Rawson, Photographers and Dealers in Photographic Albums & Oval Frames, Peru, IL; author's photograph).

Offices/Honors: Sheriff, LaSalle Co., IL, 1866–68. County Clerk, LaSalle Co., IL, 1873–77.

Miscellaneous: Resided Tonica, LaSalle Co., IL; and Lacon, Marshall Co., IL, before war; Ottawa, LaSalle Co., IL, after war

Buried: Ottawa Avenue Cemetery, Ottawa, IL (Ford Addition, Section 11, Lot 14)

References: Obituary, *Ottawa Free Trader*, March 30, 1878. Obituary, *Ottawa Republican*, March 28, 1878. Katy McCaleb Headley. *McCaleb (McKillop) Clan of Scotland and the United States.* Chillicothe, MO, 1964. Obituary, *Humboldt Union*, March 30, 1878. Pension File and Military Service File, National Archives. Letters Received, Colored Troops Branch, Adjutant General's Office, File M201(CT)1863, National Archives. *The Past and Present of LaSalle County, Illinois.* Chicago, IL, 1877. Elmer Baldwin. *History of LaSalle County, Illinois.* Chicago, IL, 1877. Harvey M. Parker. *Proceedings of the First Reunion of the Eleventh Regiment Illinois Volunteer Infantry.* Ottawa, IL, 1875.

Nathaniel McCalla

Captain, Co. A, 10 IA Infantry, Sept. 6, 1861. Major, 10 IA Infantry, Jan. 25, 1862. *Colonel*, 11 Louisiana Infantry of African Descent (later 49 U.S. Colored Infantry), April 23, 1863 (Declined, since "I consider the present condition of our regiment requires my services, and I can serve my country in my present capacity in the face of the enemy better than in any other which I at the present time could fill"). Shell wound breast, Missionary Ridge, TN, Nov. 25, 1863. Honorably mustered out, Aug. 15, 1865. Battle honors: New Madrid, Iuka, Corinth, Champion's Hill, Vicksburg Campaign, Missionary Ridge.

Born: 1827 Scott Co., KY

Died: April 30, 1878 Greenhorn, CO

Other Wars: Mexican War (Private, Co. H, 1 IN Infantry)

Occupation: Farmer

Offices/Honors: Sheriff, Polk Co., IA, 1866–68

Miscellaneous: Resided Polk City, Polk Co., IA, to 1870; Fairmont, Fillmore Co., NE; and Greenhorn, Pueblo Co., CO

Buried: Greenhorn, Pueblo Co., CO?

References: Wilbur G. Gaffney. *The Fillmore County Story.* Geneva, NE, 1968. Pension File and Military Service

Nathaniel McCalla (courtesy Iowa Gold Star Military Museum).

File, National Archives. *The History of Polk County, Iowa.* Des Moines, IA, 1880. Addison A. Stuart. *Iowa Colonels and Regiments.* Des Moines, IA, 1865. Leonard Brown. *American Patriotism; or, Memoirs of "Common Men."* Des Moines, IA, 1869. Letters Received, Colored Troops Branch, Adjutant General's Office, File M8(CT)1863, National Archives.

Lewis McCoy

Captain, Co. D, 115 OH Infantry, Sept. 18, 1862. Detached to organize 127 OH Infantry (later 5 U.S. Colored Infantry), June 1863. Upon the strong recommendation of Ohio Governor David Tod, he was appointed Colonel, 5 U.S. Colored Infantry, Oct. 27, 1863. He declined the appointment, Nov. 18, 1863, having "pledged the members (of his company) to remain with the company as captain during its term of service." Honorably mustered out, June 22, 1865.
Born: April 4, 1813, NY
Died: Dec. 16, 1867, near Alliance, OH
Occupation: Farmer
Miscellaneous: Resided Bayard, Columbiana Co., OH
Buried: Moultrie Chapel Cemetery, Moultrie, Columbiana Co., OH
References: Obituary, *New Lisbon Journal,* Jan. 10, 1868. Versalle F. Washington. *Eagles on Their Buttons: A Black Infantry Regiment in the Civil War.* Columbia, MO, 1999. Military Service File, National Archives. Letters Received, Colored Troops Branch, Adjutant General's Office, Files O46(CT)1863, C322(CT)1863, and M205(CT)1863, National Archives. *History of Columbiana County, Ohio, with Illustrations and Biographical Sketches of Some of Its Prominent Men and Pioneers.* Philadelphia, PA, 1879. www.ancestry.com.

Augustus O. Millington

Hospital Steward, 9 IL Infantry (3 months), April 26, 1861. Honorably mustered out, July 26, 1861. Captain, Co. I, 29 IL Infantry, Sept. 14, 1861. *Major,* 29 IL Infantry, May 6, 1862. Found guilty by a Board of Examination of drunkenness on duty, he was dismissed Oct. 14, 1862. Dismissal revoked, and honorably mustered out, Nov. 18, 1862, upon the strong recommendation of Major Gen. John A. McClernand, who described him as "a brave and skillful officer, enforcing rigid discipline and having one of the best, if not the best, drilled regiment in the brigade." *Lieutenant Colonel,* 121 IL Infantry, Oct. 1862. Regiment failed to complete organization. Lieutenant Colonel, 3 MO Infantry of African Descent, Feb. 18, 1864. Designation of regiment changed to 67 U.S. Colored Infantry, March 11, 1864. Honorably mustered out, Oct. 24, 1864. Colonel, 18 U.S. Colored Infantry, Oct. 25, 1864. Commanded Post of Bridgeport (AL), District of the Etowah, Department of the Cumberland, Dec. 1864–Jan. 1865. Tried by court-martial, Feb. 14, 1865, on charges of "Drunkenness on duty" and "Neglect of duty," he was found guilty and sentenced to be cashiered, June 2, 1865. Battle honors: Fort Donelson, Shiloh.
Born: June 7, 1828, Worthington, OH
Died: Feb. 18, 1902, Chattanooga, TN
Other Wars: Mexican War (Sergeant, Co. A, 4 IL Infantry)

Occupation: Brick mason, contractor, and builder

Miscellaneous: Resided Springfield, Sangamon Co., IL; Leavenworth, Leavenworth Co., KS (1870); Montgomery, Montgomery Co., AL (1880); and Chattanooga, Hamilton Co., TN

Buried: Chattanooga National Cemetery, Chattanooga, TN (Post Plot, Section C, Site 4)

References: John C. Power. *History of the Early Settlers of Sangamon County, Illinois.* Springfield, IL, 1876. Obituary, *Chattanooga Daily Times*, Feb. 19, 1902. Pension File and Military Service File, National Archives. Letters Received, Volunteer Service Branch, Adjutant General's Office, File M1227(VS)1862, National Archives. Court-martial Case Files, 1809–1894, File MM-2565, National Archives. "Incidents of the Great Fight," *Daily Illinois State Journal*, April 16, 1862. www.ancestry.com.

James Montgomery

Colonel, 3 KS Infantry, July 25, 1861. Honorably mustered out, April 3, 1862, upon consolidation of 3 KS Infantry and 4 KS Infantry to form 10 KS Infantry. Colonel, 34 U.S. Colored Infantry, March 5, 1863. Commanded 4 Brigade, 1 Division, U.S. Forces, Morris Island (SC), Department of the South, Aug.–Nov. 1863. Commanded 3 Brigade, 1 Division, 10 Army Corps, U.S. Forces, Morris Island (SC), Department of the South, Nov. 1863–Jan. 1864. Commanded 3 Brigade, 2 Division, District of Florida, Department of the South, Feb.–April 1864. Resigned Sept. 23, 1864, on account of ill health, due to "a hydrocele of the left side of a large size and chronic bronchitis." Colonel, 6 KS State Militia, Oct. 15, 1864. Battle honors: Dry Wood Creek, Morristown, Jacksonville, Palatka, Darien, Olustee, Price's Missouri Expedition (Big Blue, Westport).

Born: Dec. 22, 1814 Ashtabula Co., OH

Died: Dec. 6, 1871 near Mound City, KS

Occupation: Farmer

Miscellaneous: Resided Mound City, Linn Co., KS. One of the acknowledged leaders of the Free State movement in Kansas during 1857–61.

Buried: Woodland Cemetery, Mound City, KS (National Cemetery Plot, Grave 76)

References: William Ansel Mitchell. *Linn County, Kansas: A History.* Kansas City, MO, 1928. Allen Johnson and Dumas Malone, editors. *Dictionary of American Biography.* New York City,

James Montgomery (KansasMemory.org, Kansas Historical Society, Item No. 209263).

James Montgomery (KansasMemory.org, Kansas Historical Society, Item No. 499). **James Montgomery (New Hampshire Historical Society [S1993.513.47]).**

NY, 1964. Brian R. Dirck, "By the Hand of God: James Montgomery and Redemptive Violence," *Kansas History: A Journal of the Central Plains*, Vol. 27, No. 1–2 (Spring-Summer 2004). Alfred T. Andreas. *History of the State of Kansas.* Chicago, IL, 1883. Frank William Blackmar, editor. *Kansas: A Cyclopedia of State History.* Chicago, IL, 1912. George W. Martin, editor. *Transactions of the Kansas State Historical Society, 1897–1900.* Topeka, KS, 1900. George W. Martin, editor. *Transactions of the Kansas State Historical Society, 1901–1902.* Topeka, KS, 1902. Obituary, *Fort Scott Daily Monitor*, Dec. 9, 1871. Obituary, *Lawrence Republican Daily Journal*, Dec. 10, 1871. William E. Connelley. *A Standard History of Kansas and Kansans.* Chicago and New York, 1918. Pension File and Military Service File, National Archives. Letters Received, Colored Troops Branch, Adjutant General's Office, File W261(CT)1863, National Archives. Russell Duncan, editor. *Blue-Eyed Child of Fortune: The Civil War Letters of Colonel Robert Gould Shaw.* Athens, GA, 1992.

Andrew Brown Morrison

Captain, Co. H, 26 IL Infantry, Nov. 1, 1861. Chaplain, 26 IL Infantry, Jan. 1, 1862. Major, 4 AR Infantry of African Descent, Sept. 17, 1863. Designation of regiment changed to 57 U.S. Colored Infantry, March 11, 1864. Colonel, 57 U.S. Colored Infantry, May 23, 1864. Commanded Post of Huntersville (AR), District of Little Rock, 7 Army Corps, Department of Arkansas, June–Sept. 1864. Commanded 1 Brigade, 2 Division, 7 Army Corps, Department of Arkansas, Sept.–Oct. 1864. Resigned

Oct. 22, 1864, since "I am a minister and not a military man ... and the labor and exposure incident to camp life has occasioned serious disease of the heart." Battle honors: Vicksburg Campaign.

Born: May 26, 1831 Guernsey Co., OH

Died: Oct. 6, 1916 Glendale, CA

Occupation: Methodist clergyman

Miscellaneous: Resided Lawrenceville, Lawrence Co., IL (1860); Olney, Richland Co., IL (1861); Anna, Union Co., IL (1870); Carbondale, Jackson Co., IL (1880); Chillicothe, Livingston Co., MO; Danville, Des Moines Co., IA; Visalia, Tulare Co., CA; and Glendale, Los Angeles Co., CA, after 1887

Buried: Rosedale Cemetery, Los Angeles, CA (Section D, Lot 49)

References: Pension File and Military Service File, National Archives. Obituary, *Los Angeles Times*, Oct. 8, 1916. Letters Received, Colored Troops Branch, Adjutant General's Office, Files M179(CT)1863 and M774(CT)1864, National Archives. www.ancestry.com.

Andrew Brown Morrison (courtesy Henry Deeks).

John A. Nelson

Captain, Co. E, 3 CT Infantry (3 months), May 11, 1861. Honorably mustered out, Aug. 12, 1861. Captain, Co. H, 30 MA Infantry, Dec. 9, 1861. Provost Marshal, Post of Ship Island (MS), Department of the Gulf, March–May 1862. Honorably mustered out, May 30, 1862. Lieutenant Colonel, 1 LA Native Guards (later 73 U.S. Colored Infantry), Sept. 27, 1862. Colonel, 3 LA Native Guards, Nov. 26, 1862. Designation of regiment changed to 3 Infantry, Corps d'Afrique (later 75 U.S. Colored Infantry), June 6, 1863. Arrested for "conduct unbecoming an officer and a gentleman in appropriating to himself and his own use the property of a widow lady," he resigned Aug. 14, 1863. Colonel, 10 U.S. Colored Infantry, Oct. 6, 1863. Dismissed, Jan. 9, 1864, for "having authorized and permitted the impressment of Negro recruits into his regiment, thereby hindering recruiting, and spreading distrust and alarm among the Negroes." He appealed his dismissal to President Lincoln, who disapproved the dismissal and ordered Major Gen. Ben Butler to reinstate him or conduct a fuller investigation of the facts. He was discharged, March 15, 1864, upon the adverse report of a Court of Inquiry, which found "that he is of very limited general education, that he is grossly deficient in his knowledge of tactics and regulations, that his conduct as an officer has been improper since his arrest, and that large numbers of Negroes were impressed by the officers under his command ... and he was grossly and culpably negligent in preventing such impressment." Battle honors: Port Hudson Campaign.

Born: 1834? Ireland
Died: Oct. 27, 1880 Park City, UT
Other Wars: Mexican War (Powder boy, USS Albany)
Occupation: Machinist and saloon keeper before war. Miner and merchant after war.
Miscellaneous: Resided Boston, MA; and Hartford, CT, before war; Virginia City, Madison Co., MT, 1865–71; and Park City, Summit Co., UT, after 1871
Buried: City Cemetery, Park City, Summit Co., UT
References: Obituary, *Salt Lake Tribune*, Oct. 28, 1880. Pension File and Military Service File, National Archives. Letters Received, Colored Troops Branch, Adjutant General's Office, Files F85(CT)1863 and N18(CT)1863, National Archives. James G. Hollandsworth, Jr. *The Louisiana Native Guards: The Black Military Experience During the Civil War.* Baton Rouge, LA, 1995. Clare P. Weaver, editor. *Thank God My Regiment an African One: The Civil War Diary of Colonel Nathan W. Daniels.* Baton Rouge, LA, 1998. Joseph T. Wilson. *The Black Phalanx: A History of the Negro Soldiers of the United States in the Wars of 1775–1812, 1861–65.* Hartford, CT, 1888.

Charles Ledyard Norton

Private, Co. F, 7 NY State Militia, May 25, 1862. Honorably discharged Aug. 19, 1862. 1 Lieutenant, Co. A, 25 CT Infantry, Sept. 4, 1862. Captain, Co. A, 25 CT Infantry, Jan. 16, 1863. Acting ADC, Staff of Brig. Gen. Henry W. Birge, 3 Brigade, 4 Division, 19 Army Corps, Department of the Gulf, Jan.–June 1863. Honorably mustered out, Aug. 26, 1863. Captain, Co. C, 29 CT Infantry, Dec. 5, 1863. Resigned Feb. 9, 1864, to accept promotion. Colonel, 4 Engineers, Corps d'Afrique, March 3, 1864. Designation of regiment changed to 98 U.S. Colored Infantry, April 4, 1864. Commanded Post of Brashear City (LA), Southern Division of Louisiana, Department of the Gulf, May 1865. Commanded Post of New Iberia (LA), Eastern District of Louisiana, Department of Louisiana and Texas, June–Oct. 1865. Colonel, 78 U.S. Colored Infantry, Aug. 26,

Charles Ledyard Norton (post-war) (Anderson, 785 Broadway, New York; author's photograph).

1865, upon consolidation of 98 U.S. Colored Infantry with 78 U.S. Colored Infantry. Honorably mustered out, Jan. 6, 1866. Battle honors: Irish Bend, Port Hudson Campaign.

Born: June 11, 1837 Farmington, CT

Died: Dec. 14, 1909 Sandwich, MA

Education: Graduated Yale College, New Haven, CT, 1859

Occupation: Journalist and author of numerous works on outdoor life and sports

Miscellaneous: Resided Farmington, Hartford Co., CT, before war; New York City, NY, 1861-1891; and Sandwich, Barnstable Co., MA, after 1891

Buried: Riverside Cemetery, Farmington, CT

References: Arthur W. Wright. *History of the Class of 1859, Yale College: A Record of Fifty-Nine Years.* New Haven, CT, 1914. Obituary Circular, Whole No. 1011, New York MOLLUS. Obituary, *Boston Globe*, Dec. 15, 1909. Pension File and Military Service File, National Archives. Letters Received, Colored Troops Branch, Adjutant General's Office, File C353(CT)1863, National Archives. *Obituary Record of Graduates of Yale University Deceased from June 1900 to June 1910.* New Haven, CT, 1910. James Grant Wilson and John Fiske, editors. *Appletons' Cyclopedia of American Biography.* New York City, NY, 1888. Edward T. Fairbanks. *Yale College Class of 1859, Decennial Record.* New Haven, CT, 1870. Henry C. Johnson, editor. *The Tenth General Catalogue of the Psi Upsilon Fraternity.* Bethlehem, PA, 1888.

Henry Taylor Noyes

1 Lieutenant, Adjutant, 148 NY Infantry, Aug. 22, 1862. Major, 148 NY Infantry, Dec. 29, 1863. GSW Cold Harbor, VA, June 3, 1864. Acting AIG, Staff of Brig. Gen. John H. Martindale and Brig. Gen. Adelbert Ames, 2 Division, 18 Army Corps, Army of the James, June–Sept. 1864. Colonel, 38 U.S. Colored Infantry, Sept. 28, 1864. Resigned Dec. 10, 1864, since "during the past two months I have been under medical treatment and unfit for duty by reason of disease which now disables me to rejoin my regiment." Battle honors: Cold Harbor, Richmond Campaign.

Born: Aug. 10, 1838 Starkey, Yates Co., NY

Died: Oct. 15, 1903 Rochester, NY

Education: Attended Columbia College Law School, New York City, NY

Occupation: Law student before war. Engaged in lumber trade in Michigan, 1865–70, after which he managed several manufacturing enterprises in New York, including the National

Henry Taylor Noyes (post-war) (Lloyd, 44 Third Street, Troy, NY; author's photograph).

Yeast Company in Seneca Falls and the German-American Button Company in Rochester.

Offices/Honors: Postmaster, East Tawas, Iosco Co., MI, 1869–70. Unsuccessful candidate for U.S. House of Representatives, 1890.

Miscellaneous: Resided Starkey, Yates Co., NY, before war; Iosco Co., MI, 1865–70; Seneca Falls, Seneca Co., NY, 1870–87; and Rochester, Monroe Co., NY, after 1887

Buried: Glenwood Cemetery, Watkins Glen, NY

References: Obituary Circular, Whole No. 792, New York MOLLUS. *The Men of New York.* Buffalo, NY, 1898. Obituary, *Rochester Democrat and Chronicle,* Oct. 16, 1903. Obituary, *New York Tribune,* Oct. 16, 1903. Henry E. and Harriette E. Noyes, compilers. *Genealogical Record of Some of the Noyes Descendants of James, Nicholas and Peter Noyes.* Boston, MA, 1904. Military Service File, National Archives.

James Turner Organ

Recruiting 2 Lieutenant, 30 MO Infantry, July 30, 1862. Captain, Co. D, 30 MO Infantry, Sept. 25, 1862. Captain, Co. A, 2 MS Heavy Artillery of African Descent, Sept. 12, 1863. Designation of regiment changed to 5 U.S. Colored Heavy Artillery, March 11, 1864. Designation of regiment changed to 6 U.S. Colored Heavy Artillery, April 26, 1864. Detached as Colonel, 70 U.S. Colored Infantry, April 1, 1864. Honorably mustered out as colonel, Nov. 7, 1864. Honorably mustered out as Captain, Co. A, 6 U.S. Colored Heavy Artillery, May 13, 1866. Battle honors: Vidalia.

Born: 1822 Wilson Co., TN

Died: Oct. 7, 1879 Harrisburg, IL

Occupation: Blacksmith before war. Physician after war.

Miscellaneous: Resided Fairfield, Wayne Co., IL (1850); Crab Orchard, Williamson Co., IL (1860); Walpole, Hamilton Co., IL; and Harrisburg, Saline Co., IL (1870)

Buried: Wolf Creek Cemetery, Eldorado, Saline Co., IL

References: *History of Gallatin, Saline, Hamilton, Franklin, and Williamson Counties, Illinois, from the Earliest Time to the Present.* Chicago, IL, 1887. Obituary, *Wayne County Press,* Oct. 16, 1879. Pension File and Military Service File, National Archives. Letters Received, Colored Troops Branch, Adjutant General's Office, File O70(CT)1863, National Archives.

Joseph Griswold Perkins

Private, Rifle Co. A, 1 CT Infantry, April 22, 1861. Honorably mustered out, July 31, 1861. Captain, Co. L, 1 CT Heavy Artillery, March 12, 1862. Resigned Dec. 3, 1863. Lieutenant Colonel, 19 U.S. Colored Infantry, Dec. 9, 1863. Colonel, 19 U.S. Colored Infantry, March 1, 1865. Commanded 3 Brigade, 1 Division, 25 Army Corps, Department of Texas, Sept.–Oct. 1865. Commanded 1 Brigade, 1 Division, 25 Army Corps, Department of Texas, Dec. 1865–Jan. 1866. Commanded 1 Division, 25 Army Corps, Department of Texas, Jan. 1866. Honorably mustered out, Jan. 15, 1867. Battle honors: Yorktown, Petersburg Campaign.

Born: April 20, 1838 New London, CT

Died: Jan. 27, 1913 Old Lyme, CT

Education: Attended Brown University, Providence, RI

Occupation: Lawyer

Offices/Honors: Connecticut Senate, 1872–73

Miscellaneous: Resided Hartford, CT, to 1868; and Old Lyme, New London Co., CT, after 1868

Buried: Duck River Cemetery, Old Lyme, CT

References: Obituary, *Norwich Bulletin*, Jan. 30, 1913. Obituary, *Hartford Courant*, Jan. 29, 1913. Pension File and Military Service File, National Archives. Letters Received, Colored Troops Branch, Adjutant General's Office, File P118(CT)1863, National Archives. John C. Taylor and Samuel P. Hatfield, compilers. *History of the First Connecticut Artillery and of the Siege Trains of the Armies Operating Against Richmond, 1862–1865.* Hartford, CT, 1893. Glenn E. Griswold, compiler. *The Griswold Family, England-America: Edward of Windsor, Connecticut; Matthew of Lyme, Connecticut; Michael of Wethersfield, Connecticut.* Rutland, VT, 1943.

Joseph Griswold Perkins (Gil Barrett Collection).

Mardon Wilson Plumly

Private, Co. I, 71 PA Infantry, June 28, 1861. 2 Lieutenant, Co. D, 40 NY Infantry, July 1, 1862. GSW left breast, 2nd Bull Run, VA, Aug. 29, 1862. Resigned Nov. 23, 1862, "having been afflicted with chronic diarrhea for the past year, which has rendered me totally unfit for duty most of that time." Colonel, 7 LA (Colored) Infantry, July 10, 1863. Honorably mustered out, Sept. 7, 1863. Colonel, 86 U.S. Colored Infantry, Sept. 7, 1863. Commanded 1 Brigade, District of West Florida, Department of the Gulf, Feb. 1864. Resigned Aug. 8, 1864, since "I feel that.... I shall not be able to pass so rigorous an examination in all branches of education as is required by the General Order requiring my appearance before the Board of Examination." Private, Co. K, 1 LA Cavalry, Dec. 29, 1864. Sergeant, Co. K, 1 LA Cavalry, Dec. 31, 1864. 1 Sergeant, Co. K, 1 LA Cavalry, Feb. 26, 1865. Reduced to Private. June 13, 1865. Honorably mustered out, Aug. 28, 1865. Battle honors: Ball's Bluff, Fair Oaks, 2nd Bull Run.

Born: Dec. 12, 1841 Trenton, NJ

Died: Nov. 5, 1889 near Fort Ross, Sonoma Co., CA

Education: Attended Jefferson Medical College, Philadelphia, PA

Occupation: Medical student before war. Laborer after war.

Miscellaneous: Resided San Francisco, CA; and Sea View, Sonoma Co., CA. Brother-in-law of Bvt. Brig. Gen. John W. Ames (6 U.S. Colored Infantry).

Buried: Sea View Cemetery, Sea View, CA (unmarked)

References: Pension File and Military Service File, National Archives. Letters Received, Colored Troops Branch, Adjutant General's Office, File 371(CT)1879, National Archives. Obituary, *Sonoma Democrat*, Nov. 16, 1889. www.ancestry.com.

Richard Root

1 Lieutenant, Co. K, 19 IA Infantry, Aug. 22, 1862. Captain, Co. E, 8 IA Cavalry, Sept. 30, 1863. Major, 8 IA Cavalry, May 1, 1864. Commanded 1 Brigade, 1 Division, Cavalry Corps, Army of the Cumberland, Aug. 1864. Colonel, 136 U.S. Colored Infantry, July 15, 1865. Honorably mustered out Jan. 4, 1866. Battle honors: Prairie Grove, Marmaduke's Expedition into Missouri (Springfield), Atlanta Campaign (Lovejoy's Station, Newnan).

Born: Jan. 27, 1834 Johnsville, Frederick Co., MD

Died: July 28, 1903 Camden, ME

Occupation: Farmer and carpenter before war. After war engaged in hotel business and held a number of public offices in local and federal government.

Offices/Honors: Deputy U.S. Marshal, Southern District of Iowa, 1871–83. U.S. Marshal, Southern District of Iowa, 1883–85. Sheriff, Lee County (IA), 1887–89. Postmaster, Keokuk, IA, 1889–93. Acting Assistant Doorkeeper, U.S. Senate, 1901–03.

Richard Root (post-war) (State Historical Society of Iowa, Des Moines).

Miscellaneous: Resided Mount Pleasant, Henry Co., IA, 1865–77; Keokuk, Lee Co., IA, 1877-1900; and Washington, D.C.

Buried: Arlington National Cemetery, Arlington, VA (Section 3, Lot 1414)

References: *Portrait and Biographical Album of Lee County, Iowa*. Chicago, IL, 1887. *History of Des Moines County, Iowa*. Chicago, IL, 1879. Obituary, *Frederick News*, Aug. 19, 1903. Obituary, *Muscatine News-Tribune*, July 30, 1903. Obituary, *Washington Evening Star*, July 30, 1903. Pension File and Military Service File, National Archives. Letters Received, Volunteer Service Branch, Adjutant General's Office, File R771(VS)1863, National Archives. J. Irvine Dungan. *History of the Nineteenth Regiment Iowa Volunteer Infantry*. Davenport, IA, 1865.

Clark Esek King Royce

Private, Co. B, 44 NY Infantry, Aug. 15, 1861. 2 Lieutenant, Co. B, 44 NY Infantry, Sept. 13, 1861. 1 Lieutenant, Co. B, 44 NY Infantry, July 4, 1862. Captain, Co. A, 44 NY Infantry, Aug. 26, 1862. Captain, Co. E, 44 NY Infantry, April 16, 1863. Lieutenant Colonel, 6 U.S. Colored Infantry, Sept. 23, 1863. Commanded 3 Brigade, 3

Division, 18 Army Corps, Army of the James, Sept. 1864. Shell wound foot, New Market Heights, VA, Sept. 29, 1864. Colonel, 29 U.S. Colored Infantry, Jan. 1, 1865. Honorably mustered out, Nov. 6, 1865. Battle honors: Peninsular Campaign (Hanover Court House, Gaines' Mill, Malvern Hill), 2nd Bull Run, Antietam, Fredericksburg, Gettysburg, Bermuda Hundred, Petersburg Campaign (New Market Heights), Appomattox Campaign.

Born: Jan. 13, 1837 New Lebanon Springs, NY

Died: Oct. 1, 1897 New York City, NY (committed suicide by inhaling illuminating gas)

Education: Graduated Williams College, Williamstown, MA, 1859. Attended Columbia College Law School, New York City, NY.

Occupation: Lawyer

Miscellaneous: Resided Sag Harbor, Suffolk Co., NY, 1865–69; Scranton, Lackawanna Co., PA, 1869–76; San Francisco, CA, 1876–97. Convicted of embezzlement while serving as Treasurer of Soldiers' Home, Yountville, CA, 1893.

Clark Esek King Royce (Turner's First Floor Atelier, 808 Chestnut Street, Philadelphia, PA; Ken Turner Collection).

Buried: Cemetery of the Evergreens, New Lebanon, NY

References: Eben B. Parsons. *1855–1859–1884. Class of Fifty-Nine, Williams College--Four Years in College and Twenty-Five Years Out of College.* Syracuse, NY, 1884. *The Bay of San Francisco, the Metropolis of the Pacific Coast and Its Suburban Cities: A History.* Chicago, IL, 1892. Obituary, *San Francisco Call,* Oct. 2, 1897. Obituary, *San Francisco Chronicle,* Oct. 2, 1897. Obituary, *New York Sun,* Oct. 2, 1897. William H. Ward, editor. *Records of Members of the Grand Army of the Republic with a Complete Account of the Twentieth National Encampment.* San Francisco, CA, 1886. Pension File and Military Service File, National Archives. Letters Received, Colored Troops Branch, Adjutant General's Office, File R65(CT)1863, National Archives. Letters Received, Commission Branch, Adjutant General's Office, File R401(CB)1866, National Archives. Eugene A. Nash. *A History of the Forty-Fourth Regiment New York Volunteer Infantry in the Civil War, 1861–1865.* Chicago, IL, 1911. John McMurray. *Recollections of a Colored Troop.* Brookville, PA, 1994. Edward A. Miller, Jr. *The Black Civil War Soldiers of Illinois: The Story of the Twenty-Ninth U.S. Colored Infantry.* Columbia, SC, 1998.

Gustavus Adolphus Scroggs

Authorized Aug. 19, 1861 to raise and organize "Eagle Brigade" of four regiments in New York. Although he raised forty-one companies of volunteers, including the 21st, 78th, and 100th New York Infantry regiments and parts of two

Gustavus Adolphus Scroggs (George H. Stowits. *History of the One Hundredth Regiment of New York State Volunteers.* **Buffalo, NY, 1870**).

other regiments, the "Eagle Brigade" never came into existence. Nominated as Brig. Gen., USV, June 18, 1862. Assigned to command 2 Brigade, 2 Division, 2 Army Corps, Army of Virginia, July 7, 1862, but did not take command because the U.S. Senate adjourned without confirming him. Provost Marshal, 30 District of New York, April 1863–Feb. 1864. Colonel, 25 U.S. Colored Infantry, March 4, 1864. While awaiting transportation to take his regiment to the Department of the Gulf, he was charged with "disobedience of orders" when he refused to obey an order from Major Gen. John J. Peck to move his regiment temporarily to New Bern, NC. Although found guilty by court martial, April 25, 1864, he escaped punishment due to "many mitigating considerations." Having accepted his commission for the purpose of "organizing the colored men of Texas into U.S. regiments," he resigned July 6, 1864, upon learning that "no attempt would be made for a considerable period, if at all, to carry out the object for which I was commissioned." Provost Marshal, 30 District of New York, Nov. 1864–Dec. 1865.

Born: Aug. 8, 1820 Darlington, Beaver Co., PA

Died: Jan. 24, 1887 Buffalo, NY

Occupation: Lawyer

Offices/Honors: Brig. Gen., 31 Brigade, New York State Militia, 1854–58. Sheriff of Erie Co., NY, 1859–61. U.S. Commissioner, Northern District of New York, 1875–85.

Miscellaneous: Resided Buffalo, Erie Co., NY

Buried: Forest Lawn Cemetery, Buffalo, NY (Section D, Lot 148)

References: George H. Stowits. *History of the 100th Regiment of New York State Volunteers.* Buffalo, NY, 1870. Obituary, *Buffalo Courier,* Jan. 25, 1887. Obituary, *Buffalo Times,* Jan. 25, 1887. Joseph H. Bausman. *History of Beaver County, Pennsylvania, and Its Centennial Celebration.* New York City, NY, 1904. H. Perry Smith, editor. *History of the City of Buffalo and Erie County.* Syracuse, NY, 1884. Military Service File, National Archives. Letters Received, Colored Troops Branch, Adjutant General's Office, Files P128(CT)1864 and W124(CT)1864, National Archives. Letters Received, Adjutant General's Office, File S2108(AGO)1862, National Archives. "Court Martial of Col. Scroggs," *Buffalo Courier,* May 7, 1864.

Thomas Duncan Sedgewick

Captain, Co. B, 2 KY Infantry, June 3, 1861. Major, 2 KY Infantry, June 28, 1861. Colonel, 2 KY Infantry, Jan. 27, 1862. Shell wound of thigh, Shiloh, TN, April 7, 1862.

Thomas Duncan Sedgewick (Library of Congress [LC-DIG-cwpb-07297]).

Thomas Duncan Sedgewick (Webster & Bro., Louisville, Kentucky; courtesy Everitt Bowles).

Commanded 22 Brigade, 4 Division, Army of the Ohio, April–May 1862. Commanded 1 Brigade, 2 Division, 21 Army Corps, Army of the Cumberland, July–Aug. 1863. Commanded 1 Brigade, 1 Division, 4 Army Corps, Army of the Cumberland, Oct.–Nov. 1863. Honorably mustered out, June 19, 1864. Colonel, 114 U.S. Colored Infantry, July 3, 1864. Commanded Post of Camp Nelson (KY), District of Kentucky, 23 Army Corps, Department of the Ohio, Sept.–Nov. 1864. Commanded 2 Brigade, 1 Division, 25 Army Corps, Department of Virginia, March–Sept. 1865. Commanded Post of Ringgold Barracks (TX), Department of Texas, March–July 1866. Commanded Sub-District of the Rio Grande, Department of Texas, Sept.–Dec. 1866. Honorably mustered out, April 2, 1867. Battle honors: Shiloh, Corinth, Stone's River, Chickamauga.

Born: 1837? Louisville, KY

Died: April 26, 1879 New York City, NY (found dead in a city park in an intoxicated condition)

Occupation: Mercantile clerk before war. Chief Clerk, U.S. Corps of Engineers, Louisville, KY, 1869–71. U.S. Treasury Department and U.S. War Department clerk in later years.

Miscellaneous: Resided Louisville, Jefferson Co., KY; New Albany, Floyd Co., IN; and Washington, D.C. Brother-in-law of Colonel William W. Tuley (7 IN Legion).

Buried: Cypress Hills National Cemetery, Brooklyn, NY (Section 2, Grave 12172, misidentified as T. B. Sedgwick, removed from City Cemetery, Hart's Island, New York Harbor, June 9, 1941).

References: Obituary, *New Albany Ledger-Standard*, April 28, 1879. Obituary, *New York Times*, April 27, 1879. Obituary, *Louisville Courier-Journal*, April 29, 1879. Letters Received, Volunteer Service Branch, Adjutant General's Office, File S1686(VS)1862, National Archives. Letters Received, Appointment, Commission and Personal Branch, Adjutant General's Office, File 3715(ACP)1873, National Archives. Pension File and Military Service File, National Archives. Letters Received, Colored Troops Branch, Adjutant General's Office, File F163(CT)1864, National Archives. Richard D. Sears. *Camp Nelson, Kentucky: A Civil War History*. Lexington, KY, 2002. William F. Tuley. *The Tuley Family Memoirs*. New Albany, IN, 1906. http://sedgwick.org/na/families/barnabas1810/sedgwick-thomas1837.html.

John Andrew Shannon

Captain, Co. A, 100 OH Infantry, July 15, 1862. Major, 100 OH Infantry, May 13, 1863. Provost Marshal, Staff of Brig. Gen. Milo S. Hascall, 3 Division, 23 Army

Thomas Duncan Sedgewick (standing, with Colonel David A. Enyart, 1 Kentucky Infantry) (USAHEC [RG98S-CWP58.45]).

Corps, Department of the Ohio, Aug.–Dec. 1863. Lieutenant Colonel, 1 U.S. Colored Heavy Artillery, May 11, 1864. Colonel, 1 U.S. Colored Heavy Artillery, Nov. 4, 1864. Although acquitted by court martial, March 19, 1865, of "disgraceful conduct" involving Negro laundresses, when he resigned, May 13, 1865, Major Gen. George H. Thomas, in forwarding his resignation, recommended its acceptance "for the good of

John Andrew Shannon (W.E. Prall, Photographer, Gay Street, Knoxville, TN; author's photograph).

the service" and added "dismissal would be better."

Born: Oct. 19, 1826 Wyandot Co., OH

Died: Nov. 30, 1894 Mason, MI

Education: Attended Denison University, Granville, OH

John Andrew Shannon (T.M. Schleier, Photographer, On Union and Cherry Sts., and 27 Public Square, Nashville, TN; L.M. Strayer Collection).

Occupation: Methodist clergyman before war. Lawyer after war.

Miscellaneous: Resided Fostoria, Seneca Co., OH (1860); Perrysburg, Wood Co., OH, to 1871; Bowling Green, Wood Co., OH, 1871–85; and Mason, Ingham Co., MI, after 1885

Buried: Oak Grove Cemetery, Bowling Green, OH (Southwest Mound Section)

References: *Portrait and Biographical Album of Ingham and Livingston Counties, Michigan*. Chicago, IL, 1891. Obituary, *Detroit Free Press*, Dec. 1, 1894. Obituary, *Owosso Times*, Dec. 7, 1894. Obituary, *Perrysburg Journal*, Dec. 8, 1894. *Commemorative Historical and Biographical Record of Wood County, Ohio: Its Past and Present*. Chicago, IL, 1897. Pension File and Military Service File, National Archives. Letters Received, Commission Branch, Adjutant General's Office, File S2315(CB)1865, National Archives. Court-martial Case Files, 1809–1894, File MM-1635, National Archives. Frederick W. Fout. *The Dark Days of the Civil War, 1861 to 1865*. St. Louis, MO, 1904.

Charles S. Sheley

2 Lieutenant, Co. E, 10 IL Infantry (3 months), April 22, 1861. Captain, Co. E, 10 IL Infantry (3 months), May 15, 1861. Honorably mustered out, July 29, 1861. Captain,

Co. C, 10 IL Infantry (3 years), Aug. 17, 1861. Resigned July 3, 1862, "on account of the protracted and dangerous illness of my wife, requiring my presence at home." *Colonel,* 2 AR Infantry of African Descent (later 54 U.S. Colored Infantry), May 21, 1863. Appointment revoked, Jan. 23, 1864, in response to a petition from regimental officers, asking to be relieved from his "ignorance, abusive conduct, buffoonery, and incompetency," and further describing him as "utterly destitute of dignity of character, entirely heartless in the cause we are engaged, devoid of the ability to comprehend its principles, and deficient in the requisite skill to put them into practice."

Born: Oct. 13, 1832 Watertown, NY
Died: Sept. 4, 1888 Fairbury, IL
Occupation: Moulder and hotel-keeper before war. Civil engineer after war.

Miscellaneous: Resided Quincy, Adams Co., IL, before war; and Fairbury, Livingston Co., IL, after war

Buried: Graceland Cemetery, Fairbury, IL

References: Pension File and Military Service File, National Archives. Letters Received, Colored Troops Branch, Adjutant General's Office, File S485(CT)1864, National Archives. Obituary, *Fairbury Blade,* Sept. 15, 1888. Mark K. Christ, "They Will Be Armed: Lorenzo Thomas Recruits Black Troops in Helena, April 6, 1863," *Arkansas Historical Quarterly,* Vol. 72, No. 4 (Winter 2013). William A. Dobak. *Freedom by the Sword: The U.S. Colored Troops, 1862–1867.* Washington, D.C., 2011.

Charles S. Sheley (Reeve & Watts, Photographers, No. 57 High Street, Over Post Office, Columbus, OH; courtesy Henry Deeks).

William Silliman

1 Lieutenant, Co. D, 7 NY Cavalry, Nov. 6, 1861. Honorably mustered out, March 31, 1862. 1 Lieutenant, Adjutant, 124 NY Infantry, July 16, 1862. Captain, Co. C, 124 NY Infantry, Aug. 20, 1862. Resigned Feb. 1, 1864, to accept promotion. Colonel, 26 U.S. Colored Infantry, Feb. 8, 1864. Commanded Post of Beaufort (SC), District of Beaufort, Department of the South, Sept.–Oct. 1864. Commanded 2 Separate Brigade, Department of the South, Dec. 1864. GSW right thigh, Gregory's Farm, SC, Dec. 9, 1864. Battle honors: Chancellorsville, Gettysburg, John's Island, Gregory's Farm.

Born: Oct. 18, 1837 Canterbury, Orange Co., NY

Died: Dec. 17, 1864 DOW Beaufort, SC

Education: Attended Yale Law School, New Haven, CT. Graduated Albany (NY) Law School, 1860.

Occupation: Lawyer

Miscellaneous: Resided Cornwall, Orange Co., NY; and Bloomfield, Essex Co., NJ

Buried: Bloomfield Cemetery, Bloomfield, NJ (Lot 329)

References: Edward M. Ruttenber and Lewis H. Clark, compilers. *History of Orange County, New York*. Philadelphia, PA, 1881. Obituary, *New York Times*, Jan. 5, 1865. Pension File and Military Service File, National Archives. Charles H. Weygant. *History of the One Hundred and Twenty-Fourth Regiment N.Y.S.V.* Newburgh, NY, 1877. Letters Received, Colored Troops Branch, Adjutant General's Office, File B100(CT)1864, National Archives.

William Silliman (R.A. Lewis, 152 Chatham Street, New York; author's photograph).

Absalom S. Smith

2 Lieutenant, Co. C, 14 WI Infantry, Jan. 30, 1862. Captain, Co. C, 14 WI Infantry, March 17, 1862. GSW side, Shiloh, TN, April 7, 1862. Colonel, 6 MS Infantry of African Descent (later 58 U.S. Colored Infantry), Aug. 31, 1863. Dismissed Jan. 18, 1864, for "disgracing the uniform of the United States by boisterous conduct" while "beastly drunk" at the St. Charles Hotel in New Orleans, LA. He appealed his dismissal to President Lincoln, supported by a number of testimonials, including one from Wisconsin Governor James T. Lewis, who, unaware of the facts, described his offence as "a mere matter of sport." President Lincoln referred the case to Judge Advocate General Joseph Holt, who concluded, May 5, 1864, that since "he has attempted to commend himself to Executive clemency by misrepresenting the facts in his case, ... no recommendation can be made in his favor from this office." Battle honors: Shiloh, Corinth, Vicksburg Campaign.

Born: 1834? Elimsport, Lycoming Co., PA

Died: June 9, 1865 Montana Territory (killed by Sioux Indians)

Occupation: Unknown

Miscellaneous: Resided Omro, Winnebago Co., WI; and Fond du Lac, Fond du Lac Co., WI

Buried: Place of burial unknown

References: Military Service File, National Archives. Letters Received, Colored Troops Branch, Adjutant General's Office, File S201(CT)1863, National Archives. Court-martial Case Files, 1809-1894, File NN-1285, National Archives. "Indian Troubles on the Yellowstone," *Montana Post*, June 24, 1865. David A. Langkau. *Civil War*

Veterans of Winnebago County, Wisconsin. Bowie, MD, 1993. Emerson Collins and John W. Jordan, editors. *Genealogical and Personal History of Lycoming County, Pennsylvania.* New York and Chicago, 1906. www.ancestry.com.

Michael William Smith

1 Lieutenant, Adjutant, 15 IN Infantry, June 14, 1861. Resigned Aug. 31, 1861. Major, 1 OH Cavalry, Dec. 6, 1861. Resigned June 10, 1862, since "my business ... requires my immediate presence," and "the excessive fatigues undergone since the evacuation of Corinth have so prostrated my whole system that I am compelled to admit an almost utter inability to discharge the duties of my position." Lieutenant Colonel, 140 IL Infantry, June 18, 1864. Honorably mustered out, Oct. 29, 1864. Colonel, 66 U.S. Colored Infantry, Feb. 8, 1865. Commanded Post of Vicksburg (MS), Department of Mississippi, June–July 1865. Commanded Post of Mississippi City (MS), Department of Mississippi, July–Aug, 1865. Commanded Post of Natchez (MS), Southern District of Mississippi, Department of Mississippi, Aug.–Nov. 1865. Commanded Southern District of Mississippi, Department of Mississippi, Jan.–Feb. 1866. Honorably mustered out, March 20, 1866. Battle honors: Siege of Corinth.

Michael William Smith (E. Roberts, Photograph Gallery, Base St., Fulton, IL; author's photograph).

Born: Oct. 11, 1836 Port Robinson, Ontario, Canada
Died: May 26, 1889, Bond Hill, Hamilton Co., OH
Occupation: School teacher and school principal
Offices/Honors: Superintendent of Schools, Whiteside Co., IL, 1869–73
Miscellaneous: Resided Bryan, Williams Co., OH; Fulton, Whiteside Co., IL, 1862–66; Morrison, Whiteside Co., IL, 1866–73; Sterling, Whiteside Co., IL, 1873–74; and Bond Hill, Hamilton Co., OH, after 1874
Buried: Spring Grove Cemetery, Cincinnati, OH (Section 104, Lot 301)
References: Pension File and Military Service File, National Archives. Letters Received, Colored Troops Branch, Adjutant General's Office, File S923(CT)1864, National Archives. Gunnar A. Benson. *Centennial Anniversary of Whiteside County Education Association, 1856–1956.* Sterling, IL, 1956. William W. Davis. *History of Whiteside County, Illinois, from Its Earliest Settlement to 1908.* Chicago, IL, 1908. www.ancestry.com.

Homer Baxter Sprague

Captain, Co. H, 13 CT Infantry, Feb. 18, 1862. GSW right hand and arm, Irish Bend, LA, April 14, 1863. Major, 13 CT Infantry, Oct. 5, 1863. *Colonel*, 11 Infantry, Corps d'Afrique (later 83 U.S. Colored Infantry), Nov. 11, 1863 (Declined, since "I prefer to remain in the 13th Conn."). Lieutenant Colonel, 13 CT Infantry, Dec. 30, 1863. Taken prisoner, Winchester, VA, Sept. 19, 1864. Confined Libby Prison (Richmond, VA), Salisbury, NC, and Danville, VA. Paroled Feb. 22, 1865. Honorably mustered out, April 25, 1866. Bvt. Colonel, USV, March 13, 1865, for gallant and meritorious services at Port Hudson, Louisiana. Battle honors: Irish Bend, Port Hudson Campaign, Shenandoah Valley Campaign (Winchester).

Born: Oct. 19, 1829 Sutton, MA
Died: March 23, 1918 Newton, MA
Education: Graduated Yale University, New Haven, CT, 1852
Occupation: Lawyer, educator, and author
Offices/Honors: Connecticut House of Representatives, 1868–69. President, Mills College, Oakland, CA, 1885–87. President, University of North Dakota, Grand Forks, ND, 1887–91.

Miscellaneous: Resided New Haven, New Haven Co., CT; Ithaca, Tompkins Co., NY; Needham, Norfolk Co., MA; New York City, NY; Newton, Middlesex Co., MA; and other cities during his long career in education. First cousin of Bvt. Brig. Gen. Augustus B.R. Sprague.

Buried: Evergreen Cemetery, New Haven, CT (Western Avenue, Lot 181)

Homer Baxter Sprague (courtesy Henry Deeks).

Homer Baxter Sprague (post-war) (Purdy & Frear, Photographers, Ithaca, NY; author's Photograph).

References: *The National Cyclopaedia of American Biography*. Vol. 24. New York City, NY, 1935. *Obituary Record of Graduates of Yale University Deceased during the Year Ending July, 1, 1918*. New Haven, CT, 1919. Allen Johnson and Dumas Malone, editors. *Dictionary of American Biography*. New York City, NY, 1964. Obituary, *Hartford Courant*, March 25, 1918. Obituary, *Boston Globe*, March 23, 1918. Obituary, *Grand Forks Herald*, March 23, 1918. Homer B. Sprague. *History of the 13th Infantry Regiment of Connecticut Volunteers during the Great Rebellion*. Hartford, CT, 1867. Homer B. Sprague. *Lights and Shadows in Confederate Prisons: A Personal Experience, 1864–5*. New York City, NY, 1915. Pension File and Military Service File, National Archives. Letters Received, Commission Branch, Adjutant General's Office, File S2006(CB)1865, National Archives. Obituary Circular, Whole No. 1314, California MOLLUS. Augustus B.R. Sprague. *Genealogy (in Part) of the Sprague Families in America*. Worcester, MA, 1902.

Spencer Hallenbake Stafford

Major, 6 NY State Militia (3 months), May 14, 1861. Honorably discharged, July 9, 1861. Lieutenant Colonel, 11 NY Infantry, Oct. 18, 1861. Lamenting the lack of field service and unhappy with the living conditions while assigned to court martial duty at Fort Monroe (VA), he resigned March 5, 1862. Captain, Assistant Provost Marshal, Staff of Major Gen. Benjamin F. Butler, Department of the Gulf, July–Sept. 1862. Colonel, 1 LA Native Guards, Sept. 27, 1862. Designation of regiment changed to 1 Infantry, Corps d'Afrique, June 6, 1863. Dismissed Sept. 8, 1863, for "contemptuous and disrespectful words toward the President and abusive language to the officer of a picket guard." He appealed his dismissal to President Lincoln, who referred the matter to Judge Advocate General Joseph Holt. Judge Holt recommended that the order of dismissal be disapproved, "In view of the capacity and spirit which Col. Stafford has displayed; of his valuable services; of the numerous and exceedingly laudatory testimonials that he produces; of the fact that he has had no trial by his peers; of the doubt thrown upon the accusing proofs by his own oath, as well as his whole military history; of the recommendations presented; and of all the papers in the case." On April 21, 1864, Stafford was informed that "the disability resting upon you by reason of your dismissal from the service is hereby removed, and no objection to you being re-commissioned is known to exist." The order dismissing him was finally revoked, Jan. 3, 1871, and he was honorably discharged to date, Sept. 15, 1863. Appointed *Colonel*, 10 U.S. Colored Infantry, May 3, 1864. Commanded Fort Powhatan (VA), Department of Virginia and North Carolina, May 1864. Appointment revoked, July 26, 1864. Battle honors: Wilson's Wharf.

Born: April 7, 1822 Albany, NY
Died: Dec. 25, 1888 Utica, NY
Education: Attended Williams College, Williamstown, MA
Occupation: Lawyer
Miscellaneous: Resided New York City, NY, before war; Marietta, Washington Co., OH; and Oneida, Madison Co., NY, after war. First cousin of Bvt. Brig. Gen. Lewis Benedict and Colonel David E. Gregory (144 NY Infantry).
Buried: Forest Hill Cemetery, Utica, NY (Section 22B, Lot 758)
References: Obituary, *Utica Morning Herald*, Dec. 28, 1888. Military Service

Spencer Hallenbake Stafford (Brady, Washington; Library of Congress [LC-DIG-cwpb-04592]).

File, National Archives. Letters Received, Colored Troops Branch, Adjutant General's Office, File G46(CT)1863, National Archives. Obituary, *Utica Daily Observer*, Dec. 29, 1888. *Catalogue of the Sigma Phi with the Thesaurus.* Boston, MA, 1891. Henry M. Benedict. *A Contribution to the Genealogy of the Stafford Family in America; Containing an Account of Col. Joab Stafford and a Complete Record of His Descendants in the Male Lines.* New York City, NY, 1895. James G. Hollandsworth, Jr. *The Louisiana Native Guards: The Black Military Experience During the Civil War.* Baton Rouge, LA, 1995. Stephen J. Ochs. *A Black Patriot and a White Priest: Andre Cailloux and Claude Paschal Maistre in Civil War New Orleans.* Baton Rouge, LA, 2000. Clare P. Weaver, editor. *Thank God My Regiment an African One: The Civil War Diary of Colonel Nathan W. Daniels.* Baton Rouge, LA, 1998. Benjamin F. Butler. *Autobiography and Personal Reminiscences of Major General Benjamin F. Butler: Butler's Book.* Boston, MA, 1892.

Ozora Pierson Stearns

1 Lieutenant, Co. F, 9 MN Infantry, Aug. 28, 1862. Acting ADC, Staff of Brig. Gen. Stephen Miller, District of Minnesota, Department of the Northwest, June–Aug. 1863. Colonel, 39 U.S. Colored Infantry, April 28, 1864. Commanded 1 Brigade, 3 Division, 9 Army Corps, Army of the Potomac, Sept.–Oct. 1864. Commanded 2 Brigade, 3 Division, 10 Army Corps, Department of North Carolina, June–July 1865. Honorably mustered out, Dec. 4, 1865. Battle honors: Richmond Campaign (Assault on the Crater, Boydton Plank Road), Fort Fisher Campaign.

Born: Jan. 15, 1831 DeKalb, St. Lawrence Co., NY

Died: June 2, 1896 Pacific Beach, San Diego Co., CA

Education: Attended Oberlin (OH) College. Graduated University of Michigan, Ann Arbor, MI, 1858. Graduated University of Michigan Law School, Ann Arbor, MI, 1860.

Occupation: Lawyer and judge

Offices/Honors: U.S. Register in Bankruptcy, 1867–71. U.S. Senate, 1871. District court judge, 1874–94.

Miscellaneous: Resided Rochester, Olmsted Co., MN, to 1872; Duluth, St. Louis Co., MN, after 1872

Buried: Forest Hill Cemetery, Duluth, MN (Section D, Block 9, Lot 8)

References: Consul Willshire Butterfield, "The Bench and Bar of Duluth," *Magazine of Western History*, Vol. 9, No. 5 (March 1889). Obituary, *Duluth Evening Herald*, June 2, 1896. Obituary, *Duluth News-Tribune*, June 3, 1896. Obituary, *Minneapolis Journal*, June 2, 1896. Obituary, *Saint Paul Globe*, June 3, 1896. Obituary Circular, Whole No. 167, Minnesota MOLLUS. *The United States Biographical Dictionary and Portrait Gallery of Eminent and Self-Made Men.* Minnesota Volume. New York and Chicago, 1879. Avis Stearns Van Wagenen. *Genealogy and Memoirs of Charles and Nathaniel Stearns and Their Descendants.* Syracuse, NY, 1901. William Horatio Barnes. *History of Congress. The Forty-First Congress of the United States, 1869–1871.* New York City, NY, 1872. Lyster M. O'Brien, compiler. *The Class of "Fifty Eight," University of Michigan, 1858 to 1913.* Cleveland, OH, 1913. *The National Cyclopaedia of American Biography.* Vol. 10. New York City, NY, 1909. James L. Harrison, compiler. *Biographical Directory of the*

Ozora Pierson Stearns (J.H. & J.B. Easton, Rochester, MN; Minnesota Historical Society).

Ozora Pierson Stearns (seated center, with Field and Staff, 39 U.S. Colored Infantry, including Major Quincy McNeill, seated left, and Lt. Col. Charles J. Wright, seated right) (Massachusetts MOLLUS Collection, USAHEC [Vol. 35, p. 1743]).

American Congress, 1774–1949. Washington, D.C., 1950. Dwight E. Woodbridge and John S. Pardee, editors. *History of Duluth and St. Louis County Past and Present.* Chicago, IL, 1910. Theodore R. Chase. *The Michigan University Book, 1844–1880.* Detroit, MI, 1880. Pension File and Military Service File, National Archives. Letters Received, Colored Troops Branch, Adjutant General's Office, File M122(CT)1864, National Archives.

Ozora Pierson Stearns (U.S. Senate, 1871) (Brady-Handy Photograph Collection, Library of Congress [LC-DIG-cwpbh-00125]).

Albert Stickney

Captain, Co. A, 47 MA Infantry, Sept. 19, 1862. Lieutenant Colonel, 47 MA Infantry, Nov. 7, 1862. Commanded Post of Brashear City (LA), Department of the Gulf, June 1863. Acting AIG, Staff of Brig. Gen. William H. Emory, Defenses of New Orleans, Department of the Gulf, June–July 1863. Honorably mustered out, Sept. 1, 1863. *Colonel*, 11 Infantry, Corps d'Afrique (later 83 U.S. Colored Infantry), Aug. 27, 1863 (Declined on account of illness). Battle honors: La Fourche Crossing.

Born: Feb. 1, 1839 Cambridge, MA
Died: May 4, 1908 Greenwich, CT
Education: Graduated Harvard University, Cambridge, MA, 1859. Graduated Harvard University Law School, 1862.
Occupation: Lawyer and author of works pertaining to law, government, and politics

Albert Stickney (Harvard University, 1859) (author's photograph).

Albert Stickney (Massachusetts MOLLUS Collection, USAHEC [Vol. 108, p. 5589]).

Albert Stickney (courtesy The Excelsior Brigade).

Miscellaneous: Resided Cambridge, Middlesex Co., MA, before war; New York City, NY, after war. Counsel in 1879–80 for General Gouverneur K. Warren before the military court of inquiry, which investigated General Warren's conduct in the battle of Five Forks.

Buried: Rockland Cemetery, Sparkill, NY (Section A-3, Plot 101)

References: David McAdam, et al., editors. *History of the Bench and Bar of New York.* New York City, NY, 1897. Obituary, *New York Tribune,* May 5, 1908. Obituary, *Cambridge Chronicle,* May 9, 1908. Obituary, *Boston Journal,* May 5, 1908. Military Service File, National Archives. Richard B. Irwin. *History of the Nineteenth Army Corps.* New York City and London, 1893. *Records of the Class of 1859, Harvard College.* Cambridge, MA, 1896. Francis H. Brown. *Harvard University in the War of 1861–1865.* Boston, MA, 1886. Matthew A. Stickney. *The Stickney Family: A Genealogical Memoir of the Descendants of William and Elizabeth Stickney from 1637 to 1869.* Salem, MA, 1869. Moses King. *Notable New Yorkers, 1896–1899.* New York City, NY, 1899.

Benjamin Roach Townsend

Private, Co. B, 1 U.S. Sharpshooters, Aug. 12, 1862. Honorably discharged, Nov. 25, 1862. 2 Lieutenant, Co. D, 125 NY Infantry, Oct. 21, 1862. 1 Lieutenant, Co. F, 125 NY Infantry, Dec. 12, 1862. Major, 2 U.S. Colored Infantry, Nov. 20, 1863. Lieutenant Colonel, 2 U.S. Colored Infantry, May 2, 1864. Colonel, 2 U.S. Colored Infantry, July 20, 1864. Commanded Post of Cedar Keys (FL) and U.S. Forces, West Coast of Florida, District of Key West and Tortugas, Department of the Gulf, Sept. 1864–Jan. 1865. GSW left arm, Natural Bridge, FL, March 6, 1865. Commanded Post and Sub-District of Key West (FL), Department of Florida, Sept.–Nov. 1865. Honorably mustered out, Jan. 5, 1866. Battle honors: Antietam, Bristoe Station, Natural Bridge.

Born: Nov. 27, 1838 New Orleans, LA

Died: Sept. 8, 1902 Index, Snohomish Co., WA

Occupation: Drover before war. Mine operator in later years.

Miscellaneous: Resided Floyd, Oneida Co., NY; and Austin, Travis Co., TX, to 1877; Wallingford, New Haven Co., CT, 1877–93; and Seattle, King Co., WA, after 1893. Son of Nathaniel Townsend, a prominent Texas Unionist.

Buried: In Memoriam Cemetery, Wallingford, CT

References: Ezra D. Simons. *A*

Benjamin Roach Townsend (Massachusetts MOLLUS Collection, USAHEC [Vol. 126, p. 6470L]).

Regimental History: The One Hundred and Twenty-Fifth New York State Volunteers. New York City, NY, 1888. Obituary, *New Haven Evening Register,* Sept. 9, 1902. Obituary, *Austin Daily Statesman,* Sept. 10, 1902. Obituary, *Tacoma Daily Ledger,* Sept. 9, 1902. Military Service File, National Archives. Letters Received, Colored Troops Branch, Adjutant General's Office, File T73(CT)1863, National Archives. Walter P. Webb, editor. *The Handbook of Texas.* Austin, TX, 1952. Lawrence K. Hodges, editor. *Mining in the Pacific Northwest.* Seattle, WA, 1897.

James Trimble

Private, Co. C, 20 TN Infantry, May 20, 1861. Transferred to Confederate service, Aug. 1861. Discharged Sept. 11, 1861. *Colonel,* 14 U.S. Colored Infantry, Nov. 17, 1863. On Jan. 21, 1864, the mustering officer, Captain Reuben D. Mussey, refused to muster him as colonel "upon the ground that while a citizen of the United States, he has been in arms against the same and has given aid, countenance, counsel and encouragement to persons engaged in armed hostility thereto, having been in the State service of Tennessee at a time when the State and its military force were arrayed against the Government." Adjutant General Lorenzo Thomas supported Mussey's action, with the added comment, "I object entirely to the muster of this person. I have seen Mr. Trimble and am satisfied that he should not be placed at the head of a regiment."

Born: 1838? Nashville, TN
Died: 1878? (date and place of death unknown)
Education: Graduated University of Nashville (TN), 1858
Occupation: Lawyer. In his later years he led a nomadic existence as a lecturer, leaving a trail of drunkenness and minor thievery, resulting in frequent periods of imprisonment.
Miscellaneous: Resided Gallatin, Sumner Co., TN; and Nashville, TN, before war. Cincinnati, OH; and numerous cities in New York, after war.
Buried: Place of burial unknown
References: Letters Received, Colored Troops Branch, Adjutant General's Office, File T29(CT)1864, National Archives. Leroy P. Graf and Ralph W. Haskins, editors. *The Papers of Andrew Johnson.* Volume 6, 1862–1864. Knoxville, TN, 1983. Walter T. Durham. *Rebellion Revisited: A History of Sumner County, Tennessee, from 1861 to 1870.* Franklin, TN, 1999. "James Trimble, of Tennessee: An Eccentric Fellow—Soldier, Lecturer, Philosopher, and Lunatic," *Rome Sentinel,* May 21, 1878. "A Tramp's Diary: Some of His Amusing Adventures," *Geneva Courier,* April 7, 1880. www.ancestry.com.

William Dutton Turner

Assistant Surgeon, 1 IL Light Artillery, Sept. 27, 1861. Surgeon, 97 IL Infantry, March 14, 1863. Colonel, 6 U.S. Colored Heavy Artillery, April 22, 1864. Designation of regiment changed to 7 U.S. Colored Heavy Artillery, April 26, 1864. Designation of regiment changed to 11 U.S. Colored Infantry, Jan. 23, 1865. Discharged April 28, 1865, upon adverse report of a Board of Examination, which found him "not qualified for the position he holds." Supported by Adjutant General Lorenzo Thomas, who stated, "He could only have been removed by great injustice, and on the report of officers prejudiced against him," he was restored to his position, June 3, 1865, upon the recommendation of General Ulysses S. Grant. Commanded Fort Pickering, Post of Memphis (TN), District of West Tennessee, Department of the Cumberland, July 1865. Honorably mustered out, Jan. 12, 1866. Battle honors: Fort Donelson, Shiloh, Chickasaw Bayou, Vicksburg Campaign.

Born: 1830? Jamaica, West Indies
Died: Dec. 31, 1866 Clear Lake, AR
Occupation: Physician
Miscellaneous: Resided Glasgow, Scotland; and Portage, Columbia Co., WI, before war; and Clear Lake, Pulaski Co., AR, after war. His wife, Joanna W. Turner, accompanied him throughout the war as a volunteer nurse. She received a pension in her own name, and when she died, June 15, 1901, she was buried in Arlington (VA) National Cemetery.
Buried: Place of burial unknown
References: Pension File and Military Service File, National Archives. Letters Received, Colored Troops Branch, Adjutant General's Office, File T100(CT)1864, National Archives.

William Dutton Turner (T. Lilienthal, 102 Poydras St., New Orleans, LA; author's photograph).

John Baptiste Weber

Private, Co. A, 44 NY Infantry, Aug. 30, 1861. Sergeant, Co. A, 44 NY Infantry, Jan. 2, 1862. Sergeant Major, 44 NY Infantry, April 1, 1862. 2 Lieutenant, Co. F, 44 NY Infantry, May 30, 1862. 1 Lieutenant, Adjutant, 116 NY Infantry, Aug. 8, 1862. Acting AAG, Staff of Colonel Edward P. Chapin, et al., 1 Brigade, 1 Division, 19 Army Corps, Department of the Gulf, Feb.–Aug. 1863. Colonel, 18 Infantry, Corps d'Afrique, Nov. 7, 1863. Commanded 2 Brigade, 2 Division, Corps d'Afrique, Department of the Gulf, Nov. 1863–Feb. 1864. Designation of regiment changed to 89 U.S. Colored Infantry, April 4, 1864. Resigned June 20, 1864, "in order to discharge those other duties which a son owes to a parent that is physically unable to take care of himself." Battle honors: Peninsular Campaign (Hanover Court House, Gaines' Mill, Malvern Hill), Port Hudson Campaign (Plains Store, Port Hudson, Cox's Plantation).

Born: Sept. 21, 1842 Buffalo, NY
Died: Dec. 18, 1926 West Seneca, Erie Co., NY
Occupation: Bookkeeper and clerk before war; engaged in wholesale grocery business after war
Offices/Honors: Sheriff of Erie Co., NY, 1874–76. U.S. House of Representatives,

John Baptiste Weber (John B. Weber. *Autobiography of John B. Weber.* Buffalo, NY, 1924).

John Baptiste Weber (Douglass & Co., Buffalo, NY; John B. Weber. *Autobiography of John B. Weber.* Buffalo, NY, 1924).

1885–89. Commissioner of Immigration, Port of New York, 1890–93. Commissioner General, Pan American Exposition, Buffalo, NY, 1901.

Miscellaneous: Resided Buffalo, Erie Co., NY, to 1868; and West Seneca (now Lackawanna), Erie Co., NY, after 1868

Buried: Forest Lawn Cemetery, Buffalo, NY (Section 8, Lot 150)

References: John B. Weber. *Autobiography of John B. Weber.* Buffalo, NY, 1924. Obituary, *Buffalo Courier Express*, Dec. 19, 1926. *Memorial and Family History of Erie County, New York.* New York and Buffalo, 1906–08. *The National Cyclopaedia of American Biography.* Vol. 24. New York City, NY, 1935. James L. Harrison, compiler. *Biographical Directory of the American Congress, 1774–1949.* Washington, D.C., 1950. Eugene A. Nash. *A History of the Forty-Fourth Regiment New York Volunteer Infantry in the Civil War, 1861–1865.* Chicago, IL, 1911. Orton S. Clark. *One Hundred and Sixteenth Regiment of New York State Volunteers.* Buffalo, NY, 1868. Pension File and Military Service File, National Archives. Letters Received, Volunteer Service Branch, Adjutant General's Office, File W94(VS)1869, National Archives.

Lauriston Washington Whipple

Captain, Co. G, 33 IA Infantry, Oct. 4, 1862. GSW nose, Helena, AR, July 4, 1863. Acting ADC, Staff of Brig. Gen. Samuel A. Rice, 2 Brigade, 3 Division, Army of Arkansas, Aug. 1863–Jan. 1864. Acting ADC, Staff of Brig. Gen. Samuel A. Rice, 2 Brigade, 3 Division, 7 Army Corps, Department of Arkansas, Jan.–Feb. 1864. Lieutenant Colonel, 6 AR Infantry of African Descent, June 18, 1864. Designation of regiment changed to 113 U.S. Colored Infantry, June 25, 1864. Colonel, 113 U.S. Colored Infantry, April 1, 1865. Commanded White River District, Department of Arkansas, Aug. 1865 and Feb. 1866. Honorably mustered out, April 9, 1866. Battle honors: Yazoo Pass Expedition, Helena, Advance upon and capture of Little Rock.

Born: April 19, 1825 Barre, MA

Died: Feb. 25, 1902 Sedalia, MO

Other Wars: Mexican War (Private, Co. C, 2 IL Infantry)

Occupation: Carpenter before war; Baptist clergyman after war

Miscellaneous: Resided Pella, Marion Co., IA, before war; Dresden, Pettis Co., MO, 1866–74; and Sedalia, Pettis Co., MO, after 1874

Buried: Crown Hill Cemetery, Sedalia, MO (Section 19, Lot 30)

References: Obituary, *Sedalia Daily Capital*, Feb. 26, 1902. Obituary, *Sedalia Democrat*, Feb. 25, 1902. Pension File and Military Service File, National Archives. Letters Received, Colored Troops Branch, Adjutant General's Office, File W426(CT)1865, National Archives. Andrew F. Sperry. *History of the 33d Iowa Infantry Volunteer Regiment, 1863–6*. Des Moines, IA, 1866. *The History of Pettis County, Missouri*. N.p., 1882.

Lauriston Washington Whipple (State Historical Society of Iowa, Des Moines).

Edmund Roberts Wiley, Jr.

1st Lieutenant, Adjutant, 62 IL Infantry, July 1, 1862. Adjutant, Post of Jackson (TN), 16 Army Corps, Department of the Tennessee, March–April 1863. Acting AAG, Staff of Colonel James M. True, 3 Brigade, 3 Division, 16 Army Corps, Army of the Tennessee, April–May 1863. Major, 2 TN Infantry of African Descent, June 30, 1863. Designation of regiment changed to 61 U.S. Colored Infantry, March 11, 1864. Detached as *Colonel*, 1 Regiment, Enrolled Militia (Freedmen), District of West Tennessee, Sept. 6, 1864. Assigned to recruiting service, Jan. 10, 1865. Colonel, 88 U.S. Colored Infantry (New), Aug. 10, 1865. Lieutenant Colonel, 3 U.S. Colored Heavy Artillery, Jan. 4, 1866. Judge Advocate, Department of Tennessee, March–April 1866. Honorably mustered out, April 30, 1866. Battle honors: Holly Springs.

Born: June 20, 1833 New York City, NY

Died: Nov. 2, 1917 Little Rock, AR

Education: Attended Illinois College, Jacksonville, IL

Occupation: Merchant tailor before war. Lawyer and journalist after war.

Offices/Honors: Arkansas County (AR) Clerk, 1867–71. Arkansas House of Representatives, 1871–72. Sheriff of Arkansas Co., AR, 1872–74. U.S. Internal Revenue Storekeeper, 1878–86.

Miscellaneous: Resided Springfield, Sangamon Co., IL; DeWitt, Arkansas Co., AR (1870); Atlanta, Logan Co., IL (1880); and Little Rock, Pulaski Co., AR

Buried: Oakland Cemetery, Little Rock, AR (Lilac Street, Lot 14)

References: John Carroll Power. *History of the Early Settlers of Sangamon County, Illinois.* Springfield, IL, 1876. *Catalogue of Phi Alpha Society, Illinois College, 1845–1890.* Jacksonville, IL, 1890. Pension File and Military Service File, National Archives. Obituary, *Arkansas Gazette*, Nov. 3, 1917. Letters Received, Colored Troops Branch, Adjutant General's Office, Files W852(CT)1864 and R84(CT)1865, National Archives. Letters Received, Volunteer Service Branch, Adjutant General's Office, File H101(VS)1867, National Archives.

Edmund Roberts Wiley, Jr. (author's photograph).

William Francis Wood

Captain, Spencer Artillery, 4 IN Legion (Spencer County), June 10, 1861. Captain, Co. K, 25 IN Infantry, Aug. 19, 1861. Resigned Sept. 2, 1861. Chaplain, 1 IN Cavalry, Aug. 20, 1861. Major, 1 IN Cavalry, Oct. 10, 1861. Lieutenant Colonel, 1 IN Cavalry, Nov. 7, 1861. Resigned April 2, 1863, "in consequence of a serious injury in the knee joint causing severe pain when actively engaged." Colonel Conrad Baker recommended acceptance of the resignation, with the added comment, "the harmony and efficiency of the regiment will be promoted and the public service benefited by so doing." Colonel, 1 AR Infantry of African Descent, May 1, 1863. Commanded Post of Goodrich's Landing (LA), District of Northeast Louisiana, Department of the Tennessee, June–Aug. 1863. Designation of regiment changed to 46 U.S. Colored Infantry, May 11, 1864. Commanded Post of Milliken's Bend (LA), District of Vicksburg, Department of the Tennessee, May–Aug. 1864. Still suffering from the injury to his knee joint, he resigned, Aug. 8, 1864, due to "inability to perform duties in the field from injuries received in the service." Battle honors: Fredericktown, Round Hill, Panther Creek (KY), Yazoo Pass Expedition, Goodrich's Landing.

Born: March 23, 1826 Manchester, England

Died: Aug. 13, 1890 Fernandina Beach, FL

Other Wars: Mexican War (Private, 3 Battalion, LA Volunteers)

Occupation: Baptist clergyman and farmer

Miscellaneous: Resided Sycamore Twp., Hamilton Co., OH; and Rockport,

Spencer Co., IN, to 1870; Fernandina, Nassau Co., FL, 1870–80; and Key West, Monroe Co., FL, after 1880

Buried: Bosque Bello Cemetery, Fernandina Beach, FL

References: Civil War and Mexican War Pension Files, National Archives. Military Service File, National Archives. Letters Received, Colored Troops Branch, Adjutant General's Office, File W492(CT)1864, National Archives. *Indiana in the War of the Rebellion: Official Report of W.H.H. Terrell, Adjutant General.* Indianapolis, IN, 1869. *History of Warrick, Spencer and Perry Counties, Indiana.* Chicago, IL, 1885. www.ancestry.com.

William Washington Woodward

2 Lieutenant, Co. C, 1 OH Infantry (3 months), April 29, 1861. Honorably mustered out, Aug. 16, 1861. Captain, Co. C, 44 OH Infantry, Sept. 18, 1861. Resigned July 28, 1862, due to "chronic flux, which has so reduced me that I am totally unfit for service." 2 Lieutenant, Co. K, 2 OH Cavalry, Oct. 6, 1862. Captain, Co. K, 2 OH Cavalry, Nov. 14, 1862. Acting AIG, Staff of Brig. Gen. Speed S. Fry, Camp Nelson, 1 Division, District of Kentucky, 23 Army Corps, Department of the Ohio, Sept. 1863–March 1864. Provost Marshal General and Acting AAG, Staff of Brig. Gen. Edward H. Hobson, 1 Division, District of Kentucky, 23 Army Corps, Department of the Ohio, April–July 1864. Colonel, 116 U.S. Colored Infantry, July 15, 1864. Commanded 3 Brigade, 2 Division, 25 Army Corps, Army of the James, March–May 1865. Commanded 3 Brigade, 2 Division, 25 Army Corps, Department of Texas, May–Sept. 1865. Honorably mustered out, Dec. 15, 1865. Accused in Dec. 1866 of having deposited $3300 of his soldiers' funds in a Cincinnati bank for safekeeping and then failing to return the funds, he finally in 1871 asked for relief from any further responsibility for the funds, explaining that, by order of General Thomas, he had paid the funds to Evan D. Kennedy, a disreputable agent of the Louisville (KY) Freedmen's Bureau, who failed to provide a receipt for the money. Battle honors: Vienna, 1st Bull Run, Appomattox Campaign.

William Francis Wood (courtesy David W. Taylor).

Born: July 4, 1834, Miami Co., OH

Died: April 5, 1913, Sandusky, OH

Occupation: Engaged in wholesale grocery business

Miscellaneous: Resided Dayton, Montgomery Co., OH, to 1880; Sandusky, Erie Co., OH, after 1880

Buried: Oakland Cemetery, Sandusky, OH (Section 55, Lot 1, unmarked)

William Washington Woodward (Todd & Vandegrift's Fine Art Palace, Sidney, OH; John P. Gurnish Collection).

References: *The Union Army*. Ohio Edition. Vol. 8. Madison, WI, 1908. Obituary, *Sandusky Star-Journal*, April 5, 1913. Pension File and Military Service File, National Archives. Letters Received, Colored Troops Branch, Adjutant General's Office, File W612(CT)1864, National Archives. Letters Received, Volunteer Service Branch, Adjutant General's Office, File P1767(VS)1864, National Archives. William A. Dobak. *Freedom by the Sword: The U.S. Colored Troops, 1862–1867.* Washington, D.C., 2011.

William Wierman Wright

Superintendent of Aquia Creek and Fredericksburg Military Railroad, 1862. Superintendent of Richmond, Fredericksburg & Potomac Military Railroad, 1863. Superintendent of U.S. Military Railroads, Department of the Susquehanna, 1863. Chief Engineer, U.S. Military Railroads, Military Division of the

William Wierman Wright (Massachusetts MOLLUS Collection, USAHEC [Vol. 69, p. 3428]).

William Wierman Wright (Library of Congress [LC-DIG-ppmsca-23721]).

Mississippi, 1864–65. Chief Engineer, U.S. Military Railroads, Department of North Carolina, 1865. *Colonel*, 42 U.S. Colored Infantry, March 2, 1864. Preferring to retain his position as Chief Engineer, he was never mustered as colonel, and was finally dropped from the rolls of the regiment, July 31, 1865.

Born: July 27, 1824, York Springs, PA

William Wierman Wright (in the field as Chief Engineer, Military Railroads) (Library of Congress [LC-DIG-ppmsca-23726]).

Died: March 9, 1882, Philadelphia, PA (Died in Moyamensing Prison while confined for drunkenness)
Education: Attended Gettysburg (PA) College
Occupation: Civil engineer engaged in railroad construction
Miscellaneous: Resided Philadelphia, PA
Buried: Huntington Friends Meeting House Cemetery, Latimore Twp., Adams Co., PA
References: *Proceedings of the American Society of Civil Engineers.* Vol. 8 (January to December 1882). New York City, NY, 1882. *Report of the Proceedings of the Society of the Army of the Tennessee at the Fifteenth Annual Meeting.* Cincinnati, OH, 1885. Obituary, *Gettysburg Compiler,* March 15, 1882. Obituary, *Philadelphia Times,* March 11, 1882. Obituary, *New York Times,* March 11, 1882. Obituary, *Gettysburg Star and Sentinel,* March 15, 1882. Herman Haupt. *Reminiscences of General Herman Haupt.* Milwaukee, WI, 1901. Thomas Weber. *The Northern Railroads in the Civil War, 1861–1865.* New York City, NY, 1952. Military Service File, National Archives. Letters Received, Colored Troops Branch, Adjutant General's Office, File M547(CT)1865, National Archives. William W. Wright Collection, Special Collections Division, Georgetown (DC) University. William W. Wright Papers, 1863–1870, Manuscript Division, Library of Congress, Washington, D.C.

Van Eps Young

Private, Co. E, 17 WI Infantry, Oct. 7, 1861. 1 Lieutenant, Co. H, 14 WI Infantry, March 7, 1862. 1 Lieutenant, Adjutant, 14 WI Infantry, July 17, 1862. Lieutenant Colonel, 10 LA Infantry of African Descent (later 48 U.S. Colored Infantry), April 12, 1863. Colonel, 11 LA Infantry of African Descent, Oct. 8, 1863. Designation of regiment changed to 49 U.S. Colored Infantry, March 11, 1864. Commanded Post of Milliken's Bend (LA), District of Vicksburg, Aug.–Sept. 1864. Commanded 1 Brigade, 1 Division, U.S. Colored Troops, District of Vicksburg, Sept.–Oct. 1864. Commanded 1 Brigade, 4 Division, 16 Army Corps, District of Vicksburg, Oct.–Nov. 1864. Provost Marshal, Staff of Major Gen. Napoleon J.T. Dana, District of Vicksburg, Nov.–Dec. 1864. Provost Marshal General, Department of Mississippi, Dec. 1864–Oct. 1865. Commanded Sub-District of Meridian (MS),

Van Eps Young (author's photograph).

Northern District of Mississippi, Oct. 1865. Commanded Post of Vicksburg (MS), Western District of Mississippi, Jan. 1866. Honorably mustered out, June 14, 1866. Battle honors: Shiloh.

Born: Sept. 30, 1822 Auburn, NY

Died: Dec. 12, 1895 Grand Rapids, MI

Occupation: Livery keeper and produce dealer before war. Accountant and bookkeeper after war.

Offices/Honors: Wisconsin Senate, 1867. Superintendent of Police, Grand Rapids, MI, 1881–82.

Miscellaneous: Resided Sheboygan, Sheboygan Co., WI, to 1870; and Grand Rapids, Kent Co., MI, after 1870

Buried: Oak Hill Cemetery, Grand Rapids, MI (Section A, Lot 14)

References: *History of Kent County, Michigan.* Chicago, IL, 1881. Obituary, *Grand Rapids Press*, Dec. 13, 1895. Obituary, *Grand Rapids Herald*, Dec. 13, 1895. Pension File and Military Service File, National Archives. Letters Received, Colored Troops Branch, Adjutant General's Office, File Y10(CT)1863, National Archives. "A Good Nomination," *Wisconsin State Journal*, Oct. 22, 1866.

Van Eps Young (H.S. Harmon, Sheboygan, WI; Courtesy Missouri Historical Society, St. Louis [P0233–2859]).

Ladislas Louis Zulavsky

Lieutenant Colonel, 5 Regiment, Ullmann's Brigade (later 10 Infantry, Corps d'Afrique), March 28, 1863. Colonel, 10 Infantry, Corps d'Afrique, Nov. 1, 1863. Designation of regiment changed to 82 U.S. Colored Infantry, April 4, 1864. Commanded 1 Brigade, District of West Florida, Department of the Gulf, Aug.–Nov. 1864. Commanded 3 Brigade, 1 Division, U.S. Colored Troops, Military Division of West Mississippi, March 1865. Commanded 1 Brigade, 1 Division, U.S. Colored Troops, Military Division of West Mississippi, April–May 1865. Commanded Post of Apalachicola (FL),

Ladislas Louis Zulavsky (author's photograph).

Ladislas Louis Zulavsky (E. M. Douglass, Artist, 324 Fulton St., Brooklyn, NY; author's photograph).

District of West Florida, May–Aug. 1865. Commanded Sub-District of Key West (FL), Department of Florida, Oct. 1865. Commanded Post of Pensacola Harbor, Department of Florida, Nov. 1865–June 1866. Honorably mustered out, Sept. 10, 1866. Battle honors: Marianna (FL), Mobile Campaign (Fort Blakely).

Ladislas Louis Zulavsky (courtesy Henry Deeks).

Born: March 9, 1837, Szurte, Ung County, Hungary

Died: April 22, 1884, Middletown, NY (New York State Asylum for the Insane)

Other Wars: Served as an officer in the Hungarian Legion during Giuseppe Garibaldi's 1860 campaign for the unification of Italy

Occupation: Civil engineer before war. Cotton broker after war.

Miscellaneous: Resided Brooklyn, NY; and Augusta, Richmond Co., GA. Nephew of Hungarian revolutionary hero Louis Kossuth.

Buried: Green-Wood Cemetery, Brooklyn, NY (Section 71, Lot 825, Grave 38)

References: Stephen Beszedits, "Hungarian Companions of the First Class in the Military Order of the Loyal Legion of the United States," *Vasvary Collection Newsletter,* (2015, No. 2). Istvan Kornel Vida. *Hungarian Émigrés in the American Civil War: A History and Biographical Dictionary.* Jefferson, NC, 2012. Martin W. Ofele. *German-Speaking Officers in the U.S. Colored Troops, 1863–1867.* Gainesville, FL,

2004. Obituary Circular, Whole No. 228, New York MOLLUS. Military Service File, National Archives. Letters Received, Colored Troops Branch, Adjutant General's Office, File Z3(CT)1864, National Archives. "A Sad Case: A Former Cotton Buyer in Augusta Becomes Hopelessly Insane," *Augusta Chronicle,* Nov. 8, 1883. Edmund Vasvary. *Lincoln's Hungarian Heroes: The Participation of Hungarians in the Civil War, 1861-1865.* Washington, D.C., 1939. Dale Cox. *The Battle of Marianna, Florida: Expanded Edition.* Bascom, FL, 2011. Isaac S. Bangs, "The Ullman Brigade," *War Papers Read Before the Commandery of the State of Maine, MOLLUS.* Vol. 2. Portland, ME, 1902. Ned Smith. *The 2nd Maine Cavalry in the Civil War: A History and Roster.* Jefferson, NC, 2014. Death Notice, *Brooklyn Daily Eagle,* April 23, 1884. www.findagrave.com.

U.S. Armed Forces

Regiments

1st Artillery
John Erving	Oct. 5, 1857	Retired Oct. 26, 1861
Justin Dimick	Oct. 26, 1861	Retired Aug. 1, 1863, Bvt. Brig. Gen., USV
Israel Vogdes	Aug. 1, 1863	Retired Jan. 2, 1881, Brig. Gen., USV

2nd Artillery
Matthew M. Payne	Nov. 11, 1856	Resigned July 23, 1861
John L. Gardner	July 23, 1861	Retired Nov. 1, 1861, Bvt. Brig. Gen., USA
William W. Morris	Nov. 1, 1861	Died Dec. 11, 1865, Bvt. Major Gen., USA
William F. Barry	Dec. 11, 1865	Died July 18, 1879, Brig. Gen., USV

3rd Artillery
William Gates	Oct. 13, 1845	Retired June 1, 1863, Bvt. Brig. Gen., USA
Thomas W. Sherman	June 1, 1863	Retired Dec. 31, 1870, Brig. Gen., USV

4th Artillery
Francis S. Belton	June 10, 1857	Retired Aug. 28, 1861
Charles S. Merchant	Aug. 28, 1861	Retired Aug. 1, 1863, Bvt. Brig. Gen., USA
Horace Brooks	Aug. 1, 1863	Retired Jan. 10, 1877, Bvt. Brig. Gen., USA

5th Artillery
Harvey Brown	May 14, 1861	Retired Aug. 1, 1863, Bvt. Major Gen., USA
George Nauman	Aug. 1, 1863	Died Aug. 11, 1863
Henry S. Burton	Aug. 11, 1863	Died April 4, 1869, Bvt. Brig. Gen., USA

1st Cavalry (Regiment designated as 1st U.S. Dragoons to Aug. 3, 1861)
Benjamin L. Beall	May 13, 1861	Retired Feb. 15, 1862
George A.H. Blake	Feb. 15, 1862	Retired Dec. 15, 1870, Bvt. Brig. Gen., USA

2nd Cavalry (Regiment designated as 2nd U.S. Dragoons to Aug. 3, 1861)
Philip St. George Cooke	June 14, 1858	Promoted Brig. Gen., USA, Nov. 12, 1861
Thomas J. Wood	Nov. 12, 1861	Retired June 9, 1868, Major Gen., USV

3rd Cavalry (Regiment designated as 1st Mounted Riflemen to Aug. 3, 1861)
John S. Simonson	May 13, 1861	Retired Sept. 28, 1861, Bvt. Brig. Gen., USA
Marshall S. Howe	Sept. 28, 1861	Retired Aug. 31, 1866

4th Cavalry (Regiment designated as 1st U.S. Cavalry to Aug. 3, 1861)
John Sedgwick	April 25, 1861	KIA May 9, 1864, Major Gen., USV
Lawrence P. Graham	May 9, 1864	Retired Dec. 15, 1870, Brig. Gen., USV

5th Cavalry (Regiment designated as 2nd U.S. Cavalry to Aug. 3, 1861)
George H. Thomas	May 3, 1861	Promoted Brig. Gen., USA, Oct. 27, 1863
William H. Emory	Oct. 27, 1863	Retired July 1, 1876, Major Gen., USV

6th Cavalry (Regiment designated as 3rd U.S. Cavalry to Aug. 3, 1861)
David Hunter	May 14, 1861	Retired July 31, 1866, Major Gen., USV

1st Infantry
Carlos A. Waite	June 5, 1860	Retired Feb. 8, 1864, Bvt. Brig. Gen., USA
Robert C. Buchanan	Feb. 8, 1864	Retired Dec. 31, 1870, Brig. Gen., USV

2nd Infantry
Dixon S. Miles	Jan. 19, 1859	DOW Sept. 16, 1862
Sidney Burbank	Sept. 16, 1862	Retired May 1, 1870, Bvt. Brig. Gen., USA

3rd Infantry
Benjamin L.E. Bonneville	Feb. 3, 1855	Retired Sept. 9, 1861, Bvt. Brig. Gen., USA
Charles F. Smith	Sept. 9, 1861	Died April 25, 1862, Major Gen., USV
William Hoffman	April 25, 1862	Retired May 1, 1870, Bvt. Major Gen., USA

4th Infantry
William Whistler	July 15, 1845	Retired Oct. 9, 1861
Silas Casey	Oct. 9, 1861	Retired July 8, 1868, Major Gen., USV

5th Infantry
Gustavus Loomis	March 9, 1851	Retired June 1, 1863, Bvt. Brig. Gen., USA
John F. Reynolds	June 1, 1863	KIA July 1, 1863, Major Gen., USV
Daniel Butterfield	July 1, 1863	Resigned March 14, 1870, Major Gen., USV

6th Infantry
Washington Seawell	Oct. 17, 1860	Retired Feb. 20, 1862, Bvt. Brig. Gen., USA
Electus Backus	Feb. 20, 1862	Died June 7, 1862
Hannibal Day	June 7, 1862	Retired Aug. 1, 1863, Bvt. Brig. Gen., USA
Edward A. King	Aug. 1, 1863	KIA Sept. 20, 1863
James D. Greene	Sept. 20, 1863	Resigned June 25, 1867, Bvt. Brig. Gen., USA

7th Infantry
John J. Abercrombie	Feb. 25, 1861	Retired June 12, 1865, Brig. Gen., USV

7th Infantry (continued)
John T. Sprague	June 12, 1865	Retired Dec. 15, 1870, Bvt. Brig. Gen., USA

8th Infantry
John Garland	May 7, 1849	Died June 5, 1861
Pitcairn Morrison	June 6, 1861	Retired Oct. 20, 1863, Bvt. Brig. Gen., USA
Albemarle Cady	Oct. 20, 1863	Retired May 18, 1864, Bvt. Brig. Gen., USA
James V. Bomford	May 18, 1864	Retired June 8, 1874, Bvt. Brig. Gen., USA

9th Infantry
George Wright	March 3, 1855	Died July 30, 1865, Brig. Gen., USV
John H. King	July 30, 1865	Retired Feb. 20, 1882, Brig. Gen., USV

10th Infantry
Edmund B. Alexander	March 3, 1855	Retired Feb. 22, 1869, Bvt. Brig. Gen., USA

11th Infantry
Erasmus D. Keyes	May 14, 1861	Resigned May 6, 1864, Major Gen., USV
William S. Ketchum	May 6, 1864	Retired Dec. 15, 1870, Brig. Gen., USV

12th Infantry
William B. Franklin	May 14, 1861	Resigned March 15, 1866, Major Gen., USV

13th Infantry
William T. Sherman	May 14, 1861	Promoted Brig. Gen., USA, July 4, 1863
John P. Sanderson	July 4, 1863	Died Oct. 14, 1864
Isaac V.D. Reeve	Oct. 14, 1864	Retired Jan. 1, 1871, Bvt. Brig. Gen., USA

14th Infantry
Charles P. Stone	May 14, 1861	Resigned Sept. 13, 1864, Brig. Gen., USV
Gabriel R. Paul	Sept. 13, 1864	Retired Feb. 16, 1865, Brig. Gen., USV
Charles S. Lovell	Feb. 16, 1865	Retired Dec. 15, 1870, Bvt. Brig. Gen., USA

15th Infantry
Fitz John Porter	May 14, 1861	Cashiered Jan. 21, 1863, Major Gen., USV
Oliver L. Shepherd	Jan. 21, 1863	Retired Dec. 15, 1870, Bvt. Brig. Gen., USA

16th Infantry
Andrew Porter	May 14, 1861	Resigned April 20, 1864, Brig. Gen., USV
Caleb C. Sibley	April 20, 1864	Retired Feb. 22, 1869, Bvt. Brig. Gen., USA

17th Infantry
Samuel P. Heintzelman	May 14, 1861	Retired Feb. 22, 1869, Major Gen., USV

18th Infantry
Henry B. Carrington	May 14, 1861	Retired Dec. 15, 1870, Brig. Gen., USV

19th Infantry
Edward R.S. Canby	May 14, 1861	Promoted Brig. Gen., USA, July 28, 1866

Chiefs of Bureaus or Staff Corps of the Army

Adjutant General's Department
Lorenzo Thomas	March 7, 1861	Retired Feb. 22, 1869, Brig. Gen., USA

Inspector-General's Department
Sylvester Churchill	June 25, 1841	Retired Sept. 25, 1861
Randolph B. Marcy	Aug. 9, 1861	Retired Jan. 2, 1881, Brig. Gen., USV

Judge-Advocate General's Department
Joseph Holt	Sept. 3, 1862	Retired Dec. 1, 1875, Brig. Gen., USA

Quartermaster's Department
Quartermaster General
Montgomery C. Meigs	May 15, 1861	Retired Feb. 6, 1882, Brig. Gen., USA

Assistant Quartermaster General
Daniel D. Tompkins	Dec. 22, 1856	Died Feb. 26, 1863

Subsistence Department
George Gibson	April 18, 1818	Died Sept. 29, 1861
Joseph P. Taylor	Sept. 29, 1861	Died June 29, 1864, Brig. Gen., USA
Amos B. Eaton	June 29, 1864	Retired May 1, 1874, Brig. Gen., USA

Medical Department
Surgeon General
Thomas Lawson	Nov. 30, 1836	Died May 15, 1861
Clement A. Finley	May 15, 1861	Retired April 14, 1862, Bvt. Brig. Gen., USA
William A. Hammond	April 25, 1862	Dismissed Aug. 18, 1864, Brig. Gen., USA
Joseph. K. Barnes	Aug. 22, 1864	Retired June 30, 1882, Brig. Gen., USA

Medical Inspector General
Thomas F. Perley	July 1, 1862	Resigned Aug. 10, 1863
Joseph K. Barnes	Aug. 10, 1863	Promoted to Surgeon Gen. Aug. 22, 1864

Medical Director
George E. Cooper	Feb. 25, 1865	June 30, 1865

Pay Department
Benjamin F. Larned	July 20, 1854	Died Sept. 6, 1862
Timothy P. Andrews	Sept. 6, 1862	Retired Nov. 29, 1864, Bvt. Brig. Gen., USA
Benjamin W. Brice	Nov. 29, 1864	Retired Jan. 1, 1872, Bvt. Major Gen., USA

Corps of Engineers
Joseph G. Totten	Dec. 7, 1838	Died April 22, 1864, Brig. Gen., USA
Richard Delafield	April 22, 1864	Retired Aug. 8, 1866, Brig. Gen., USA

Corps of Topographical Engineers (merged into Corps of Engineers, March 3, 1863)
John J. Abert	July 7, 1838	Retired Sept. 9, 1861

Stephen H. Long	Sept. 9, 1861	Retired June 1, 1863
James D. Graham	June 1, 1863	Died Dec. 28, 1865
Ordnance Department		
James W. Ripley	April 23, 1861	Retired Sept. 15, 1863, Brig. Gen., USA
George D. Ramsay	Sept. 15, 1863	Retired Sept. 12, 1864, Brig. Gen., USA
Alexander B. Dyer	Sept. 12, 1864	Died May 20, 1874, Brig. Gen., USA
John Symington	Aug. 3, 1861	Retired June 1, 1863
Signal Corps		
Albert J. Myer	March 3, 1863	Revoked July 21, 1864, Bvt. Brig. Gen., USA
Benjamin F. Fisher	Dec. 3, 1864	Discharged July 28, 1866, Bvt. Brig. Gen., USV

Miscellaneous

Superintendent, U.S. Military Academy

Alexander H. Bowman	March 1, 1861	Discharged July 8, 1864

Biographies

John James Abert

Colonel, Chief of U.S. Topographical Engineers, July 7, 1838. Retired Sept. 9, 1861.

Born: Sept. 17, 1788 Shepherdstown, WV

Died: Jan. 27, 1863 Washington, D.C.

Education: Graduated U.S. Military Academy, West Point, NY, 1811

Other Wars: War of 1812 (Bvt. Major, U.S. Corps of Topographical Engineers)

Occupation: Regular Army (Colonel, retired Sept. 9, 1861)

Miscellaneous: Resided Washington, D.C. Father of Bvt. Brig. Gen. William S. Abert.

Buried: Rock Creek Cemetery, Washington, D.C. (Section A, Lot 128)

References: *Dictionary of American Biography.* Supplement 1. New York City, NY, 1944. *The National Cyclopaedia of American Biography.* Vol. 4. New York City, NY, 1897. James Grant Wilson and John Fiske, editors. *Appletons' Cyclopaedia of American Biography.* New York City, NY, 1888. *Eminent and Representative*

John James Abert (Massachusetts MOLLUS Collection, USAHEC [Vol. 128, p. 6556]).

John James Abert (West Point Museum Collection, U.S. Military Academy, West Point, NY).

Men of Virginia and the District of Columbia of the Nineteenth Century. Madison, WI, 1893. George W. Cullum. *Biographical Register of the Officers and Graduates of the U.S. Military Academy at West Point, N.Y.* Third Edition. Boston and New York, 1891. Obituary, *Daily National Intelligencer,* Feb. 13, 1863. Pension File, National Archives.

Electus Backus

Lieutenant Colonel, 3 U.S. Infantry, Jan. 19, 1859. Colonel, 6 U.S. Infantry, Feb. 20, 1862.

Born: Feb. 17, 1804 Rensselaerville, NY
Died: June 7, 1862 Detroit, MI
Education: Graduated U.S. Military Academy, West Point, NY, 1824
Other Wars: Florida Indian War (Captain, 1 U.S. Infantry). Mexican War (Bvt. Major, USA, Sept. 23, 1846, for gallant and meritorious conduct in the several conflicts at Monterey, Mexico).
Occupation: Regular Army (Colonel, 6 U.S. Infantry)
Miscellaneous: Resided Detroit, Wayne Co., MI. Son-in-law of Bvt. Major Gen. Hugh Brady (War of 1812).
Buried: Elmwood Cemetery, Detroit, MI (Section A, Lot 92)
References: Belle McKinney Hays Swope. *History of the Families of McKinney-Brady-Quigley*. Chambersburg, PA, 1905. George W. Cullum. *Biographical Register of the Officers and Graduates of the U.S. Military Academy at West Point, N.Y.* Third Edition. Boston and New York, 1891. Spencer C. Tucker, editor. *The Encyclopedia of the Mexican-American War: A Political, Social, and Military History*. Santa Barbara, CA, 2013. James Grant Wilson and John Fiske, editors. *Appletons' Cyclopaedia of American Biography*. New York City, NY, 1888. Obituary, *Detroit Free Press*, June 8, 1862. Obituary, *Michigan Argus*, June 13, 1862. Reno W. Backus. *The Backus Families of Early New England*. N.p., 1966. Pension File, National Archives.

Benjamin Lloyd Beall

Lieutenant Colonel, 1 U.S. Dragoons, March 3, 1855. Commanded Department of California, Oct. 1860–Jan. 1861. Colonel, 1 U.S. Dragoons, May 13, 1861. Colonel, 1 U.S. Cavalry, Aug. 3, 1861. Commanded District of Oregon, Sept.–Oct. 1861. Retired Feb. 15, 1862.

Born: Oct. 1801 Washington, D.C.
Died: Aug. 16, 1863 Baltimore, MD
Education: Attended U.S. Military Academy, West Point, NY (Class of 1818)
Other Wars: Florida Indian War (Bvt. Major, USA, March 15, 1837, for gallantry and successful services in the war against the Florida Indians). Mexican War (Bvt. Lieutenant Colonel, USA, March 16, 1848, for gallant and meritorious conduct in the battle of Santa Cruz de Rosales, Mexico).
Occupation: Regular Army (Colonel, 1 U.S. Cavalry)
Miscellaneous: Resided Baltimore, MD. Father-in-law of Bvt. Brig. Gen. Langdon C. Easton. Brother of Colonel Lloyd J. Beall (Confederate States Marine Corps).
Buried: Green Mount Cemetery, Baltimore, MD (Area N, Lot 9)
References: Theophilus F. Rodenbough, compiler. *The Bravest Five Hundred of '61*. New York City, NY, 1891. Theophilus F. Rodenbough. *From Everglade to Canyon with the Second Dragoons (Second United States Cavalry)*. New York City, NY, 1875. David C. Reed. "Sabers and Saddles: The Second Regiment of United States Dragoons at Fort Washita, 1842–1845." Master's thesis, Oklahoma State University, 2013. Fielder M.M. Beall, editor. *Colonial Families of the United States Descended from the Immigrants Who Arrived Before 1700, Mostly from England and Scotland, and*

Who are Now Represented by Citizens of the Following Names: Bell, Beal, Bale, Beale, Beall. Washington, D.C., 1929. Pension File, National Archives. Obituary, *Baltimore Sun,* Aug. 17, 1863. Obituary, *New York Times,* Aug. 19, 1863. Theophilus F. Rodenbough and William L. Haskin, editors. *The Army of the United States: Historical Sketches of Staff and Line with Portraits of Generals-in-Chief.* New York City, NY, 1896. Will Gorenfeld and George Stammerjohn, editors, "A Death in the Family: The Letters of Maj. Lloyd J. Beall to His Brother Bvt. Maj. Benjamin L. Beall," *Military Collector and Historian,* Vol. 60, No. 2 (Summer 2008).

Francis Smith Belton

Colonel, 4 U.S. Artillery, June 10, 1857. Retired Aug. 28, 1861.

Born: Aug. 7, 1791 Baltimore, MD

Died: Sept. 10, 1861 Brooklyn, NY

Other Wars: War of 1812 (1 Lieutenant, 4 U.S. Infantry). Mexican War (Lieutenant Colonel, 3 U.S. Artillery. Bvt. Colonel, USA, Aug. 20, 1847, for gallant and meritorious conduct in the battles of Contreras and Churubusco, Mexico).

Occupation: Regular Army (Colonel, 4 U.S. Artillery)

Miscellaneous: Resided Brooklyn, NY. Uncle of CSA General Edmund Kirby Smith. Uncle of Brig. Gen. Edmund Kirby (1 U.S. Artillery). Great uncle of Colonel Joseph L. Kirby Smith (43 OH Infantry).

Buried: Holy Cross Cemetery, Brooklyn, NY (Select Ground)

References: Melatiah Everett Dwight. *The Kirbys of New England.* New York City, NY, 1898. George F. and William T.R. Marvin. *Descendants of Reinold and Matthew Marvin of Hartford, CT, 1638 and 1635, Sons of Edward Marvin, of Great Bentley, England.* Boston, MA, 1904. Obituary, *Brooklyn Daily*

Benjamin Lloyd Beall (courtesy California History Room, California State Library, Sacramento, CA [Division Commanders of California, 1847–1879]).

Francis Smith Belton (author's photograph).

Eagle, Sept. 13, 1861. Obituary, *New York Herald*, Sept. 14, 1861. Obituary, *New York Tribune*, Sept. 14, 1861. Obituary, *New York Commercial Advertiser*, Sept. 13, 1861. Obituary, *Baltimore Sun*, Sept. 14, 1861. Pension File, National Archives. Joseph M. Silinonte. *Tombstones of the Irish Born: Cemetery of the Holy Cross, Flatbush, Brooklyn.* Westminster, MD, 2006.

Alexander Hamilton Bowman

Major, U.S. Corps of Engineers, Jan. 5, 1857. Superintendent, U.S. Military Academy, with rank of Colonel, March 1, 1861–July 8, 1864. Lieutenant Colonel, U.S. Corps of Engineers, March 3, 1863.

Born: March 30, 1803 Wilkes-Barre, PA
Died: Nov. 11, 1865 Wilkes-Barre, PA
Education: Graduated U.S. Military Academy, West Point, NY, 1825
Occupation: Regular Army (Lieutenant Colonel, U.S. Corps of Engineers)
Miscellaneous: Resided Wilkes-Barre, Luzerne Co., PA. Father-in-law of Bvt. Brig. Gen. Miles D. McAlester.
Buried: Hollenback Cemetery, Wilkes-Barre, PA (Lot 1040)
References: George W. Cullum. *Biographical Register of the Officers and Graduates of the U.S. Military Academy at West Point, N.Y.* Third Edition. Boston and New York, 1891. Obituary, *Luzerne Union*, Nov. 22, 1865. Obituary, *Lancaster Intelligencer*, Nov. 14, 1865. Obituary, *New York Herald*, Nov. 12, 1865. *The National Cyclopaedia of American Biography.* Vol. 5. New York City, NY,

Alexander Hamilton Bowman (U.S. Military Academy Library).

Alexander Hamilton Bowman (Charles D. Fredricks & Co. "Specialite," 587 Broadway, New York; author's photograph).

1907. James Grant Wilson and John Fiske, editors. *Appletons' Cyclopaedia of American Biography.* New York City, NY, 1888. Pension File, National Archives. Letters Received, Commission Branch, Adjutant General's Office, File E291(CB)1865, National Archives. Oscar J. Harvey. *A History of Lodge No. 61, F. and A. M., Wilkes-Barre, PA.* Wilkes-Barre, PA, 1897.

Sylvester Churchill

Colonel, Inspector General, USA, June 25, 1841. Retired Sept. 25, 1861.

Born: Aug. 2, 1783 Woodstock, VT

Died: Dec. 7, 1862 Washington, D.C.

Other Wars: War of 1812 (Major, AIG, USA). Mexican War (Bvt. Brig. Gen, USA, Feb. 23, 1847, for gallant and meritorious conduct in the battle of Buena Vista, Mexico.).

Occupation: Regular Army (Colonel Inspector General)

Miscellaneous: Resided Washington, D.C. Distant cousin of Prime Minister Winston Churchill of Great Britain.

Buried: Oak Hill Cemetery, Washington, D.C. (North Hill, Lot 279, Baird Family Mausoleum)

References: Franklin Hunter Churchill. *Sketch of the Life of Bvt. Brig. Gen. Sylvester Churchill, Inspector General, U.S. Army, with Notes and Appendices.* New York City, NY, 1888. Gardner A. and Nathaniel W. Churchill, compilers. *The Churchill Family in America.* Boston, MA, 1904. James Grant Wilson and John Fiske, editors. *Appletons' Cyclopaedia of American Biography.* New York City, NY, 1888. Obituary, *Daily National Intelligencer,* Dec. 12, 1862. Obituary, *New York Tribune,* Dec. 10, 1862. Obituary, *Burlington Free Press,* Dec. 12, 1862. Joseph W.A. Whitehorne, "Inspector General Sylvester Churchill's Efforts to Produce a New Army Drill Manual, 1850–1862," *Civil War History,* Vol. 32, No. 2 (June 1986).

Alexander Hamilton Bowman (courtesy The Excelsior Brigade).

Sylvester Churchill (Brady's National Portrait Galleries, New York & Washington; Massachusetts MOLLUS Collection, USAHEC [Vol. 72, p. 3568L]).

George Edward Cooper

Major, Surgeon, USA, May 21, 1861. Medical Director, Staff of Major Gen. David Hunter, Department of the South, March–April 1862. Medical Director, Staff of Major Gen. George H. Thomas, Department of the Cumberland, April 1864–June 1865. Assigned to duty as Colonel, Feb. 25–June 30, 1865. Medical Director, Staff of Major Gen. George H. Thomas, Military Division of the Tennessee, June–July 1865. Medical Director, Staff of Major Gen. George Stoneman, Department of Tennessee, July–Nov. 1865. Bvt. Lieutenant Colonel, USA, Sept. 1, 1864, for faithful and meritorious services during the war. Bvt. Colonel, USA, March 13, 1865, for faithful and meritorious services during the war. Battle honors: Fort Pulaski, Atlanta Campaign, Nashville.

Born: Sept. 1824 Philadelphia, PA

Died: April 13, 1881 San Francisco, CA

Education: Attended Gettysburg (PA) College. Graduated University of Pennsylvania Medical School, Philadelphia, PA, 1847.

Other Wars: Mexican War (1 Lieutenant, Assistant Surgeon, USA)

Occupation: Regular Army (Lieutenant Colonel, Assistant Medical Purveyor, USA, Dec. 2, 1876)

Miscellaneous: Resided Fort Monroe, Elizabeth City Co., VA, 1865–70; and San Francisco, CA, 1875–81

Buried: Golden Gate National Cemetery, San Bruno, CA (Section E, Block 2, Grave 425)

References: Pension File, National Archives. Letters Received, Appointment, Commission, and Personal Branch, Adjutant General's Office, File 2438(ACP)1881, National Archives. Letters Received, Adjutant General's Office, Files P1067(AGO)1862 and C345(AGO)1863, National Archives. Letters Received, Commission Branch, Adjutant General's Office, File S276(CB)1865, National Archives. Obituary, *San Francisco Examiner*, April 15, 1881. Obituary, *San Francisco Bulletin*, April 14, 1881. Mary C. Gillett. *The Army Medical Department, 1818–1865*. Washington, DC, 1987. Guy V. Henry. *Military Record of Civilian Appointments in the United States Army*. Vol. 1. New York City, NY, 1869. Clyde B. Stover and Charles W. Beachem. *The Alumni Record of Gettysburg College, 1832–1932*. Gettysburg, PA, 1932. Ewing Jordan, compiler. *University of Pennsylvania Men Who Served in the Civil War, 1861–1865: Department of Medicine, Classes 1816–1862*. Philadelphia, PA, 1915.

George Edward Cooper (courtesy National Library of Medicine, Bethesda, MD [101416190]).

John Erving

Colonel, 1 U.S. Artillery, Oct. 5, 1857. Retired Oct. 26, 1861.
Born: 1789 Boston, MA
Died: Oct. 26, 1862 New York City, NY
Occupation: Regular Army (Colonel, 1 U.S. Artillery, retired Oct. 26, 1861)
Miscellaneous: Resided Philadelphia, PA; and New York City, NY
Buried: Green-Wood Cemetery, Brooklyn, NY (Section 170, Lot 13710)
References: "Obituary of Gallant Officers Recently Deceased," *New York Daily Tribune*, Dec. 9, 1862. Cuyler Reynolds, editor. *Genealogical and Family History of Southern New York and the Hudson River Valley.* New York City, NY, 1914. William L. Haskin, compiler. *The History of the First Regiment of Artillery from Its Organization in 1821, to January 1st, 1876.* Portland, ME, 1879. Death Notice, *New York Daily Tribune*, Oct. 28, 1862. Letters Received, Adjutant General's Office, File E295(AGO)1861, National Archives.

John Garland

Colonel, 8 U.S. Infantry, May 7, 1849.
Born: Nov. 15, 1793 VA

John Garland (Brady's National Portrait Gallery. Published by E. Anthony, 501 Broadway, New York; Author's photograph).

John Garland (Brady's National Portrait Gallery. Published by E. Anthony, 501 Broadway, New York; courtesy Henry Deeks).

Died: June 5, 1861 New York City, NY

Other Wars: War of 1812 (1 Lieutenant, 3 U.S. Infantry). Florida Indian War (Major, 1 U.S. Infantry. Mexican War (Lieutenant Colonel, 4 U.S. Infantry; Bvt. Brig. Gen., USA, Aug. 20, 1847, for gallant and meritorious conduct in the battles of Contreras and Churubusco, Mexico).

Occupation: Regular Army (Colonel, 8 U.S. Infantry)

Miscellaneous: Resided Washington, D.C. Father-in-law of CSA General James Longstreet.

Buried: Oak Hill Cemetery, Washington, D.C. (North Hill, Lot 171)

References: Obituary, *New York Herald,* June 8, 1861. Obituary, *Daily National Intelligencer,* June 8, 1861. Obituary, *Washington National Republican,* June 10, 1861. Ruth H. Early. *Campbell Chronicles and Family Sketches Embracing the History of Campbell County, Virginia, 1782–1926.* Lynchburg, VA, 1927. James Grant Wilson and John Fiske, editors. *Appletons' Cyclopaedia of American Biography.* New York City, NY, 1888.

George Gibson

Colonel, Quartermaster General, Southern Division, USA, April 29, 1816–April 14, 1818. Colonel, Commissary General of Subsistence, USA, April 18, 1818–Sept. 29, 1861.

Born: Sept. 11, 1775 Westover, Spring Twp., Perry Co., PA

Died: Sept. 29, 1861 Washington, D.C.

Other Wars: War of 1812 (Lieutenant Colonel, 5 U.S. Infantry). Florida War (Bvt.

George Gibson (Fayette Robinson. *An Account of the Organization of the Army of the United States with Biographies of Distinguished Officers of All Grades.* Philadelphia, PA, 1848).

George Gibson (The National Archives [69045]).

Brig. Gen., USA, April 29, 1826, for ten years faithful service in one grade). Mexican War (Bvt. Major Gen., USA, May 30, 1848, for meritorious conduct particularly in performing his duties in the prosecution of the War with Mexico).

Occupation: Regular Army (Colonel, Commissary General of Subsistence)
Miscellaneous: Resided Washington, D.C.
Buried: Congressional Cemetery, Washington, D.C. (Range 56, Site 140)
References: Thomas P. Roberts. *Memoirs of John Bannister Gibson, Late Chief Justice of Pennsylvania.* Pittsburgh, PA, 1890. Harry Harrison Hain. *History of Perry County, Pennsylvania.* Harrisburg, PA, 1922. James Grant Wilson and John Fiske, editors. *Appletons' Cyclopaedia of American Biography.* New York City, NY, 1888. Fayette Robinson. *An Account of the Organization of the Army of the United States With Biographies of Distinguished Officers of All Grades.* Philadelphia, PA, 1848. Obituary, *Washington National Republican,* Oct. 1, 1861. Obituary, *Bedford Inquirer,* Oct. 11, 1861. Obituary, *Philadelphia Press,* Oct. 1, 1861. Obituary, *Philadelphia Inquirer,* Oct. 3, 1861. John W. Barriger. *Legislative History of the Subsistence Department of the United States Army from June 16, 1775, to August 15, 1876.* Washington, D.C., 1877. https://quartermaster.army.mil/bios/previous-qm-generals/quartermaster_general_bio-gibson.html.

James Duncan Graham

Major, U.S. Corps of Topographical Engineers, July 7, 1838. Lieutenant Colonel, U.S. Corps of Topographical Engineers, Aug. 6, 1861. Superintending Engineer of the harbor improvements on the North and Northwestern Lakes, Aug. 1861–April 1864. Lieutenant Colonel, U.S. Corps of Engineers, March 3, 1863. Colonel, U.S. Corps of Engineers, June 1, 1863. Superintending Engineer of sea-walls in Boston Harbor, and in charge of the preservation and repairs of harbor works on the Atlantic Coast, Aug. 1864–Dec. 1865.

Born: April 4, 1799 Prince William Co., VA
Died: Dec. 28, 1865 Boston, MA
Education: Graduated U.S. Military Academy, West Point, NY, 1817
Other Wars: Mexican War (Major, U.S. Corps of Topographical Engineers; Bvt. Lieutenant Colonel, USA, Jan. 1, 1847, for valuable and highly distinguished services, particularly on the boundary line between the United States and the provinces of Canada and New Brunswick)
Occupation: Regular Army (Colonel, U.S. Corps of Engineers)
Miscellaneous: Resided Chicago, IL; Detroit, MI; and Boston, MA. Brother of Brig. Gen. Lawrence P. Graham. Father of Bvt. Brig. Gen. William M. Graham. Brother-in-law of Major Gen. George G. Meade.
Buried: Congressional Cemetery, Washington, D.C. (Range 51, Site 215)
References: Necrology (James Duncan Graham), *The New England Historical & Genealogical Register,* Vol. 21, No. 2 (April 1867). Allen Johnson and Dumas Malone, editors. *Dictionary of American Biography.* New York City, NY, 1964. James Grant Wilson and John Fiske, editors. *Appletons' Cyclopaedia of American Biography.* New York City, NY, 1888. George W. Cullum. *Biographical Register of the Officers and Graduates of the U.S. Military Academy at West Point, N.Y.* Third Edition. Boston and New York, 1891. *The National Cyclopaedia of American Biography.* Vol. 23. New

James Duncan Graham (R.A. Miller, No. 63 Court St., Cor. Cornhill, Boston, MA; author's photograph).

James Duncan Graham (R.A. Miller, No. 63 Court St., Cor. Cornhill, Boston, MA; author's photograph).

York City, NY, 1933. Obituary, *New York Herald*, Dec. 30, 1865. Obituary, *Chicago Tribune*, Jan. 3, 1866. Obituary, *Boston Daily Advertiser*, Dec. 30, 1865. Obituary, *New York Times*, Jan. 7, 1866. Pension File, National Archives. Letters Received, Adjutant General's Office, Files E138(AGO)1864 and G333(AGO)1864, National Archives. Letters Received, Commission Branch, Adjutant General's Office, File G586(CB)1864, National Archives.

Marshall Spring Howe

Lieutenant Colonel, 2 U.S. Dragoons, June 14, 1858. Lieutenant Colonel 2 U.S. Cavalry, Aug. 3, 1861. Colonel, 3 U.S. Cavalry, Sept. 28, 1861. Commanded Southern Military District of New Mexico, July–Dec. 1862. Commanded U.S. Troops, City and Harbor of New York, Department of the East, Sept. 1863–June 1865. Retired Aug. 31, 1866.

Born: June 12, 1804 Standish, ME

Died: Dec. 8, 1878 Harrodsburg, KY

Education: Attended U.S. Military Academy, West Point, NY (Class of 1827). Attended Bowdoin College Medical School, Brunswick, ME (Class of 1829).

Other Wars: Florida Indian War (1 Lieutenant, 2 U.S. Dragoons). Mexican War (Major, 2 U.S. Dragoons).

Marshall Spring Howe (Massachusetts MOLLUS Collection, USAHEC [Vol. 72, p. 3592L]).

Marshall Spring Howe (Library of Congress [LC-DIG-cwpb-04711]).

Occupation: Regular Army (Colonel 3 U.S. Cavalry, retired Aug. 31, 1866)

Miscellaneous: Resided Harrodsburg, Mercer Co., KY, after war. Brother of Brig. Gen. Albion P. Howe.

Buried: Forest Lawn Cemetery, Buffalo, NY (Section 3, Lot 22)

References: Obituary (Marshall S. Howe), *Army and Navy Journal*, Vol. 16, No. 20 (Dec. 21, 1878). Daniel W. Howe. *Howe Genealogies.* Boston, MA, 1929. Mrs. Lucien Howe. *Frontiersmen.* Cambridge, MA, 1931. Obituary, *Louisville Courier-Journal*, Dec. 10, 1878. Letters Received, Adjutant General's Office, File R120(AGO)1866, National Archives. Letters Received, Commission Branch, Adjutant General's Office, File H767(CB)1866, National Archives. *General Catalogue of the Non-Graduates of Bowdoin College, 1794–1915.* Brunswick, ME, 1916.

Edward Augustine King

Lieutenant Colonel, 19 U.S. Infantry, May 14, 1861. Colonel, 68 IN Infantry, Aug. 20, 1862. Taken prisoner and paroled, Munfordville, KY, Sept. 17, 1862. Colonel, 6 U.S. Infantry, Aug. 1, 1863. Commanded 2 Brigade, 4 Division, 14 Army Corps, Army of the Cumberland, Aug.–Sept. 1863. GSW head, Chickamauga, GA, Sept. 20, 1863. Battle honors: Munfordville, Chickamauga.

Born: April 3, 1814 Cambridge, NY

Died: Sept. 20, 1863 KIA Chickamauga, GA

Other Wars: Texas War for Independence. Mexican War (Captain, 15 U.S. Infantry).

Occupation: Lawyer

Offices/Honors: Postmaster, Dayton, OH, 1853–61

Miscellaneous: Resided Dayton, Montgomery Co., OH. Uncle of the wife of Major Gen. Thomas J. Wood.

Buried: Woodland Cemetery, Dayton, OH (Section 68, Lot 177)

References: *The Biographical Cyclopedia and Portrait Gallery with an Historical Sketch of the State of Ohio.* Vol. 3. Cincinnati, OH, 1884. Cameron H. King, compiler. *The King Family of Suffield, Connecticut.* San Francisco, CA, 1908. Augustus W. Drury. *History of the City of Dayton and Montgomery County, Ohio.* Chicago and Dayton, 1909. John F. Edgar. *Pioneer Life in Dayton and Vicinity, 1796–1840.* Dayton, OH, 1896. Edwin W. High. *History of the Sixty-Eighth Regiment Indiana Volunteer Infantry, 1862–1865.* N.p., 1902. *Indiana at Chickamauga, 1863–1900. Report of Indiana Commissioners Chickamauga National Military Park.* Indianapolis, IN, 1901. *A Genealogy of the King Family.* Buffalo, NY, 1930. Pension File and Military Service File, National Archives. Death report, *Cincinnati Daily Commercial,* Sept. 30, 1863.

Edward Augustine King (Webster & Bro., Louisville, KY; courtesy Everitt Bowles).

Benjamin Franklin Larned

Colonel, Paymaster General, USA, July 20, 1854.

Born: Sept. 6, 1794 Pittsfield, MA

Died: Sept. 6, 1862 Washington, D.C. (chronic inflammation of bladder and prostate gland)

Other Wars: War of 1812 (1 Lieutenant, 5 U.S. Infantry, and Bvt. Captain, USA, Aug. 15, 1814, for gallant conduct in the defense of Fort Erie, Upper Canada)

Occupation: Regular Army (Colonel, Paymaster General)

Miscellaneous: Resided Pittsfield, Berkshire Co., MA; Detroit, Wayne Co., MI; and Washington, DC. Fort Larned, KS, was named in his honor.

Buried: Pittsfield Cemetery, Pittsfield, MA

References: Johney Larned. *Though Silent They Speak: The Larned Family History.* Bloomington, IN, 2006. William L. Learned, compiler. *The Learned Family (Learned, Larned, Learnard, Larnard and Lerned) Being Descendants of William Learned, Who Was of Charlestown, Massachusetts, in 1632.* Albany, NY, 1898. Obituary, *Berkshire County Eagle,* Sept. 11, 1862. Obituary, *Pittsfield Sun,* Sept. 11, 1862.

Obituary, *Daily National Intelligencer,* Sept. 8, 1862. Obituary, *New York Daily Tribune,* Sept. 26, 1862. James Grant Wilson and John Fiske, editors. *Appletons' Cyclopaedia of American Biography.* New York City, NY, 1888. Pension File, National Archives.

Thomas Lawson

Colonel, Surgeon General, USA, Nov. 30, 1836.

Born: Aug. 29, 1789 Princess Anne Co., VA

Died: May 15, 1861 Norfolk, VA

Other Wars: War of 1812 (Surgeon, 6 U.S. Infantry). Florida Indian War (Lieutenant Colonel of Volunteers). Mexican War (Bvt. Brig. Gen., USA, May 30, 1848, for meritorious conduct in the Mexican War).

Occupation: Colonel, Surgeon General, USA (died May 15, 1861)

Miscellaneous: Resided Washington, D.C.

Buried: Place of burial unknown

References: Mary C. Gillett, "Thomas Lawson, Second Surgeon General of the U.S. Army: A Character Sketch," *Prologue: Quarterly of the National Archives and Records Administration,* Vol. 14, No. 1 (Spring 1982). James E. Pilcher. *The Surgeon Generals of the Army of the United States of America.* Carlisle, PA, 1905. Obituary, *Daily National Intelligencer,* May 29, 1861. Obituary, *New York Herald,* May 28, 1861. Lyon G. Tyler, editor. *Encyclopedia of Virginia Biography.* New York City, NY, 1915. Howard A. Kelly. *A Cyclopedia of American Medical Biography.* Philadelphia and London, 1912. *The National Cyclopaedia of American Biography.* Vol. 4. New York City, NY, 1897. Mary C. Gillett. *The Army Medical Department, 1818–1865.* Washington, DC, 1987. https://history.amedd.army.mil/surgeongenerals/T_Lawson.html.

Stephen Harriman Long

Major, U.S. Corps of Topographical Engineers, July 7, 1838. Colonel, U.S. Corps of

Benjamin Franklin Larned (Library of Congress [LC-USZ62–39250]).

Thomas Lawson (courtesy National Library of Medicine, Bethesda, MD [101416076]).

Topographical Engineers, Sept. 9, 1861. Colonel, U.S. Corps of Engineers, March 3, 1863. Retired June 1, 1863.

Born: Dec. 30, 1784 Hopkinton, NH
Died: Sept. 4, 1864 Alton, IL
Education: Graduated Dartmouth College, Hanover, NH, 1809
Occupation: Regular Army (Colonel, U.S. Corps of Engineers)
Miscellaneous: Resided Alton, Madison Co., IL. Best known for his exploration of the American West, the highest peak of the Rocky Mountains being named for him.
Buried: Alton Cemetery, Alton, IL (Old Yard Section, Lot 567)
References: Richard G. Wood. *Stephen Harriman Long, 1784–1864, Army Engineer, Explorer, Inventor.* Glendale, CA, 1966. Allen Johnson and Dumas Malone, editors. *Dictionary of American Biography.* New York City, NY, 1964. Obituary, *Alton Telegraph,* Sept. 9, 1864. *The National Cyclopaedia of American Biography.* Vol. 11. New York City, NY, 1901. James Grant Wilson and John Fiske, editors. *Appletons' Cyclopaedia of American Biography.* New York City, NY, 1888. John Halliday, "Stephen Long, a Famed Explorer," *Military Images,* Vol. 23, No. 4 (Jan.–Feb. 2002). Charles C. Lord. *Life and Times in Hopkinton, New Hampshire.* Concord, NH, 1890. George T. Chapman. *Sketches of the Alumni of Dartmouth College.* Cambridge, MA, 1867. Wilbur T. Norton, editor. *Centennial History of Madison County, Illinois, and Its People, 1812–1912.* Chicago and New York, 1912. Harvey Reid. *Biographical Sketch of Enoch Long, an Illinois Pioneer.* Chicago, IL, 1884.

Stephen Harriman Long (B.P. Paige, Plumb Gallery, Washington, D.C.; author's photograph).

Stephen Harriman Long (author's photograph).

Dixon Stansbury Miles

Colonel, 2 U.S. Infantry, Jan. 19, 1859. Commanded 5 Division, Army of Northeastern Virginia, July 1861. Accused of drunkenness at First Bull Run, he was removed from command soon after the battle. Commanded Railroad Brigade, Middle Department, March–Sept. 1862. The Harper's Ferry Military Commission, convened to investigate the surrender of Harper's Ferry, Sept. 15, 1862, concluded that "Colonel Miles' incapacity, amounting to almost imbecility, led to the shameful surrender of this important post." Shell wound both legs, Harper's Ferry, WV, Sept. 15, 1862. Battle honors: First Bull Run, Harper's Ferry.

Born: May 4, 1804 Baltimore Co., MD

Died: Sept. 16, 1862 DOW Harper's Ferry, WV

Education: Graduated U.S. Military Academy, West Point, NY, 1824

Other Wars: Florida Indian War (Captain, 7 U.S. Infantry). Mexican War (Major, 5 U.S. Infantry; Bvt. Major, USA, May 9, 1846, for gallant and distinguished conduct in the defense of Fort Brown, Texas; Bvt. Lieutenant Colonel, USA, Sept. 23, 1846, for gallant and meritorious conduct in the several conflicts at Monterey, Mexico).

Occupation: Regular Army (Colonel, 2 U.S. Infantry, died Sept. 16, 1862)

Miscellaneous: Resided Sweet Air, Baltimore Co., MD

Buried: St. James Episcopal Churchyard, Our Lady's Manor, Monkton, Baltimore Co., MD

References: Paul R. Teetor. *A Matter of Hours: Treason at Harper's*

Dixon Stansbury Miles (author's photograph).

Dixon Stansbury Miles (E. & H.T. Anthony, 501 Broadway, New York, from photographic negative in Brady's National Portrait Gallery; courtesy Steve Meadow).

Ferry. Rutherford, NJ, 1982. Dennis E. Frye, "Stonewall Attacks!—The Siege of Harpers Ferry," *Blue & Gray Magazine*, Vol. 5, Issue 1 (September 1987). George W. Cullum. *Biographical Register of the Officers and Graduates of the U.S. Military Academy at West Point, N.Y.* Third Edition. Boston and New York, 1891. Obituary, *Baltimore Sun*, Sept. 17, 1862. Obituary, *Boston Morning Journal*, Sept. 17, 1862. Don Wickman. *"We Are Coming Father Abra'am," The History of the 9th Vermont Volunteer Infantry, 1862–1865*. Lynchburg, VA, 2005. Thomas P. Lowry. *Tarnished Eagles: The Courts-Martial of Fifty Union Colonels and Lieutenant Colonels*. Mechanicsburg, PA, 1997. James Grant Wilson and John Fiske, editors. *Appletons' Cyclopaedia of American Biography*. New York City, NY, 1888. *The War of the Rebellion: A Compilation of the Official Records of the Union and Confederate Armies*. Series 1, Vol. 19, Part 1, pp. 799–800. Pension File, National Archives.

Dixon Stansbury Miles (E. & H.T. Anthony, 501 Broadway, New York, from photographic negative in Brady's National Portrait Gallery; Library of Congress [LC-DIG-ppmsca-53947]).

George Nauman

Major, 3 U.S. Artillery, Dec. 24, 1853. Lieutenant Colonel, 1 U.S. Artillery, July 23, 1861. Chief of Artillery, Newport News, VA, Nov. 1861–July 1862. Colonel, 5 U.S. Artillery, Aug. 1, 1863.

Born: Oct. 7, 1802 Lancaster, PA

Died: Aug. 11, 1863 Philadelphia, PA

Education: Graduated U.S. Military Academy, West Point, NY, 1823

Other Wars: Florida Indian War (1 Lieutenant, 1 U.S. Artillery). Mexican War (Captain, 1 U.S. Artillery; Bvt. Major, USA, April 18, 1847, for gallant and meritorious conduct in the battle of Cerro Gordo, Mexico; Bvt. Lieutenant Colonel, USA, Aug. 20, 1847, for gallant and meritorious conduct in the battles of Contreras and Churubusco, Mexico).

Occupation: Regular Army (Colonel, 5 U.S. Artillery, died Aug. 11, 1863)

Miscellaneous: Resided Lancaster, Lancaster Co., PA

Buried: Lancaster Cemetery, Lancaster, PA (Lot 484)

References: Alexander Harris. *A Biographical History of Lancaster County.* Lancaster, PA, 1872. Obituary (George Nauman), *Army and Navy Journal,* Vol. 1, No. 4 (Sept. 19, 1863). Obituary, *Lancaster Intelligencer,* Aug. 18, 1863. Obituary, *Lancaster Daily Evening Express,* Aug. 17, 1863. *Biographical Annals of Lancaster County, Pennsylvania.* Chicago, IL, 1903. George W. Cullum. *Biographical Register of the Officers and Graduates of the U.S. Military Academy at West Point, N.Y.* Third Edition. Boston and New York, 1891. William J. Tenney. *The Military and Naval History of the Rebellion in the United States.* New York City, NY, 1865. Letters Received, Adjutant General's Office, File N204(AGO)1861, National Archives. Pension File, National Archives.

Matthew Mountjoy Payne

Colonel, 2 U.S. Artillery, Nov. 11, 1856. Resigned July 23, 1861.

Born: Jan. 17, 1784 Goochland Co., VA

Died: Aug. 1, 1862 Goochland, VA

Other Wars: War of 1812 (Captain, 20 U.S. Infantry). Florida Indian War (Major, 2 U.S. Artillery). Mexican War (Lieutenant Colonel, 4 U.S. Artillery; Bvt. Colonel, USA, May 9, 1846, for gallant and distinguished services in the battles of Palo Alto and Resaca de la Palma, Texas).

Occupation: Regular Army (Colonel, 2 U.S. Artillery, resigned July 23, 1861)

Miscellaneous: Resided Goochland, Goochland Co., VA

Buried: Grace Episcopal Churchyard, Goochland, VA

References: Fayette Robinson. *An Account of the Organization of the Army of the United States with Biographies of Distinguished Officers of All Grades.* Philadelphia, PA, 1848. Rosa F. Yancey. *Lynchburg and Its Neighbors.* Richmond, VA, 1935. Francis S. Drake. *Dictionary of American Biography Including Men of the Time.* Boston, MA, 1872. Letters Received, Adjutant General's Office, File G347(AGO)1865, National Archives.

Matthew Mountjoy Payne (Fayette Robinson. *An Account of the Organization of the Army of the United States with Biographies of Distinguished Officers of All Grades.* **Philadelphia, PA, 1848).**

Thomas Fitch Perley

Surgeon, USV, Oct. 23, 1861. Colonel, Medical Inspector General, July 1, 1862. Charged with issuing blank soldier's discharges to persons not authorized to have them and recommended for dismissal as incompetent, he was allowed to resign as Medical Inspector General, Aug. 10, 1863, "in consequence of the state of health of my wife." Honorably mustered out, July 27, 1865. Bvt. Lieutenant Colonel, USV, June 1, 1865, for faithful and meritorious services.

Born: Feb. 23, 1815 Bridgton, ME

Died: March 21, 1889 Portland, ME

Education: Graduated Bowdoin College, Brunswick, ME, 1837. Graduated Medical School of Maine, Brunswick, ME, 1841.

Occupation: Physician. An enthusiastic entomologist, he had one of the finest collections of butterflies in the country.

Miscellaneous: Resided Hazzard's Bluff, near Jacksonville, FL, 1853–61; Bridgton, Cumberland Co., ME; and Portland, Cumberland Co., ME, after war

Buried: Evergreen Cemetery, Portland, ME (Section A, Lot 717)

References: Nehemiah Cleaveland and Alpheus S. Packard. *History of Bowdoin College with Biographical Sketches of Its Graduates from 1806 to 1879, Inclusive.* Boston, MA, 1882. Obituary, *Portland Daily Press*, March 22, 1889. Obituary, *Portland Daily Eastern Argus*, March 23, 1889. Obituary, *Boston Herald*, March 22, 1889. Martin Van Buren Perley, compiler. *History and Genealogy of the Perley Family.* Salem, MA, 1906. Letters Received, Commission Branch, Adjutant General's Office, Files P253(CB)1863 and P283(CB)1863, National Archives. "Resignation of the Medical Inspector of the Army," *New York Herald,* Aug. 14, 1863.

Thomas Fitch Perley (Brady's National Photographic Galleries, No. 352 Pennsylvania Av., Washington, D.C.; courtesy Henry Deeks).

Thomas Fitch Perley (Brady's National Photographic Galleries, No. 352 Pennsylvania Av., Washington, D.C.; courtesy Steve Meadow).

John Phillip Sanderson

Lieutenant Colonel, 15 U.S. Infantry, May 14, 1861. Commanded Fort Adams (RI), Department of the East,

Jan.–July 1863. Colonel, 13 U.S. Infantry, July 4, 1863. Provost Marshal General, Staff of Major Gen. William S. Rosecrans, Department of the Missouri, March–Oct. 1864. Best known for his efforts to expose the activities of the Order of American Knights, a subversive secret society, in Missouri. Battle honors: Chickamauga.

Born: Feb. 13, 1818 East Hanover, Lebanon Co., PA

Died: Oct. 14, 1864 St. Louis, MO

Occupation: Lawyer and newspaper editor before war. Regular Army (Colonel, 13 U.S. Infantry, died Oct. 14, 1864).

Offices/Honors: Pennsylvania House of Representatives, 1845. Pennsylvania Senate, 1846–48. Chief Clerk, U.S. War Department, March–May 1861.

Miscellaneous: Resided Lebanon, Lebanon Co., PA; Philadelphia, PA; and Springfield, Greene Co., OH

Buried: Ferncliff Cemetery, Springfield, OH (Section A, Lot 37)

References: E. Benjamin Bierman. *Lebanon County in Our State Legislature. A Paper Read Before the Lebanon County Historical Society, February 19, 1904.* Lebanon, PA, 1904. Obituary, *Daily Missouri Democrat,* Oct. 15, 1864. Obituary, *Daily Missouri Republican,* Oct. 15, 1864. Obituary, *New York Daily Tribune,* Oct. 19, 1864. Obituary (John P. Sanderson), *Army and Navy Journal,* Vol. 2, No. 9 (Oct. 22, 1864). James Grant Wilson and John Fiske, editors. *Appletons' Cyclopaedia of American Biography.* New York City, NY, 1888. *The National Cyclopaedia of American Biography.* Vol. 6. New York City, NY, 1896. Frank L. Klement. *The Copperheads in the Middle West.* Chicago, IL, 1960. Frank L. Klement. *Dark Lanterns: Secret Political Societies, Conspiracies, and Treason*

John Phillip Sanderson (author's photograph).

John Phillip Sanderson (Col. Joseph Leffel's Excelsior Art Palace, 82 Main Street, Springfield, OH; L.M. Strayer Collection).

Trials in the Civil War. Baton Rouge, LA, 1984. Mark W. Johnson. *That Body of Brave Men: The U.S. Regular Infantry and the Civil War in the West.* Cambridge, MA, 2003. Pension File, National Archives. Letters Received, Adjutant General's Office, Files S575(AGO)1861 and S1534(AGO)1863, National Archives. J.P. Sanderson Papers, 1846–1865 (MSS 209), Ohio Historical Society.

John Symington

Major, Ordnance Department, USA, March 27, 1842. Commanded Allegheny Arsenal, Pittsburgh, PA, 1857–62. Colonel, Ordnance Department, USA, Aug. 3, 1861. Although initially charged with negligence resulting in the explosion which destroyed the Allegheny Arsenal, Sept. 17, 1862, and killed 78 workers, he was later found innocent of any wrongdoing by a military tribunal. Retired June 1, 1863.

Born: Dec. 24, 1796 Brandywine, New Castle Co., DE

Died: April 4, 1864 Harford Co., MD

Education: Graduated U.S. Military Academy. West Point, NY, 1815

Other Wars: Mexican War (Commanded Harper's Ferry, VA, Arsenal)

Occupation: Regular Army (Colonel, Ordnance Department)

Miscellaneous: Resided Lawrenceville, Allegheny Co., PA (1860); and Harford Co., MD. Father-in-law of CSA Brig. Gen. William R. Boggs. His wife, Elizabeth McCaw (Johnston) Symington, was the aunt of CSA Brig. Gen. George E. Pickett. His son, William Newton Symington, served on engineer duty in the Confederate Army in 1865.

Buried: Green Mount Cemetery, Baltimore, MD (Area U, Lot 58)

References: Obituary, *Pittsburgh Daily Post*, May 17, 1864. George W. Cullum. *Biographical Register of the Officers and Graduates of the U.S. Military Academy at West Point, N.Y.* Third Edition. Boston and New York, 1891. Joseph Barry. *The Strange Story of Harper's Ferry with Legends of the Surrounding Country.* Martinsburg, WV, 1903. Pension File, National Archives. Letters Received, Commission Branch, Adjutant General's Office, File S1203(CB)1864, National Archives. Letters Received, Adjutant General's Office, File S1194(AGO)1862, National Archives. www.ancestry.com.

John Symington (Massachusetts MOLLUS Collection, USAHEC [Vol. 135, p. 6946L]).

Daniel D. Tompkins

Colonel, Assistant Quartermaster General, Dec. 22, 1856. Chief Quartermaster, New York City (NY) Quartermaster Depot, April 1861–Feb. 1863. Nominated (Feb. 23, 1863) as Bvt. Brig. Gen., USA, July 1, 1862, for meritorious services in charge of the Quartermaster's Department at New York, but not confirmed.

Born: Nov. 30, 1798 NY

Died: Feb. 26, 1863 Brooklyn, NY

Education: Graduated U.S. Military Academy, West Point, NY, 1820

Other Wars: Florida War (Captain, 1 U.S. Artillery. Bvt. Major, USA, Sept. 11, 1836, for gallant and meritorious conduct in the war against the Florida Indians) and Mexican War (Major, Quartermaster, USA. Bvt. Lieutenant Colonel, USA, May 30, 1848, for meritorious conduct particularly in the performance of his duties in the prosecution of the war with Mexico.)

Occupation: Regular Army (Colonel, Assistant Quartermaster General)

Miscellaneous: Resided Brooklyn, NY. Nephew of U.S. Vice President Daniel D. Tompkins. Father of Bvt. Brig. Gen. Charles H. Tompkins (Quartermaster). Father-in-law of Bvt. Brig. Gen. William J. Sloan (Surgeon, USA).

Daniel D. Tompkins (Augustus Morand, 297 Fulton St., Cor. Johnson, Brooklyn, NY; author's photograph).

Buried: Oakwood Cemetery, Troy, NY (Section F, Lot 21)

References: George W. Cullum. *Biographical Register of the Officers and Graduates of the U.S. Military Academy at West Point, N.Y.* Third Edition. Boston and New York, 1891. Robert A. and Clare F. Tompkins, compilers. *The Tomkins-Tompkins Genealogy.* Los Angeles, CA, 1942. Obituary, *New York Evening Post,* Feb. 27, 1863. Obituary, *New York Daily Tribune,* Feb. 28, 1863. James Grant Wilson and John Fiske, editors. *Appletons' Cyclopaedia of American Biography.* New York City, NY, 1888. Obituary, *New York Times,* Feb. 28, 1863. John Cornell. *Genealogy of the Cornell Family, Being an Account of the Descendants of Thomas Cornell of Portsmouth, R.I.* New York City, NY, 1902. Pension File, National Archives. Letters Received, Appointment, Commission and Personal Branch, Adjutant General's Office, File 887(ACP)1886, National Archives.

William Whistler

Colonel, 4 U.S. Infantry, July 15, 1845. Retired Oct. 9, 1861.

Born: Dec. 3, 1780 Hagerstown, MD

Died: Dec. 4, 1863 Newport, KY

Other Wars: War of 1812 (Captain, 1 U.S. Infantry). Florida Indian War

(Lieutenant Colonel, 7 U.S. Infantry). Mexican War (Colonel, 4 U.S. Infantry).

Occupation: Regular Army (Colonel, 4 U.S. Infantry, retired Oct. 9, 1861)

Miscellaneous: Resided Newport, Campbell Co., KY. Father of Bvt. Brig. Gen. Joseph N.G. Whistler. Father-in-law of Brig. Gen. Gabriel R. Paul. Grandfather of Colonel Edward Bloodgood (22 WI Infantry). Uncle of the artist, James McNeill Whistler.

Buried: Evergreen Cemetery, Southgate, Campbell Co., KY (Section 17, Lot 73, unmarked in Helm family lot)

References: Carolyn Thomas Foreman, "Colonel William Whistler," *The Chronicles of Oklahoma*, Vol. 18, No. 4 (December 1940). Albert A. Nofi, "Colonel Whistler Retires," *North & South Magazine*, Vol. 10, No. 6 (June 2008). Joseph Smith, "The Whistlers—A Family Illustrious in War and Peace," *The Journal of the American-Irish Historical Society*, Vol. 2, 1899. Joseph Kirkland. *The Chicago Massacre of 1812 with Illustrations and Historical Documents.* Chicago, IL, 1893. Joseph Kirkland. *The Story of Chicago.* Chicago, IL, 1892. Obituary, *Detroit Free Press*, Dec. 16, 1863. Obituary, *Cincinnati Daily Enquirer*, Dec. 7, 1863. James Grant Wilson and John Fiske, editors. *Appletons' Cyclopaedia of American Biography.* New York City, NY, 1888. *The National Cyclopaedia of American Biography.* Vol. 9. New York City, NY, 1899. Letters Received, Commission Branch, Adjutant General's Office, File E115(CB)1863, National Archives. William H. Powell. *A History of the Organization and Movements of the Fourth Regiment of Infantry, United States Army.* Washington, D.C., 1871. www.ancestry.com.

William Whistler (Joseph Kirkland. *The Story of Chicago*. Chicago, IL, 1892).

William Whistler (courtesy Scott Boulton).

U.S. Marine Corps

William Dulany	July 26, 1861	Retired June 6, 1864
William L. Shuttleworth	June 10, 1864	Retired Dec. 4, 1867
Colonel Commandant		
John Harris	Jan. 7, 1859	Died May 12, 1864
Jacob Zeilin	June 10, 1864	Retired Nov. 1, 1876

Biographies

William Dulany

Major, U.S. Marine Corps, Nov. 17, 1847. Colonel, U.S. Marine Corps, July 26, 1861. Commanded Norfolk (VA) Marine Station, 1862–65. Retired June 6, 1864.

Born: June 4, 1800, Alexandria, VA

Died: July 4, 1868, near Beltsville, MD

Other Wars: Seminole Indian War (Bvt. Major, USMC, March 3, 1843, for meritorious conduct in Florida). Mexican War (Bvt. Lieutenant Colonel, USMC, Sept. 14, 1847, for gallant and meritorious conduct at the storming and capture of the castle of Chapultepec and the capture of the Belen Gate and the City of Mexico).

Occupation: U.S. Marine Corps (Colonel, retired June 6, 1864)

Miscellaneous: Resided Brooklyn, NY; Charlestown, Middlesex Co., MA; and Beltsville, Prince George's Co., MD

Buried: Baltimore Cemetery, Baltimore, MD (Area S, Lot 555)

References: Pension File, National Archives. Obituary, *New York Herald*, July 10, 1868. Obituary, *New York Commercial Advertiser*, July 10, 1868. David M. Sullivan. *The United States Marine Corps in the Civil War.* 4 vols. Shippensburg, PA, 1997–2000. Edward W. Callahan, editor. *List of Officers of the Navy of the United States and of the Marine Corps from 1775 to 1900.* New York City, NY, 1901. James Grant Wilson and John Fiske, editors. *Appletons' Cyclopaedia of American Biography.* New York City, NY, 1888.

John Harris

Colonel Commandant, U.S. Marine Corps, Jan. 7, 1859.

Born: May 20, 1790, East Whiteland Twp., Chester Co., PA

Died: May 12, 1864, Washington, D.C.

Other Wars: War of 1812 (1 Lieutenant, USMC). Florida Indian War (Captain, USMC; Bvt. Major, USMC, Jan. 27, 1837, for gallantry and good conduct in the war against Florida Indians, particularly in the affair of the Hatchee Lustee).

John Harris (E. & H.T. Anthony, 501 Broadway, New York, from photographic negative in Brady's National Portrait Gallery; Library of Congress [LC-DIG-cwpb-05525]).

John Harris (Brady-Handy Photograph Collection, Library of Congress [LC-DIG-cwpbh-01055]).

Occupation: U.S. Marine Corps (Colonel Commandant)

Miscellaneous: Resided Washington, D.C.

Buried: Oak Hill Cemetery, Washington, D.C. (Chapel Hill, Lot 568). Cenotaph at Great Valley Presbyterian Church Cemetery, Malvern, PA.

References: Allan R. Millett and Jack Shulimson. *Commandants of the Marine Corps*. Annapolis, MD, 2004. David M. Sullivan. *The United States Marine Corps in the Civil War*. 4 vols. Shippensburg, PA, 1997–2000. Obituary, *Washington Evening Star*, May 13, 1864. Joseph S. Harris. *Record of the Harris Family Descended from John Harris, Born 1680 in Wiltshire, England*. Philadelphia, PA, 1903. Joseph S. Harris. *Notes on the Ancestry of the Children of Joseph Smith Harris and Delia Silliman Brodhead*. Philadelphia, PA, 1898. Edward W. Callahan, editor. *List of Officers of the Navy of the United States and of the Marine Corps from 1775 to 1900*. New York City, NY, 1901.

William Louis Shuttleworth

Captain, U.S. Marine Corps, Sept. 28, 1857. Major, U.S. Marine Corps, Feb. 6, 1864. Colonel, U.S. Marine Corps, June 10, 1864. Retired Dec. 4, 1867. Battle honors: Capture of Confederate batteries at Hatteras Inlet, NC.

Born: Jan. 6, 1812 Piscataway, NJ
Died: Sept. 27, 1871 Brooklyn, NY

Other Wars: Mexican War (1 Lieutenant, USMC; Bvt. Captain, USMC, March 16, 1847, for gallant and meritorious conduct in the bombardment and capture of Vera Cruz)

Occupation: U.S. Marine Corps (Colonel, retired Dec. 4, 1867)

Miscellaneous: Resided Brooklyn, NY. His son, John G. Shuttleworth, served in the Confederate Army as a Private in the 2 FL Infantry.

Buried: Green-Wood Cemetery, Brooklyn, NY (Section F, Lot 20157)

References: David M. Sullivan. *The United States Marine Corps in the Civil War.* 4 vols. Shippensburg, PA, 1997–2000. *Fourth Annual Report of the Bureau of Military Statistics, State of New York.* Albany, NY, 1867. Obituary, *Brooklyn Daily Union,* Sept. 29, 1871. Obituary, *Brooklyn Daily Eagle,* Sept. 29, 1871. Obituary, *New York Herald,* Sept. 29, 1871. Edward W. Callahan, editor. *List of Officers of the Navy of the United States and of the Marine Corps from 1775 to 1900.* New York City, NY, 1901. www.annefield.net/shuttleworthlinks.htm.

William Louis Shuttleworth (Silsbee, Case & Co., Photographic Artists, 299½ Washington St., Boston, MA; courtesy Anne Healy Field).

Jacob Zeilin

Captain, U.S. Marine Corps, Sept. 14, 1847. GSW left arm, First Bull Run, VA, July 21, 1861. Major, U.S. Marine Corps, July 26, 1861. Colonel Commandant, U.S. Marine Corps, June 10, 1864. Retired Nov. 1, 1876. Battle honors: First Bull Run, Siege of Battery Wagner.

Born: July 16, 1806 Philadelphia, PA
Died: Nov. 18, 1880 Washington, D.C.
Education: Attended U.S. Military Academy, West Point, NY (Class of 1826)
Other Wars: Mexican War (Captain, USMC; Bvt. Major, USMC, Jan. 9, 1847, for gallant conduct at San Gabriel and La Mesa)
Occupation: Brigadier General Commandant, USMC, March 2, 1867; retired Nov. 1, 1876
Miscellaneous: Resided Philadelphia, PA; and Washington, D.C.

Jacob Zeilin (Brady-Handy Photograph Collection, Library of Congress [LC-DIG-cwpbh-00448]).

Buried: Laurel Hill Cemetery, Philadelphia, PA (Section 18, Lots 33–36)

References: Allan R. Millett and Jack Shulimson. *Commandants of the Marine Corps.* Annapolis, MD, 2004. Allen Johnson and Dumas Malone, editors. *Dictionary of American Biography.* New York City, NY, 1964. James Grant Wilson and John Fiske, editors. *Appletons' Cyclopaedia of American Biography.* New York City, NY, 1888. *The National Cyclopaedia of American Biography.* Vol. 11. New York City, NY, 1901. Obituary Circular, unnumbered, Pennsylvania MOLLUS. David M. Sullivan. *The United States Marine Corps in the Civil War.* 4 vols. Shippensburg, PA, 1997–2000. William H. Powell and Edward Shippen, editors. *Officers of the Army and Navy (Regular) Who Served in the Civil War.* Philadelphia, PA, 1892. Obituary (Jacob Zeilin), *Army and Navy Journal,* Vol. 18, No. 16 (Nov. 20, 1880). Obituary, *Washington Evening Star,* Nov. 19, 1880. Obituary, *New York Herald,* Nov. 19, 1880. Obituary, *New York Daily Tribune,* Nov. 19, 1880. Edward W. Callahan, editor. *List of Officers of the Navy of the United States and of the Marine Corps from 1775 to 1900.* New York City, NY, 1901.

U.S. Sharpshooters

Regiments

1st U.S. Sharpshooters
Hiram Berdan Nov. 30, 1861 Resigned Jan. 2, 1864, Bvt. Major Gen., USV

2nd U.S. Sharpshooters
Henry A.V.Z. Post Jan. 1, 1862 Resigned Nov. 18, 1862
Homer R. Stoughton Jan. 19, 1864 Mustered out Jan. 23, 1865

Biographies

Henry Albertson Van Zo Post

Lieutenant Colonel, 2 U.S. Sharpshooters, Nov. 2, 1861. Colonel, 2 U.S. Sharpshooters, Jan. 1, 1862. GSW left arm, Antietam, MD, Sept. 17, 1862. Resigned Nov. 18, 1862. Battle honors: Peninsular Campaign, Second Bull Run, Antietam.

Born: May 16, 1832 New York City, NY

Died: Jan. 25, 1914 New York City, NY

Occupation: Mechanical engineer before war. Manufacturer of railroad supplies and railroad banker after war.

Miscellaneous: Resided New York City, NY; and Cincinnati, OH,

Henry Albertson Van Zo Post (Brady's National Photographic Portrait Gallery, No. 352 Pennsylvania Av., Washington, D.C.; Massachusetts MOLLUS Collection, USAHEC [Vol. 52, p. 2584]).

1864–70. Son-in-law of Brig. Gen. Nathaniel C. McLean.

Buried: Woodlawn Cemetery, New York City, NY (Section 46/47, Cypress Plot, Lots 5808–5810)

References: Marie Caroline De Trobriand Post. *The Post Family.* New York City, NY, 1905. Obituary, *New York Sun,* Jan. 26, 1914. Obituary, *New York Times,* Jan. 27, 1914. Pension File, National Archives. Letters Received, Volunteer Service Branch, Adjutant General's Office, File P1047(VS)1862, National Archives. Charles A. Stevens. *Berdan's United States Sharpshooters in the Army of the Potomac, 1861–1865.* St. Paul, MN, 1892.

Homer Richard Stoughton

Captain, Co. E, 2 U.S. Sharpshooters, Oct. 30, 1861. Major, 2 U.S. Sharpshooters, Sept. 17, 1862. Lieutenant Colonel, 2 U.S. Sharpshooters, June 24, 1863. *Colonel,* 2 U.S. Sharpshooters, Jan. 19, 1864. GSW left breast, Spotsylvania, VA, May 10, 1864. Taken prisoner, Petersburg, VA, June 21, 1864. Confined Richmond, VA; Macon, GA; and Columbia, SC. Paroled Dec. 10, 1864. Honorably mustered out, Jan. 23, 1865. Battle honors: Fredericksburg, Chancellorsville, Gettysburg, Bristoe Station, Mine Run, Wilderness, Spotsylvania, Petersburg.

Born: Nov. 13, 1836 Quechee, VT

Died: Sept. 17, 1902 Otsego, Allegan Co., MI

Education: Attended Royalton (VT) Academy

Occupation: Railroad station agent. Vice President and General Manager, Shelby (AL) Iron Co., 1885–91.

Offices/Honors: Postmaster, West Randolph, VT, 1866–72

Miscellaneous: Resided Randolph, Orange Co., VT, 1858–72; Palmer, Hampden Co., MA, 1872-83; New London, New London

Henry Albertson Van Zo Post (Gil Barrett Collection).

Homer Richard Stoughton (Library of Congress [LC-DIG-cwpb-05356]).

Co., CT, 1883–85; Shelby, Shelby Co., AL, 1885–91; Oberlin, Lorain Co., OH; and Barre, Washington Co., VT, 1892–1902

Buried: Elmwood Cemetery, Barre, VT (Lot 396½)

References: Obituary, *Randolph Herald and News*, Sept. 25, 1902. Obituary, *Montpelier Daily Journal*, Sept. 18, 1902. Obituary, *Barre Evening Telegram*, Sept. 18, 1902. Evelyn M. Wood Lovejoy. *History of Royalton, Vermont, with Family Genealogies, 1769–1911*. Burlington, VT, 1911. Pension File, National Archives. Letters Received, Volunteer Service Branch, Adjutant General's Office, Files S18(VS)1864 and S168(VS)1865, National Archives. Charles A. Stevens. *Berdan's United States Sharpshooters in the Army of the Potomac, 1861–1865*. St. Paul, MN, 1892. George W. Fuller. *Descendants of Thomas Stoughton (1600–1661) of Dorchester, Mass*. Potsdam, NY, 1929.

U.S. Veteran Volunteers

Regiments

1st Engineers
William E. Merrill		Aug. 30, 1864		Mustered out Sept. 26, 1865

1st Infantry
Charles Bird		May 30, 1865		Mustered out Jan. 19, 1866

2nd Infantry
Oscar Malmborg		Jan. 1, 1865		Discharged May 30, 1865
James A. Hall		Aug. 15, 1865		Mustered out March 1, 1866,
					Bvt. Brig. Gen., USV

3rd Infantry
William H. Morgan		Jan. 10, 1865		Discharged March 6, 1866,
					Bvt. Brig. Gen., USV

4th Infantry
Oliver Wood		Dec. 29, 1864		Mustered out March 1, 1866,
					Bvt. Brig. Gen., USV

5th Infantry
John G. Hazard		July 14, 1865		Mustered out March 5, 1866,
					Bvt. Brig. Gen., USV

6th Infantry
Charles E. La Motte		Aug. 22, 1865		Discharged March 22, 1866,
					Bvt. Brig. Gen., USV

7th Infantry
Philip P. Brown, Jr.		July 15, 1865		Mustered out Feb. 9, 1866,
					Bvt. Brig. Gen., USV

8th Infantry
Francis E. Pierce		June 15, 1865		Mustered out March 22, 1866,
					Bvt. Brig. Gen., USV

9th Infantry
Daniel Macauley		Aug. 10, 1865		Discharged March 12, 1866,
					Bvt. Brig. Gen., USV

Unassigned
George W. Gist		March 10, 1865		Resigned June 9, 1865
Benjamin A.F. Greer		Dec. 24, 1864		Discharged July 3, 1865
James M. Pomeroy		Feb. 15, 1865		Mustered as Lt. Col.,
					July 20, 1865
Nathaniel P. Richmond		March 6, 1865		Resigned May 29, 1865
Dudley Wickersham		Feb. 14, 1865		Mustered as Major,
					July 1, 1865

Biographies

Charles Bird

1 Lieutenant, Co. K, 1 DE Infantry (3 months), May 20, 1861. Honorably mustered out, Aug. 16, 1861. 2 Lieutenant, Co. E, 2 DE Infantry, April 11, 1862. 1 Lieutenant, Co. E, 2 DE Infantry, Oct. 1, 1862. GSW face, Fredericksburg, VA, Dec. 13, 1862. Captain, Co. E, 2 DE Infantry, March 15, 1863. Acting ADC, Chief of Pioneers, Staff of Brig. Gen. Francis C. Barlow, 1 Division, 2 Army Corps, Army of the Potomac, April–June 1864. GSW groin, Petersburg, VA, June 18, 1864. Honorably mustered out, June 30, 1864. Lieutenant Colonel, 9 DE Infantry, Sept. 3, 1864. Honorably mustered out, Dec. 23, 1864. Lieutenant Colonel, 1 U.S. Veteran Volunteer Infantry, Jan. 25, 1865. Colonel, 1 U.S. Veteran Volunteer Infantry, May 30, 1865. Honorably mustered out, Jan. 19, 1866. Bvt. 1 Lieutenant, USA, and Bvt. Captain, USA, March 2, 1867, for gallant and meritorious services in the battle of Fredericksburg, VA. Bvt. Major, USA, March 2, 1867, for gallant and meritorious services in the battle of Spotsylvania, VA. Bvt. Lieutenant Colonel, USA, March 2, 1867, for gallant and meritorious services in the battle of Petersburg, VA, June 20, 1864. Battle honors: Fredericksburg, Chancellorsville, Spotsylvania, Petersburg, Operations in the Shenandoah Valley (Hamilton).

Born: June 17, 1838, Wilmington, DE
Died: March 22, 1920, Brooklyn, NY
Education: Attended Lawrenceville School, Lawrenceville, NJ
Other Wars: Spanish American War
(Colonel, Quartermaster, USV)

Charles Bird (post-war) (USAHEC [RG641S-MO-PA3.1]).

Charles Bird (Brig. Gen., USV, 1901) (*Companions of the Military Order of the Loyal Legion of the United States*. Second Edition. New York City, NY, 1901).

Occupation: Regular Army (Brig. Gen., USA, retired June 17, 1902)

Miscellaneous: Resided Wilmington, New Castle Co., DE. Active in American Red Cross and Young Men's Christian Association after retirement from U.S. Army.

Buried: Wilmington and Brandywine Cemetery, Wilmington, DE

References: Obituary, *Wilmington Evening Journal*, March 22, 1920. Obituary, *Wilmington Morning News*, March 23, 1920. Obituary, *Brooklyn Daily Eagle*, March 23, 1920. *Who Was Who in America, 1897–1942*. Chicago, IL, 1942. Pension File and Military Service File, National Archives. Constance W. Altshuler. *Cavalry Yellow & Infantry Blue*. Tucson, AZ, 1991. *A Military Album Containing Over One Thousand Portraits of Commissioned Officers Who Served in the Spanish-American War*. New York City, NY, 1902. Register of Army Commissions in Hancock's First Army Corps, 1864–65, Record Group 94, Entry 328, National Archives.

George Washington Gist

1 Lieutenant, Adjutant, 17 KY Infantry, May 26, 1862. Captain, Co. D, 17 KY Infantry, April 23, 1863. Acting ACS, Staff of Brig. Gen. Samuel Beatty, 1 Brigade, 3 Division, 21 Army Corps, Army of the Cumberland, July 1863. Acting AAG, Staff of Colonel Frederick Knefler, 3 Brigade, 3 Division, 4 Army Corps, Army of the Cumberland, March–April 1864. Honorably mustered out, Jan. 23, 1865. Appointed *Colonel*, U.S. Veteran Volunteer Infantry, March 10, 1865. Resigned June 9, 1865. Battle honors: Fort Donelson, Shiloh, Siege of Corinth, Chickamauga, Missionary Ridge, Atlanta Campaign.

Born: July 20, 1819 Frederick Co., MD

Died: Nov. 9, 1891 Washington, D.C.

Education: Attended Transylvania University, Lexington, KY

Offices/Honors: Judge, Montgomery County (KY) Court, 1851–58

Occupation: Lawyer, judge, and U.S. Treasury Department clerk

Miscellaneous: Resided Mount Sterling, Montgomery Co., KY, to 1867; Cincinnati, OH, 1867–69; and Washington, D.C., after 1869. Grandson of Revolutionary War General Mordecai Gist.

Buried: Arlington National Cemetery, Arlington, VA (Section 1, Site 44-B)

References: Obituary, *Washington Evening Star*, Nov. 10, 1891. *Society of the Army of the Cumberland. Twenty-Fourth Reunion, Cleveland, Ohio*. Cincinnati, OH, 1894. Jean M. Dorsey and Maxwell J. Dorsey. *Christopher Gist of Maryland and Some of His Descendants, 1679–1957*.

George Washington Gist (post-war, 1890) (W.L. Spedden, Photographer, 808 7th St., N.W., Washington, D.C.; USAHEC [RG127S-DCC.207]).

Chicago, IL, 1958. Pension File and Military Service File, National Archives. Obituary, *Frederick News,* Nov. 12, 1891. Obituary, *Louisville Courier-Journal,* Nov. 11, 1891. John Blackburn. *A Hundred Miles A Hundred Heartbreaks.* Owensboro, KY, 1972. Thomas Speed, Robert M. Kelly, and Alfred Pirtle. *The Union Regiments of Kentucky.* Louisville, KY, 1897. Register of Army Commissions in Hancock's First Army Corps, 1864–65, Record Group 94, Entry 328, National Archives.

Benjamin A.F. Greer

Private, Co. B, 4 OH Infantry (3 months), May 4, 1861. Honorably mustered out, Aug. 21, 1861. 1 Lieutenant, Co. E, 20 OH Infantry, Oct. 15, 1861. Captain, Co. B, 20 OH Infantry, May 16, 1862. Honorably mustered out, Oct. 27, 1864. Appointed *Colonel,* U.S. Veteran Volunteer Infantry, Dec. 24, 1864. Honorably discharged, July 3, 1865, "not having passed the required examination before a duly authorized Examining Board." Battle honors: Fort Donelson, Shiloh, Champion's Hill, Vicksburg Campaign, Atlanta Campaign (Kenesaw Mountain).

Born: 1834? Knox Co., OH

Died: Jan. 28, 1883 Mount Vernon, OH

Occupation: Lawyer

Offices/Honors: Probate Judge, Knox Co., OH, 1875–78

Miscellaneous: Resided Mount Vernon, Knox Co., OH

Benjamin A. F. Greer (USAHEC [RG98S-CWP74.101]).

Buried: Mound View Cemetery, Mount Vernon, OH (Section 1, Lot 40, unmarked)

References: Pension File, National Archives. Letters Received, Volunteer Service Branch, Adjutant General's Office, File C492(VS)1867, National Archives. Norman N. Hill, Jr., compiler. *History of Knox County, Ohio, Its Past and Present.* Mount Vernon, OH, 1881. *The Biographical Record of Knox County, Ohio.* Chicago, IL, 1902. Obituary, *Cincinnati Commercial Gazette,* Jan. 29, 1883. Obituary, *Cincinnati Enquirer,* Jan. 29, 1883. Register of Army Commissions in Hancock's First Army Corps, 1864–65, Record Group 94, Entry 328, National Archives. David W. Wood, compiler. *History of the 20th O.V.V.I. Regiment and Proceedings of the First Reunion.* Columbus, OH, 1876.

Oscar Malmborg

Lieutenant Colonel, 55 IL Infantry, Oct. 31, 1861. Commanded 2 Brigade, 5 Division, Army of the Tennessee, April 6, 1862. Colonel, 55 IL Infantry, Dec. 19, 1862.

Oscar Malmborg (S.M. Fassett, Artist, 122 & 124 Clark Street, Chicago, IL; courtesy Karl E. Sundstrom).

GSW near right eye, Vicksburg, MS, May 19, 1863. Shell wound near left eye, Vicksburg, MS, May 22, 1863. Commanded 2 Brigade, 2 Division, 15 Army Corps, Army of the Tennessee, Aug. 6–Sept. 10, 1863. Chief Engineer, Staff of Major Gen. James B. McPherson, 17 Army Corps, Army of the Tennessee, April 26–July 18, 1864. Resigned

Oscar Malmborg (Abraham Lincoln Presidential Library & Museum).

Oscar Malmborg (USAHEC [RG98S-CWP7.129]).

Sept. 20, 1864, since "my health has become so impaired by fatigue and exposure in the discharge of the double duties as regimental commander and engineer that I deem it my duty to my country no longer to hold my commission in so reduced a command." Colonel, 2 U.S. Veteran Volunteer Infantry, Jan. 1, 1865. Honorably discharged, May 30, 1865, on account of physical disability. Battle honors: Shiloh, Chickasaw Bayou, Arkansas Post, Vicksburg Campaign, Atlanta Campaign.

Born: Feb. 29, 1820 Kraklingbo, Gotland, Sweden

Died: April 29, 1880 Visby, Sweden

Education: Attended Karlberg Military Academy, Stockholm, Sweden

Occupation: Immigration agent for the Illinois Central Railroad before war. Accountant and U.S. Treasury Department clerk after war.

Miscellaneous: Resided Chicago, IL; Washington, D.C.; and Visby, Gotland, Sweden, after 1874

Buried: Eastern Cemetery (Ostra Kyrkogarden), Visby, Sweden

References: Ernst W. Olson, editor. *History of the Swedes of Illinois.* Chicago, IL, 1908. Obituary, *Chicago Inter Ocean,* May 28, 1880. Pension File and Military Service File, National Archives. Letters Received, Volunteer Service Branch, Adjutant General's Office, File M392(VS)1868, National Archives. Otto Eisenschiml, "The 55th Illinois at Shiloh," *Journal of the Illinois State Historical Society,* Vol. 56, No. 2 (Summer 1963). *The Story of the Fifty-Fifth Regiment Illinois Volunteer Infantry in the Civil

War, 1861–1865. Huntington, WV, 1993. Nels Hokanson. *Swedish Immigrants in Lincoln's Time.* New York and London, 1942. Thomas M. Eddy. *The Patriotism of Illinois.* Chicago, IL, 1865. Register of Army Commissions in Hancock's First Army Corps, 1864-65, Record Group 94, Entry 328, National Archives.

William Emery Merrill

2 Lieutenant, U.S. Corps of Engineers, Feb. 20, 1861. 1 Lieutenant, U.S. Corps of Engineers, Aug. 6, 1861. Taken prisoner, Cheat Mountain, WV, Sept. 12, 1861. Confined Richmond, VA. Exchanged Feb. 23, 1862. Shell wound shoulder, Lee's Mill, VA, April 16, 1862. Chief Engineer, Staff of Major Gen. Gordon Granger, Army of Kentucky, Oct. 1862–May 1863. Captain, U.S. Corps of Engineers, March 3, 1863. Chief Topographical Engineer, Staff of Major Gen. William S. Rosecrans, Army of the Cumberland, May 1863–Jan. 1864. Chief Engineer, Staff of Major Gen. George H. Thomas, Army of the Cumberland, Jan.–July 1864 and Sept. 1864–May 1865. Colonel, 1 U.S. Veteran Volunteer Engineers, Aug. 30, 1864. Honorably mustered out as Colonel, Sept. 26, 1865. Bvt. Captain, USA, April 16, 1862, for gallant and meritorious conduct in an engagement with the enemy before Yorktown, VA. Bvt. Major, USA, Sept. 19, 1863, for faithful and meritorious services in the battle of Chickamauga, GA. Bvt. Lieutenant Colonel, USA, March 13, 1865, for faithful and meritorious services in the battles of Lookout Mountain and Missionary Ridge, TN. Bvt. Colonel, USA, March 13, 1865, for faithful and meritorious services in the battles of Resaca and New Hope Church, GA. Battle honors: Peninsular Campaign (Yorktown,

William Emery Merrill (West Point cadet) (U.S. Military Academy Library).

William Emery Merrill (courtesy Henry Deeks).

William Emery Merrill (courtesy Henry Deeks).

William Emery Merrill (Henry Ulke, 278 Pennsylvania Avenue, Washington, D.C.; author's photograph).

Lee's Mill), Cedar Mountain, Second Bull Run, Tullahoma Campaign, Chickamauga, Chattanooga Campaign (Lookout Mountain, Missionary Ridge), Atlanta Campaign (Resaca, New Hope Church).

    Born: Oct. 11, 1837 Fort Howard, Green Bay, WI

    Died: Dec. 14, 1891 aboard train en route to Shawneetown, IL

    Education: Graduated U.S. Military Academy, West Point, NY, 1859

    Occupation: Regular Army (Lieutenant Colonel, U.S. Corps of Engineers, Feb. 20, 1883)

    Miscellaneous: Resided Newport, Campbell Co., KY

    Buried: Arlington National Cemetery, Arlington, VA (Section 1, Site 68-A)

    References: *Twenty-Third Annual Reunion of the Association of the Graduates of the United States Military Academy at West Point, New York.* Saginaw, MI, 1892. Obituary Circular, Whole No. 202, Ohio MOLLUS. *Society of the Army of the Cumberland. Twenty-Third Reunion, Chickamauga, Georgia.* Cincinnati, OH, 1892. George W. Cullum. *Biographical Register of the Officers and Graduates of the U.S. Military Academy at West Point, N.Y.* Third Edition. Boston and New York, 1891. Leland R. Johnson. *The Falls City Engineers: A History of the Louisville District Corps of Engineers, United States Army.* Louisville, KY, 1974. Allen Johnson and Dumas Malone, editors. *Dictionary of American Biography.* New York City, NY, 1964. *The National Cyclopaedia of American Biography.* Vol. 10. New York City, NY, 1900. James Grant Wilson and John Fiske, editors. *Appletons' Cyclopaedia of American Biography.* New York City, NY, 1888. Obituary, *Cincinnati Enquirer,* Dec. 15, 1891. Obituary, *New York Times,* Dec. 15, 1891. Obituary (William E. Merrill), *Army and Navy Journal,* Vol. 29, No. 17 (Dec. 19, 1891). Letters Received, Volunteer Service Branch, Adjutant General's Office, File W2669(VS)1864, National Archives.

James Morgarum Pomeroy

Captain, Co. B, 16 NY Infantry, May 15, 1861. Resigned July 9, 1861, since "a fundamental disagreement exists between myself and the two other commissioned officers of my company, occasioning on their part a failure to yield the cooperation and support indispensable to the thorough discipline and efficiency of my command." Major, 2 KS Cavalry, Feb. 28, 1862. GSW right thigh, Little Santa Fe, MO, March 22, 1862. Major, 9 KS Cavalry, March 27, 1862. Appointed *Colonel,* 4 Indian Home Guards, KS Infantry, Dec. 26, 1862. Declined appointment, April 26, 1863. Regiment did not complete organization. Honorably mustered out, Jan. 16, 1865. Appointed *Colonel,* U.S. Veteran Volunteer Infantry, Feb. 15, 1865. Lieutenant Colonel, 4 U.S. Veteran Volunteer Infantry, July 20, 1865. Honorably mustered out, April 27, 1866. Bvt. Colonel, USV, March 13, 1865, for gallant and meritorious services during the war. Battle honors: Little Santa Fe, Newtonia, Fort Gibson.

Born: Aug. 8, 1836 Belleville, NJ
Died: Nov. 27, 1887 St. Louis, MO
Education: Graduated Wesleyan University, Middletown, CT, 1856
Occupation: Lawyer and author
Offices/Honors: Adjutant General of Arkansas, 1877–79
Miscellaneous: Resided Little Rock, Pulaski Co., AR. Author of several works on the Constitution of the State of Arkansas.
Buried: Jefferson Barracks National Cemetery, St. Louis, MO (Section 59, Grave 11579)

References: *Alumni Record of Wesleyan University, Middletown, Connecticut.* Third Edition, 1881–83. Hartford, CT, 1883. Albert A. Pomeroy. *History and Genealogy of the Pomeroy Family.* Toledo, OH, 1912. *Obituary Record of Alumni of Wesleyan University, for the Academic Year Ending June 28, 1888.* Middletown, CT, 1888. Henry C. Johnson, editor. *The Tenth General Catalogue of the Psi Upsilon Fraternity.* Bethlehem, PA, 1888. Pension File and Military Service File, National Archives. Letters Received, Volunteer Service Branch, Adjutant General's Office, File P97(VS)1864, National Archives. Register of Army Commissions in Hancock's First Army Corps, 1864–65, Record Group 94, Entry 328, National Archives. Obituary, *Daily Arkansas Gazette,* Dec. 4, 1887.

Nathaniel Pendleton Richmond

2 Lieutenant, Co. E, 13 IN Infantry, April 25, 1861. Acting ADC, Staff of Brig. Gen. William S. Rosecrans, July–Aug. 1861. Discharged for promotion, Aug. 20, 1861. Lieutenant Colonel, 1 WV Cavalry, Sept. 7, 1861. Colonel, 1 WV Cavalry, Oct. 16, 1862. Resigned March 18, 1863, on account of physical disability due to "hemorrhoids, with which he has been afflicted for the past twelve months." Colonel, 1 WV Cavalry, June 12, 1863. Commanded 1 Brigade, 3 Division, Cavalry Corps, Army of the Potomac, July 4–9, 1863. Resigned Nov. 11, 1863, due to injuries to right hip and back caused by fall of his horse at Raccoon Ford, VA, Sept. 16, 1863. Colonel, Howard County Regiment, Indiana Legion, April 1, 1864. Appointed *Colonel,* U.S. Veteran Volunteer Infantry, March 6, 1865. Resigned May 29, 1865, since he was "not prepared to pass the examination required in infantry tactics." Battle honors: Kelly's Ford, Second Bull Run, Antietam, Gettysburg Campaign (Gettysburg, Hagerstown, Boonsborough), Raccoon Ford.

Born: July 26, 1833, Indianapolis, IN
Died: June 28, 1919, Malvern, AR
Education: Attended Brown University, Providence, RI
Occupation: Lawyer and farmer
Offices/Honors: Indiana Senate, 1865–1869. Mayor of Kokomo, IN, 1873–79.
Miscellaneous: Resided Kokomo, Howard Co., IN; and Malvern, Hot Spring Co., AR, after 1882
Buried: Oakridge Cemetery, Malvern, AR (Block 5, Lot 14)
References: Kingman Brothers, compilers. *Combination Atlas Map of Howard County, Indiana.* Chicago, IL, 1877. Obituary, *Kokomo Daily Tribune*, July 7, 1919. *A Biographical History of Eminent and Self-Made Men of the State of Indiana.* Cincinnati, OH, 1880. Pension File and Military Service File, National Archives. Letters Received, Volunteer Service Branch, Adjutant General's Office, File R184(VS)1870, National Archives. Rebecca A. Shepherd, Charles W. Calhoun, Elizabeth Shanahan-Shoemaker, and Alan F. January, editors. *A Biographical Directory of the Indiana General Assembly.* Vol. 1, 1816–1899. Indianapolis, IN, 1980. Joshua B. Richmond. *The Richmond Family, 1594–1896.* Boston, MA, 1897. Register of Army Commissions in Hancock's First Army Corps, 1864–65, Record Group 94, Entry 328, National Archives.

Nathaniel Pendleton Richmond (post-war) (author's photograph).

Dudley Wickersham

Lieutenant Colonel, 10 IL Cavalry, Nov. 25, 1861. Colonel, 10 IL Cavalry, May 16, 1862. Commanded 1 Brigade, 3 Division, Army of the Frontier, Department of the Missouri, Dec. 1862. Commanded Post of Fayetteville, AR, Department of the Missouri, Dec. 1862. Commanded 2 Division, Army of the Frontier, Department of the Missouri, March–April 1863. Commanded Cavalry Brigade, 2 Division, Army of the Frontier, Department of the Missouri, June 1863. Suffering from hemorrhoids, he resigned, May 10, 1864, since "the horse back exercise attendant on field duty constantly aggravates the disease." Appointed *Colonel*, U.S. Veteran Volunteer Infantry, Feb. 14, 1865. Major, 3 U.S. Veteran Volunteer Infantry, July 1, 1865. Honorably mustered out, April 30, 1866. Battle honors: Prairie Grove, Advance upon Little Rock (Bayou Meto).

Born: Nov. 21, 1819 Woodford Co., KY
Died: Aug. 8, 1898 Springfield, IL
Other Wars: Mexican War (Sergeant, Co. A, 4 IL Infantry)

Occupation: Dry goods merchant and grocer

Offices/Honors: Assessor of U.S. Internal Revenue for several years after war

Miscellaneous: Resided Springfield, Sangamon Co., IL

Buried: Oak Ridge Cemetery, Springfield, IL (Block 10, Lot 243)

References: Obituary, *Illinois State Journal*, Aug. 9, 1898. *History of Sangamon County, Illinois*. Chicago, IL, 1881. Obituary, *Illinois State Register*, Aug. 9, 1898. *The United States Biographical Dictionary and Portrait Gallery of Eminent and Self-Made Men*. Illinois Volume. Chicago, Cincinnati, and New York, 1876. Newton Bateman and Paul Selby, editors. *Historical Encyclopedia of Illinois and History of Sangamon County*. Chicago, IL, 1912. Thomas M. Eddy. *The Patriotism of Illinois*. Chicago, IL, 1865. Pension File and Military Service File, National Archives. Letters Received, Volunteer Service Branch, Adjutant General's Office, File O787(VS)1865, National Archives. Register of Army Commissions in Hancock's First Army Corps, 1864–65, Record Group 94, Entry 328, National Archives.

Dudley Wickersham (C.S. German, Photographer, National Gallery, Springfield, IL; Abraham Lincoln Presidential Library & Museum).

U.S. Volunteers

Regiments

1st Volunteer Infantry
Charles A.R. Dimon	Aug. 7, 1864	Mustered out Nov. 27, 1865, Bvt. Brig. Gen., USV

2nd Volunteer Infantry
Andrew P. Caraher	Feb. 18, 1865	Mustered out Nov. 7, 1865

3rd Volunteer Infantry
Christopher H. McNally	March 31, 1865	Mustered out Nov. 29, 1865

4th Volunteer Infantry *(regiment not entitled to a colonel since it never attained full strength)*

5th Volunteer Infantry
Henry E. Maynadier	March 27, 1865	Mustered out Aug. 30, 1866, Bvt. Brig. Gen., USV

6th Volunteer Infantry
Carroll H. Potter	March 27, 1865	Mustered out Oct. 10, 1866, Bvt. Brig. Gen., USV

Biographies

Andrew Patrick Caraher

Captain, Co. A, 28 MA Infantry, Dec. 13, 1861. Major, 28 MA Infantry, July 26, 1862. Shell wound head, Fredericksburg, VA, Dec. 13, 1862. GSW right groin, Chancellorsville, VA, May 3, 1863. Honorably mustered out, Sept. 20, 1863. Major, Veteran Reserve Corps, Sept. 21, 1863. Lieutenant Colonel, 4 Veteran Reserve Corps, Sept. 29, 1863. Provost Marshal of Prisoners, Rock Island (IL) Prison, March 1864–Feb. 1865. Colonel, 2 U.S. Volunteer Infantry, Feb. 18, 1865. Commanded Post of Fort Riley (KS), District of the Upper Arkansas, March–April 1865. Commanded Post of Fort Leavenworth (KS), District of North Kansas, Department of the Missouri, June–Aug. 1865. Honorably mustered out as Colonel, Nov. 7, 1865. Honorably mustered out as Lieutenant Colonel, Jan. 6, 1867. Bvt. Captain, USA, March 2, 1867, for gallant and meritorious services in the battle of Fredericksburg, VA. Bvt. Major, USA, March 2, 1867, for gallant and meritorious services in the battle of Gettysburg, PA. Battle honors: Second Bull Run, Chantilly, South Mountain, Antietam, Fredericksburg, Chancellorsville, Gettysburg.

Born: Nov. 25, 1829 County Armagh, Ireland
Died: April 4, 1885 Langtry, Val Verde Co., TX
Occupation: Regular Army (Captain, 8 U.S. Cavalry)

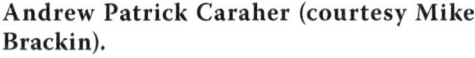

Andrew Patrick Caraher (courtesy Mike Brackin).

Andrew Patrick Caraher (author's photograph).

Miscellaneous: Resided Lynn, Essex Co., MA

Buried: San Antonio National Cemetery, San Antonio, TX (Section A, Grave 57)

References: Obituary, *San Antonio Daily Express*, April 7, 1885. Obituary, *Boston Journal*, April 20, 1885. Obituary, *Boston Herald*, April 19, 1885. Letters Received, Appointment, Commission and Personal Branch, Adjutant General's Office, File 5154(ACP)1874, National Archives. Letters Received, Volunteer Service Branch, Adjutant General's Office, File F136(VS)1866, National Archives. Dee Brown. *The Galvanized Yankees*. Urbana, IL, 1963. Benton McAdams. *Rebels at Rock Island: The Story of a Civil War Prison*. DeKalb, IL, 2000. David P. Conyngham. *The Irish Brigade and Its Campaigns*. Boston, MA, 1869. James L. Bowen. *Massachusetts in the War, 1861-1865*. Springfield, MA, 1889. *Field Record of Officers of the Veteran Reserve Corps from the Commencement to the Close of the Rebellion*. Washington, D.C., 1865. Obituary (Andrew P. Caraher), *Army and Navy Journal*, Vol. 22, No. 38 (April 18, 1885).

Christopher Hely McNally

2 Lieutenant, U.S. Mounted Rifles, May 23, 1855. 1 Lieutenant, U.S. Mounted Rifles, May 5, 1861. GSW left lung, Mesilla, NM, July 25, 1861. Taken prisoner and paroled, Fort Fillmore, NM, July 27, 1861. 1 Lieutenant, 3 U.S. Cavalry, Aug. 3, 1861. Captain, 3 U.S. Cavalry, Sept. 28, 1861. Exchanged, Aug. 27, 1862. Commanded Post of Fort Wayne (MI), Oct.–Nov. 1862. Chief Inspector of Horses and Mules, Department of the Missouri, May 1863–July 1864. Colonel, 3 U.S. Volunteer Infantry, March 31, 1865. Commanded Fort Sedgwick (CO), District of the Plains, Department of

the Missouri, Sept.–Oct. 1865. Honorably mustered out as Colonel, Nov. 29, 1865. Bvt. Captain, USA, July 25, 1861, for gallant and meritorious services in action near Mesilla, New Mexico. Bvt. Major, USA, March 13, 1865, for meritorious services during the war. Battle honors: Mesilla.

Born: June 1820 Middlesex, England

Died: Feb. 14, 1889 East Orange, NJ

Occupation: Regular Army (Captain, 3 U.S. Cavalry, retired Dec. 24, 1866)

Miscellaneous: Resided Roslyn, Nassau Co., NY; and East Orange, Essex Co., NJ

Buried: Holy Sepulchre Cemetery, East Orange, NJ (Section K, Block 370, Plot 5)

References: Pension File and Military Service File, National Archives. Letters Received, Commission Branch, Adjutant General's Office, File M201(CB)1868, National Archives. Letters Received, Volunteer Service Branch, Adjutant General's Office, File M1576(VS)1865, National Archives. Guy V. Henry. *Military Record of Civilian Appointments in the United States Army.* Vol. 1. New York City, NY, 1869. Dee Brown. *The Galvanized Yankees.* Urbana, IL, 1963. Benton McAdams. *Rebels at Rock Island: The Story of a Civil War Prison.* DeKalb, IL, 2000. Death notice, *New York Herald,* Feb. 17, 1889. www.crossedsabers.blogspot.com/2012/05/fiddlers-green-christopher-h-mcnally.html.

Veteran Reserve Corps

Regiments

1st Regiment
Richard H. Rush   Oct. 1, 1863   Resigned July 1, 1864
John R. Lewis   Sept. 8, 1864   Mustered out March 31, 1867,
                                                     Bvt. Brig. Gen., USV

2nd Regiment
George N. Morgan   Dec. 10, 1863   Mustered out Feb. 12, 1866,
                                                     Bvt. Brig. Gen., USV

3rd Regiment
Frederick D. Sewall   Sept. 25, 1863   Mustered out Jan. 1, 1868,
                                                     Bvt. Brig. Gen., USV

4th Regiment
Adolphus J. Johnson   Sept. 28, 1863   Mustered out July 10, 1866

5th Regiment
Ambrose A. Stevens   Sept. 25, 1863   Mustered out Nov. 23, 1865,
                                                     Bvt. Brig. Gen., USV

6th Regiment
Moses N. Wisewell   Sept. 25, 1863   Resigned Oct. 1, 1865,
                                                     Bvt. Brig. Gen., USV

7th Regiment
Absalom Y. Johnson   Sept. 25, 1863   Resigned June 18, 1864
Edward P. Fyffe   June 18, 1864   Mustered out Aug. 20, 1866,
                                                     Bvt. Brig. Gen., USV

8th Regiment
Benjamin J. Sweet   Sept. 25, 1863   Resigned Sept. 19, 1865,
                                                     Bvt. Brig. Gen., USV

9th Regiment
George W. Gile   Sept. 29, 1863   Mustered out Jan. 4, 1867,
                                                     Bvt. Brig. Gen., USV

10th Regiment
David P. DeWitt   Sept. 29, 1863   Mustered out June 6, 1866,
                                                     Bvt. Brig. Gen., USV

11th Regiment
Benjamin S. Porter   Sept. 29, 1863   Resigned Feb. 15, 1864
John Egbert Farnum   July 26, 1864   Mustered out June 30, 1866,
                                                     Bvt. Brig. Gen., USV

12th Regiment
Addison Farnsworth   Sept. 29, 1863   Resigned Dec. 10, 1864,
                                                     Bvt. Brig. Gen., USV

John Mansfield   Dec. 3, 1864   Mustered out Nov. 20, 1866,
                                                     Bvt. Brig. Gen., USV

13th Regiment
John Hendrickson	Oct. 5, 1863	Mustered out June 30, 1866, Bvt. Brig. Gen., USV

14th Regiment
Frank P. Cahill	Sept. 30, 1863	To 20 Veteran Reserve Corps, Jan. 12, 1864
Samuel D. Oliphant	Dec. 4, 1863	Mustered out June 30, 1866, Bvt. Brig. Gen., USV

15th Regiment
James C. Strong	Sept. 29, 1863	Discharged July 7, 1866, Bvt. Brig. Gen., USV

16th Regiment
Charles M. Prevost	Sept. 29, 1863	Discharged June 30, 1866, Bvt. Brig. Gen., USV

17th Regiment
Adoniram J. Warner	Nov. 15, 1863	Mustered out Nov. 17, 1865, Bvt. Brig. Gen., USV

18th Regiment
Charles F. Johnson	Dec. 7, 1863	Died July 28, 1867

19th Regiment
Oscar V. Dayton	Dec. 4, 1863	Mustered out Aug. 20, 1866, Bvt. Brig. Gen., USV

20th Regiment
Frank P. Cahill	Jan. 12, 1864	To 24 Veteran Reserve Corps, Feb. 9, 1864
Noah L. Jeffries	Feb. 12, 1864	Mustered out Aug. 26, 1866, Bvt. Brig. Gen., USV

21st Regiment
John Ely	Dec. 14, 1863	Mustered out Oct. 31, 1867, Bvt. Brig. Gen., USV

22nd Regiment
George A. Woodward	Dec. 4, 1863	Mustered out July 20, 1866

23rd Regiment
William H. Browne	Dec. 19, 1863	To 24 Veteran Reserve Corps, April 5, 1864
Frank P. Cahill	April 5, 1864	Mustered out Dec. 1, 1865

24th Regiment
Frank P. Cahill	Feb. 9, 1864	To 23 Veteran Reserve corps, April 5, 1864
William H. Browne	April 5, 1864	Mustered out June 30, 1866, Bvt. Brig. Gen., USV

Biographies

Frank Patrick Cahill

Captain, Co. H, 1 KY Infantry, June 6, 1861. Major, 1 KY Infantry, Jan. 22, 1862. GSW left foot, Shiloh, TN, April 7, 1862. Lieutenant Colonel, 1 KY Infantry, Nov. 6, 1862. Resigned Aug. 17, 1863, "on account of ill health." Major, Veteran Reserve Corps, Aug. 17, 1863. Colonel, 14 Veteran Reserve Corps, Sept. 30, 1863. Colonel, 20 Veteran Reserve Corps, Jan. 12, 1864. Colonel, 24 Veteran Reserve Corps, Feb. 9, 1864. Colonel, 23 Veteran Reserve Corps, April 5, 1864. Commanded Veteran Reserve Corps, Post of Nashville (TN), Nov. 1864–April 1865. Commanded District of Wisconsin, Department of the Northwest, June–July 1865. Acting Assistant Provost Marshal

General, State of Minnesota, Aug.–Nov. 1865. Honorably mustered out, Dec. 1, 1865. Battle honors: Shiloh, Siege of Corinth.

Born: April 29, 1832, Thurles, Ireland

Died: April 27, 1879, Edgefield, near Nashville, TN

Occupation: Journalist and hotelkeeper before war. Lawyer and insurance agent after war.

Offices/Honors: Tennessee Senate, 1877–79

Miscellaneous: Resided Cincinnati, Hamilton Co., OH, before war; and Nashville, Davidson Co., TN, after war

Buried: Mount Olivet Cemetery, Nashville, TN (Section 1, Lot 124, unmarked)

References: Obituary, *Nashville Daily American*, April 29, 1879. Obituary, *Cincinnati Daily Gazette*, April 30, 1879. Pension File and Military Service File, National Archives. Letters Received, Volunteer Service Branch, Adjutant General's Office, File P2116(VS)1864, National Archives. Robert M. McBride and Dan M. Robison. *Biographical Directory of the Tennessee General Assembly.* Vol. 2, 1861–1901. Nashville, TN, 1979. James D. Richardson. *Tennessee Templars: A Register of Names with Biographical Sketches of the Knights Templar of Tennessee.* Nashville, TN, 1883. "War Matters," *Cincinnati Daily Press,* May 15, 1861. "The First and Second Kentucky Regiments in the Pittsburg Battle," *Cincinnati Enquirer,* April 16, 1862. "The State Senate—Col. Frank Cahill," *Nashville Daily American,* Sept. 16, 1876.

Frank Patrick Cahill (Massachusetts MOLLUS Collection, USAHEC [Vol. 98, p. 5011]).

Absalom Yarborough Johnson

Lieutenant Colonel, 28 KY Infantry, Nov. 6, 1861. Taken prisoner and paroled, Lebanon, KY, July 12, 1862. Exchanged Sept. 16, 1862. Resigned March 14, 1863, being unfit for duty due to direct inguinal hernia on both sides. Major, 7 Veteran Reserve Corps, Aug. 13, 1863. Colonel, 7 Veteran Reserve Corps, Sept. 25, 1863. Resigned June 18, 1864. Battle honors: Morgan's First Kentucky Raid.

Born: Dec. 24, 1821 Lynchburg, VA

Died: March 12, 1907 Louisville, KY

Occupation: Coach maker before war. U.S. Internal Revenue gauger after war.

Miscellaneous: Resided Louisville, Jefferson Co., KY. Organized the Louisville Fire Department in 1858 and served as its first Chief Engineer.

Buried: Cave Hill Cemetery, Louisville, KY (Section O, Lot 328)

References: Obituary, *Louisville Courier-Journal,* March 13, 1907. Pension File and Military Service File, National Archives. Letters Received, Volunteer Service Branch, Adjutant General's Office, File J116(VS)1868, National Archives. Thomas Speed, Robert M. Kelly, and Alfred Pirtle. *The Union Regiments of Kentucky.* Louisville, KY, 1897. James J. Holmberg, "Browsing in OurArchives: Louisville Fire Fighting," *The Filson,* Vol. 11, No. 2 (Summer 2011).

Adolphus James Johnson

Colonel, 1 NJ Militia, April 30, 1861. Honorably mustered out, July 31, 1861. Colonel, 8 NJ Infantry, Sept. 14, 1861. GSW entering left side abdomen and exiting right side, Williamsburg, VA, May 5, 1862. Resigned March 19, 1863, on account of disability arising from his wounds. Major, Veteran Reserve Corps, July 16, 1863. Colonel, 4 Veteran Reserve Corps, Sept. 28, 1863. Commanded Rock Island (IL) Prison, Jan. 1864–July 1865. Commanded Camp Butler, Springfield, IL, Nov. 1865–June 1866. Honorably mustered out, July 10, 1866. Battle honors: Peninsular Campaign (Williamsburg).

Born: March 26, 1816, Newark, NJ

Died: May 29, 1893, Newark, NJ

Occupation: Barber and hatter before war. Warden of Essex Co. (NJ) Jail, 1866–88.

Miscellaneous: Resided Newark, Essex Co., NJ. Active in pre-war militia, serving as Captain, Co. D (City Blues), 12 NY State Militia, in 1850.

Buried: Evergreen Cemetery, Hillside, NJ (Section O, Lot 15)

References: Obituary, *Newark Daily Advertiser,* May 30, 1893. Pension File and Military Service File, National Archives. Obituary, *New York Herald,* May 31, 1893. Obituary, *New York Sun,* May 31, 1893. Joseph Atkinson. *The History of Newark, New Jersey.* Newark, NJ, 1878. Benton McAdams. *Rebels at Rock Island.* DeKalb, IL, 2000. *Report Annual Reunion and Dinner of the Old Guard*

Adolphus James Johnson (J. Gurney & Son, Photographic Artists, 707 Broadway, New York; author's photograph).

Association, 12th Regiment, N.G.S. N.Y. New York City, NY, 1894. Letters Received, Volunteer Service Branch, Adjutant General's Office, File J115(VS)1862, National Archives.

Charles Francis Johnson

Lieutenant Colonel, 81 PA Infantry, Sept. 16, 1861. Colonel, 81 PA Infantry, June 1, 1862. GSW both thighs and groin, Glendale, VA, June 30, 1862. Resigned Nov. 24, 1862, on account of physical disability from "sympathetic inflammation of the spermatic cord," caused by his wounds. Major, Veteran Reserve Corps, June 5, 1863. Lieutenant Colonel, 16 Veteran Reserve Corps, Sept. 29, 1863. Colonel, 18 Veteran Reserve Corps, Dec. 7, 1863. Commanded 2 Provisional Brigade, Garrison of Washington, D.C., Aug. 1865. Battle honors: Peninsular Campaign (Fair Oaks, Glendale).
Born: Sept. 22, 1827 Philadelphia, PA
Died: July 28, 1867 Bowling Green, KY (chronic diarrhea and cystitis)
Occupation: Clerk and engraver
Miscellaneous: Resided Philadelphia, PA; and Camden, Camden Co., NJ
Buried: Fairview Cemetery, Bowling Green, KY
References: Fred Pelka, editor. *The Civil War Letters of Colonel Charles F. Johnson, Invalid Corps.* Amherst and Boston, 2004. Pension File and Military Service File, National Archives. Obituary, *Louisville Daily Journal,* Aug. 2, 1867. Death notice, *Philadelphia Public Ledger,* Aug. 3, 1867. Charles F. Johnson Papers, U.S. Army Heritage & Education Center. Letters Received, Volunteer Service Branch, Adjutant General's Office, File J356(VS)1865, National Archives. George C. Groce and David H. Wallace. *The New-York Historical Society's Dictionary of Artists in America, 1564–1860.* New Haven, CT, 1957. *Field Record of Officers of the Veteran*

Charles Francis Johnson (Charles G. Crane, No. 532 Arch Street, Philadelphia, PA; USAHEC [RG98S-CWP68.76]).

Charles Francis Johnson (M.M. Griswold, Photographer, Johnson Building, Columbus, OH; author's photograph).

Reserve Corps from the Commencement to the Close of the Rebellion. Washington, D.C., 1865.

Benjamin Sabin Porter

Captain, Co. B, 49 OH Infantry, Aug. 17, 1861. Major, 49 OH Infantry, Sept. 30, 1862. GSW left shoulder, Stone's River, TN, Dec. 31, 1862. Taken prisoner and paroled, Murfreesboro, TN, Jan. 1, 1863. Lieutenant Colonel, 49 OH Infantry, Jan. 24, 1863. Major, Veteran Reserve Corps, July 18, 1863. Colonel, 11 Veteran Reserve Corps, Sept. 29, 1863. Commissary of Prisoners, Rock Island (IL) Prison, Jan. 1864. Resigned Feb. 15, 1864. Battle honors: Shiloh, Stone's River.

Born: Jan. 26, 1828 Ithaca, NY
Died: March 18, 1905 Council Bluffs, IA
Other Wars: Mexican War (Corporal, Co. F, 1 OH Volunteers)
Occupation: Carriage maker
Miscellaneous: Resided Green Springs, Seneca Co., OH, before war; Peru, LaSalle Co., IL (1870); Ottawa, LaSalle Co., IL (1880); Red Oak, Montgomery Co., IA; and Council Bluffs, Pottawattamie Co., IA, 1888–1905
Buried: Evergreen Cemetery, Red Oak, IA (Red Oak Junction Section, Lot 605)
References: Obituary, *Red Oak*

Benjamin Sabin Porter (USAHEC [RG98S-CWP37.85]).

Benjamin Sabin Porter (C.C. Doty, No. 3 Union Block, Water St., Elmira, NY; author's photograph).

Richard Henry Rush (author's photograph).

Richard Henry Rush (F. Gutekunst, Photographer, 704 & 706 Arch Street, Philadelphia, PA; Ken Turner Collection).

Express, March 24, 1905. Obituary, *Council Bluffs Daily Nonpareil*, March 19, 1905. Pension File and Military Service File, National Archives. Letters Received, Volunteer Service Branch, Adjutant General's Office, File G758(VS)1863, National Archives. *History of Seneca County, Ohio*. Chicago, IL, 1886.

Richard Henry Rush

Colonel, 6 PA Cavalry, Oct. 5, 1861. Commanded 3 Brigade, Pleasanton's Cavalry Division, Army of the Potomac, Sept.–Nov. 1862. Detailed as Assistant to the Provost Marshal General, in charge of the organization of the Veteran Reserve Corps, May 10, 1863. Resigned Sept. 29, 1863, to accept appointment in Veteran Reserve Corps. Colonel, 1 Veteran Reserve Corps, Oct. 1, 1863. Commanded Rock Island (IL) Prison, Nov.–Dec. 1863. Commanded 1 Brigade, Veteran Reserve Corps, District of Washington, 22 Army Corps, Department of Washington, March–May 1864. Resigned July 1, 1864. Battle honors: Peninsular Campaign (Hanover Court House, Gaines' Mill, White Oak Swamp), South Mountain, Antietam.

Born: Jan. 14, 1825 London, England
Died: Oct. 17, 1893 Philadelphia, PA
Education: Graduated U.S. Military Academy, West Point, NY, 1846
Other Wars: Mexican War (1 Lieutenant, 2 U.S. Artillery)
Occupation: Regular Army (1 Lieutenant, 2 U.S. Artillery, resigned July 1, 1854). Gentleman of leisure.
Miscellaneous: Resided Philadelphia, PA. Descended from two Signers of the Declaration of Independence, being the grandson of Benjamin Rush, who married

the daughter of Richard Stockton.

Buried: Laurel Hill Cemetery, Philadelphia, PA (Section P, Lots 37/40)

References: *Twenty-Fifth Annual Reunion of the Association of the Graduates of the United States Military Academy at West Point, New York.* Saginaw, MI, 1894. Frederick W. Pyne. *Descendants of the Signers of the Declaration of Independence.* Camden, ME, 1998. Obituary, *Philadelphia Times,* Oct. 19, 1893. Obituary, *Philadelphia Public Ledger,* Oct. 18, 1893. Letters Received, Volunteer Service Branch, Adjutant General's Office, File P615(VS)1863, National Archives. Samuel L. Gracey. *Annals of the Sixth Pennsylvania Cavalry.* Philadelphia, PA, 1868. George W. Cullum. *Biographical Register of the Officers and Graduates of the U.S. Military Academy at West Point, N.Y.* Third Edition. Boston and New York, 1891. Military Service File, National Archives.

Richard Henry Rush (Broadbent & Co., 814 Chestnut Street, Philadelphia, PA; Ronn Palm Collection).

George Abisha Woodward

Captain, Co. A, 2 PA Reserves, Aug. 1, 1861. Major, 2 PA Reserves, April 2, 1862. Lieutenant Colonel, 2 PA Reserves, June 30, 1862. GSW right foot and left leg, Glendale, VA, June 30, 1862. Taken prisoner, Glendale, VA, June 30, 1862. Confined Libby Prison, Richmond, VA. Paroled July 17, 1862. Exchanged Aug. 27, 1862. Major, Veteran Reserve Corps, Aug. 24, 1863. Lieutenant Colonel, 9 Veteran Reserve Corps, Sept. 25, 1863. Colonel, 22 Veteran Reserve Corps, Dec. 4, 1863. Honorably mustered out, July 20, 1866. Bvt. Colonel, USA, March 2, 1867, for gallant and meritorious services in the battle of Gettysburg, PA. Battle honors: Peninsular Campaign (Mechanicsville, Gaines' Mill, Glendale), Gettysburg.

Born: Feb. 14, 1835 Wilkes-Barre, PA
Died: Dec. 22, 1916 Washington, D.C.

George Abisha Woodward (W. Ogilvie, Successor to S. S. Hull, Photographer, No. 14 Public Square, Wilkes-Barre, PA: Gil Barrett Collection).

George Abisha Woodward (post-war) (*Companions of the Military Order of the Loyal Legion of the United States*. Second Edition. New York City, NY, 1901).

Education: Graduated Trinity College, Hartford, CT, 1855

Occupation: Lawyer before war. Regular Army (Colonel 15 U.S. Infantry, retired March 20, 1879; Brigadier Gen., USA, retired April 23, 1904).

Miscellaneous: Resided Milwaukee, WI, before war; Philadelphia, PA; and Washington, D.C., after 1887

Buried: Arlington National Cemetery, Arlington, VA (Section 1, Site 54-B)

References: William H. Powell and Edward Shippen, editors. *Officers of the Army and Navy (Regular) Who Served in the Civil War.* Philadelphia, PA, 1892. *The National Cyclopaedia of American Biography.* Vol. 10. New York City, NY, 1909. Obituary, *Washington Evening Star,* Dec. 23, 1916. Obituary, *Washington Post,* Dec. 23, 1916. Obituary, *New York Times,* Dec. 23, 1916. Norma S. Woodward. *Descendants of Richard Woodward, New England, 1589–1982.* Baltimore, MD, 1982. Military Service File, National Archives. Evan M. Woodward. *Our Campaigns; or, the Marches, Bivouacs, Battles, Incidents of Camp Life and History of Our Regiment During Its Three Years Term of Service.* Philadelphia, PA, 1865. Josiah R. Sypher. *History of the Pennsylvania Reserve Corps.* Lancaster, PA, 1865.

Aides-de-Camp

Anselme I. Albert	March 31, 1862	Resigned June 8, 1864
James Belger	July 11, 1862	Dismissed Nov. 30, 1863
Tristam Burges	May 1862	Dec. 1862
Speed Butler	June 30, 1862	Resigned Aug. 22, 1864
Le Grand B. Cannon	Feb. 1, 1862	Resigned June 11, 1862
George W. Coolbaugh	Oct. 1862	Sept. 1863
Philip Daum	May 26, 1862	Dismissed April 7, 1863
John H. Devereux	March 1862	Resigned March 20, 1864
John V.D. DuBois	Feb. 19, 1862	Mustered out Feb. 9, 1866
Charles Ellet, Jr.	April 28, 1862	DOW June 21, 1862
John T. Fiala	March 31, 1862	Resigned June 8, 1864
Philip Figyelmesy	March 31, 1862	Resigned Dec. 20, 1864
Thomas T. Gantt	Aug. 26, 1861	Resigned July 5, 1862
John A. Gurley	Aug. 6, 1861	Resigned Oct. 1, 1861
Alexander Hamilton, Jr.	April 24, 1861	July 18, 1863
Charles F. Havelock	Nov. 23, 1861	Resigned July 31, 1863
Robert N. Hudson	March 31, 1862	Resigned Aug. 26, 1863
Amos B. Jones	May 31, 1862	Dismissed May 8, 1865
Thomas M. Key	Aug. 19, 1861	Discharged March 31, 1863
Gustavus Koerner	Sept. 28, 1861	Discharged Nov. 2, 1861
Owen Lovejoy	Sept. 25, 1861	Nov. 4, 1861
John N. Macomb	May 15, 1862	Mustered out May 31, 1866
Louis H. Marshall	June 30, 1862	Discharged July 28, 1865
Joseph C. McKibbin	Nov. 29, 1861	Resigned Jan. 29, 1864
William H. Merritt	Jan. 29, 1862	Discharged March 21, 1862
Christopher A. Morgan	June 30, 1862	Died Jan. 20, 1866
George G. Pride	Feb. 1862	April 1863
George L. Schuyler	April 24, 1861	July 18, 1863
John G. Stephenson	Nov. 27, 1861	July 1863
Albert Tracy	March 31, 1862	Mustered out Nov. 25, 1863
Benjamin Welch, Jr.	July 11, 1862	Sept. 1862
Edward H. Wright	Aug. 19, 1861	Discharged March 31, 1863
Charles Zagonyi	March 31, 1862	Resigned June 4, 1864

Biographies

Anselme Ignacz Albert

Captain, Co. A, 3 MO Infantry (3 months), May 8, 1861. Lieutenant Colonel, 3 MO Infantry, July 16, 1861. GSW hip, Wilson's Creek, MO, Aug. 10, 1861. Taken prisoner, Wilson's Creek, MO, Aug. 10, 1861. Paroled Aug. 20, 1861. Honorably mustered out, Aug. 22, 1861. Colonel, ADC, Staff of Major Gen. John C. Fremont, Western Department, Sept.–Oct. 1861. Commanded 1 Brigade, 4 Division, Southwestern District of Missouri, Department of the Missouri, October 1861–Jan. 1862. Chief of Staff to Brig. Gen. Franz Sigel, 1 and 2 Divisions, Southwestern District of Missouri, Department of the Missouri. Colonel, Additional ADC, USA, March 31, 1862. Chief of Staff to Major Gen. John C. Fremont, Mountain Department, March–June 1862. Nominated as Brig. Gen., USV, April 28, 1862. Nomination tabled by U.S. Senate, July 16, 1862. Resigned June 8, 1864. Battle honors: Carthage, Wilson's Creek, Operations in the Shenandoah Valley (Cross Keys).

Born: Dec. 1819 Budapest, Hungary

Died: Nov. 20, 1893 St. Louis, MO

Other Wars: Major in Hungarian revolutionary army of 1848–49

Occupation: Bookkeeper before war. Banker, journalist, interpreter, and district assessor after war.

Miscellaneous: Resided St. Louis, MO

Buried: St. Matthew Cemetery, St. Louis, MO (Block 7, Lot 151)

References: Edmund Vasvary. *Lincoln's Hungarian Heroes: The Participation of Hungarians in the Civil War, 1861–1865.* Washington, D.C., 1939. Obituary, *St. Louis Globe-Democrat,* Nov. 21, 1893. Obituary, *St. Louis Republic,* Nov. 21, 1893. Istvan Kornel Vida. *Hungarian Émigrés in the American Civil War: A History and Biographical Dictionary.* Jefferson, NC, 2012. Stephen Beszedits, "Hungarians with General John C. Fremont in the American Civil War," *Vasvary Collection Newsletter,* (2003, No. 2). Pension File and Military Service File, National Archives. Letters Received, Commission Branch, Adjutant General's Office, File A225(CB)1864, National Archives. Correspondence Concerning Fremont's Appointments, 1861–1864, Record Group 94, Entry 164, National Archives. Pamela Herr and Mary Lee Spence, editors.

Anselme Ignacz Albert (courtesy Henry Deeks).

The Letters of Jessie Benton Fremont. Urbana, IL, 1993. Al Benson, Jr., and Walter D. Kennedy. *Lincoln's Marxists.* Gretna, LA, 2011. Carded Records Relating to Staff Officers, National Archives.

James Belger

Captain, AQM, USA, June 18, 1846. Chief Quartermaster, Department of Washington, April 1861. Chief Quartermaster, Department of Pennsylvania, May–Aug. 1861. Major, Quartermaster's Department, USA, Aug. 3, 1861. Chief Quartermaster, Dix's Division, Army of the Potomac, Nov. 1861–March 1862. Chief Quartermaster, Middle Department, March–July 1862. Colonel, Additional ADC, USA, July 11, 1862. Chief Quartermaster, 8 Army Corps and Middle Department, July 1862–March 1863. Although acquitted by General Court Martial of "neglect and violation of duty to the prejudice of good order and military discipline" in purchasing supplies and chartering vessels at higher rates than the cash market price, he was dishonorably dismissed, Nov. 30, 1863, when the proceedings of the court were disapproved by Secretary of War Stanton, since "the evidence fully establishes that Colonel Belger is guilty of gross neglect and violation of duty." President Andrew Johnson revoked the dismissal, Nov. 11, 1867, but Attorney General Orville Browning ruled that the President did not have the authority to overturn a dismissal. He was finally restored to the rank of major and quartermaster in the U.S. Army, by Act of Congress, March 3, 1871.

Born: Aug. 7, 1816 Sackets Harbor, NY

Died: Dec. 10, 1891 New York City, NY

Other Wars: Mexican War (Captain, AQM, USA. Bvt. Major, USA, May 30, 1848, for meritorious conduct particularly in the performance of his duty in the prosecution of the War with Mexico.)

Occupation: Supervisor of Internal Revenue for the State of Texas, 1868–69. Regular Army (Major, Quartermaster's Department, retired June 19, 1879).

Miscellaneous: Resided Washington, D.C.; Atlanta, GA; and New York City, NY. Brother-in-law of noted Confederate officers John Robert Baylor and George Wythe Baylor.

Buried: Post Cemetery, West Point, NY (Section 25, Row A, Grave 13)

References: Letters Received, Commission Branch, Adjutant General's Office, File B2273(CB)1867, National Archives. Pension File, National Archives. Court-martial Case Files, 1809–1894, File NN-0784, National Archives. "Appointment to Texas," *New Orleans Daily Picayune*, Dec. 31, 1868. "A Veteran Officer," *Atlanta Constitution*, June 19, 1884. Orval Walker Baylor and Henry Bedinger Baylor, editors. *Baylor's History of the Baylors: A Collection of Records and Important Family Data.* Le Roy, IL, 1914. Carded Records Relating to Staff Officers, National Archives.

Tristam Burges

Colonel, Volunteer ADC, Staff of Brig. Gen. George Stoneman, Chief of Cavalry, Army of the Potomac, May–Dec. 1862. Shell wound thigh, Williamsburg, VA, May 4, 1862. Battle honors: Peninsular Campaign (Williamsburg).

Born: July 24, 1817, MA

Died: May 23, 1863, East Providence, RI

Education: Attended Brown University, Providence, RI

Occupation: Lawyer and farmer

Offices/Honors: Rhode Island Senate, 1862–63

Miscellaneous: Resided Seekonk, Bristol Co., MA; and Providence, Providence Co., RI

Buried: North Burial Ground, Providence, RI (Section 6, Lot 700)

References: Ebenezer Burgess. *Burgess Genealogy: Memorial of the Family of Thomas and Dorothy Burgess, Who Were Settled at Sandwich, in the Plymouth Colony in 1637.* Boston, MA, 1865. Obituary, *Providence Daily Post,* May 25, 1863. Obituary, *Providence Evening Press,* May 23, 1863. Horace S. Foote, editor. *Pen Pictures from the Garden of the World, or Santa Clara County, California.* Chicago, IL, 1888.

Tristam Burges (Massachusetts MOLLUS Collection, USAHEC [Vol. 72, p. 3561]).

Speed Butler

Captain, Commissary of Subsistence, USV, Aug. 3, 1861. Acting AAG, Staff of Brig. Gen. John Pope, District of North Missouri, July–Aug. 1861. Major, 5 IL Cavalry, Sept. 1, 1861. Major, Acting AAG, Staff of Major Gen. John Pope, Army of the Mississippi, Feb.–June 1862. Colonel, Additional ADC, June 30, 1862. ADC, Staff of Major Gen. John Pope, Army of Virginia, June–Aug. 1862. ADC, Staff of Major Gen. John Pope, Department of the Northwest, Sept. 1862–Aug. 1864. Resigned Aug. 22, 1864. Battle honors: New Madrid, Island No. 10, Farmington, 2nd Bull Run.

Born: Aug. 7, 1837 Springfield, IL

Died: April 8, 1885 Springfield, IL

Education: Attended Lutheran College, Springfield, IL

Occupation: Lawyer before war. Grocer and broker after war. Engaged in coal mining and manufacturing pursuits in later years.

Miscellaneous: Resided Springfield, Sangamon Co., IL

Buried: Oak Ridge Cemetery, Springfield, IL (Block 7, Lot 113)

References: John C. Power. *History of the Early Settlers of Sangamon County, Illinois.* Springfield, IL, 1876. Obituary, *Daily Illinois State Journal,* April 9, 1885. Obituary, *Daily Illinois State Register,* April 9, 1885. *History of Sangamon County, Illinois.* Chicago, IL, 1881. Pension File and Military Service File, National Archives. Letters Received, Commission Branch, Adjutant General's Office, File B1179(CB)1864, National Archives.

Le Grand Bouton Cannon

Volunteer ADC, Staff of Brig. Gen. John E. Wool, Department of the East, April–Aug. 1861. Major, Additional ADC, Aug. 28, 1861. ADC, Staff of Major Gen. John E. Wool, Department of Virginia, Aug. 1861–June 1862. Colonel, Additional ADC, Feb. 1, 1862. Resigned June 11, 1862, due to "Mrs. Cannon's frail condition and also my own impaired health."

Le Grand Bouton Cannon (Johnston Bros., 867 & 869 Broadway, Near 18th St., New York; courtesy Everitt Bowles).

Born: Nov. 1, 1815 New York City, NY
Died: Nov. 3, 1906 Burlington, VT
Education: Attended Rensselaer Polytechnic Institute, Troy, NY
Occupation: Engaged in iron industry and dry goods business before war. Railroad promoter and capitalist after war.
Miscellaneous: Resided Troy, Rensselaer Co., NY; New York City, NY; and Burlington, Chittenden Co., VT
Buried: Oakwood Cemetery, Troy, NY (Section I-1, Lot 36)
References: *American Biography: A New Cyclopedia.* Vol. 3. New York City, NY, 1918. Hiram Carleton, editor. *Genealogical and Family History of the State of Vermont.* New York and Chicago, 1903. Obituary Circular, Whole No. 903, New York MOLLUS. Obituary, *Burlington Free Press,* Nov. 5, 1906. Obituary, *New York Times,* Nov. 4, 1906. Obituary, *Troy Times,* Nov. 3, 1906. Le Grand B. Cannon. *Personal Reminiscences of the Rebellion, 1861–1866.* New York City, NY, 1895. Letters Received, Adjutant General's Office, File C668(AGO)1861, National Archives. Henry B. Nason, editor. *Biographical Record of the Officers and Graduates of the Rensselaer Polytechnic Institute, 1824–1886.* Troy, NY, 1887.

Le Grand Bouton Cannon (Johnston Bros., 867 Broadway, New York; author's photograph).

George W. Coolbaugh

Colonel, Volunteer ADC, and Superintendent of Military Railroads, Staff of Major Gen. James B. McPherson, 17 Army Corps, Army of the Tennessee, Oct. 1862–Sept. 1863. With Lt. Col. William E. Strong, he raised the flag over the Vicksburg (MS) Court House after the surrender of Vicksburg. Battle honors: Corinth, Expedition on the Big Black River toward Canton, MS (Robinson's Mills).

Born: July 28, 1834 Monroe Co., PA
Died: Jan. 21, 1883 San Antonio, TX
Occupation: Civil engineer
Miscellaneous: Resided Middle

George W. Coolbaugh ("Specialite," Hoag & Quick's Art Palace, No. 100 4th St., opp. Post Office, Cincinnati, Ohio; author's photograph).

George W. Coolbaugh (Barr & Young, Army Photographers, Fort Pickering, Memphis, Tennessee; author's photograph).

George W. Coolbaugh (Outley's Photographic Palace of Art, 39 4th St., Opposite Planters' House, St. Louis, MO; author's photograph).

George W. Coolbaugh (Outley's Photographic Palace of Art, 39 4th St., Opposite Planters' House, St. Louis, MO; author's photograph).

Smithfield Twp., Monroe Co., PA; St. Louis, MO; Arkansas; Colorado; Laredo, Webb Co., TX; Monterey, Mexico; and San Antonio, Bexar Co., TX. Upon leaving his staff position with Gen. McPherson, he began a long shameful career as an adventurer and swindler, accepting large sums of money while masquerading as a Major General in the Mexican Liberal Army in 1864–65, and serving a lengthy term in an Arkansas prison in the 1870s for mail fraud. His shameful conduct was reported to be a contributing factor in the suicide of his brother, William F. Coolbaugh, a well-known Chicago banker, in 1877.

Buried: San Antonio National Cemetery, San Antonio, TX (Section C, Grave 371)

References: Edward C. Hoagland. *The Coolbaugh Family in America.* Towanda, PA, 1938. John Y. Simon, editor. *The Papers of Ulysses S. Grant.* Vol. 10: January 1–May 31, 1864. Carbondale, IL, 1982. James Harrison Wilson. *Under the Old Flag.* New York and London, 1912. Obituary, *San Antonio Daily Express,* Jan. 23, 1883. Obituary, *San Antonio Evening Light,* Jan. 22, 1883. Obituary, *Leavenworth Standard,* Jan. 24, 1883. "General Coolbaugh, the Mexican Filibustero," *Daily Missouri Democrat,* Sept. 22, 1864. "Extraordinary Case of Swindling," *New York World,* May 27, 1865. "Arrest of General Coolbaugh," *Daily Missouri Democrat,* Feb. 3, 1866. "More About Gen. Coolbaugh," *Daily Missouri Democrat,* Feb. 5, 1866. "Arrest of General Coolbaugh," *New York Daily Herald,* Feb. 16, 1866. "A Distinguished Visitor," *Harrisburg Telegraph,* Aug. 25, 1866. "A Bogus Special Mail Agent in Colorado," *Wilmington Morning Star,* May 14, 1868. "Particulars of the Coolbaugh Suicide: The Skeleton in the Closet," *Decatur Weekly Republican,* Nov. 22. 1877.

Philip Daum

Captain, Battery A, 1 WV Light Artillery, June 28, 1861. *Lieutenant Colonel,* 1 WV Light Artillery, Feb. 4, 1862. Chief of Artillery, Staff of Brig. Gen. James Shields, 1 Division, Department of the Rappahannock, March–June 1862. Colonel, Additional ADC, May 26, 1862. Dismissed April 7, 1863, for "attempting to defraud the Government by the presentation of false vouchers." Battle honors: Campaign in West Virginia (Scary Creek), Greenbrier River, Kernstown, Port Republic.

Born: 1829? Prussia
Died: Nov. 14, 1902 Brooklyn, NY?
Other Wars: Prussian army service
Occupation: Tailor?
Miscellaneous: Resided New York City, NY; and Brooklyn, NY
Buried: Evergreens Cemetery, Brooklyn, NY?
References: Military Service File, National Archives. Letters Received, Volunteer Service Branch, Adjutant General's Office, File D640(VS)1862, National Archives. Letters Received, Commission Branch, Adjutant General's Office, File D4(CB)1863, National Archives. Letters Received, Adjutant General's Office, File D463(AGO)1862, National Archives. Wilhelm Kaufmann. *The Germans in the American Civil War.* Translated by Steven Rowan and edited by Don Heinrich Tolzmann with Werner D. Mueller and Robert E. Ward. Carlisle, PA, 1999. "A Well Deserved Appointment," *Wheeling Daily Intelligencer,* Feb. 4, 1862. "Fighting Them Over, What Our Veterans Have to Say About Their Old Campaigns. Port Republic, Capt. Huntington Replies to Dr. Capehart," *Washington National Tribune,* Dec. 5, 1889.

John Henry Devereux

Colonel, Volunteer ADC, Staff of Major Gen. Nathaniel P. Banks, 5 Army Corps, Army of the Potomac, March 1862. Appointed Superintendent, U.S. Military Railroads of Virginia, Army of the Potomac, April 22, 1862. Resigned March 20, 1864.

Born: April 5, 1832, Boston, MA
Died: March 17, 1886, Cleveland, OH
Education: Attended Portsmouth (NH) Academy
Occupation: Civil engineer and railroad executive

Miscellaneous: Resided Cleveland, OH
Buried: Lake View Cemetery, Cleveland, OH (Section 8, Lots 180–181)

References: J.H. Kennedy, "General J.H. Devereux," *Magazine of Western History*, Vol. 4, No. 2 (June 1886). Allen Johnson and Dumas Malone, editors. *Dictionary of American Biography.* New York City, NY, 1964. *The National Cyclopaedia of American Biography.* Vol. 12. New York City, NY, 1904. J. Fletcher Brennan, editor. *The Biographical Cyclopedia and Portrait Gallery of Distinguished Men, with an Historical Sketch of the State of Ohio.* Cincinnati, OH, 1879. *The Biographical Cyclopedia and Portrait Gallery with an Historical Sketch of the State of Ohio.* Vol. 4. Cincinnati, OH, 1887. Obituary, *Cleveland Plain Dealer,* March 18, 1886. Obituary, *Cleveland Leader and Morning Herald,* March 18, 1886. Obituary Circular, Whole No. 72, Ohio MOLLUS. Herman Haupt. *Reminiscences of General Herman Haupt.* Milwaukee, WI, 1901. Mrs. Frank M. Angellotti, "John Devereux of Marblehead, Mass., and Some of His Descendants," *New England Historical and Genealogical Register,* Vol. 74, No. 4 (Oct. 1920). "General Devereux," *Cleveland Leader and Morning Herald,* March 24, 1886.

John Van Deusen DuBois

1 Lieutenant, U.S. Mounted Riflemen, May 13, 1861. 1 Lieutenant, 3 U.S. Cavalry, Aug. 3, 1861. Major, 1 MO Light Artillery, Sept. 1, 1861. Colonel, Additional ADC, Feb. 19, 1862. Captain, 3 U.S. Cavalry, Feb. 21, 1862. Chief of Artillery, Staff of Major Gen. Henry W. Halleck, Department of the Missouri, Feb. 21–March 11, 1862. Chief of Artillery, Staff of Major Gen. Henry W. Halleck, Department of the Mississippi, March 11–July 11, 1862. Colonel, 1 MO Light Artillery, Aug. 7, 1862. Resigned Oct. 14, 1862. Commanded 3 Brigade, 2 Division, Army of West Tennessee, Oct. 4–14, 1862. Nominated Brig. Gen., USV, Jan. 19, 1863, to rank from Nov.

John Henry Devereux (Library of Congress [LC-DIG-ppmsca-33987]).

John Henry Devereux (Frederick Hill Meserve. Historical Portraits, A Part of the Collection of Americana of Frederick Hill Meserve. New York City, 1913–1915; courtesy of the New York State Library, Manuscripts and Special Collections).

29, 1862. Nomination as Brig. Gen., USV, withdrawn Feb. 12, 1863. Chief of Cavalry, Staff of Major Gen. John M. Schofield and Major Gen. William S. Rosecrans, Department of the Missouri, Sept. 29, 1863–Sept. 25, 1864. Chief of Staff, Staff of Major Gen. William S. Rosecrans, Department of the Missouri, Sept. 25–Dec. 7, 1864. Inspector General, Staff of Major Gen. Grenville M. Dodge, Department of the Missouri, Dec. 9, 1864–Aug. 5, 1865. Inspector General, Staff of Major Gen. John Pope, Department of the Missouri, Aug. 5, 1865–Feb. 9, 1866. Honorably mustered out as Additional ADC, Feb. 9, 1866. He initially accepted brevets of captain, major, and lieutenant colonel, but becoming aware of the post-war proliferation of brevets, he withdrew his acceptance of these brevets, July 5, 1867, dissatisfied with the inadequate recognition of his war-time services as compared with others. Battle honors: Wilson's Creek, Farmington, Iuka, Corinth, Price's Missouri Expedition.

John Van Deusen DuBois (Nichols & Bro's Photographic Gallery, No. 60 N. 4th Street, St. Louis, MO; courtesy Marcus S. McLemore).

Born: Aug. 7, 1833 Livingston, Columbia Co., NY
Died: July 31, 1879 Hudson, NY
Education: Graduated U.S. Military Academy, West Point, NY, 1855
Occupation: Regular Army (Major, 3 U.S. Cavalry, retired May 17, 1876)
Miscellaneous: Resided Hudson, Columbia Co., NY
Buried: Rhinebeck Cemetery, Rhinebeck, NY
References: *Eleventh Annual Reunion of the Association of the Graduates of the U.S. Military Academy at West Point, NY.* East Saginaw, MI, 1880. George W. Cullum. *Biographical Register of the Officers and Graduates of the U.S. Military Academy.* Third Edition. Boston, MA, 1891. William Heidgerd. *The American Descendants of Chretien Du Bois of Wicres, France.* Part 7. New Paltz, NY, 1973. Jared C. Lobdell, editor, "The Civil War Journal and Letters of Colonel John Van Deusen Du Bois, April 12, 1861 to October 16, 1862," *Missouri Historical Review,* Vol. 60, No. 4 (July 1966) and Vol. 61, No. 1 (Oct. 1966). Letters Received, Commission Branch, Adjutant General's Office, File R390(CB)1870, National Archives. Military Service File, National Archives. Obituary, *New York Times,* Aug. 1, 1879. Obituary, Circular No. 8, Series of 1879–80, New York MOLLUS. Obituary, *Poughkeepsie Daily Eagle,* Aug. 1, 1879.

Charles Ellet, Jr.

Colonel, Additional ADC, April 28, 1862. Commanded Mississippi Ram Fleet, May–June 1862. GSW knee, Memphis, TN, June 6, 1862. Battle honors: Memphis.

Born: Jan. 1, 1810 Penn's Manor, Bucks Co., PA

Died: June 21, 1862 DOW Cairo, IL

Education: Attended Ecole Polytechnique, Paris, France

Occupation: Civil engineer and author. Designer of suspension bridges over the Niagara, Ohio, and Schuylkill Rivers. Author of numerous engineering works, and also of two pamphlets, *The Army of the Potomac and Its Mismanagement,* and *Military Incapacity and What It Costs the Country,* containing scathing criticism of the competency of General George B. McClellan and other Union generals.

Miscellaneous: Resided Philadelphia, PA; and Washington, D.C. Brother of Brig. Gen. Alfred W. Ellet. Father of Colonel Charles Rivers Ellet (1 Infantry, Mississippi Marine Brigade).

Buried: Laurel Hill Cemetery, Philadelphia, PA (Section C, Lot 12)

References: Gene D. Lewis. *Charles Ellet, Jr., The Engineer as Individualist, 1810–1862.* Urbana, IL, 1968. Allen Johnson and Dumas Malone, editors. *Dictionary of American Biography.* New York City, NY, 1964. *The National Cyclopaedia of American Biography.* Vol. 4. New York City, NY, 1897. Charles B. Stuart. *Lives and Works of Civil and Military Engineers of America.* New York City, NY, 1871. Warren D. Crandall and Isaac D. Newell. *History of the Ram Fleet and the Mississippi Marine Brigade in the War for the Union on the Mississippi and Its Tributaries.* St. Louis, MO, 1907. Charles Perrin Smith. *Lineage of the Lloyd and Carpenter Family.* Camden, NJ, 1870. Obituary, *Philadelphia North American,* June 23, 1862. Obituary, *Philadelphia Inquirer,* June 23, 1862. Obituary, *New York Tribune,* June 24, 1862. Obituary, *Chicago Daily Tribune,* June 26, 1862. "The Colonels Ellet," *Army and Navy Journal,* Vol. 1, No. 14 (Nov. 28,

Charles Ellet, Jr. (Charles B. Stuart. *Lives and Works of Civil and Military Engineers of America.* New York City, NY, 1871).

Charles Ellet, Jr. (Warren D. Crandall and Isaac D. Newell. *History of the Ram Fleet and the Mississippi Marine Brigade in the War for the Union on the Mississippi and Its Tributaries.* St. Louis, MO, 1907).

John Thomas Fiala

Lieutenant Colonel, 2 U.S. Reserve Corps, MO Infantry (3 months), May 7, 1861. Honorably mustered out, Aug. 16, 1861. Colonel, Brigade Inspector, Staff of Major Gen. John C. Fremont, Western Department, Aug. 16, 1861. Colonel, Topographical Engineer, Staff of Major Gen. John C. Fremont, Western Department, Sept. 20, 1861. Honorably discharged, Nov. 12, 1861. Colonel, Additional ADC, March 31, 1862. Chief of Topographical Engineers, Staff of Major Gen. John C. Fremont, Mountain Department, April–June 1862. Resigned June 8, 1864.

Born: Jan. 26, 1822 Temesvar, Hungary

Died: Dec. 1, 1911 San Francisco, CA

Other Wars: Officer in Hungarian revolutionary army of 1848–49.

Occupation: Topographical engineer before war. Engineering draftsman after war.

Offices/Honors: Treasurer of St. Louis Co., MO, 1865–71

Miscellaneous: Resided St. Louis, MO, to 1872; and San Francisco, CA, and Alameda, Alameda Co., CA, after 1872. Brother-in-law of Colonel Robert J. Rombauer (1 U.S. Reserve Corps, MO Infantry). Collaborated with Edward Haren in the publication in 1860 of *Fiala & Haren's New Sectional Map of the State of Missouri,* the first large topographical map of Missouri.

Buried: Cremated at Cypress Lawn Cemetery, Colma, CA (Cremains to Truman Funeral Home)

John Thomas Fiala (Robert J. Rombauer. *The Union Cause in St. Louis in 1861: An Historical Sketch.* St. Louis, MO, 1909).

References: Edmund Vasvary. *Lincoln's Hungarian Heroes: The Participation of Hungarians in the Civil War, 1861–1865.* Washington, D.C., 1939. Istvan Kornel Vida. *Hungarian Émigrés in the American Civil War: A History and Biographical Dictionary.* Jefferson, NC, 2012. Stephen Beszedits, "Hungarians with General John C. Fremont in the American Civil War," *Vasvary Collection Newsletter,* (2003, No. 2). "Hon. Frank P. Blair, Jr., and Col. J.T. Fiala," *Daily Missouri Democrat,* Oct. 16, 1862. Pension File, National Archives. Obituary, *San Francisco Chronicle,* Dec. 2, 1911. Obituary, *Oakland Tribune,* Dec. 2, 1911. Robert J. Rombauer. *The Union Cause in St. Louis in 1861: An Historical Sketch.* St. Louis, MO, 1909. Pamela Herr and Mary Lee Spence, editors. *The Letters of Jessie Benton Fremont*. Urbana, IL, 1993. Letters Received, Commission Branch, Adjutant General's Office, File F279(CB)1864, National Archives.

Philip Figyelmesy

Colonel, Additional ADC, March 31, 1862. ADC and Acting AIG, Staff of Major Gen. John C. Fremont, Mountain Department, April–June 1862. ADC, Staff of Major Gen. Julius Stahel, Cavalry Division, Department of Washington, March–June 1863. ADC, Staff of Major Gen. Julius Stahel, Chief of Cavalry, Department of the Susquehanna, July 1863–March 1864. ADC, Staff of Major General Julius Stahel, 1 Cavalry Division, Department of West Virginia, April–August 1864. Resigned Dec. 20, 1864. Battle honors: Strasburg.

Born: Jan. 1, 1822 Budapest, Hungary

Died: July 25, 1907 Philadelphia, PA

Other Wars: Major in the Hungarian revolutionary army of 1848–49. Colonel, Hungarian Legion, with General Garibaldi in Sicily and Italy, 1860–61.

Occupation: Hungarian patriot and foreign diplomat

Offices/Honors: U.S. Consul, Demerara, British Guiana, 1865–88

Miscellaneous: Resided Marietta, Lancaster Co., PA; Georgetown, British Guiana, 1865–88; Geneva, Switzerland, 1890–94; and Philadelphia, PA

Buried: Marietta Cemetery, Marietta, PA

References: Stephen Beszedits, "The Life and Times of Philip Figyelmessy (1822–1907)," *Vasvary Collection Newsletter*, (2006, No. 2). Edmund Vasvary. *Lincoln's Hungarian Heroes: The Participation of Hungarians in the Civil War, 1861–1865*. Washington, D.C., 1939. Istvan Kornel Vida. *Hungarian Émigrés in the American Civil War: A History and Biographical Dictionary*. Jefferson, NC, 2012. Eugene

Philip Figyelmesy (Hungarian Legion, 1860; author's photograph).

Pivany. *Hungarians in the American Civil War.* Cleveland, OH, 1913. Obituary, *Lancaster Daily New Era,* July 26, 1907. Obituary, *Lancaster Daily Intelligencer,* July 26, 1907. Obituary, *Philadelphia Inquirer,* July 26, 1907. "Under Four Flags," *Lancaster Inquirer,* Aug. 3, 1907. Pension File, National Archives. Letters Received, Commission Branch, Adjutant General's Office, File F97(CB)1865, National Archives. Letters Received, Adjutant General's Office, Files F137(AGO)1862 and F128(AGO)1864, National Archives.

Thomas Tasker Gantt

Colonel, Additional ADC, Aug. 26, 1861. Judge Advocate, Staff of Major Gen. George B. McClellan, Army of the Potomac, Aug. 1861–July 1862. Resigned July 5, 1862, due to "a disqualification for active military duty growing out of a lameness of long standing recently much aggravated." Provost Marshal General, District of Missouri and Iowa, Sept.–Nov. 1862.

Born: July 22, 1814, Georgetown, DC
Died: June 17, 1889, St. Louis, MO
Education: Attended U.S. Military Academy, West Point, NY (Class of 1835)
Occupation: Lawyer and judge
Offices/Honors: Judge, St. Louis Court of Appeals, 1875–77
Miscellaneous: Resided St. Louis, MO. First cousin of CSA General Richard S. Ewell.
Buried: Bellefontaine Cemetery, St. Louis, MO (Block 26, Lot 1920)
References: William Hyde and Howard L. Conard, editors. *Encyclopedia of the History of St. Louis.* New York, Louisville, and St. Louis, 1899. Obituary, *St. Louis Post-Dispatch,* June 17, 1889. Obituary, *St. Louis Globe-Democrat,* June 18, 1889. J. Thomas Scharf. *History of Saint Louis City and County.* Philadelphia, PA, 1883. John F. Darby. *Personal Recollections of Many Prominent People Whom I Have Known, and of Events, Especially of Those Relating to the History of St. Louis, During the First Half of the Present Century.* St. Louis, MO, 1880. A.J.D. Stewart, editor. *The History of the Bench and Bar of Missouri.* St. Louis, MO, 1898. Letters Received, Adjutant General's Office, Files G323(AGO)1861 and G385(AGO)1862, National Archives.

Thomas Tasker Gantt (William Hyde and Howard L. Conard, editors. *Encyclopedia of the History of St. Louis.* New York, Louisville, and St. Louis, 1899).

John Addison Gurley

Colonel, IN Legion, Aug. 1, 1861. Colonel, Volunteer ADC, Staff of Major Gen. John C. Fremont, Western Department, Aug. 6, 1861. Resigned Oct. 1, 1861.

Born: Dec. 9, 1813 East Hartford, CT

Died: Aug. 19, 1863 Green Twp., Hamilton Co., OH

Occupation: Universalist clergyman, newspaper editor, and farmer

Offices/Honors: U.S. House of Representatives, 1859–63. Appointed Governor of Arizona Territory, but died before assuming office.

Miscellaneous: Resided Green Twp., Hamilton Co., OH

Buried: Spring Grove Cemetery, Cincinnati, OH (Section 36, Lot 28)

References: Albert E. Gurley. *The History and Genealogy of the Gurley Family.* Hartford, CT, 1897. James L. Harrison, compiler. *Biographical Directory of the American Congress, 1774–1949.* Washington, D.C., 1950. Obituary, *Cincinnati Daily Commercial*, Aug. 20, 1863. Obituary, *New York Evening Post*, Aug. 20, 1863. Obituary, *Chicago Daily Tribune*, Aug. 22, 1863.

John Addison Gurley (courtesy Sharlot Hall Museum Library & Archives [1020.0154.0006]).

Alexander Hamilton, Jr.

Colonel, Volunteer ADC, Staff of Major Gen. John E. Wool, Department of the East, April 24, 1861–July 18, 1863. Battle honors: New York Draft Riots.

Born: Jan. 26, 1816 New York City, NY

Died: Dec. 30, 1889 Irvington, NY

Education: Attended U.S. Military Academy, West Point, NY (Class of 1836)

Occupation: Lawyer

Offices/Honors: Secretary, U.S. Legation, Madrid, Spain, 1842–46

Miscellaneous: Resided New York City, NY; and Irvington, Westchester Co., NY. Grandson of Alexander Hamilton. Brother-in-law of George L. Schuyler (Volunteer ADC). Often confused with his first cousin, Major Gen. Alexander Hamilton (1815–1907), New York State Militia.

Buried: Sleepy Hollow Cemetery, Tarrytown, NY (Section 27, Plots 239–249)

References: Cuyler Reynolds, editor. *Genealogical and Family History of Southern New York and the Hudson River Valley.* New York City, NY, 1914. Obituary, *New York Times*, Dec. 31, 1889. Obituary, *New York Tribune*, Dec. 31, 1889. Florence Van Rensselaer, compiler. *The Livingston Family in America and Its Scottish Origins.* New

Charles Frederick Havelock

Colonel, Additional ADC, Nov. 23, 1861. Inspector of Cavalry, Staff of Major Gen. George B. McClellan, Army of the Potomac, 1861–62. ADC, Staff of Brig. Gen. James S. Wadsworth, Military District of Washington, 1862–63. Resigned July 31, 1863, upon revocation of an order of April 13, 1863, mustering him out of service.

Born: Oct. 16, 1803 Ingress Park, Greenhithe, Kent, England

Died: May 14, 1868, Titchfield, Hampshire, England

Other Wars: Crimean War (Brig. Gen., Irregular Osmanli Cavalry, and Major Gen., Imperial Ottoman Army, 1856)

Occupation: English army officer (Major, 53 Regiment of Foot, placed on half pay, 1849)

Miscellaneous: Resided Titchfield, Hampshire, England. Brother of Major Gen. Sir Henry Havelock.

Buried: Titchfield, Hampshire, England?

References: Rosemary Meszaros, "From the Archives: In the Matter of Charles Frederick Havelock," *North & South*, Vol. 13, No. 4 (Nov. 2011). Frederic Boase. *Modern English Biography*. London, England, 1965. H.G. Hart. *The New Annual Army List for 1852*. London, England, 1852. Letters Received, Adjutant General's Office, File H814(AGO)1861, National Archives. Letters Received, Commission Branch, Adjutant General's Office, File H312(CB)1863, National Archives.

Charles Frederick Havelock (author's photograph).

Robert Noble Hudson

Colonel, ADC, Staff of Major Gen. John C. Fremont, Western Department, Sept.–Nov. 1861. Colonel, Additional ADC, March 31, 1862. *Colonel,* 2 IN Cavalry,

April 5, 1862. Declined. Provost Marshal, Staff of Major Gen. John C. Fremont, Mountain Department, April–June 1862. Resigned Aug. 26, 1863, "to enable me to take a command in the Indiana Legion." Colonel, 133 IN Infantry, May 17, 1864. Honorably mustered out, Sept. 5, 1864.

Born: Nov. 7, 1819 Brookville, IN

Died: Aug. 30, 1889 Terre Haute, IN

Education: Graduated Indiana Asbury (now DePauw) University, Greencastle, IN, 1844

Occupation: Lawyer and newspaper editor

Offices/Honors: Indiana House of Representatives, 1851–52, 1855

Miscellaneous: Resided Terre Haute, Vigo Co., IN

Buried: Highland Lawn Cemetery, Terre Haute, IN (Section 3, Lot 142)

References: Hiram W. Beckwith. *History of Vigo and Parke Counties, Together with Historic Notes on the Wabash Valley.* Chicago, IL, 1880. Obituary, *Terre Haute Express,* Aug. 31, 1889. Mike McCormick, "Wabash Valley Profiles: Robert N. Hudson," *Terre Haute Tribune-Star,* Sept. 18, 1999. Pension File, National Archives. Letters Received, Commission Branch, Adjutant General's Office, File H330(CB)1863, National Archives. Rebecca A. Shepherd, Charles W. Calhoun, Elizabeth Shanahan-Shoemaker, and Alan F. January, editors. *A Biographical Directory of the Indiana General Assembly.* Vol. 1, 1816–1899. Indianapolis, IN, 1980. Charles A. Martin, editor. *DePauw University: Alumnal Register of Officers, Faculties and Graduates, 1837–1900.* Greencastle, IN, 1901. William Raimond Baird. *Betas of Achievement.* New York City, NY, 1914.

Robert Noble Hudson (Charles D. Fredricks & Co. "Specialite," 587 Broadway, New York; author's photograph).

Amos Balfour Jones

Captain, Co. E, 1 U.S. Sharpshooters, Sept. 9, 1861. Major, 2 U.S. Sharpshooters, Dec. 3, 1861. Colonel, Additional ADC, May 31, 1862. ADC, Staff of Major Gen. Robert C. Schenck, 8 Army Corps, Middle Department, May 1863. Acting AIG, Staff of Brig. Gen. Eliakim P. Scammon, 3 Division, 8 Army Corps, July 1863. Acting AIG, Staff of Major Gen. Franz Sigel, Department of West Virginia, April–May 1864. Commissary of Musters, Staff of Major Gen. Winfield S. Hancock, Department of West Virginia, Feb.–March 1865. Dismissed May 8, 1865, upon

Amos Balfour Jones (Richard F. Carlile Collection).

Amos Balfour Jones (Rutherford B. Hayes Presidential Library & Museums).

a report by General Hancock, April 11, 1865, that "upon the 27th day of March 1865, Col. Jones left his duties at Cumberland, MD, without authority, and without reporting the fact, leaving all business without attention, and is still absent, and that his whereabouts are unknown at these Headquarters." Battle honors: Morgan's Ohio Raid.

Born: Jan. 27, 1837 Washington, NH

Died: May 4, 1914 Charleston, WV

Education: Graduated Dartmouth College, Hanover, NH, 1861

Occupation: School teacher before war. Engaged in mining and railroad enterprises after war.

Miscellaneous: Resided Washington, Sullivan Co., NH, before war; and Charleston, Kanawha Co., WV; and Lake Charles, Calcasieu Co., LA, after war. Brother-in-law of Bvt. Brig. Gen. Samuel A. Duncan (4 U.S. Colored Infantry).

Buried: Spring Hill Cemetery, Charleston, WV (Section 30, Lot 1)

References: *History of Washington, New Hampshire, from the First Settlement to the Present Time, 1768–1886.* Claremont, NH, 1886. Obituary, *Charleston Daily Mail,* May 5, 1914. Letters Received, Commission Branch, Adjutant General's Office, File J35(CB)1864, National Archives. "The New Hampshire Sharpshooters," *Harper's Weekly,* Vol. 5, No. 249 (Oct. 5, 1861). Edward D. Redington, compiler. *Military Record of the Sons of Dartmouth in the Union Army and Navy, 1861-1865.* Cambridge, MA, 1907. George T. Chapman. *Sketches of the Alumni of Dartmouth College.* Cambridge, MA, 1867. Charles A. Stevens. *Berdan's United States Sharpshooters in the Army of the Potomac, 1861–1865.* St. Paul, MN, 1892. Military Service File, National Archives.

Thomas Marshall Key

Volunteer ADC, Staff of Major Gen. George B. McClellan, June 20, 1861. Colonel, Additional ADC, Aug. 19, 1861. ADC, Staff of Major Gen. George B. McClellan, Army of the Potomac, Aug. 1861–March 1863. Honorably discharged, March 31, 1863. Battle honors: Western Virginia Campaign (Rich Mountain), Peninsular Campaign, Antietam.

Born: Aug. 8, 1819 Washington, KY

Died: Jan. 15, 1869 Lebanon, OH

Education: Attended Augusta (KY) College. Graduated Yale University, New Haven, CT, 1838.

Occupation: Lawyer and judge

Offices/Honors: Judge, Cincinnati Commercial Court, 1848–53. Ohio Senate, 1860–62.

Miscellaneous: Resided Cincinnati, OH. Author of the District of Columbia Compensated Emancipation Act.

Buried: Spring Grove Cemetery, Cincinnati, OH (Section 24, Lot 10)

References: William B. Styple. *McClellan's Other Story: The Political Intrigue of Colonel Thomas M. Key, Confidential Aide to General George B. McClellan.* Kearny, NJ, 2012. Obituary, *Cincinnati Commercial,* Jan. 16, 1869. Obituary, *Cincinnati Daily Gazette,* Jan. 16, 1869. Obituary, *Lebanon Western Star,* Jan. 21, 1869. "Washington Letter: Col. Tom M. Key," *Cincinnati Commercial,* Jan. 20, 1869. *Obituary Record of Graduates of Yale College Deceased during the Academical Year Ending in July 1869.* New Haven, CT, 1869. *History of Cincinnati and Hamilton County, Ohio: Their Past and Present.* Cincinnati, OH, 1894. James Grant Wilson and John Fiske, editors. *Appletons' Cyclopaedia of American Biography.* New York City, NY, 1888. William M. Paxton. *The Marshall Family.* Cincinnati, OH, 1885. Letters Received, Adjutant General's Office, File K228(AGO)1861, National Archives.

Gustavus Koerner

Colonel, Additional ADC, Staff of Major Gen. John C. Fremont, Western Department, Sept. 28, 1861. Honorably discharged, Nov. 2, 1861.

Born: Nov. 20, 1809 Frankfort, Germany

Died: April 9, 1896 Belleville, IL

Education: Attended University of Jena (Germany), University of Munich (Germany), and University of Heidelberg (Germany)

Occupation: Lawyer and judge

Offices/Honors: Illinois House of Representatives, 1842–44. Judge, Illinois Supreme Court, 1845-48. Lieutenant Governor of Illinois, 1853–57. U.S. Minister to Spain, 1862–64.

Gustavus Koerner (Thomas J. McCormack, editor. **Memoirs of Gustave Koerner, 1809–1896. Cedar Rapids, IA, 1909).**

Miscellaneous: Resided Belleville, St. Clair Co., IL
Buried: Walnut Hill Cemetery, Belleville, IL
References: Thomas J. McCormack, editor. *Memoirs of Gustave Koerner, 1809–1896.* Cedar Rapids, IA, 1909. Allen Johnson and Dumas Malone, editors. *Dictionary of American Biography.* New York City, NY, 1964. *Portrait and Biographical Record of St. Clair County, Illinois.* Chicago, IL, 1892. Obituary, *St. Louis Republic,* April 10, 1896. Obituary, *Chicago Record,* April 10, 1896. Obituary, *St. Louis Globe-Democrat,* April 10, 1896. *The United States Biographical Dictionary and Portrait Gallery of Eminent and Self-Made Men.* Illinois Volume. Chicago, Cincinnati, and New York, 1876. *The National Cyclopaedia of American Biography.* Vol. 8. New York City, NY, 1898. Alvin L. Nebelsick. *A History of Belleville.* Belleville, IL, 1951. Letters Received, Adjutant General's Office, File K303(AGO)1861, National Archives.

Owen Lovejoy

Colonel, Volunteer ADC, Staff of Major Gen. John C. Fremont, Western Department, Sept. 25, 1861–Nov. 4, 1861.

Born: Jan. 6, 1811 Albion, ME

Died: March 25, 1864 Brooklyn, NY

Education: Attended Bowdoin College, Brunswick, ME

Occupation: Congregational clergyman

Owen Lovejoy (U.S. Congress, 1859) (Library of Congress [LC-DIG-ppmsca-26795]).

Owen Lovejoy (J. Gurney & Son, Photographic Artists, 707 Broadway, New York; courtesy Henry Deeks).

Offices/Honors: Illinois House of Representatives, 1854–56. U.S. House of Representatives, 1857-64.

Miscellaneous: Resided Princeton, Bureau Co., IL. His step-daughter married Bvt. Brig. Gen. Isaac H. Elliott (33 IL Infantry). Brother of abolitionist Elijah P. Lovejoy (killed in Alton, IL, 1837).

Buried: Oakland Cemetery, Princeton, IL

References: Edward Magdol. *Owen Lovejoy: Abolitionist in Congress.* New Brunswick, NJ, 1967. Allen Johnson and Dumas Malone, editors. *Dictionary of American Biography.* New York City, NY, 1964. *The Biographical Record of Bureau, Marshall and Putnam Counties, Illinois.* Chicago, IL, 1896. Obituary, *Chicago Daily Tribune,* March 29, 1864. Obituary, *New York Tribune,* March 28, 1864. Clarence E. Lovejoy. *The Lovejoy Genealogy With Biographies and History, 1460–1930.* New York City, NY, 1930. George B. Harrington. *Past and Present of Bureau County, Illinois.* Chicago, IL, 1906. James L. Harrison, compiler. *Biographical Directory of the American Congress, 1774–1949.* Washington, D.C., 1950. Thomas J. McCormack, editor. *Memoirs of Gustave Koerner, 1809–1896.* Cedar Rapids, IA, 1909. James Grant Wilson and John Fiske, editors. *Appletons' Cyclopaedia of American Biography.* New York City, NY, 1888.

John Navarre Macomb

Major, U.S. Corps of Topographical Engineers, Aug. 6, 1861. Chief Topographical Engineer, Staff of Major Gen. George B. McClellan, Army of the Potomac, Aug. 1861–April 1862. Lieutenant Colonel, Additional ADC, Sept. 28, 1861. Chief Topographical Engineer, Staff of Major Gen. Irvin McDowell, Department of the Rappahannock, April–June 1862. Colonel, Additional ADC, May 15, 1862. Chief Engineer, Staff of Major Gen. John Pope, Army of Virginia, July–Sept. 1862. Lieutenant Colonel, U.S. Corps of Engineers, March 3, 1863. Honorably mustered out as Additional ADC, May 31, 1866. Bvt. Colonel, USA, March 13, 1865, for faithful and meritorious services during the war. Battle honors: Cedar Mountain.

Born: April 9, 1811, New York City, NY

Died: March 16, 1889, Washington, D.C.

Education: Graduated U.S. Military Academy, West Point, NY, 1832

Occupation: Regular Army (Colonel, U.S. Corps of Engineers, retired June 30, 1882)

Miscellaneous: Resided Washington, D.C. Brother-in-law of Brig. Gen. Montgomery C. Meigs. Nephew of Major Gen. Alexander Macomb (War of 1812). Son-in-law of Commodore John Rodgers (War of 1812).

Buried: Arlington National Cemetery, Arlington, VA (Section 1, Site 75)

John Navarre Macomb (R.W. Addis, Photographer, 308 Penna. Avenue, Washington, D.C.; author's photograph).

References: George W. Cullum. *Biographical Register of the Officers and Graduates of the U.S. Military Academy at West Point, N.Y.* Third Edition. Boston and New York, 1891. *Twentieth Annual Reunion of the Association of the Graduates of the U.S. Military Academy at West Point, NY.* East Saginaw, MI, 1889. Letters Received, Appointment, Commission and Personal Branch, Adjutant General's Office, File 1525(ACP)1889, National Archives. *Portrait and Biographical Record of Leavenworth, Douglas, and Franklin Counties, Kansas.* Chicago, IL, 1899. Obituary, *New York Sun*, March 22, 1889. Obituary, *Washington National Tribune*, March 21, 1889. Obituary (John N. Macomb), *Army and Navy Journal*, Vol. 26, No. 30 (March 23, 1889). Obituary, *Washington Evening Star*, March 19, 1889. Pension File, National Archives. Henry A. Macomb, compiler. *Macomb Family Record: Being an Account of the Family Since the Settlement in America.* Camden, NJ, 1917. Letters Received, Adjutant General's Office, Files M926(AGO)1861 and M596(AGO)1862, National Archives. http://www.arlingtoncemetery.net/jnmacomb.htm.

Louis Henry Marshall

Captain, 10 U.S. Infantry, Dec. 29, 1860. Colonel, Benton Cadets, MO Infantry, Sept. 24, 1861. Honorably mustered out of volunteer service, Jan. 8, 1862. Acting ADC, Staff of Major Gen. John Pope, Army of the Mississippi, Feb.–June 1862. Colonel, Additional ADC, Staff of Major Gen. John Pope, Army of Virginia (and Department of the Northwest), June 30, 1862–July 28, 1865. Mustering and Disbursing Officer, Department of the Northwest, Feb. 1863–July 1865. Major, 14 U.S. Infantry, Oct. 16, 1863. Bvt. Lieutenant Colonel, USA, March 13, 1865, for gallant and meritorious services during the war. Battle honors: New Madrid, Island No. 10, Siege of Corinth, Northern Virginia Campaign (Cedar Mountain, 2nd Bull Run).

Born: May 23, 1828 VA

Died: Oct. 8, 1891 Monrovia, CA

Education: Graduated U.S. Military Academy, West Point, NY, 1849

Occupation: Regular Army (Major, 23 U.S. Infantry, resigned Nov. 23, 1868). Rancher and claims collector and agent.

Miscellaneous: Resided Baltimore, MD, before war; Cucamonga, San Bernardino Co., CA; and Monrovia, Los Angeles Co., CA, after war. Nephew of CSA General Robert E. Lee, who told his

Louis Henry Marshall (Brady's National Photographic Portrait Gallery, 352 Pennsylvania Avenue, Washington, D.C.; Frederick Hill Meserve. *Historical Portraits, a Part of the Collection of Americana of Frederick Hill Meserve.* New York City, 1913–1915; courtesy of the New York State Library, Manuscripts and Special Collections).

daughter, "I could forgive [him] fighting against us, if he had not joined such a miscreant as Pope."

Buried: Evergreen Cemetery, Los Angeles, CA (Section G, Lot 250, unmarked)

References: William M. Paxton. *The Marshall Family.* Cincinnati, OH, 1885. Pension File and Military Service File, National Archives. Letters Received, Commission Branch, Adjutant General's Office, File M460(CB)1868, National Archives. George W. Cullum. *Biographical Register of the Officers and Graduates of the U.S. Military Academy at West Point, N.Y.* Third Edition. Boston, MA, 1891. Death notice, *Los Angeles Herald,* Oct. 9, 1891. Gregory Michno. *The Deadliest Indian War in the West: The Snake Conflict, 1864–1868.* Caldwell, ID, 2007.

Joseph Chambers McKibbin

Colonel, Additional ADC, Nov. 29, 1861. Judge Advocate, Staff of Major Gen. Henry W. Halleck, Department of the Mississippi, April June 1862, Sept. 1862, Jan. 1863. Acting AIG, Staff of Major Gen. William S. Rosecrans, Feb. 22, 1863. ADC, Staff of Major Gen. William S. Rosecrans, Department of the Cumberland, April–Nov. 1863. ADC, Staff of Major Gen. George H. Thomas, Department of the Cumberland, Nov. 1863. Describing him as a "worthless fellow," Assistant Secretary of War Charles A. Dana reported on Nov. 22, 1863, "Colonel McKibbin, Additional Aide, under arrest for attempting to break through pickets while drunk, was released by Thomas on condition he should apply to be relieved from duty in this department." Resigned Jan. 29, 1864. Battle honors: Chickamauga.

Born: May 14, 1824, Chambersburg, PA

Died: July 1, 1896, Marshall Hall, MD

Education: Attended Princeton (NJ) University. Graduated Hanover (IN) College, 1843.

Occupation: Lawyer before war. General contractor after war.

Offices/Honors: California Senate, 1852–53. U.S. House of Representatives, 1857–59.

Miscellaneous: Resided Downieville, Sierra Co., CA, before war; Washington, D.C.; and Marshall Hall, Charles Co., MD, after war. Brother of Bvt. Brig. Gen. David B. McKibbin (214 PA Infantry).

Buried: Arlington National Cemetery, Arlington, VA (Section 1, Site 773)

References: Obituary, *Washington Evening Times,* July 2, 1896. Obituary, *Washington Evening Star,* July 2, 1896. Obituary, *Philadelphia Inquirer,* July 3, 1896. Obituary, *Washington National Tribune,* July 9, 1896. James L. Harrison, compiler. *Biographical Directory of the American*

Joseph Chambers McKibbin (post-war) (Obituary, *Washington Evening Times,* July 2, 1896).

Congress, 1774–1949. Washington, D.C., 1950. Letters Received, Commission Branch, Adjutant General's Office, File M728(CB)1863, National Archives. Letters Received, Appointment, Commission and Personal Branch, Adjutant General's Office, File 5429(ACP)1883, National Archives. *The War of the Rebellion: A Compilation of the Official Records of the Union and Confederate Armies.* (Vol. 31, Part 2, pp. 54, 64). Washington, D.C., 1890. "Hon. J.C. McKibbin," *Philadelphia Press,* Sept. 23, 1864.

William Hilton Merritt

Lieutenant Colonel, 1 IA Infantry (3 months), May 14, 1861. Honorably mustered out, Aug. 21, 1861. Colonel, Additional ADC, Staff of Brig. Gen. James H. Lane, Jan. 29, 1862. Honorably discharged, March 21, 1862, upon cancellation of the appointment of Gen. Lane. Battle honors: Wilson's Creek.

Born: Sept. 12, 1820 New York City, NY

Died: July 23, 1891 Cedar Rapids, IA

Education: Attended Genesee Wesleyan Seminary, Lima, NY

Occupation: Newspaper editor and banker before war. Railroad contractor and superintendent after war.

Offices/Honors: Iowa State Printer, 1851–53. Surveyor of the Port of Dubuque (IA), 1854–55. Register of the U.S. Land Office, Fort Dodge (IA), 1855–58. Mayor, Des Moines (IA), 1880–82. Postmaster, Des Moines (IA), 1886–90.

William Hilton Merritt (author's photograph).

William Hilton Merritt (courtesy Everitt Bowles).

Miscellaneous: Resided Dubuque, Dubuque Co., IA; Cedar Rapids, Linn Co., IA; and Des Moines, Polk Co., IA, after 1863

Buried: Woodland Cemetery, Des Moines, IA (Block 18, Lot 18)

References: *Portrait and Biographical Album of Polk County, Iowa.* Chicago, IL, 1890. *The United States Biographical Dictionary and Portrait Gallery of Eminent and Self-Made Men.* Iowa Volume. Chicago and New York, 1878. *History of Polk County, Iowa.* Des Moines, IA, 1880. Obituary, *Iowa State Register,* July 24, 1891. Obituary, *Davenport Morning Democrat,* July 25, 1891. Obituary, *Cedar Rapids Evening Gazette,* July 23, 1891. Pension File, National Archives. Eugene F. Ware. *The Lyon Campaign in Missouri: Being a History of the First Iowa Infantry.* Topeka, KS, 1907. "Gen. Lane's Staff Appointed by the President," *Leavenworth Times,* Jan. 31, 1862. William Garrett Piston, "The 1st Iowa Volunteers: Honor and Community in a Ninety-Day Regiment," *Civil War History,* Vol. 44, No. 1 (March 1998). Douglas Merritt, compiler. *Revised Merritt Records.* New York City, NY, 1916.

Christopher Anthony Morgan

Captain, Co. D, 39 OH Infantry, July 31, 1861. Resigned Aug. 23, 1861. Major, 1 IL Cavalry, Sept. 1, 1861. Acting ADC, Staff of Major Gen. John Pope, Army of the Mississippi, Feb.–June 1862. Colonel, Additional ADC, June 30, 1862. ADC, Staff of Major Gen. John Pope, Army of Virginia, June–Sept. 1862. AIG, Staff of Major Gen. John Pope, Department of the Northwest, Sept. 1862–Feb. 1865. AIG, Staff of Major Gen. John Pope, Department of the Missouri, March 1865–Jan. 1866. Battle honors: New Madrid, Island No. 10, Northern Virginia Campaign (2nd Bull Run).

Born: Dec. 18, 1821 Cincinnati, OH

Died: Jan. 20, 1866 St. Louis, MO

Education: Attended Woodward College, Cincinnati, OH

Occupation: Printer and book publisher

Miscellaneous: Resided Cincinnati, OH; and St. Louis, MO. Morgan County, CO, was named in his honor.

Buried: Spring Grove Cemetery, Cincinnati, OH (Section 69, Lot 21, unmarked)

References: "Colonel Christopher A. Morgan," *Fort Morgan Times,* Dec. 6, 1889. Appleton Morgan. *A History of the Family of Morgan from the Year 1089 to Present Times.* New York City, NY, 1902. *Old Woodward: A Memorial Relating to Woodward High School, 1831–36, and Woodward College, 1836–51.* Cincinnati, OH, 1884. Obituary, *Daily Missouri Republican,* Jan. 21, 1866. Obituary, *Cincinnati Daily Gazette,* Jan. 22, 1866. Letters Received, Commission Branch, Adjutant General's Office, File M550(CB)1864, National Archives. Letters

Christopher Anthony Morgan (author's photograph).

Received, Adjutant General's Office, File M783(AGO)1862, National Archives. Military Service File, National Archives.

George Greenwood Pride

Colonel, Volunteer ADC, Staff of Major Gen. Ulysses S. Grant, Department of the Tennessee, Feb.–Oct. 1862. Chief Engineer, Military Railroads, Department of the Tennessee, Nov. 1862–April 1863. Battle honors: Shiloh, Vicksburg Campaign (Duckport Canal).

Born: June 4, 1828 Wrentham, MA

Died: Dec. 11, 1906 Huntington, IN

Occupation: Civil engineer engaged in railroad construction

Offices/Honors: Postmaster, Harford, PA, 1850–52

Miscellaneous: Resided Harford, Susquehanna Co., PA; and Galena, Jo Daviess Co., IL, before war; New York City, NY; and Huntington, Huntington Co., IN, 1881–1906

Buried: Mount Hope Cemetery, Huntington, IN (Section B, Block 9, Lot 6)

References: Obituary, *Huntington Evening Herald*, Dec. 11, 1906. Obituary, *Huntington Daily News-Democrat*, Dec. 11, 1906. Obituary, *Fort Wayne Evening Sentinel*, Dec. 12, 1906. "Some Light Is Thrown on Romantic Life of Col. Pride," *Fort Wayne Evening Sentinel*, Dec. 13, 1906. Frank S. Bash, "Memories of Col. George G. Pride Are Related by Bash in Reviewing City History," *Huntington Herald*, Jan. 6, 1923.

George Greenwood Pride (Massachusetts MOLLUS Collection, USAHEC [Vol. 73, p. 3617L]).

George Greenwood Pride (Massachusetts MOLLUS Collection, USAHEC [Vol. 134, p. 6857]).

"The Sole Survivor of General Grant's Staff Lives as a Hermit," *Indianapolis Star,* Jan. 29, 1905. Pension File, National Archives. John Y. Simon, editor. *The Papers of Ulysses S. Grant.* Vol. 6: September 1–December 8, 1862. Carbondale, IL, 1977. John Y. Simon, editor. *The Papers of Ulysses S. Grant.* Vol. 7: December 9, 1862–March 31, 1863. Carbondale, IL, 1979. John Y. Simon, editor. *The Papers of Ulysses S. Grant.* Vol. 8: April 1–July 6, 1863. Carbondale, IL, 1979. Edwin Cole Bearss. *The Vicksburg Campaign.* 3 vols. Dayton, OH, 1985–86.

George Lee Schuyler

Colonel, Volunteer ADC, Staff of Major Gen. John E. Wool, Department of the East, April 24, 1861–July 18, 1863. Appointed agent to purchase arms in Europe for the War Department, July 29, 1861. Returned from Europe, March 30, 1862. Battle honors: New York Draft Riots.

Born: June 9, 1811, Rhinebeck, NY

Died: July 31, 1890, near New London, CT, on board flagship of New York Yacht Club

Education: Attended Columbia University, New York City, NY

Occupation: Civil engineer engaged in various steamboat and railroad enterprises before war; stock broker and philanthropist after war

Miscellaneous: Resided New York City, NY; and Dobbs Ferry, Westchester Co., NY. Grandson of Major Gen. Philip Schuyler. Brother-in-law of Colonel Alexander Hamilton, Jr. (Volunteer ADC). Best known as a yachtsman, owner of the world champion yacht, *America,* and donor of the well-known America's Cup.

Buried: Sleepy Hollow Cemetery, Tarrytown, NY (Section 27, Plots 239–249)

References: *The National Cyclopaedia of American Biography.* Vol. 1. New York City, NY, 1898. Florence A. Christoph. *Schuyler Genealogy: The Schuyler Families in America Prior to 1900.* Albany, NY, 1992. Cuyler Reynolds, compiler. *Genealogical and Family History of Southern New York and the Hudson River Valley.* New York City, NY, 1914. Obituary, *New York Times,* Aug. 1, 1890. Obituary, *New York Herald,* Aug. 1, 1890. Obituary, *Boston Herald,* Aug. 1, 1890. Obituary (George L. Schuyler), *The Illustrated American,* Vol. 3, No. 26 (Aug. 16, 1890).

George Lee Schuyler (post-war) (*The National Cyclopaedia of American Biography.* Vol. 1. New York City, NY, 1898).

John Gould Stephenson

Volunteer Surgeon, 19 IN Infantry, Oct.–Nov. 1861. Colonel, IN Legion, Nov. 27, 1861. Colonel, Volunteer ADC, Staff of Brig. Gen. Solomon Meredith, 1 Brigade, 1

Division, 1 Army Corps, Army of the Potomac, May–July 1863. Battle honors: Chancellorsville, Gettysburg

Born: March 1, 1828 Lancaster, NH

Died: Nov. 11, 1883 Washington, D.C.

Education: Attended Dartmouth College, Hanover, NH. Graduated Castleton (VT) Medical College, 1849.

Occupation: Physician

Offices/Honors: Librarian of Congress, 1861–64

Miscellaneous: Resided Terre Haute, Vigo Co., IN, before war; Washington, D.C., after war

Buried: Congressional Cemetery, Washington, D.C. (Range 6, Site 244)

References: Constance Carter, "John Gould Stephenson: Largely Known and Much Liked," *Quarterly Journal of the Library of Congress*, Vol. 33 (April 1976). Richard G. Wood, "Librarian-in-Arms: The Career of John G. Stephenson," *Library Quarterly*, Vol. 19 (Oct. 1949). Bohdan S. Wynar, editor. *Dictionary of American Library Biography*. Littleton, CO, 1978. Obituary, *Washington Post*, Nov. 12, 1883. Obituary, *Washington Daily National Republican*, Nov. 13, 1883. Obituary, *Washington National Tribune*, Nov. 29, 1883. Pension File of Davis E. Castle (19 IN Infantry), National Archives. Letters Received, Commission

John Gould Stephenson (Charles D. Fredricks & Co. "Specialite," 587 Broadway, New York; author's photograph).

John Gould Stephenson (Librarian of Congress) (Library of Congress [LC-USZ62–57283]).

Branch, Adjutant General's Office, File S519(CB)1863, National Archives. https://www.loc.gov/item/n96035157/john-g-stephenson-1828-1883/.

Albert Tracy

Captain, 10 U.S. Infantry, March 3, 1855. Colonel, Chief Commissary of Subsistence, Staff of Major Gen. John C. Fremont, Western Department, Oct.–Nov. 1861. Colonel, Additional ADC, March 31, 1862. Acting AAG, Staff of Major Gen. John C. Fremont, Mountain Department, March–June 1862 Major, 15 U.S. Infantry, June 1, 1863. Honorably mustered out as Additional ADC, Nov. 25, 1863. Commanded 1 Battalion, 15 U.S. Infantry, 2 Brigade, 1 Division, 14 Army Corps, Department of the Cumberland, Jan.–May 1864. Commanded 2 Battalion, 15 U.S. Infantry, 1 Brigade, 1 Separate Division, District of the Etowah, Department of the Cumberland, Feb.–April 1865. Retired Nov. 4, 1865. Bvt. Lieutenant Colonel, USA, March 13, 1865, for meritorious services during the campaign of 1862 under General Fremont in Virginia. Bvt. Colonel, USA, March 13, 1865, for faithful and meritorious services during the war. Battle honors: Western Virginia Campaign, Operations in Shenandoah Valley (Cross Keys), Atlanta Campaign (Rocky Face Ridge).

Born: April 28, 1818, Buffalo, NY

Died: June 3, 1893, New York City, NY

Other Wars: Mexican War (Bvt. Captain, USA, Sept. 13, 1847, for gallant and meritorious conduct in the battle of Chapultepec, Captain, 9 U.S. Infantry, Feb. 23, 1848). Utah War (Captain, 10 U.S. Infantry).

Occupation: Regular Army (Retired Nov. 4, 1865)

Offices/Honors: Maine Adjutant General, 1852–55

Miscellaneous: Resided Portland, Cumberland Co., ME; and New York City, NY. Born the son of John and Sarah (Kimball) Haddock, he assumed the name of the family benefactor, Albert H. Tracy, a local lawyer and civic leader.

Buried: Evergreen Cemetery, Portland, ME (Section G, Lot 26)

References: William H. Powell and Edward Shippen, editors. *Officers of the Army and Navy (Regular) Who Served in the Civil War.* Philadelphia, PA, 1892. Obituary Circular, Whole No. 108, Maine MOLLUS. Obituary, *Portland Daily Press*, June 5, 1893. Obituary, *Boston Globe*, June 5, 1893. Obituary, *Buffalo Commercial*, June 5, 1893. Letters Received, Appointment, Commission and Personal Branch, Adjutant General's Office, File 972(ACP)1885, National

Albert Tracy (Brady-Handy Photograph Collection, Library of Congress [LC-DIG-cwpbh-01770]).

Archives. Pension File, National Archives. Francis F. Wayland, editor, "Fremont's Pursuit of Jackson in the Shenandoah Valley: The Journal of Colonel Albert Tracy, March–July 1862," *Virginia Magazine of History and Biography*, Vol. 70, No. 2–3 (April–July 1962). Ray W. Irwin, editor, "Missouri in Crisis: The Journal of Captain Albert Tracy, 1861," *Missouri Historical Review*, Vol. 51, No. 1–3 (Oct. 1956, Jan. 1957, April 1957). J. Cecil Alter and Robert J. Dwyer, editors, "The Utah War: Journal of Captain Albert Tracy, 1858–1860," *Utah Historical Quarterly*, Vol. 13 (1945). Charles H. Farnam. *History of the Descendants of John Whitman of Weymouth, Mass.* New Haven, CT, 1889.

Benjamin Welch, Jr.

Colonel, Additional ADC, July 11, 1862. ADC, Staff of Major General John Pope, Army of Virginia, July–Sept. 1862 Battle honors: Northern Virginia Campaign.
Born: 1818? Kingston, NY
Died: April 14, 1863 Clifton Springs, NY
Occupation: Newspaper editor
Offices/Honors: New York State Treasurer, 1852–53. Commissary General, New York State Militia, 1859–62.
Miscellaneous: Resided Buffalo, Erie Co., NY
Buried: Sylvan Lawn Cemetery, Greene, Chenango Co., NY
References: Obituary, *Buffalo Commercial*, April 16, 1863. Obituary, *Buffalo Weekly Express*, April 21, 1863. Obituary, *New York Tribune*, April 15, 1863. Obituary, *Buffalo Daily Courier*, April 15, 1863. William J. Tenney. *The Military and Naval History of the Rebellion in the United States.* New York City, NY, 1865. Letters Received, Adjutant General's Office, File W811(AGO)1862, National Archives.

Edward Henry Wright

Major, 3 U.S. Cavalry, May 14, 1861. Lieutenant Colonel, ADC, Staff of Lieutenant General Winfield Scott, June 1, 1861–Aug. 19, 1861. Major, 6 U.S. Cavalry, Aug. 3, 1861. Colonel, Additional ADC, Aug. 19, 1861. ADC, Staff of Major Gen. George B. McClellan, Army of the Potomac, Aug.–Nov. 1861. Honorably discharged as Additional ADC, Nov. 1, 1861. Colonel Additional ADC, Jan. 15, 1862. ADC, Staff of Major Gen. George B. McClellan, Army of the Potomac, Jan.–Sept. 1862. Honorably discharged as Additional ADC, March 31, 1863. Resigned April 25, 1863. Battle honors: Peninsular Campaign, Antietam.
Born: April 5, 1824 Newark, NJ
Died: Sept. 17, 1913 Newark, NJ
Education: Graduated Princeton (NJ) University, 1844. Attended Harvard University Law School, Cambridge, MA.
Occupation: Lawyer and insurance company executive
Offices/Honors: Secretary of U.S. Legation, St. Petersburg, Russia, 1849–53
Miscellaneous: Resided Newark, Essex Co., NJ
Buried: Mount Pleasant Cemetery, Newark, NJ (Section R, Lot 123)
References: Francis Bazley Lee, editor. *Genealogical and Memorial History of the State of New Jersey.* New York City, NY, 1910. Samuel F. Bigelow and George J.

Edward Henry Wright (E. & H.T. Anthony, 501 Broadway, New York, from photographic negative in Brady's National Portrait Gallery; courtesy Steve Meadow).

Edward Henry Wright (Library of Congress [LC-DIG-cwpb-04668]).

Hagar, editors. *The Biographical Cyclopedia of New Jersey.* New York City, NY, 1908. Obituary, *Jersey Journal,* Sept. 18, 1913. Obituary, *Patterson Morning Call,* September 23, 1913. Obituary, *New York Sun,* Sept. 18, 1913. William H. Shaw, compiler. *History of Essex and Hudson Counties, New Jersey.* Philadelphia, PA, 1884. Pension File, National Archives. Letters Received, Commission Branch, Adjutant General's Office, File W177(CB)1863, National Archives.

Charles Zagonyi

Captain, Fremont's Body Guard, MO Cavalry, July 12, 1861. Major, Fremont's Body Guard, MO Cavalry, Sept. 19, 1861. Honorably mustered out, Nov. 30, 1861. Colonel, Additional ADC, March 31, 1862. Chief of Cavalry, Staff of Major Gen. John C. Fremont, Mountain Department, March–June 1862. Resigned June 4, 1864. Battle honors: Springfield, Operations in Shenandoah Valley (Woodstock, Cross Keys).

Born: 1824? Szatmar, Hungary

Died: Date and place of death unknown

Other Wars: Officer in Hungarian revolutionary army of 1848–49

Occupation: House painter and riding master before war. Reported by journalist and world traveler Junius Henri Browne, who knew Zagonyi in Missouri in 1861, to be the owner of a cigar shop in Pesth, Hungary, in 1869. This report, which was widely recirculated in 1871, has been discounted by most historians, who believe Zagonyi stayed in the United States.

Miscellaneous: Resided Philadelphia, PA; Boston, MA; and New York City,

Charles Zagonyi (H. E. Hoelke, Photographer, S. E. Cor. Fourth & Market, St. Louis, MO; author's photograph).

Charles Zagonyi (E. & H.T. Anthony, 501 Broadway, New York, from photographic negative in Brady's National Portrait Gallery; Massachusetts MOLLUS Collection, USAHEC [Vol. 73, p. 3643]).

NY. Best known for his heroic cavalry charge at Springfield (MO), Oct. 25, 1861, which became known as "Zagonyi's Death Ride."

Buried: Place of burial unknown

References: Istvan Kornel Vida. *Hungarian Émigrés in the American Civil War: A History and Biographical Dictionary*. Jefferson, NC, 2012. Stephen Beszedits, "Hungarians with General John C. Fremont in the American Civil War," *Vasvary Collection Newsletter*, (2003, No. 2). Edmund Vasvary. *Lincoln's Hungarian Heroes: The Participation of Hungarians in the Civil War, 1861-1865*. Washington, D.C., 1939. Eugene Pivany. *Hungarians in the American Civil War*. Cleveland, OH, 1913. Robert E. Miller, "Zagonyi," *Missouri Historical Review*, Vol. 76, No. 2 (Jan. 1982). Jessie Benton Fremont. *The Story of the Guard: A Chronicle of the War*. Boston, MA, 1863. Kip Lindberg and Jeff Patrick, "In the Shadow of the Light Brigade: The Charge of Fremont's Body Guard," *North & South*, Vol. 7, No. 3 (May 2004). Emil Lengyel. *Americans From Hungary*. Philadelphia and New York, 1948. Junius Henri Browne, "Letter from Hungary,"

Charles Zagonyi (Massachusetts MOLLUS Collection, USAHEC [Vol. 73, p. 3643L]).

Cincinnati Daily Enquirer, Aug. 22, 1869. Military Service File, National Archives. Letters Received, Adjutant General's Office, File Z4(AGO)1862, National Archives. Letters Received, Commission Branch, Adjutant General's Office, File Z4(CB)1864, National Archives.

Quartermasters

Alexander Bliss	May 7, 1866	Jan. 1, 1867
George W. Bradley	Nov. 7, 1864	Oct. 18, 1866
Raymond Burr	Dec. 3, 1864	Nov. 3, 1866
Byron O. Carr	Aug. 2, 1864	Jan. 31, 1865
George F. Clark	Sept. 19, 1864	Jan. 18, 1866
John C. Crane	Aug. 2, 1864	Jan. 1, 1867
Joel D. Cruttenden	Aug. 2, 1864	Nov. 3, 1866
John A. Elison	Aug. 2, 1864	Aug. 9, 1865
Herbert M. Enos	June 3, 1865	Jan. 8, 1866
John G. Farnsworth	Nov. 1, 1864	July 26, 1865
John H. Ferry	Aug. 2, 1864	Sept. 19, 1864
Michael C. Garber	Aug. 2, 1864	July 31, 1866
John B. Howard	May 26, 1865	Aug. 1, 1865
Henry Howland	June 23, 1865	Nov. 17, 1865
James G. Johnson	Aug. 2, 1864	June 19, 1865
George W. Lee	Feb. 18, 1865	May 31, 1866
William W. McKim	Aug. 2, 1864	March 8, 1866
Charles W. Moulton	Feb. 9, 1865	Oct. 4, 1865
Henry T. Noble	June 16, 1865	Oct. 5, 1866
William H. Owen	Aug. 2, 1864	Feb. 16, 1865
Gilbert A. Pierce	Aug. 24, 1864	May 13, 1865
Perley P. Pitkin	Aug. 2, 1864	Nov. 7, 1864
Charles K. Smith, Jr.	Nov. 4, 1865	Oct. 18, 1866
Ralph C. Webster	Aug. 2, 1864	July 11, 1865
Morris D. Wickersham	Oct. 6, 1865	Sept. 24, 1866

Biographies

Alexander Bliss

Captain, AQM, USV, Feb. 3, 1862. Acting Chief Quartermaster, 6 Army Corps, Army of the Potomac, Dec. 1862–March 1863. Captain, AQM, USA, March 13, 1863. AQM, Staff of Brig. Gen. Charles Griffin, 1 Division, 5 Army Corps, Army of the Potomac, March–May 1863. Assigned to duty as Lieutenant Colonel, April 20, 1863–Aug. 1, 1865. Chief Quartermaster, 8 Army Corps and Middle Department, May 1863–Oct. 1864. Acting Chief of 4 Division (River and Rail Transportation), Quartermaster General's Office, April 1865–May 1866. Assigned to duty as Colonel, Chief of 4 Division (Rail and River Transportation), Quartermaster General's Office, May 7, 1866–Jan. 1, 1867. Resigned March 30, 1868, having accepted a diplomatic appointment in Germany. Bvt. Major, USA, Bvt. Lieutenant Colonel, USA, and Bvt. Colonel, USA,

March 13, 1865, for faithful and meritorious services during the war. Battle honors: Peninsular Campaign, Fredericksburg, Chancellorsville, Monocacy.

Born: Dec. 29, 1827 Boston, MA

Died: April 30, 1896 Washington, D.C.

Education: Graduated Harvard University, Cambridge, MA, 1847

Occupation: Lawyer and diplomat

Offices/Honors: Secretary of Legation, Berlin, Germany, 1867–74

Miscellaneous: Resided Washington, D.C. Step-son of historian and diplomat George Bancroft. An original copy of Lincoln's Gettysburg Address, once owned by Alexander Bliss, is now on display in the Lincoln Room of the White House.

Buried: Arlington National Cemetery, Arlington, VA (Section 1, Site 537)

References: John Homer Bliss, compiler. *Genealogy of the Bliss Family in America from About the Year 1550 to 1880.* Boston, MA, 1881. James Grant Wilson, editor. *Appletons' Cyclopaedia of American Biography.* Vol. 7. New York City, NY, 1901. Obituary, *Washington Post,* May 1, 1896. Letters Received, Commission Branch, Adjutant General's Office, File B1160(CB)1863, National Archives. Carded Records Relating to Staff Officers, National Archives. Aaron T. Bliss. *Genealogy of the Bliss Family in America.* Midland, MI, 1982. Francis H. Brown. *Harvard University in the War of 1861–1865.* Boston, MA, 1886.

Alexander Bliss (The National Archives [Photographic Prints of Quartermaster Officers]).

George Willett Bradley

Captain, AQM, USV, Nov. 26, 1862. Quartermaster, Staff of Brig. Gen. Innis N. Palmer, 1 Division, 18 Army Corps, Department of North Carolina, March–June 1863. Quartermaster, Post of New Berne (NC), Department of Virginia and North Carolina, July 1863–Aug. 1864. Assigned to duty as Lieutenant Colonel, Chief Quartermaster, 10 Army Corps, Army of the James, Sept. 17–Nov. 6, 1864. Assigned to duty as Colonel, Nov. 7, 1864–Oct. 18, 1866. Chief Quartermaster, City Point (VA) Depot, Nov. 1864–June 1865. Chief Quartermaster, Department of Pennsylvania, June–July 1865. Chief Quartermaster, Middle Military Department, July 1865–Sept. 1866. Captain, AQM, USA, Nov. 4, 1865. Bvt. Major, USV, Bvt. Lieutenant Colonel, USV, and Bvt. Colonel, USV, March 13, 1865, for faithful and meritorious services during the war.

Born: April 8, 1830 Syracuse, NY

Died: Feb. 20, 1882 Philadelphia, PA

Occupation: Regular Army (Captain, AQM, USA) after war

Miscellaneous: Resided Syracuse, Onondaga Co., NY

Buried: Arlington National Cemetery, Arlington, VA (Sec. 1, Site 4-A). Cenotaph, Oakwood Cemetery, Syracuse, NY (Sec. 14, Lot 133)

References: Obituary, *Syracuse Morning Standard,* Feb. 22, 1882. Obituary, *Philadelphia Inquirer,* Feb. 22, 1882. Obituary, *Rochester Democrat and Chronicle,* Feb. 23, 1882. Pension File, National Archives. Letters Received, Appointment, Commission and Personal Branch, Adjutant General's Office, File 5073(ACP)1878, National Archives. Carded Records Relating to Staff Officers, National Archives. William M. Beauchamp. *Past and Present of Syracuse and Onondaga County, New York, From Prehistoric Times to the Beginning of 1908.* New York and Chicago, 1908.

George Willett Bradley (Stayner & Smith, New Bern, NC; author's photograph).

Raymond Burr

1 Lieutenant, Co. B, 55 OH Infantry, April 4, 1862. Captain, AQM, USV, July 14, 1862. Assigned to duty as Colonel, Chief Quartermaster, Columbus (OH) Quartermaster Depot, Dec. 3, 1864–Nov. 3, 1866. Honorably mustered out, Nov. 3, 1866. Bvt. Major, USV, Bvt. Lieutenant Colonel, USV, and Bvt. Colonel, USV, March 13, 1865, for faithful and meritorious services during the war.

Born: April 2, 1821 Meredith, Delaware Co., NY

Died: Jan. 26, 1892 Columbus, OH

Education: Attended Oberlin (OH) College

Occupation: Watch maker and jeweler before war. Assistant postmaster, penitentiary warden, hardware merchant and railroad inspector of watches after war.

Offices/Honors: Ohio House of Representatives, 1860–62. Assistant

Raymond Burr (Reports of Examining Boards as to Qualifications of Quartermaster Officers, 1864–65, Record Group 92, Entry 418, National Archives).

Postmaster, Columbus, OH, 1867–69 and 1875–85. Warden, Ohio Penitentiary, Columbus, OH, 1869–74.

Miscellaneous: Resided Delaware, Delaware Co., OH, before war; and Columbus, Franklin Co., OH, after war

Buried: Greenlawn Cemetery, Columbus, OH (Section R, Lot 144)

References: *The Biographical Encyclopaedia of Ohio of the Nineteenth Century.* Cincinnati and Philadelphia, 1876. Charles B. Todd. *A General History of the Burr Family.* New York City, NY, 1902. Obituary, *Ohio State Journal,* Jan. 28, 1892. Pension File, National Archives. Reports of Examining Boards as to Qualifications of Quartermaster Officers, 1864–65, Record Group 92, Entry 418, National Archives. Letters Received, Commission Branch, Adjutant General's Office, File B1534(CB)1864, National Archives. W. Cooper. *Sketches of the Senators and Representatives in the Fifty-Fourth General Assembly of the State of Ohio.* Columbus, OH, 1861.

Byron Oscar Carr

1 Lieutenant, RQM, 3 IL Cavalry, Sept. 6, 1861. Acting AQM, Staff of Major Gen. Samuel R. Curtis, Army of the Southwest, Department of the Mississippi, March–Sept. 1862. Captain, AQM, USV, Sept. 29, 1862. Chief Quartermaster, Staff of Major Gen. John M. Schofield, Army of the Frontier, Department of the Missouri, Oct. 1862–April 1863. Chief Quartermaster, Staff of Brig. Gen. John W. Davidson, Cavalry Division, Department of the Missouri, July–Aug. 1863. Chief Quartermaster, Staff of Major Gen. Frederick Steele, Army of Arkansas, Department of the Missouri, Aug. 1863–Jan. 1864. Chief Quartermaster, Staff of Major Gen. Frederick Steele, 7 Army Corps, Department of Arkansas, Feb.–May 1864. Assigned to duty as Lieutenant Colonel, May 12–Aug. 2, 1864. Chief Quartermaster, Staff of Major Gen. Frederick Steele, 7 Army Corps, Department of Arkansas, May–Aug. 1864. Assigned to duty as Colonel, Aug. 2, 1864–Jan. 31, 1865. Chief Quartermaster, Staff of Major Gen. Frederick Steele, Department of Arkansas, Aug.–Dec. 1864. Honorably mustered out, July 28, 1865. Battle honors: Pea Ridge, Cache Bayou, Springfield, Advance Upon Little Rock.

Born: April 24, 1832 Concord, Erie Co., NY

Died: Nov. 1, 1913 St. Helena, CA

Education: Attended Knox College, Galesburg, IL

Occupation: Railroad conductor

Byron Oscar Carr (Hoelke & Benecke, S.E. Cor. 4th and Market Sts., St. Louis, MO; Reports of Examining Boards as to Qualifications of Quartermaster Officers, 1864–65, Record Group 92, Entry 418, National Archives).

before war. Railroad superintendent, farmer, and bank manager after war.

Offices/Honors: Supervising Inspector of Steamboats, Louisville, KY, 1873–82

Miscellaneous: Resided Galesburg, Knox Co., IL, before war; Chicago, IL (1869); Louisville, Jefferson Co., KY, 1873–82; St. Helena, Napa Co., CA, 1882–89 and 1912–13; San Francisco, CA, 1889–91; Lemoore, Tulare Co., CA, 1891–99; Seattle, King Co., WA, 1899–1912. Brother of Brig. Gen. Eugene A. Carr.

Buried: St. Helena Public Cemetery, St. Helena, CA (Block C, Lot 23)

References: Obituary, *St. Helena Star*, Nov. 7, 1913. Obituary, *Napa Weekly Journal*, Nov. 14, 1913. Arthur A. Carr. *The Carr Book: Sketches of the Lives of Many of the Descendants of Robert and Caleb Carr, Whose Arrival on This Continent in 1635 Began the American Story of Our Family.* Ticonderoga, NY, 1947. Obituary, *Seattle Daily Times*, Nov. 6, 1913. Edson I. Carr. *The Carr Family Records.* Rockton, IL, 1894. Pension File and Military Service File, National Archives. Reports of Examining Boards as to Qualifications of Quartermaster Officers, 1864–65, Record Group 92, Entry 418, National Archives. Letters Received, Commission Branch, Adjutant General's Office, File C628(CB)1865, National Archives. Obituary Circular, Whole No. 223, Washington MOLLUS. *Directory of Knox People.* Galesburg, IL, 1923.

Byron Oscar Carr (author's photograph).

George F. Clark

Captain, AQM, USV, March 24, 1862. Post Quartermaster, Yorktown (VA), Aug. 1862–July 1864. Assigned to duty as Colonel, Chief Quartermaster, Louisville (KY) Quartermaster Depot, Sept. 19, 1864–Jan. 18, 1866. Honorably mustered out, Feb. 8, 1866. Bvt. Major, USV, Feb. 8, 1866, for faithful services in the Quartermaster's Department.

Born: 1828? Medina Co., OH

Died: Sept. 4, 1878 Medina, OH

Occupation: Miller and dry goods merchant before war. Wholesale grain and produce dealer after war.

Miscellaneous: Resided Kendallville, Noble Co., IN, before war; Louisville, Jefferson Co., KY, 1867–76; and Coldwater, Branch Co., MI, after war

Buried: Spring Grove Cemetery, Medina, OH (Section 4, Row 4)

References: Reports of Examining Boards as to Qualifications of Quartermaster Officers, 1864–65, Record Group 92, Entry 418, National Archives. Obituary,

Medina County Gazette, Sept. 6, 1878. Letters Received, Commission Branch, Adjutant General's Office, File C84(CB)1866, National Archives. Pension File, National Archives. *History of Medina County and Ohio.* Chicago, IL, 1881. *Counties of LaGrange and Noble, Indiana. Historical and Biographical.* Chicago, IL, 1882.

John C. Crane

1 Lieutenant, RQM, 1 MO Cavalry, Sept. 6, 1861. Despite widespread accusations of defrauding the Government, he was never brought to trial, and he resigned Feb. 24, 1862. Captain, AQM, USV, June 11, 1862. AQM, Staff of Brig. Gen. Andrew A. Humphreys, 3 Division, 5 Army Corps, Army of the Potomac, Dec. 1862–April 1863. AQM, U.S. Military Railroads, Military Division of the Mississippi, Dec. 1863–Nov. 1864. Assigned to duty as Colonel, Inspector, Quartermaster's Department, Aug. 2, 1864–Jan. 1, 1867. *Colonel,* 2 Regiment, Quartermaster's Forces, Department of the Cumberland, Sept. 3, 1864. *Colonel,* 4 Regiment (and commanding 2 Brigade), Quartermaster's Forces, Department of the Cumberland, Sept. 14, 1864. Court-martialed on charges of "Accepting valuable considerations from persons engaged in furnishing supplies to the Government, Corrupt and fraudulent conduct, and Willful and fraudulent neglect of duty," he was convicted in Dec. 1865, after a lengthy trial, and sentenced to be dismissed from the service. Upon appeal to Secretary of War Stanton and President Andrew Johnson, the sentence was remitted, "in view of the faithful and efficient and arduous services rendered by Col. Crane in his department at critical periods of the war," and he was honorably mustered out to date, Jan. 31, 1867.

George F. Clark (**Reports of Examining Boards as to Qualifications of Quartermaster Officers, 1864–65, Record Group 92, Entry 418, National Archives**).

Born: March 21, 1832 Johnstonburgh, Warren Co., NJ

Died: Feb. 15, 1883 Knoxville, TN

Occupation: Druggist before war. Commission merchant and pork packer in Cincinnati. Hotel steward in Knoxville.

Miscellaneous: Resided St. Louis, MO, to 1867; Cincinnati, OH, 1867–78; and Knoxville, Knox Co., TN, 1878–83

Buried: Spring Grove Cemetery, Cincinnati, OH (Section 100-A, Grave 365)

John C. Crane (J.H. Van Stavoren's Metropolitan Gallery, 53 College Street, Nashville, Tenn., H. Hall, Photographer; author's photograph).

John C. Crane (Tennessee Historical Society [34797]).

John C. Crane (J.H. Van Stavoren, Nashville, Tennessee; courtesy Ronald S. Coddington).

References: Letters Received, Appointment, Commission and Personal Branch, Adjutant General's Office, File 2856(ACP)1882, National Archives. Court-martial Case Files, 1809–1894, File MM-3216, National Archives. Letters Received, Adjutant General's Office, File C557(AGO)1862, National Archives. Leroy P. Graf and Ralph W. Haskins, editors. *The Papers of Andrew Johnson.* Vol. 6, 1862–1864. Knoxville, TN, 1983. Obituary, *Knoxville Daily Chronicle*, Feb. 17, 1883. Death notice, *Cincinnati Enquirer*, Feb. 19, 1883. "Letter from Nashville," *Cleveland Morning Leader*, Oct. 4, 1864. "Lamar House Change of Management," *Knoxville Daily Chronicle*, Feb. 19, 1882. Military Service File, National Archives. Personal Histories of Volunteer Officers in the Quartermaster Department, 1861–1865, National

Archives. *The War of the Rebellion: A Compilation of the Official Records of the Union and Confederate Armies.* Series 1, Vol. 52, Part 1, pp. 635–638. Washington, D.C., 1898. www.ancestry.com.

Joel Douglas Cruttenden

Captain, AQM, USV, Feb. 19, 1862. Taken prisoner, Strasburg, VA, May 25, 1862. Confined Salisbury, NC; and Richmond, VA. Exchanged Sept. 21, 1862. AQM, Artillery Brigade, 1 Army Corps, Army of the Potomac, May 1863–March 1864. AQM, Artillery Brigade, 5 Army Corps, Army of the Potomac, March–Aug. 1864. Assigned to duty as Colonel, Inspector, Quartermaster's Department, Aug. 2, 1864–Nov. 3, 1866. Honorably mustered out, Nov. 3, 1866. Bvt. Major, Bvt. Lieutenant Colonel, and Bvt. Colonel, USV, March 13, 1865, for faithful and meritorious services during the war.

Born: March 2, 1822, Georgetown, DC

Died: April 17, 1899, Columbus, OH

Occupation: Merchant, farmer, and real estate agent

Offices/Honors: Minnesota House of Representatives, 1857–59. Minnesota Senate, 1859–61. Register of U.S. Land Office, St. Cloud, MN, 1860–61. Register of Deeds, Bayfield Co., WI, 1872-90. Postmaster, Bayfield, WI, 1896–98.

Joel Douglas Cruttenden (Minnesota Legislature, 1858) (Hill, Kelley & Company; Minnesota Historical Society [por 23694 r1]).

Miscellaneous: Resided St. Anthony, Ramsey Co., MN; and St. Cloud, Stearns Co., MN, before war; and Bayfield, Bayfield Co., WI, after 1869

Buried: Maple Grove Cemetery, Granville, Licking Co., OH (Section 3, Lot 90)

References: Obituary, *Milwaukee Journal,* April 20, 1899. Pension File, National Archives. Alfred T. Andreas. *History of Northern Wisconsin.* Chicago, IL, 1881. Thomas M. Newson. *Pen Pictures of St. Paul, Minnesota, and Biographical Sketches of Old Settlers.* St. Paul, MN, 1886. Letters Received, Commission Branch, Adjutant General's Office, Files C336(CB)1864 and C591(CB)1866, National Archives. J. Fletcher Williams. *A History of the City of Saint Paul and of the County of Ramsey, Minnesota.* Saint Paul, MN, 1876. William Bell Mitchell. *History of Stearns County, Minnesota.* Chicago, IL, 1915. https://www.leg.state.mn.us/legdb/fulldetail?ID=11719.

John A. Elison

1 Lieutenant, RQM, 2 PA Cavalry, Oct. 23, 1861. Post Quartermaster, Convalescent Camp and Rendezvous of Distribution, Alexandria, VA, Jan. 1863–Aug. 1864.

Captain, AQM, USV, May 27, 1863. Assigned to duty as Colonel, Chief Quartermaster, Department of Washington, Aug. 2–Oct. 15, 1864. *Lieutenant Colonel*, 4 Regiment, Quartermaster's Volunteers, Department of Washington, Aug. 5, 1864. *Colonel*, 4 Quartermaster's Volunteers, Department of Washington, Sept. 8, 1864. Assigned to duty as Colonel, Chief Quartermaster, Chicago (IL) Quartermaster Depot, Feb. 27–Aug. 9, 1865. Honorably mustered out, Nov. 11, 1865.

Born: Dec. 1, 1825 Philadelphia, PA

Died: Sept. 26, 1893 Chicago, IL

Occupation: Boot and shoe merchant before war. Auctioneer after war.

Miscellaneous: Resided Philadelphia, PA, before war; and Chicago, IL, after war

Buried: Rosehill Cemetery, Chicago, IL (Section D, Lot 24, unmarked)

John A. Elison (Ronn Palm Collection).

References: Alfred T. Andreas. *History of Chicago from the Earliest Period to the Present Time.* Chicago, IL, 1884. Obituary, *Chicago Daily Tribune*, Sept. 27, 1893. Pension File and Military Service File, National Archives. Letters Received, Commission Branch, Adjutant General's Office, Files Q47(CB)1864 and E264(CB)1865, National Archives. Reports of Examining Boards as to Qualifications of Quartermaster Officers, 1864–65, Record Group 92, Entry 418, National Archives. *The War of the Rebellion: A Compilation of the Official Records of the Union and Confederate Armies.* Series 3, Vol. 4, pp. 699–700. Washington, D.C., 1900.

Herbert Merton Enos

1 Lieutenant, 6 U.S. Cavalry, May 14, 1861. Captain, AQM, USA, Aug. 3, 1861. Chief Quartermaster, District of Arizona, Jan.–Oct. 1863. Acting Chief Quartermaster, Department of New Mexico, Feb.–April 1864. Depot Quartermaster, Fort Union (NM), May 1864–Oct. 1865. Assigned to duty as Major, AQM, USV, Aug. 2, 1864–June 3, 1865. Chief Quartermaster, Department of New Mexico, Sept. 1864. Assigned to duty as Colonel, AQM, USV, June 3, 1865–Jan. 8, 1866. Chief Quartermaster, Department of New Mexico, June–Sept. 1865. Chief Quartermaster, District of New Mexico, Sept. 1865–Jan. 1866. Bvt. Major, Bvt. Lieutenant Colonel, and Bvt. Colonel, USA, March 13, 1865, for faithful and meritorious services during the war. Battle honors: Glorieta.

Born: March 10, 1833 Johnstown, NY

Died: Aug. 9, 1912 Waukesha, WI

Education: Graduated U.S. Military Academy, West Point, NY, 1856

Occupation: Regular Army (Major, Quartermaster's Department, retired May 29, 1876)

Miscellaneous: Resided Waukesha, Waukesha Co., WI
Buried: Oak Hill Cemetery, Watertown, WI (Block 4, Lot 20)
References: David I. Nelke. *The Columbian Biographical Dictionary and Portrait Gallery of the Representative Men of the United States.* Wisconsin Volume. Chicago, IL, 1895. *Forty-Fourth Annual Reunion of the Association of the Graduates of the United States Military Academy at West Point, New York, June 11, 1913.* Saginaw, MI, 1913. Obituary Circular, Whole No. 507, Wisconsin MOLLUS. Obituary, *Watertown Gazette,* Aug. 15, 1912. Obituary, *Watertown Weekly Leader,* Aug. 16, 1912. *Portrait and Biographical Record of Waukesha County, Wisconsin.* Chicago, IL, 1894. Theron W. Haight, editor. *Memoirs of Waukesha County.* Madison, WI, 1907. George W. Cullum. *Biographical Register of the Officers and Graduates of the U.S. Military Academy at West Point, N.Y.* Third Edition. Boston and New York, 1891. Jerry D. Thompson. *A Civil War History of the New Mexico Volunteers & Militia.* Albuquerque, NM, 2015. Letters Received, Appointment, Commission and Personal Branch, Adjutant General's Office, File 1372(ACP)1871, National Archives.

John Gosman Farnsworth

Captain, AQM, USV, April 14, 1862. Assigned to duty as Lieutenant Colonel, Chief Quartermaster, 4 Army Corps, Department of Virginia, Jan. 1, 1863–Aug. 10, 1863. Depot Quartermaster, Wheeling (WV), Department of West Virginia, Feb.–Oct. 1864. Assigned to duty as Colonel, Chief Quartermaster, Department of West Virginia, Nov. 1, 1864–July 26, 1865. Honorably mustered out, Oct. 23, 1865. Bvt. Major, Bvt. Lieutenant Colonel, and Bvt. Colonel, USV, March 13, 1865, for faithful and meritorious services during the war. Battle honors: Chattanooga Campaign.

Born: Jan. 21, 1832 Elmira, NY
Died: April 6, 1895 Washington, D.C.
Occupation: Wholesale lumber merchant
Offices/Honors: Colonel, 10 NY National Guard, 1868–71. Adjutant General, State of New York, 1883–85.
Miscellaneous: Resided Albany, Albany Co., NY
Buried: Rural Cemetery, Albany, NY (Section 30, Lot 53)
References: Amasa J. Parker, editor. *Landmarks of Albany County, New York.* Syracuse, NY, 1897. Obituary, *Albany Evening Journal,* April 8, 1895. Obituary, *New York Times,* April 7, 1895. Obituary, *Washington Evening Star,* April 8, 1895. Obituary

John Gosman Farnsworth (The National Archives [Photographic Prints of Quartermaster Officers]).

Circular, Whole No. 463, New York MOLLUS. Claudius B. Farnsworth. *Matthias Farnsworth and his Descendants in America.* Pawtucket, RI, 1891. Letters Received, Adjutant General's Office, File F172(AGO)1862, National Archives. Letters Received, Appointment, Commission and Personal Branch, Adjutant General's Office, File 4813(ACP)1884, National Archives. Personal Histories of Volunteer Officers in the Quartermaster Department, 1861–1865, National Archives.

John Hardin Ferry

Captain, Co. E, 7 IN Infantry (3 months), April 22, 1861. Honorably mustered out, Aug. 2, 1861. Captain, Co. A, 7 IN Infantry (3 years), Sept. 11, 1861. Acting AQM, Staff of Brig. Gen. Ebenezer Dumont, 17 Brigade, 3 Division, Department of the Ohio, Jan.–Feb. 1862. Captain, AQM, USV, April 14, 1862. Chief Quartermaster, Army of Kentucky, Sept.–Oct. 1862. Chief Quartermaster, 3 Army Corps, Army of the Ohio, Oct. 1862. Taken prisoner, Oct. 18, 1862. Exchanged Nov. 25, 1862. Superintendent of Railroad Transportation, Louisville (KY) Quartermaster Depot, Dec. 1862–Aug. 1864. Assigned to duty as Colonel, Chief Quartermaster, Louisville (KY) Quartermaster Depot, Aug. 2, 1864–Sept. 19, 1864. Failing to report for duty at Memphis (TN) after being relieved at Louisville, he was arrested, Nov. 9, 1864, and charged with "Disobedience of Orders." Explaining that he was busy settling his accounts, he was acquitted by Court-Martial, May 15, 1865, and he resigned May 27, 1865. Battle honors: Cumberland Gap Campaign.

Born: June 18, 1830 Wood Co., WV

Died: Jan. 27, 1884 Indianapolis, IN

Occupation: Railroad brakeman and telegraph operator before war. Lawyer, pension claim agent and notary public after war.

Miscellaneous: Resided Aurora, Dearborn Co., IN, before war; Washington, D.C., 1870–80; and Jersey City, Hudson Co., NJ, 1880–84. Nephew of Ohio Governor John Brough.

Buried: Crown Hill Cemetery, Indianapolis, IN (Section 27, Lot 69)

References: Pension File and Military Service File, National Archives. Obituary, *Indianapolis Journal*, Jan. 28, 1884. Obituary, *Indianapolis Daily Sentinel*, Jan. 28, 1884. Obituary, *Indianapolis News*, Jan. 28, 1884. Letters Received, Commission Branch, Adjutant General's Office, File F132(CB)1865, National Archives. Court-martial Case Files, 1809–1894, File OO-1102, National Archives. Letters Received, Adjutant General's Office, File F29(AGO)1865, National Archives. Carded Records Relating to Staff Officers, National Archives. Personal Histories of Volunteer Officers in the Quartermaster Department, 1861–1865, National Archives.

Michael Christian Garber

Captain, AQM, USV, Oct. 31, 1861. AQM, Staff of Brig. Gen. George W. Morgan, 7 Division, Army of the Ohio, March–Oct. 1862. AQM, Staff of Brig. Gen. George W. Morgan, 3 Division, Right Wing, 13 Army Corps, Army of the Tennessee, Dec. 1862. AQM, Staff of Brig. Gen. George W. Morgan, 13 Army Corps, Army of the Mississippi, Jan. 1863. AQM, Staff of Major Gen. John A. McClernand, 13 Army Corps, Department of the Tennessee, March–June 1863. AQM, Staff of Major Gen.

John A. McClernand, 13 Army Corps, Department of the Gulf, March–April 1864. Chief Quartermaster, Staff of Brig. Gen. William P. Benton, Detachment, 13 Army Corps, Department of the Gulf, May 1864. Assigned to duty as Colonel, Aug. 2, 1864–Aug. 7, 1865. Chief Quartermaster, Staff of Major Gen. Oliver O. Howard, Department of the Tennessee, Aug.–Nov. 1864. Senior Chief Quartermaster, Staff of Major Gen. Oliver O. Howard, Department of the Tennessee, Nov. 1864–Jan. 1865. Chief Quartermaster, Staff of Major Gen. William T. Sherman, Military Division of the Mississippi, Jan.–Aug. 1865. Assigned to duty as Colonel, Dec. 20, 1865–July 31, 1866. Chief Quartermaster, Staff of Major Gen. Thomas H. Ruger, Department of North Carolina, Dec. 1865–June 1866. Honorably mustered out, July 31, 1866. Bvt. Major, USV; Bvt. Lieutenant Colonel, USV; and Bvt. Colonel, USV, March 13, 1865, for faithful and meritorious services during the war. Battle honors: Mill Springs, Cumberland Gap Campaign, Chickasaw Bluffs, Arkansas Post, Vicksburg Campaign (Champion Hills, Black River Bridge), Campaign of the Carolinas.

Michael Christian Garber (author's photograph).

Born: April 7, 1813, Staunton, VA
Died: April 8, 1881, Madison, IN
Occupation: Newspaper editor and publisher
Offices/Honors: Postmaster, Madison, IN, 1875–81
Miscellaneous: Resided Madison, Jefferson Co., IN
Buried: Springdale Cemetery, Madison, IN (Plat 3, Lot 297)
References: George Irving Reed, editor. *Encyclopedia of Biography of Indiana.* Chicago, IL, 1895. Obituary, *Madison Daily Courier,* April 11, 1881. William W. Woollen. *Biographical and Historical Sketches of Early Indiana.* Indianapolis, IN, 1883. *Biographical and Historical Souvenir for the Counties of Clark, Crawford, Harrison, Floyd, Jefferson, Jennings, Scott and Washington, Indiana.* Chicago, IL, 1889. Mark A. Furnish, editor. *The Civil War Letters of Col. Michael C. Garber.* Madison, IN, 2009. Rolla Doolittle, "Colonel Michael C. Garber," *The Indianian: An Illustrated Monthly Magazine,* Vol. 5, No. 2 (Feb. 1900). Obituary, *Indianapolis News,* April 9, 1881. Letters Received, Commission Branch, Adjutant General's Office, File G72(CB)1863, National Archives.

John Brainard Howard

1 Lieutenant, Co. K, 84 NY Infantry, May 23, 1861. Acting AQM, Staff of Brig. Gen. Andrew Porter, 1 Brigade, 2 Division, Army of Northeastern Virginia, July–Aug. 1861.

John Brainard Howard (USAHEC [RG98S-CWP28.8]).

John Brainard Howard (Gardner, Corner 7th & D Sts., Washington, D.C.; courtesy Olaf]).

Acting AQM, Staff of Brig. Gen. Andrew Porter, Provost Marshal General, Army of the Potomac, Oct. 1861–Aug. 1862. Captain, AQM, USV, June 30, 1862. Assigned to duty as Lieutenant Colonel, July 7, 1863–May 26, 1865. Chief Quartermaster, Staff of Major Gen. William H. French, 3 Army Corps, Army of the Potomac, July 1863–March 1864. Acting Chief Quartermaster, Staff of Major Gen. Philip H. Sheridan, Cavalry Corps, Army of the Potomac, March–July 1864. Chief Quartermaster, Staff of Major Gen. Edward O.C. Ord, 18 Army Corps, Department of Virginia and North Carolina, July–Sept. 1864. Chief Quartermaster, Staff of Major Gen. John Gibbon, 24 Army Corps, Army of the James, Feb.–April 1865. Chief Quartermaster, Staff of Major Gen. Edward O.C. Ord, Army of the James, April–June 1865. Assigned to duty as

John Brainard Howard (center, Staff of Major Gen. William H. French, Sept. 1863) (Massachusetts MOLLUS Collection, USAHEC [Vol. 32, p. 1551]).

Colonel, May 26–Aug. 1, 1865. Honorably mustered out, July 30, 1867. Bvt. Major, USV; Bvt. Lieutenant Colonel, USV; and Bvt. Colonel, USV, March 13, 1865, for faithful and meritorious services during the war. Battle honors: First Bull Run.

Born: Nov. 8, 1829 Ulster Co., NY
Died: May 8, 1876 Brooklyn, NY
Occupation: Merchant and clerk
Miscellaneous: Resided Brooklyn, NY. Born the son of James H. and Eliza (Howell) Longbotham, he officially changed his name in 1857.
Buried: Trinity Cemetery, Hewlett, Nassau Co., NY (Range 14, Lot 18)
References: Pension File and Military Service File, National Archives. Letters Received, Commission Branch, Adjutant General's Office, File H1018(CB)1865, National Archives. Letters Received, Adjutant General's Office, File H618(AGO)1862, National Archives. Death notice, *Brooklyn Daily Eagle*, May 9, 1876. Death notice, *New York Herald*, May 10, 1876. C.V. Tevis and D.R. Marquis, compilers. *The History of the Fighting Fourteenth*. Brooklyn, NY, 1911.

Henry Howland

1 Lieutenant, RQM, 51 IL Infantry, Sept. 20, 1861. Acting AQM, Staff of Brig. Gen. Eleazer A. Paine and Brig. Gen. James D. Morgan, 1 Division, Army of the Mississippi, March–Oct. 1862. Captain, AQM, USV, June 9, 1862. AQM, Staff of Brig. Gen. John M. Palmer, 2 Division, Left Wing, 14 Army Corps, Army of the Cumberland, Dec. 1862–Jan. 1863. AQM, Staff of Major Gen. John M. Palmer, 2 Division, 21 Army Corps Army of the Cumberland, Jan.–Oct. 1863. AQM, Staff of Major Gen. David S. Stanley, 1 Division, 4 Army Corps, Army of the Cumberland, Nov. 1863–Jan. 1864. Chief Quartermaster, Bridgeport (AL) Quartermaster Depot, Jan.–Aug. 1864. Chief Quartermaster, Johnsonville (TN) Quartermaster Depot, Aug.–Nov. 1864. Chief Quartermaster, Staff of Major Gen. John M. Palmer, Department of Kentucky, March–Nov. 1865. Assigned to duty as Colonel, June 23–Nov. 17, 1865. Although he was later found guilty by court martial of embezzlement and related charges while Chief Quartermaster, Department of Kentucky, his sentence was remitted upon review, and he was mustered out, Jan. 19, 1867. In remitting his sentence, the Bureau of Military Justice found "a reasonable

Henry Howland (Hesler, Artist, No. 113 Lake Street, Chicago, IL; author's photograph).

Henry Howland (C.C. Giers' Photograph Gallery, Cor. Square and Deadrick St., Nashville, TN; courtesy Steve Meadow).

Henry Howland (D.C. Bettison, Photographer, Main Street, below Second, Over Telegraph Office, Louisville, KY; author's photograph).

doubt upon the imputation of fraudulent intent" on his part, but also found that "he fell far short of the strict vigilance and business accuracy which were demanded by his official responsibility and position." Bvt. Major, USV, March 13, 1865, for faithful and meritorious services during the war. Battle honors: Stone's River, Chickamauga, Forrest's Raid into West Tennessee (Johnsonville).

Born: March 29, 1827, Conway, MA

Died: May 6, 1883, Rochester, NY (accidentally drowned)

Occupation: Lumber merchant. Later engaged in a short-lived mining operation. Traveling sales agent at his death.

Miscellaneous: Resided Chicago, IL; and Leadville, Lake Co., CO

Buried: Rosehill Cemetery, Chicago, IL (Section 101, Lot 19)

References: Obituary, *Chicago Daily Tribune*, May 8, 1883. Pension File and Military Service File, National Archives. Letters Received, Commission Branch, Adjutant General's Office, File H24(CB)1864, National Archives. Reports of Examining Boards as to Qualifications of Quartermaster Officers, 1864–65, Record Group 92, Entry 418, National Archives. John Fitch. *Annals of the Army of the Cumberland*. Philadelphia, PA, 1863. Obituary, *Rochester Democrat and Chronicle*, May 7, 1883. Myron J. Smith, Jr. *Civil War Biographies from the Western*

Waters. Jefferson, NC, 2015. Frederick Clifton Pierce. *Field Genealogy.* Chicago, IL, 1901.

James Gould Johnson

Captain, AQM, USV, July 3, 1862. Depot Quartermaster, Harrisburg (PA) Quartermaster Depot, July 1863–March 1864. Chief Quartermaster, Staff of Major Gen. Darius N. Couch, Department of the Susquehanna, March–Nov. 1864. Assigned to duty as Colonel, Aug. 2, 1864–June 19, 1865. Chief Quartermaster, Staff of Major Gen. George Cadwalader, Department of Pennsylvania, Dec. 1864–June 1865. Dismissed, June 19, 1865, for "Disobedience of Orders," having "disobeyed the orders he received ... with regard to the repair of the hospital buildings at Carlisle Barracks, substituting his own judgment in the matter for a clearly expressed order of the War Department."

Born: Sept. 13, 1811 Bloomfield, Ontario Co., NY

Died: Jan. 3, 1882 Olean, NY

Occupation: Merchant, lumber manufacturer, and oil producer

Offices/Honors: New York State Assembly, 1848–49. Postmaster, Olean, NY, 1871–77.

Miscellaneous: Resided Allegany, Cattaraugus Co., NY; and Olean, Cattaraugus Co., NY

Buried: Mount View Cemetery, Olean, NY (Section B, Lot 117)

James Gould Johnson (Franklin Ellis. *History of Cattaraugus Co., New York.* Philadelphia, PA, 1879).

References: Franklin Ellis. *History of Cattaraugus County, New York.* Philadelphia, PA, 1879. Obituary, *Olean Daily Herald,* Jan. 4, 1882. Obituary, *Olean Democrat,* Jan. 5, 1882. William R. Cutter, editor. *Genealogical and Family History of Western New York.* New York City, NY, 1912. William Adams, editor. *Historical Gazetteer and Biographical Memorial of Cattaraugus County, N.Y.* Syracuse, NY, 1893. Obituary, *Buffalo Morning Express,* Jan. 7, 1882. Letters Received, Commission Branch, Adjutant General's Office, File J127(CB)1865, National Archives. Letters Received, Adjutant General's Office, File J170(AGO)1862, National Archives.

George Washington Lee

Captain, AQM, USV, Oct. 31, 1861. AQM, Detroit (MI) Quartermaster Depot, Nov. 1861–Feb. 1865. Assigned to duty as Colonel, Feb. 18, 1865–May 31, 1866. Chief

Quartermaster, Detroit (MI) Quartermaster Depot, Feb. 1865–May 1866. Honorably mustered out, May 31, 1866. Bvt. Major, USV; Bvt. Lieutenant Colonel, USV; and Bvt. Colonel, USV, March 13, 1865, for faithful and meritorious services during the war.

Born: Oct. 24, 1812 Greene, Chenango Co., NY

Died: June 8, 1882 Ypsilanti, MI

Occupation: Merchant and farmer before war. Lake vessel owner and Indian agent after war.

Offices/Honors: Postmaster, Howell, MI, 1849–53. U.S. Indian Agent, Mackinac (MI) Agency, 1876–82.

Miscellaneous: Resided Howell, Livingston Co., MI, before war. Detroit, Wayne Co., MI; and Ypsilanti, Washtenaw Co., MI, after war.

Buried: Highland Cemetery, Ypsilanti, MI (Block 92, Lot 22)

References: *American Biographical History of Eminent and Self-Made Men.* Michigan Volume. Cincinnati, OH, 1878.

George Washington Lee (Reports of Examining Boards as to Qualifications of Quartermaster Officers, 1864–65, Record Group 92, Entry 418, National Archives).

Obituary, *Ypsilanti Commercial,* June 10, 1882. Obituary, *Detroit Evening News,* June 8, 1882. Obituary, *Saginaw Herald,* June 15, 1882. *History of Washtenaw County, Michigan.* Chicago, IL, 1881. Reports of Examining Boards as to Qualifications of Quartermaster Officers, 1864–65, Record Group 92, Entry 418, National Archives. Letters Received, Adjutant General's Office, File L348(AGO)1861, National Archives. Letters Received, Commission Branch, Adjutant General's Office, File S166(CB)1865, National Archives.

William Walker McKim

Captain, AQM, USV, Aug. 3, 1861. AQM, Boston (MA) Quartermaster Depot, Aug. 1861–Aug. 1864. Captain, AQM, USA, July 2, 1864. Assigned to duty as Colonel, Aug. 2, 1864–March 8, 1866. Chief Quartermaster, Cincinnati (OH) Quartermaster Depot, Sept. 1864–Feb. 1865. Chief Quartermaster, Philadelphia (PA) Quartermaster Depot, Feb. 1865–March 1866. Resigned March 8, 1866. Bvt. Major, USA; Bvt. Lieutenant Colonel, USA; and Bvt. Colonel, USA, March 13, 1865, for faithful and meritorious services during the war.

Born: Jan. 2, 1828 Charlestown, MA

Died: April 2, 1895 Boston, MA

Occupation: Bookseller before war. U.S. Customs official and Purchasing Agent, New York and New England Railroad, after war.

Offices/Honors: Deputy Collector, Boston Custom House, 1873–74

Miscellaneous: Resided Buffalo, Erie Co., NY, before war; and Boston, MA, after war

Buried: Originally Forest Hills Cemetery, Jamaica Plain, MA. Removed to Warwick, MA, May 25, 1895. Removed to Mount Auburn Cemetery, Cambridge, MA (Bigelow Chapel Columbarium), Dec. 9, 1918.

References: Obituary, *Boston Journal*, April 3, 1895. Obituary, *Boston Evening Transcript*, April 3, 1895. Letters Received, Commission Branch, Adjutant General's Office, File M200(CB)1866, National Archives. www.ancestry.com. www.findagrave.com.

Charles William Moulton

Captain, AQM, USV, June 26, 1861. AQM, Gallipolis (OH) Quartermaster Depot, March 1862–March 1863. Captain, AQM, USA, March 13, 1863. AQM, Cincinnati (OH) Quartermaster Depot, May 1863–Oct. 1864. Resigned Oct. 7, 1864. Order accepting resignation revoked, Jan. 5, 1865. Assigned to duty as Colonel, Feb. 9–Oct. 4, 1865. Chief Quartermaster, Cincinnati (OH) Quartermaster Depot, Feb.–Oct. 1865. Resigned Oct. 4, 1865. Bvt. Major, USA; Bvt. Lieutenant Colonel, USA; and Bvt. Colonel, USA, March 13, 1865, for faithful and meritorious services during the war.

Born: Dec. 16, 1830 Richfield, Summit Co., OH

Died: Jan. 24, 1888 New York City, NY

Occupation: Lawyer

Miscellaneous: Resided Mansfield, Richland Co., OH; and Toledo, Lucas Co., OH, before war; Cincinnati, OH; and New York City, NY; after war. Brother-in-law of Major Gen. William T. Sherman. First cousin of Bvt. Brig. Gen. Russell A. Alger (5 MI Cavalry).

Buried: Spring Grove Cemetery, Cincinnati, OH (Section 103, Lot 24)

References: Henry W. Moulton. *Moulton Annals*. Chicago, IL, 1906. James A. Blanchard, "An Eloquent Memorial Tribute," *Grand Army Review*, Vol. 3, No. 10 (March

William Walker McKim (Massachusetts MOLLUS Collection, USAHEC [Commandery Series, Vol. 6, p. 228L]).

Charles William Moulton (The National Archives [Photographic Prints of Quartermaster Officers]).

1888). Obituary, *New York Tribune*, Jan. 25, 1888. Obituary, *New York Herald*, Jan. 25, 1888. Obituary, *Atchison Daily Globe*, Feb. 4, 1888. Absalom H. Mattox. *A History of the Cincinnati Society of Ex-Army and Navy Officers*. Cincinnati, OH, 1880. *The Biographical Encyclopaedia of Ohio of the Nineteenth Century*. Cincinnati and Philadelphia, 1876. *Appletons' Annual Cyclopaedia and Register of Important Events of the Year 1888*. New Series, Vol. 13. New York City, NY, 1889. *Report of the Proceedings of the Society of the Army of the Tennessee at the Twenty-First Meeting*. Cincinnati, OH, 1893. Letters Received, Commission Branch, Adjutant General's Office, File M236(CB)1863, National Archives. George Alfred Townsend, "Colonel C.W. Moulton and His Habits," *Cincinnati Enquirer*, Jan. 28, 1888.

Henry Theophilus Noble

Captain, Co. A, 13 IL Infantry, May 24, 1861. Acting ADC, Staff of Colonel John B. Wyman, 1 Brigade, 2 Division, Army of the Southwest, May–Oct. 1862. Acting AQM, Staff of Brig. Gen. Willis A. Gorman, District of Eastern Arkansas, Department of the Tennessee, Dec. 1862–Feb. 1863. Acting AQM, Staff of Brig. Gen. Leonard F. Ross, 13 Division, 13 Army Corps, Army of the Tennessee, Feb.–April 1863. Acting ADC, Staff of Brig. Gen. Peter J. Osterhaus, 9 Division, 13 Army Corps, Army of the Tennessee, April–July 1863. Captain, AQM, USV, July 8, 1863. AQM, District of Eastern Arkansas, Army of the Tennessee, July 1863–Jan. 1864. AQM, Staff of Brig. Gen. Frederick Salomon, 3 Division (and 1 Division), 7 Army Corps, Department of

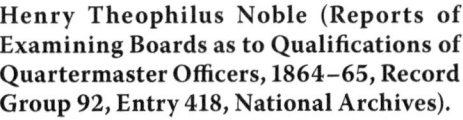

Henry Theophilus Noble (Reports of Examining Boards as to Qualifications of Quartermaster Officers, 1864–65, Record Group 92, Entry 418, National Archives).

Henry Theophilus Noble (post-war) (*Military History and Reminiscences of the Thirteenth Regiment of Illinois Volunteer Infantry in the Civil War in the United States, 1861–1865*. Chicago, IL, 1892).

Arkansas, Jan.–July 1864. AQM, District of Eastern Arkansas, Department of Arkansas, Aug.–Nov. 1864. Acting Chief Quartermaster, Staff of Major Gen. Joseph J. Reynolds, Department of Arkansas, Dec. 1864–May 1865. Assigned to duty as Colonel, June 16, 1865–Oct. 5, 1866. Chief Quartermaster, Staff of Major Gen. Joseph J. Reynolds and Major Gen. Edward O.C. Ord, Department of Arkansas, June 1865–Oct. 1866. Honorably mustered out, Oct. 5, 1866. Bvt. Major, USV; Bvt. Lieutenant Colonel, USV; and Bvt. Colonel, USV, March 13, 1865, for faithful and meritorious services during the war. Battle honors: Yazoo Pass Expedition, Vicksburg Campaign.

Born: May 3, 1829, Otis, Berkshire Co., MA

Died: April 15, 1891, Dixon, IL

Occupation: Farmer and banker before war. Plow manufacturer after war.

Miscellaneous: Resided Dixon, Lee Co., IL. Nephew of Colonel Silas Noble (2 IL Cavalry).

Buried: Oakwood Cemetery, Dixon, IL (Lot 376)

References: John Moses, editor. *Biographical Dictionary and Portrait Gallery of the Representative Men of the United States.* Illinois Volume. Chicago, IL, 1896. *Portrait and Biographical Record of Lee County, Illinois.* Chicago, IL, 1892. *History of Lee County.* Chicago, IL, 1881. Obituary, *Dixon Telegraph,* April 15, 1891. Obituary Circular, Whole No. 156, Illinois MOLLUS. Lucius M. Boltwood, compiler. *History and Genealogy of the Family of Thomas Noble of Westfield, Massachusetts.* Hartford, CT, 1878. *Military History and Reminiscences of the Thirteenth Regiment of Illinois Volunteer Infantry in the Civil War in the United States, 1861–1865.* Chicago, IL, 1892. *Report of the Proceedings of the Society of the Army of the Tennessee at the Twenty-Third Meeting.* Cincinnati, OH, 1893. Pension File and Military Service File, National Archives. Letters Received, Commission Branch, Adjutant General's Office, File N150(CB)1863, National Archives. Reports of Examining Boards as to Qualifications of Quartermaster Officers, 1864–65, Record Group 92, Entry 418, National Archives. Myron J. Smith, Jr. *Civil War Biographies from the Western Waters.* Jefferson, NC, 2015.

William Henry Owen

1 Lieutenant, Co. K, 3 ME Infantry, Aug. 19, 1861. Captain, AQM, USV, Oct. 31, 1861. AQM, 2 Brigade, 1 Division, 3 Army Corps, Army of the Potomac, March–Nov. 1862. AQM, Staff of Major Gen. David B. Birney, 1 Division, 3 Army Corps, Army of the Potomac, Nov.–Dec. 1862. AQM, Staff of Brig.

William Henry Owen (R.W. Addis, Photographer, 308 Penna. Avenue, Washington, D.C.; Craig T. Johnson Collection).

William Henry Owen (Craig T. Johnson Collection).

William Henry Owen (Bogardus, Photographer, 363 Broadway, New York; author's photograph).

Gen. Oliver O. Howard, 2 Division, 2 Army Corps, Army of the Potomac, Dec. 1862–April 1863. Assigned to duty as Lieutenant Colonel, May 22, 1863–Aug. 2, 1864. Chief Quartermaster, 5 Army Corps, Army of the Potomac, May 1863–Aug. 1864. Assigned to duty as Colonel, Aug. 2, 1864–Feb. 16, 1865. Inspector, Quartermaster's Department, Aug. 1864–Feb. 1865. Honorably mustered out, June 19, 1865. Battle honors: Peninsular Campaign, Gettysburg.

Born: Feb. 5, 1830 Brookhaven, Suffolk Co., NY

Died: Dec. 31, 1903 Washington, D.C.

Education: Graduated Bowdoin College, Brunswick, ME, 1851. Graduated Columbia University Law School, 1861.

Occupation: Lawyer and civil engineer

Miscellaneous: Resided Brooklyn, NY, before war; Washington, D.C.; and San Antonio, Bexar Co., TX (1877–83), after war

Buried: Arlington National Cemetery, Arlington, VA (Section 3, Site 1701). Cenotaph at Union Cemetery, Middle Island, Suffolk Co., NY.

References: Nehemiah Cleaveland and Alpheus S. Packard. *History of Bowdoin College with Biographical Sketches of Its Graduates from 1806 to 1879, Inclusive.* Boston, MA, 1882. Obituary, *Washington Post,* Jan. 1, 1904. Obituary, *Washington Evening Star,* Jan. 1, 1904. Obituary, *New York Daily Tribune,* Jan. 5, 1904. Pension File, National Archives. Letters Received, Commission Branch, Adjutant General's Office,

File O152(CB)1866, National Archives. Letters Received, Volunteer Service Branch, Adjutant General's Office, File O21(VS)1869, National Archives. *General Catalogue of Bowdoin College and the Medical School of Maine: A Biographical Record of Alumni and Officers, 1794–1950.* Brunswick, ME, 1950. *Catalogue of Alpha Delta Phi.* New York City, NY, 1899. Obituary Circular, Whole No. 372, District of Columbia MOLLUS.

Gilbert Ashville Pierce

2 Lieutenant, Co. H, 9 IN Infantry, April 22, 1861. Honorably mustered out, July 29, 1861. Captain, AQM, USV, Aug. 3, 1861. Chief Quartermaster, Paducah (KY) Quartermaster Depot, Dec. 1861–Dec. 1862. AQM, Staff of Brig. Gen. John McArthur, 6 Division, 17 Army Corps, Army of the Tennessee, Feb.–May 1863. AQM, Vicksburg (MS) Quartermaster Depot, July–Sept. 1863. Assigned to duty as Lieutenant Colonel, Sept. 12, 1863–March 2, 1864. Assistant Chief Quartermaster, Department of the Tennessee, Dec. 1863–Feb. 1864. Chief Quartermaster, Staff of Major Gen. John A. McClernand, 13 Army Corps, Department of the Gulf, March–April 1864. Assigned to duty as Colonel, Aug. 24, 1864–May 13, 1865. Inspector, Quartermaster's Department, Aug. 1864–May 1865. Volunteer ADC, Staff of Brig. Gen. John P. Hatch, Coast Division, Department of the South, Nov. 1864. GSW Honey Hill, SC, Nov. 30, 1864. Honorably mustered out, Oct. 7, 1865. Bvt. Major, USV; Bvt. Lieutenant Colonel, USV; and Bvt. Colonel, USV, July 25, 1865, for faithful and meritorious services during the war. Battle honors: Vicksburg Campaign, Honey Hill.

Born: Jan. 11, 1838 East Otto, Cattaraugus Co., NY

Died: Feb. 15, 1901 Chicago, IL

Education: Attended Old University of Chicago (IL)

Occupation: Lawyer, newspaper editor, and author

Offices/Honors: Indiana House of Representatives, 1867–69. Governor of Dakota Territory, 1884–87. U.S. Senate, 1889–91. U.S. Minister to Portugal, 1893.

Miscellaneous: Resided Valparaiso, Porter Co., IN; Chicago, IL; and Minneapolis, MN. Author of *The Dickens Dictionary* and several novels.

Buried: Adams Cemetery, near Malden, Porter Co., IN

References: Allen Johnson and Dumas Malone, editors. *Dictionary of American Biography.* New York City,

Gilbert Ashville Pierce (Swymmer's Gallery, 147 Canal St., New Orleans. LA; author's photograph).

NY, 1964. Thomas A. McMullin and David Walker. *Biographical Directory of American Territorial Governors.* Westport, CT, 1984. *The Biographical Encyclopaedia of Illinois of the Nineteenth Century.* Philadelphia, PA, 1875. Obituary Circular, Whole No. 249, Minnesota MOLLUS. James L. Harrison, compiler. *Biographical Directory of the American Congress, 1774–1949.* Washington, D.C., 1950. Obituary, *Chicago Daily Inter Ocean,* Feb. 16, 1901. Obituary, *Minneapolis Tribune,* Feb. 16, 1901. Clark J. Pahlas, "Gilbert A. Pierce: Eighth Territorial Governor," *The WI–IYOHI, Monthly Bulletin of the South Dakota Historical Society,* Vol. 12, No. 5 (August 1958). *The National Cyclopaedia of American Biography.* Vol. 1. New York City, NY, 1898. *Report of the Proceedings of the Society of the Army of the Tennessee at the Thirty-Third Meeting.* Cincinnati, OH, 1902. George W. Kingsbury. *History of Dakota Territory.* Chicago, IL, 1915. *History of Porter County, Indiana.* Chicago and New York, 1912. Pension File, National Archives. Carded Records Relating to Staff Officers, National Archives. Reports of Examining Boards as to Qualifications of Quartermaster Officers, 1864–65, Record Group 92, Entry 418, National Archives. Letters Received, Commission Branch, Adjutant General's Office, Files P693(CB)1864, P1040(CB)1864, P404(CB)1865, and Q58(CB)1865, National Archives.

Perley Peabody Pitkin

1 Lieutenant, RQM, 2 VT Infantry, June 20, 1861. Captain, AQM, USV, Feb. 19, 1862. AQM, Harper's Ferry (WV) Quartermaster Depot, Sept.–Oct. 1862. Depot Quartermaster, Belle Plain (VA), Nov. 1862–May 1863. AQM, Aquia Creek (VA) Quartermaster Depot, May–June 1863. Depot Quartermaster, Warrenton Junction (VA), July–Dec. 1863. Depot Quartermaster, Brandy Station (VA), Jan.–May 1864. Depot Quartermaster, City Point (VA), June–July 1864. Assigned to duty as Colonel, Aug. 2–Nov. 7, 1864. Chief Quartermaster, City Point (VA) Quartermaster Depot, Aug.–Nov. 1864. Acting Chief Quartermaster, Armies Operating Against Richmond, Sept. 1864. Resigned, Nov. 7, 1864, to accept the position of Quartermaster General of the State of Vermont.

Born: March 9, 1826, Marshfield, VT
Died: July 28, 1891, Montpelier, VT
Occupation: Farmer before war. Manufacturer of saw mills after war.
Offices/Honors: Vermont House of Representatives, 1859–60 and 1872–73. Quartermaster General, State of Vermont, 1864–71.

Perley Peabody Pitkin (A. N. Blanchard, Photographer, Barre, VT; USAHEC [RG98S-CWP90.25]).

Miscellaneous: Resided Montpelier, Washington Co., VT

Buried: Green Mount Cemetery, Montpelier, VT (Lot 608)

References: Hiram Carleton, editor. *Genealogical and Family History of the State of Vermont.* New York and Chicago, 1903. Jacob G. Ullery, compiler. *Men of Vermont: An Illustrated Biographical History of Vermonters and Sons of Vermont.* Brattleboro, VT, 1894. Abby Maria Hemenway. *The History of Washington County in the Vermont Historical Gazetteer.* Montpelier, VT, 1882. George G. Benedict. *Vermont in the Civil War: A History of the Part Taken by the Vermont Soldiers and Sailors in the War for the Union, 1861–65.* Burlington, VT, 1886. Lucius E. Chittenden. *Personal Reminiscences, 1840–1890, Including Some Not Hitherto Published of Lincoln and the War.* New York City, NY, 1893. Obituary, *Vermont Watchman & State Journal,* Aug. 5, 1891. Obituary, *Burlington Free Press,* July 30, 1891. Obituary, *Montpelier Argus and Patriot,* July 29, 1891. Albert P. Pitkin. *Pitkin Family of America: A Genealogy of the Descendants of William Pitkin.* Hartford, CT, 1887. Paul G. Zeller. *The Second Vermont Volunteer Infantry Regiment, 1861–1865.* Jefferson, NC, 2002. Pension File and Military Service File, National Archives. Letters Received, Commission Branch, Adjutant General's Office, File P756(CB)1864, National Archives. Letters Received, Adjutant General's Office, File P280(AGO)1862, National Archives. Carded Records Relating to Staff Officers, National Archives.

Perley Peabody Pitkin (post-war) (Jacob G. Ullery, compiler. *Men of Vermont: An Illustrated Biographical History of Vermonters and Sons of Vermont.* Brattleboro, VT, 1894).

Charles Kilgore Smith, Jr.

1 Lieutenant, RQM, 26 OH Infantry, July 25, 1861. Captain, AQM, USV, May 12, 1862. AQM, Staff of Majr Gen. Lovell H. Rousseau, 1 Division, 14 Army Corps, Army of the Cumberland, Jan.–Sept. 1863. AQM, Chattanooga (TN) Quartermaster Depot,

Charles Kilgore Smith, Jr. (H. Goldsticker, Photographer, Army of the Cumberland; author's photograph).

Nov. 1863–June 1865. Chief Assistant Quartermaster, Department of the Cumberland, July–Nov. 1864. Chief Quartermaster, Staff of Major Gen. James B. Steedman, Department of Georgia, July 1865–Oct. 1866. Assigned to duty as Colonel, Nov. 4, 1865–Oct. 18, 1866. Honorably mustered out, Oct. 26, 1866. Bvt. Major, USV, March 13, 1865, for faithful and meritorious services during the war.

    Born: Oct. 22, 1835 Hamilton, OH
    Died: Dec. 30, 1870 Columbia, SC
    Education: Attended U.S. Military Academy, West Point, NY (Class of 1854)
    Occupation: Farmer
    Miscellaneous: Resided Hamilton, Butler Co., OH
    Buried: Greenwood Cemetery, Hamilton, OH (Zion Section, Lot 233)
    References: *A History and Biographical Cyclopaedia of Butler County, Ohio.* Cincinnati, OH, 1882. Obituary, *Columbia Daily Phoenix*, Dec. 31, 1870. Death Notice, *Cincinnati Daily Gazette*, Jan. 5, 1871. Military Service File, National Archives. Reports of Examining Boards as to Qualifications of Quartermaster Officers, 1864–65, Record Group 92, Entry 418, National Archives. Letters Received, Commission Branch, Adjutant General's Office, File S61(CB)1868, National Archives. Carded Records Relating to Staff Officers, National Archives.

Charles Kilgore Smith, Jr. (The National Archives [Photographic Prints of Quartermaster Officers]).

Ralph Cushing Webster

    Captain, AQM, USV, Sept. 30, 1861. AQM, Staff of Brig. Gen. Albin Schoepf, 1 Brigade, 1 Division, Department of the Ohio, Dec. 1861–March 1862. AQM, Staff of Brig. Gen. Henry W. Wessells, 3 Brigade, Peck's Division, Department of Virginia, Dec. 1862. AQM, Staff of Brig. Gen. Henry W. Wessells, 4 Division, 18 Army Corps, Department of North Carolina, Dec. 1862–May 1863. Chief Quartermaster, Staff of Major Gen. John J. Peck and Brig. Gen. Innis N. Palmer, District of North Carolina, Department of Virginia and North Carolina, Aug. 1863–Aug. 1864. Assigned to duty as Colonel, Aug. 2, 1864–July 11, 1865. Chief Quartermaster, Staff of Major Gen. Benjamin F. Butler, Department of Virginia and North Carolina, Aug. 1864–Feb. 1865. Chief Quartermaster, Staff of Major Gen. Edward O.C. Ord, Department of Virginia, April 1865. AQM, Fort Sedgwick, Julesburg, CO, Dec. 1865–Oct 1866. Honorably mustered out, Nov. 3, 1866. Bvt. Major, USV; Bvt. Lieutenant Colonel, USV; and Bvt. Colonel, USV, March 13, 1865, for faithful and meritorious services during the war. Battle honors: Mill Springs, Kinston, White Hall, Goldsborough.

Ralph Cushing Webster (The National Archives [Photographic Prints of Quartermaster Officers]).

Ralph Cushing Webster (Kimberly Bros., National Gallery, Fortress Monroe, VA; author's photograph).

Born: Oct. 9, 1826 Cincinnati, OH
Died: Jan. 17, 1911 Denver, CO
Occupation: U.S. Customs officer before war. After the war held positions in the U.S. Revenue Service, the U.S. Land Office, and finally the U.S. Mint, Denver, CO, 1889–1911.

Miscellaneous: Resided West Roxbury and Dedham, Norfolk Co., MA, to 1867; Denver, CO, 1867–78 and 1887–1911; Deadwood, Lawrence Co., SD, 1878–83; and Miles City, Custer Co., MT, 1883–87

Buried: Cremated at Riverside Cemetery, Denver, CO (No. 549). Place of burial unknown, but possibly with his widow, Caroline (Manley) Webster (died Feb. 25, 1919), Block 12, Lot 24.

References: Obituary Circular, Whole No. 211, Colorado MOLLUS. Pension File, National Archives. Letters Received, Commission Branch, Adjutant General's Office, File W1080(CB)1866, National Archives. Obituary, *Denver Post*, Jan. 18, 1911. Obituary, *Deadwood Daily Pioneer-Times*, Feb. 15, 1911. Obituary, *Rocky Mountain News*, Jan. 19, 1911.

Morris Dickenson Wickersham

Captain, Co. E, 79 PA Infantry, Oct. 1, 1861. Acting AQM, Staff of Colonel Henry A. Hambright, 3 Brigade (and 2 Brigade), 1 Division, 14 Army Corps, Army of the Cumberland, March–July 1863. Acting AQM, Staff of Major Gen. Lovell H. Rousseau and Brig. Gen. Absalom Baird, 1 Division, 14 Army Corps, Army of the Cumberland, July–Oct. 1863. Acting AQM, Staff of Major Gen. George H. Thomas, Department of

Morris Dickenson Wickersham (H. Goldsticker, Photographer, Army of the Cumberland; Ronn Palm Collection).

Morris Dickenson Wickersham (H. A. Olwell, 78 Dauphin Street, Mobile, AL; Ken Turner Collection).

the Cumberland, Nov. 1863–April 1864. Captain, AQM, USV, April 7, 1864. AQM, Staff of Major Gen. George H. Thomas, Department of the Cumberland, April–Sept. 1864. Chief Assistant Quartermaster, Department of the Cumberland, May–June 1865. Assigned to duty as Colonel, Oct. 6, 1865–Sept. 24, 1866. Chief Quartermaster, Staff of Major Gen. Charles R. Woods, Department of Alabama, Oct. 1865–June 1866. Chief Quartermaster, Staff of Major Gen. Charles R. Woods, Department of the South, June–Aug. 1866. Honorably mustered out, Sept. 22, 1866. Bvt. Major, USV; Bvt. Lieutenant Colonel, USV; and Bvt. Colonel, USV, March 13, 1865, for faithful and meritorious services during the war. Battle honors: Chickamauga Campaign, Missionary Ridge, Atlanta Campaign.

Born: March 14, 1839, Unionville, Chester Co., PA

Died: Jan. 1, 1904 Mobile, AL

Education: Attended Millersville (PA) State Normal School

Occupation: School teacher before war. Lawyer after war.

Offices/Honors: Postmaster, Mobile, AL, 1873–82. U.S. District Attorney, Southern District of Alabama, 1889–93 and 1897–1904.

Miscellaneous: Resided Millersville, Lancaster Co., PA, before war; and Mobile, Mobile Co., AL, after war. Brother of Colonel James P. Wickersham (47 PA Militia).

Buried: Catholic Cemetery, Mobile, AL (Section F, Lot 21)

References: *Memorial Record of Alabama*. Madison, WI, 1893. *The National Cyclopaedia of American Biography*. Vol. 8. New York City, NY, 1900. Thomas M. Owen. *History of Alabama and Dictionary of Alabama Biography*. Chicago, IL, 1921. Obituary Circular, Whole No. 600, Ohio MOLLUS. *Society of the Army of the Cumberland. Thirty-Second Reunion, Indianapolis, Indiana*. Cincinnati, OH, 1905.

Obituary, *Mobile Register,* Jan. 1, 1904. Obituary, *West Chester Daily Local News,* Jan. 2, 1904. Obituary, *Lancaster Semi-Weekly New Era,* Jan. 2, 1904. Obituary, *Montgomery Advertiser,* Jan. 2, 1904. Pension File and Military Service File, National Archives. Letters Received, Commission Branch, Adjutant General's Office, File W774(CB)1866, National Archives. Reports of Examining Boards as to Qualifications of Quartermaster Officers, 1864–65, Record Group 92, Entry 418, National Archives.

Commissaries of Subsistence

George W. Campbell	July 29, 1865	Sept. 10, 1866
George D. Harrington	July 24, 1865	Aug. 21, 1866
Joseph C. Read	June 9, 1865	March 13, 1866
Egbert T.S. Schenck	July 29, 1865	May 9, 1867
Gideon Scull, Jr.	July 1, 1865	May 31, 1866
Joseph J. Slocum	Oct. 23, 1865	July 7, 1866
Samuel H. Sturdevant	May 26, 1865	Oct. 14, 1865
Richard B. Treat	May 29, 1865	Sept. 23, 1865

Biographies

George Whitaker Campbell

Captain, Commissary of Subsistence, USV, Sept. 9, 1861. Assigned to duty as Colonel, July 29, 1865–Sept. 10, 1866. Chief Commissary of Subsistence, Chicago (IL) Commissary Depot, July 1865–Sept. 1866. Honorably mustered out, Sept. 10, 1866. Bvt. Major, USV, March 13, 1865, for meritorious services in his department during the war.

Born: Nov. 11, 1806 King William Co., VA

Died: Sept. 16, 1881 Chicago, IL

Occupation: Grocer and commission merchant before war. Assignee in bankruptcy after war.

Miscellaneous: Resided Galena, Jo Daviess Co., IL, before war; and Chicago, IL, after war. Father of Colonel Wallace Campbell (110 U.S. Colored Infantry). His niece, Anna Elizabeth Campbell, was the wife of Bvt. Brig. Gen. Orville E. Babcock of General Grant's Staff.

Buried: Graceland Cemetery, Chicago, IL (Section B, Lot 349, unmarked)

References: Obituary, *Chicago Daily Tribune*, Sept. 18, 1881. Obituary, *Chicago Inter Ocean*, Sept. 19, 1881. Letters Received, Commission Branch, Adjutant General's Office, File C713(CB)1865, National Archives. Letters Received, Adjutant General's Office, File C699(AGO)1861, National Archives. *The History of Jo Daviess County, Illinois*. Chicago, IL, 1878. John Y. Simon, editor. *The Papers of Ulysses S. Grant*. Vol. 15: May 1–December 31, 1865. Carbondale, IL, 1988. www.findagrave.com.

George Dana Harrington

Captain, Commissary of Subsistence, USV, May 2, 1862. Commissary of Subsistence, Columbus (OH) Commissary Depot, May 1862–June 1866. Assigned to duty as Colonel, July 24, 1865–Aug. 21, 1866. Honorably mustered out, Aug. 21, 1866. Bvt. Major, USV; and Bvt. Lieutenant Colonel, USV, March 13, 1865, for meritorious services in his department during the war.

Born: July 28, 1823, Londonderry, VT

Died: March 13, 1879, Washington, D.C.

Education: Graduated Yale University, New Haven, CT, 1845

Occupation: Civil engineer before war. Jewelry merchant and U.S. Census Bureau clerk after war.

Offices/Honors: Chief Clerk, U.S. Census Bureau, 1870–79

Miscellaneous: Resided Bennington, Bennington Co., VT, before war; Columbus, OH, 1862–70; and Washington, D.C., after 1870

Buried: Old First Church Cemetery, Bennington, VT

References: *Record of the Class of 1845 of Yale College.* New York City, NY, 1881. Obituary, *Bennington Banner,* March 20, 1879. Obituary, *Rutland Daily Herald & Globe,* March 26, 1879. Obituary, *Manchester Journal,* March 20, 1879. *Obituary Record of Graduates of Yale College Deceased during the Academical Year Ending in June 1879.* New Haven, CT, 1880. Lyman Coleman. *Genealogy of the Lyman Family in Great Britain and America.* Albany, NY, 1872. Pension File, National Archives. Letters Received, Commission Branch, Adjutant General's Office, File H569(CB)1864, National Archives.

George Dana Harrington (post-war) (*Record of the Class of 1845 of Yale College.* **New York City, NY, 1881**).

Joseph Corson Read

Sergeant, Co. B, 4 PA Infantry (3 months), April 20, 1861. Honorably mustered out, July 27, 1861. 2 Lieutenant, Co. F, 51 PA Infantry, Sept. 2, 1861. Captain, Commissary of Subsistence, USV, July 22, 1862. Commissary of Subsistence, Staff of Major Gen. Jesse L. Reno, 9 Army Corps, Army of the Potomac, Sept. 1862. Assistant to Chief Commissary of Subsistence, Department of the Cumberland, Feb.–Dec. 1864. Chief Commissary of Subsistence, Staff of Major Gen. James H. Wilson, Cavalry Corps, Military Division of the Mississippi, Dec. 1864–Feb. 1865. Chief Commissary of Subsistence, Staff of Major Gen. George H. Thomas, Department of the Cumberland, Feb.–June 1865. Assigned to duty as Colonel, June 9, 1865–March 13, 1866. Chief Commissary of Subsistence, Staff of Major Gen. George H. Thomas, Military Division of the Tennessee, June 1865–Feb. 1866. Honorably mustered out, March 13, 1866. Bvt. Major, USV; and Bvt. Lieutenant Colonel, USV, March 13, 1865, for meritorious services in his department during the war. Battle honors: Antietam, Nashville.

Born: May 28, 1831 Norristown, PA

Died: Oct. 4, 1889 Fernandina Beach, FL

Occupation: Druggist in early life. Lumber manufacturer after war.

Miscellaneous: Resided Norristown, Montgomery Co., PA; and Fernandina Beach, Nassau Co., FL, after 1868

Buried: Evergreen Cemetery, Jacksonville, FL (Section C)

References: *Society of the Army of the Cumberland. Twenty-first Reunion, Toledo, Ohio.* Cincinnati, OH, 1891. Hiram Corson. *The Corson Family: A History of the Descendants of Benjamin Corson.* Philadelphia, PA, 1896. Obituary, *Florida Times-Union*, Oct. 7, 1889. Pension File and Military Service File, National Archives. Letters Received, Commission Branch, Adjutant General's Office, File R92(CB)1866, National Archives. Thomas H. Parker. *History of the 51st Regiment of P.V. and V.V.* Philadelphia, PA, 1869.

Joseph Corson Read (J.H. Van Stavoren, Metropolitan Gallery, 53 College St., Nashville, TN; courtesy Steve Meadow).

Egbert Tangier Smith Schenck

Captain, Commissary of Subsistence, USV, Sept. 7, 1861. Post Commissary of Subsistence, Huntsville (AL), Feb.–April 1864. Post Commissary of Subsistence, Pilot Knob (MO), May–Oct. 1864. Post Commissary of Subsistence, Rock Island (IL), March–July 1865. Assigned to duty as Colonel, July 29, 1865–May 9, 1867. Chief Commissary of Subsistence, Cairo (IL) Commissary Depot, July 1865–May 1867. Honorably mustered out, Oct. 1, 1867. Bvt. Major, USV, March 13, 1865, for meritorious services in his department during the war. Bvt. Lieutenant Colonel, USV, Nov. 14, 1865, for faithful services. Battle honors: Price's Missouri Expedition (Pilot Knob).

Egbert Tangier Smith Schenck (State Historical Society of Iowa, Des Moines).

Born: Jan. 18, 1820 Franklin, OH
Died: Oct. 26, 1910 Muscatine, IA
Occupation: Farmer
Miscellaneous: Resided West Liberty, Muscatine Co., IA, to 1873; and Downey, Cedar Co., IA, after 1873. Brother of Major Gen. Robert C. Schenck.
Buried: Oak Ridge Cemetery, West Liberty, IA (Section B, Lot 24)
References: Obituary, *Muscatine Journal,* Oct. 26, 1910. Obituary, *Muscatine News-Tribune,* Oct. 27, 1910. *The History of Cedar County, Iowa.* Chicago, IL, 1878. Pension File, National Archives. Letters Received, Commission Branch, Adjutant General's Office, File Q100(CB)1867, National Archives. Letters Received, Adjutant General's Office, File S1057(AGO)1861, National Archives.

Gideon Scull, Jr.

Captain, Commissary of Subsistence, USV, Aug. 3, 1861. Chief Commissary of Subsistence, Staff of Major Gen. Ormsby M. Mitchel, Department of the South, Oct. 1862. Inspecting Commissary, Department of the Missouri, Jan.–June 1864. Chief Commissary of Subsistence, Staff of Major Gen. William S. Rosecrans, Major Gen. Grenville M. Dodge, and Major Gen. John Pope, Department of the Missouri, Aug. 1864–May 1866. Assigned to duty as Colonel, July 1, 1865–May 31, 1866. Honorably mustered out, May 31, 1866. Bvt. Major, USV; and Bvt. Lieutenant Colonel, USV, March 13, 1865, for meritorious services in his department during the war.

Born: May 26, 1833, Philadelphia, PA
Died: June 28, 1899, Venice, Italy
Education: Graduated University of Pennsylvania, Philadelphia, PA, 1853
Occupation: Admiral's Secretary, USN, 1858–61. Fire insurance executive after war.

Gideon Scull, Jr. (Massachusetts MOLLUS Collection, USAHEC [Vol. 118, p. 6056]).

Miscellaneous: Resided Philadelphia, PA, to 1871; and Boston, MA, after 1871
Buried: Mount Auburn Cemetery, Cambridge, MA (Excelsior Path, Lot 5280)
References: Obituary, *Boston Herald,* June 29, 1899. Obituary, *Boston Evening Transcript,* June 29, 1899. Obituary, *Boston Globe,* June 29, 1899. William Ellis Scull. *The Family of Scull.* Philadelphia, PA, 1930. *University of Pennsylvania: Biographical Catalogue of the Matriculates of the College, 1749–1893.* Philadelphia, PA, 1894. *Zeta Psi Fraternity of North America: Semicentennial Biographical Catalogue.* New York City, NY, 1899. Letters Received, Adjutant General's Office, File S955(AGO)1861, National Archives. Letters Received, Commission Branch, Adjutant General's Office, Files D278(CB)1865 and S2191(CB)1865, National Archives.

Joseph Jermain Slocum

Captain, Commissary of Subsistence, USV, Feb. 19, 1862. Commissary of Subsistence, Staff of Major Gen. Ormsby M. Mitchel, May–July 1862. Assigned to duty as Colonel, Oct. 23, 1865–July 7, 1866. Chief Commissary of Subsistence, Indianapolis (IN) Commissary Depot, Oct. 1865–July 1866. Honorably mustered out, July 7, 1866. Bvt. Major, USV, March 13, 1865, for meritorious services in his department during the war.

Born: June 24, 1833 Syracuse, NY
Died: Oct. 2, 1924 New York City, NY
Occupation: Commission merchant before war. Banker after war. Business associate of the prominent financier Russell Sage, his brother-in-law, from whose widow he inherited $8,000,000, upon her death in 1918.

Miscellaneous: Resided Cincinnati, OH, to 1874; Chicago, IL, 1874–78; and New York City, NY, after 1878. He and Bvt. Brig. Gen. George D. Ruggles married sisters.

Buried: Woodlawn Cemetery, New York City, NY (Section 98/99, Oak Hill Plot, Lot 8754)

Joseph Jermain Slocum (Hoag Quick & Co., Art Palace, No. 100 4th St., opp. Post Office, Cincinnati, OH; courtesy Jim Rivest).

References: Henry Whittemore. *History of the Sage and Slocum Families of England and America.* New York City, NY, 1908. Charles E. Slocum. *History of the Slocums, Slocumbs, and Slocombs of America: Genealogical and Biographical.* Defiance, OH, 1908. Arthur W. L'Hommedieu. *L'Hommedieu Genealogy.* Chicago, IL, 1951. Obituary, *Syracuse Post-Standard*, Oct. 4, 1924. Obituary, *New York Times*, Oct. 3, 1924. Pension File, National Archives. www.ancestry.com.

Samuel Henry Sturdevant

Captain, Commissary of Subsistence, USV, Aug. 3, 1861. AQM, Staff of Brig. Gen. Henry W. Slocum, 1 Division, 6 Army Corps, Army of the Potomac, May–Oct. 1862. Acting Chief Commissary of Subsistence, Staff of Major General William B. Franklin, Left Grand Division, Army of the Potomac, Nov. 1862–Jan. 1863. Assigned to duty as Lieutenant Colonel, Jan. 1, 1863–Jan. 31, 1865. Chief Commissary of Subsistence, Staff of Major Gen. Henry W. Slocum, 12 Army Corps, Army of the Potomac, Jan.–Sept. 1863. Chief Commissary of Subsistence, Staff of Major Gen. Henry W. Slocum, 12 Army Corps, Department of the Cumberland, Sept. 1863–April 1864. Chief Commissary of Subsistence, Staff of Major Gen. Henry W. Slocum, District of Vicksburg (MS), Department of the Tennessee, April–Sept. 1864. Chief Commissary of Subsistence, Staff of Major Gen. Henry W. Slocum, Army of Georgia, Dec. 1864–May 1865. Assigned to duty as Colonel, May 26–Oct. 14, 1865. Chief Commissary of

Samuel Henry Sturdevant (R.W. Addis, Photographer, McClees Gallery, 308 Penna. Avenue, Washington, D.C.; USAHEC [RG98S-CWP109.21]).

Samuel Henry Sturdevant (post-war) (William H. Powell, editor. *Officers of the Army and Navy (Volunteer) Who Served in the Civil War*. Philadelphia, PA, 1893).

Subsistence, Staff of Major Gen. Henry W. Slocum, Department of Mississippi, May–Sept. 1865. Honorably mustered out, Oct. 14, 1865. Battle honors: Peninsular Campaign, Antietam, Fredericksburg, Chancellorsville, Gettysburg.

    Born: March 29, 1832 Braintrim Twp., Wyoming Co., PA
    Died: Feb. 24, 1898 Wilkes-Barre, PA
    Education: Attended Wyoming Seminary, Kingston, PA
    Occupation: Lumber merchant
    Miscellaneous: Resided Wilkes-Barre, Luzerne Co., PA
    Buried: Hollenback Cemetery, Wilkes-Barre, PA (Lot 285)
    References: William H. Powell, editor. *Officers of the Army and Navy (Volunteer) Who Served in the Civil War*. Philadelphia, PA, 1893. Obituary Circular, Whole No. 357, Pennsylvania MOLLUS. Horace E. Hayden, Alfred Hand and John W. Jordan, editors. *Genealogical and Family History of the Wyoming and Lackawanna Valleys, Pennsylvania*. New York and Chicago, 1906. Obituary, *Wilkes-Barre Record*, Feb. 25, 1898. Obituary, *Wilkes-Barre Evening Leader*, Feb. 24, 1898. Henry C. Bradsby, editor. *History of Luzerne County, Pennsylvania, with Biographical Selections*. Chicago, IL, 1893. Charles E. Slocum. *The Life and Services of Major General Henry Warner Slocum*. Toledo, OH, 1913.

Richard Bryan Treat

1 Sergeant, Co. F, 4 OH Infantry (3 months), April 20, 1861. 2 Lieutenant, Co. F, 4 OH Infantry, May 18, 1861. Captain, AQM, USV, May 20, 1861. Discharged Sept.

23, 1861. Major, 6 OH Cavalry, Oct. 23, 1861. Resigned May 22, 1862. Captain, Commissary of Subsistence, USV, Aug. 26, 1862. Commissary of Subsistence, Staff of Brig. Gen. Jacob D. Cox, 9 Army Corps, Army of the Potomac, Sept.–Oct. 1862. Assigned to duty as Lieutenant Colonel, Jan. 25, 1864–May 28, 1865. Chief Commissary of Subsistence, Staff of Brig. Gen. Jacob D. Cox, Major Gen. George Stoneman, and Major Gen. John M. Schofield, 23 Army Corps, Department of the Ohio, Jan. 1864–Feb. 1865. Chief Commissary of Subsistence, Staff of Major Gen. John M. Schofield and Major Gen. Jacob D. Cox, 23 Army Corps, Department of North Carolina, Feb.–May 1865. Assigned to duty as Colonel, May 29–Sept. 23, 1865. Chief Commissary of Subsistence, Staff of Major Gen. John M. Schofield, Department of North Carolina, May–Sept. 1865. Honorably mustered out, Sept. 23, 1865. Bvt. Major, USV; Bvt. Lieutenant Colonel, USV; and Bvt. Colonel, USV, Aug. 29, 1865, for faithful and meritorious services. Battle honors: Antietam.

Born: Oct. 31, 1835 Tallmadge, OH

Died: July 7, 1917 San Francisco, CA

Education: Graduated Harvard University Law School, Cambridge MA, 1859

Occupation: Lawyer

Miscellaneous: Resided Canton, Stark Co., OH, before war; New York City, NY, 1865–75; Modesto, Stanislaus Co., CA, 1875–82; San Luis Obispo, San Luis Obispo Co., CA, 1882–88; Los Angeles, CA, 1888–98; and San Francisco, CA, after 1898

Buried: San Francisco National Cemetery, San Francisco, CA (Section OS, Plot 94, Grave 6)

References: *An Illustrated History of Los Angeles County, California.* Chicago, IL, 1889. John Harvey Treat. *The Treat Family: A Genealogy of Trott, Tratt, and Treat for Fifteen Generations, and Four Hundred and Fifty Years in England and America.* Salem, MA, 1893. Joseph C. Bates, editor. *History of the Bench and Bar of California.* San Francisco, CA, 1912. Circular, Whole No. 984, California MOLLUS. Obituary Circular, Whole No. 1259, California MOLLUS. Obituary, *San Francisco Chronicle,* July 11, 1917. Obituary, *San Francisco Examiner,* July 10, 1917. Pension File, National Archives. Letters Received, Volunteer Service Branch, Adjutant General's Office, File T24(VS)1862, National Archives. Francis H. Brown. *Roll of Students of Harvard University Who Served in the Army or Navy of the United States During the War of the Rebellion.* Cambridge, MA, 1866.

Miscellaneous Organizations

Acting Provost Marshal General, Department of the Missouri
Joseph Darr, Jr.   Oct. 1864   Dec. 1864
Superintendent of Mails, Army of the United States
Absalom H. Markland   Feb. 6, 1862   April 1865
Chief of Transportation, Staff of Major Gen. John C. Fremont
Isaiah C. Woods   Sept. 20, 1861   Resigned Nov. 30, 1861
Inspector General, Staff of Major Gen. John C. Fremont
Juan Napoleon Zerman   Aug. 7, 1861   Discharged Feb. 4, 1862
Superintendent of Railroads, Staff of Major Gen. John C. Fremont
Edward H. Castle   Aug. 6, 1861   Superseded Dec. 9, 1861
1st AL Cavalry
George E. Spencer   Sept. 11, 1863   Resigned July 22, 1865, Bvt. Brig. Gen., USV
1st FL Cavalry (regiment failed to complete organization)
Eugene von Kielmansegge   March 29, 1864   Mustered as Lt. Col., Nov. 4, 1864
2nd FL Cavalry (regiment failed to complete organization)
1st Battalion, GA State Troops Infantry
John H. Ashworth   July 15, 1864   Died May 15, 1865
New York Light Artillery
Alexander Doull   Jan. 1863   Resigned Aug. 3, 1863
Volunteer Cavalry
Ulric Dahlgren   July 20, 1863   KIA March 2, 1864
Enrolled Militia, District of Vicksburg
1st Regiment
William B. Holbrook   Sept. 30, 1864   June 1865
Ira A. Batterton   June 1865   July 1865
2nd Regiment
Solomon Bostwick   Oct. 1864   Feb. 1865
William Woods   April 1865   June 1865
George M. Sabin   June 1865   July 1865
1st Regiment (Freedmen)
Matthew M. Miller   Nov. 5, 1864   Resigned May 29, 1865
William T. Sullivan   June 1865   July 1865
Enrolled Militia, Post of Natchez
3rd Regiment
Charles B. Smith   Nov. 1864   Jan. 1865
Ernest A. Denicke   Jan. 7, 1865   Dec. 1865
1st Infantry, Mississippi Marine Brigade
Charles Rivers Ellet   March 26, 1863   Resigned Sept. 8, 1863
1st NC Infantry
Joseph M. McChesney   Sept. 18, 1863   Resigned May 13, 1865
Oscar Eastmond   June 20, 1865   Mustered out June 27, 1865
2nd NC Infantry (regiment consolidated with 1st Infantry, Feb. 27, 1865)

2nd NC Mounted Infantry (regiment not entitled to a colonel since it never attained full strength)
3rd NC Mounted Infantry
George W. Kirk   March 14, 1865   Mustered out Aug. 8, 1865
154th PA Infantry
Charles R. Doron   Aug. 22, 1862   Superseded Oct. 29, 1862
Quartermaster's Forces, Department of the Cumberland
1st Regiment
Charles H. Irvin   Sept. 3, 1864
2nd Regiment
John C. Crane   Sept. 3, 1864   To 4th Regiment, Sept. 14, 1864

John C. Peterson   Sept. 14, 1864
3rd Regiment
Sylvanus H. Stevens   Sept. 3, 1864   To 6th Regiment, Sept. 14, 1864

James F. Rusling   Sept. 14, 1864   Bvt. Brig. Gen., USV
4th Regiment
Thomas J. Cox   Sept. 3, 1864   To 7th Regiment, Sept. 14, 1864

John C. Crane   Sept. 14, 1864
5th Regiment
John F. Isom   Sept. 3, 1864   To 8th Regiment, Sept. 14, 1864

George Isenstein   Sept. 14, 1864
6th Regiment
Sylvanus H. Stevens   Sept. 14, 1864
7th Regiment
Thomas J. Cox   Sept. 14, 1864
8th Regiment
John F. Isom   Sept. 14, 1864
9th Regiment
Simon B. Brown   Jan. 23, 1865
Quartermaster's Volunteers, Department of Washington
1st Regiment
Charles H. Tompkins   Aug. 2, 1864   Bvt. Brig. Gen., USA
2nd Regiment
Elisha E. Camp   Aug. 2, 1864
3rd Regiment
James G.C. Lee   Aug. 3, 1864
4th Regiment
Elias M. Greene   Aug. 5, 1864
John A. Elison   Sept. 8, 1864
5th Regiment
James A. Ekin   Aug. 2, 1864   Bvt. Brig. Gen., USA
6th Regiment (regiment not entitled to a colonel since it never attained full strength)
7th Regiment (originally 2nd Colored Regiment)
Thomas G. Whytal   Aug. 4, 1864

Biographies

John H. Ashworth

Private, Co. F, 1 SC Cavalry, CSA, Dec. 4, 1861. Absent without leave since Oct. 1862. Dropped from the rolls as deserter, March 1, 1864. *Colonel*, 1 Battalion, GA

State Troops Infantry, July 15, 1864. Taken prisoner, Bucktown, Gilmer Co., GA, Nov. 5, 1864. Confined Castle Thunder, Richmond, VA, and Raleigh, NC.
Born: 1830? NC
Died: May 15, 1865 Raleigh, NC (Died of starvation while imprisoned)
Occupation: Physician
Miscellaneous: Resided Gilmer Co., GA, and Fannin Co., GA
Buried: Place of Burial unknown
References: Pension File and Military Service File, National Archives. Robert S. Davis, Jr. "Forgotten Union Guerrillas of the North Georgia Mountains," *A North Georgia Journal of History*, Vol. 1 (1989). Letters Received, Volunteer Service Branch, Adjutant General's Office, File R882(VS)1865, National Archives. "From North West Georgia: Capture of the Notorious Ashworth and His Command," *Augusta Chronicle*, Dec. 4, 1864.

Ira Abbott Batterton

Private, Co. K, 8 IL Infantry, Aug. 1, 1861. Discharged Feb. 16, 1863. *Colonel*, 1 Enrolled Militia, District of Vicksburg, Department of Mississippi, June–July 1865.
Born: Nov. 11, 1838 Lawndale, McLean Co., IL
Died: July 15, 1865 Vicksburg, MS (accidentally shot by Charles Fontaine)
Occupation: Newspaper editor. Editor and publisher of the *Vicksburg Herald*, 1864–65.
Miscellaneous: Resided Lexington, McLean Co., IL
Buried: Wiley Cemetery, Colfax, McLean Co., IL
References: www.findagrave.com. www.ancestry.com. Obituary, *Chicago Daily Tribune*, July 26, 1865. Obituary, *Daily Illinois State Journal*, July 29, 1865. *The History of McLean County, Illinois.* Chicago, IL, 1879. *Transactions of the McLean County Historical Society, Bloomington, Ill.* Vol. 1 (War Record of McLean County with Other Papers). Bloomington, IL, 1899. Dr. E. Duis. *The Good Old Times in McLean County, Illinois.* Bloomington, IL, 1874. John Y. Simon, editor. *The Papers of Ulysses S. Grant.* Vol. 6: September 1–December 8, 1862. Carbondale, IL, 1977.

Solomon Bostwick

Sergeant Major, 11 IL Infantry, Sept. 9, 1861. Taken prisoner, Fort Donelson, TN, Feb. 15, 1862. Confined Memphis, TN, and Montgomery, AL. Paroled Oct. 17, 1862. 1 Lieutenant, Co. E, 11 IL Infantry, Nov. 29, 1862. Captain, Co. E, 11 IL Infantry, May 31, 1863. Acting AIG, Staff of Brig. Gen. Elias S. Dennis, 1 Division, 17 Army Corps, Army of

Solomon Bostwick (Fassett's Gallery, 122 & 124 Clark St., Chicago, IL; author's photograph).

Solomon Bostwick (Massachusetts MOLLUS Collection, USAHEC [Vol. 130, p. 6654L]).

Solomon Bostwick (Washington Gallery, Odd Fellows' Hall, Vicksburg MS; USAHEC [RG98S-CWP72.81]).

the Tennessee, April–Sept. 1864. Detached as *Colonel*, 2 Enrolled Militia, District of Vicksburg, Department of Mississippi, Oct. 1864–Feb. 1865. Honorably mustered out, July 14, 1865. Battle honors: Fort Donelson, Mobile Campaign.

Born: March 21, 1835 Champlain, NY

Died: Dec. 2, 1888 Leavenworth, KS

Occupation: Railroad construction engineer, bookkeeper, and farmer

Miscellaneous: Resided Pana, Christian Co., IL; Council Bluffs, Pottawattamie Co., IA; Champlain, Clinton Co., NY, 1872–79; Alpena, Alpena Co., MI (1880); Chillicothe, Livingston Co., MO; and Leavenworth, Leavenworth Co., KS

Buried: Leavenworth National Cemetery, Leavenworth, KS (Section 9, Row 2, Grave 46)

References: Henry A. Bostwick, compiler. *Genealogy of the Bostwick Family in America: The Descendants of Arthur Bostwick of Stratford, Conn.* Hudson, NY, 1901. Obituary, *The Weekly Knight and Soldier*, Dec. 12, 1888. Obituary, *Kansas Newspaper Union*, Dec. 20, 1888. Pension File and Military Service File, National Archives. "Organization of the Militia," *Vicksburg Herald*, Oct. 7, 1864.

Simon Benjamin Brown

Captain, AQM, USV, Sept. 21, 1861. Post Quartermaster, Lexington (KY), Dec. 1861–Sept. 1862. Post Quartermaster, Clarksville (TN), Feb. 1863–April 1864. Superintendent of Transportation, U.S. Military Railroads, Nashville (TN), May 1864–Feb. 1866. *Colonel*, 9 Regiment, Quartermaster's Forces, Department of the Cumberland, Jan. 23, 1865. Honorably mustered out, March 20, 1866. Bvt. Major, USV, March 13, 1865, for faithful and meritorious services in the Quartermaster's Department.

Born: Oct. 3, 1816 Strafford, VT
Died: March 19, 1889 Chicago, IL
Occupation: Engaged in mercantile pursuits, especially metallic roofing, 1873–75
Offices/Honors: U.S. Internal Revenue gauger, 1875–87
Miscellaneous: Resided Joliet, Will Co., IL; Chicago, IL; and Bloomington, McLean Co., IL, before war; Nashville, Davidson Co., TN; and Chicago, IL, after war
Buried: Oakwoods Cemetery, Chicago, IL (Section D, Division 1, Lot 100)
References: *Transactions of the McLean County Historical Society*. Vol. 1 (War Record of McLean County with Other Papers). Bloomington, IL, 1899. Pension File, National Archives. Letters Received, Commission Branch, Adjutant General's Office, File B205(CB)1866, National Archives. Reports of Examining Boards as to Qualifications of Quartermaster Officers, 1864–65, Record Group 92, Entry 418, National Archives. Obituary, *Chicago Daily Tribune*, March 21, 1889. Obituary, *Chicago Inter Ocean*, March 21, 1889. "Major Simon B. Brown: In Memoriam," *Chicago Inter Ocean*, May 20, 1889. *The War of the Rebellion: A Compilation of the Official Records of the Union and Confederate Armies.* Series 1, Vol. 52, Part 1, p. 673. Washington, D.C., 1898.

Simon Benjamin Brown (Reports of Examining Boards as to Qualifications of Quartermaster Officers, 1864–65, Record Group 92, Entry 418, National Archives).

Elisha Ely Camp

1 Lieutenant, 9 U.S. Infantry, May 14, 1861. Captain, AQM, USA, Aug. 3, 1861. *Colonel*, 2 Regiment, Quartermaster's Volunteers, Department of Washington, Aug. 2, 1864. Bvt. Major, USA, and Bvt. Lieutenant Colonel, USA, March 13, 1865, for faithful and meritorious services during the war.
Born: Dec. 21, 1824 Sackets Harbor, NY
Died: Aug. 4, 1867 Washington, D.C.
Other Wars: Mexican War (2 Lieutenant, 3 U.S. Dragoons)
Occupation: Regular Army (Captain, AQM)
Miscellaneous: Resided Hounsfield, Jefferson Co., NY; and Washington, D.C.
Buried: Congressional Cemetery, Washington, D.C. (Range 31, Site 174)
References: Pension File, National Archives. Letters Received, Commission

Elisha Ely Camp (Brady, Washington; author's photograph).

Elisha Ely Camp (USAHEC [RG98S-CWP230.58]).

Branch, Adjutant General's Office, File C1063(CB)1867, National Archives. Obituary, *New-York Daily Reformer (Watertown, NY)*, Aug. 14, 1867. Obituary, *Daily National Intelligencer*, Aug. 6, 1867. Obituary, *Washington Evening Star*, Aug. 8, 1867. Obituary, *New York Herald*, Aug. 6, 1867. "Parade of the Quartermaster's Brigade," *Washington Evening Star*, Aug. 2, 1864. Fred R. Brown. *History of the Ninth U.S. Infantry, 1799–1909*. Chicago, IL, 1909. Letters Received, Commission Branch, Adjutant General's Office, File Q47(CB)1864, National Archives. *The War of the Rebellion: A Compilation of the Official Records of the Union and Confederate Armies*. Series 1, Vol. 37, Part 2, pp. 385–387. Washington, D.C., 1891. *The War of the Rebellion: A Compilation of the Official Records of the Union and Confederate Armies*. Series 3, Vol. 4, pp. 699–700. Washington, D.C., 1900.

Edward Herrick Castle

Colonel, Superintendent of Railroads, Staff of Major Gen. John C. Fremont, Department of the West, Aug. 6, 1861. Superseded, Dec. 9, 1861, by Colonel Lewis B. Parsons, who, in a letter to Major Gen. Halleck, Jan. 24, 1862, expounded, "My only object in writing is that you may not be deceived, as to the character of this man Castle, than whom, if his reputation speaks truly, few greater scamps 'go unwhipt of justice.' I have such evidence that I do not hesitate to charge him, while in that position under Gen. Fremont, with having received bribes to a large amount, and I have no doubt other charges equally infamous can be proved against him." Although he claimed to have received the thanks of both Houses of Congress and also of President

Edward Herrick Castle (meeting his son, Ephraim, in Washington, D.C., Sept. 5, 1862) (author's photograph).

Lincoln for his valuable railroad services throughout the war, as described in some detail in his autobiography, there is no evidence of any service after 1861.

Born: Aug. 5, 1811 Amenia, NY
Died: July 25, 1894, Chicago, IL
Occupation: Capitalist engaged in real estate and railroad enterprises
Miscellaneous: Resided Chicago, IL
Buried: Rosehill Cemetery, Chicago, IL (Section P, Lot 38)
References: *Life of Edward Herrick Castle.* Chicago, IL, 1893. *Album of Genealogy and Biography Cook County, Illinois.* Chicago, IL, 1897. Alfred T. Andreas. *History of Chicago from the Earliest Period to the Present Time.* Chicago, IL, 1884. Joseph Kirkland. *The Story of Chicago.* Chicago, IL, 1892. Obituary, *Chicago Inter Ocean,* July 26, 1894. Obituary, *Chicago Daily Tribune,* July 26, 1894. "Capt. Castle's Four Score Years," *Chicago Daily Tribune,* Aug. 5, 1891. "Octogenarian Castle," *Chicago Inter Ocean,* Aug. 6, 1891. Letters Received, Commission Branch, Adjutant General's Office, File C934(CB)1863, National Archives. Union Citizens File, Edward H. Castle, Record Group 109, National Archives. *Report of the Joint Committee on the Conduct of the War.* Part 3-Department of the West. Washington, D.C., 1863.

Thomas Jefferson Cox

Captain, AQM, USV, June 11, 1862. AQM, in charge of Clothing, Camp and Garrison Equipage, and Stationery, Nashville (TN) Quartermaster Depot, Oct. 1862–Sept. 1866. *Colonel,* 4 Regiment, Quartermaster's Forces, Department of the Cumberland, Sept. 3, 1864. *Colonel,* 7 Regiment, (and commanding 3 Brigade), Quartermaster's Forces, Department of the Cumberland, Sept. 14, 1864. Bvt. Major, USV, March 13, 1865, for faithful and meritorious services during the war. Bvt. Lieutenant Colonel, USV, May 25, 1866, for faithful services in the Quartermaster's Department. Bvt. Colonel, USV, July 25, 1866, for faithful and meritorious services.

Born: March 9, 1823 Zanesville, OH
Died: Sept. 17, 1866 Nashville, TN (cholera)
Education: Attended Granville (now Denison) College, Granville, OH
Occupation: Farmer
Miscellaneous: Resided Springfield Twp., Muskingum Co., OH. Brother of Congressman Samuel Sullivan Cox.
Buried: Woodlawn Cemetery, Zanesville, OH (Section X, Block 2, Lot 2)

Thomas Jefferson Cox (Reports of Examining Boards as to Qualifications of Quartermaster Officers, 1864–65, Record Group 92, Entry 418, National Archives).

References: J. Hope Sutor. *Past and Present of the City of Zanesville and Muskingum County, Ohio, Together with Biographical Sketches of Many of Its Leading and Prominent Citizens and Illustrious Dead*. Chicago, IL, 1905. Obituary, *Daily Ohio Statesman*, Sept. 24, 1866. Pension File, National Archives. Reports of Examining Boards as to Qualifications of Quartermaster Officers, 1864–65, Record Group 92, Entry 418, National Archives. Letters Received, Commission Branch, Adjutant General's Office, File C614(CB)1864, National Archives. Frederick A. Virkus, editor. *The Abridged Compendium of American Genealogy*. Vol. 3. Chicago, IL, 1928. Obituary, *Nashville Tennessean*, Sept. 18, 1866. William Van Zandt Cox and Milton Harlow Northrup. *Life of Samuel Sullivan Cox*. Syracuse, NY, 1899. *The War of the Rebellion: A Compilation of the Official Records of the Union and Confederate Armies*. Series 1, Vol. 52, Part 1, pp. 635–638. Washington, DC, 1898.

Thomas Jefferson Cox (Frederick A. Virkus, editor. *The Abridged Compendium of American Genealogy*. Vol. 3. Chicago, IL, 1928).

Ulric Dahlgren

Captain, Additional ADC, May 29, 1862. ADC, Staff of Brig. Gen. Rufus Saxton, Post of Harper's Ferry (WV), May 1862. ADC, Staff of Major Gen. Franz Sigel, 1 Army Corps, Army of Virginia (and later 11 Army Corps, Army of the Potomac), June 1862–Jan. 1863. ADC, Staff of Major Gen. Joseph Hooker, Army of the Potomac, March–June 1863. GSW right foot (amputated), Hagerstown, MD, July 6, 1863. Colonel, Volunteer Cavalry, July 20, 1863. Battle honors: Harper's Ferry, Cedar Mountain, Rappahannock Station, 2nd Bull Run, Fredericksburg, Chancellorsville, Beverly Ford, Hagerstown, Kilpatrick's Expedition against Richmond.

Born: April 3, 1842, near Neshaminy, Bucks Co., PA

Died: March 2, 1864, KIA near Stevensville, King and Queen Co., VA

Ulric Dahlgren (M.B. Brady & Co., National Photographic Portrait Galleries, No. 352 Penna. Ave., Washington, D.C. & New York; Ken Turner Collection).

Education: Attended University of Pennsylvania, Philadelphia PA

Occupation: Law student

Miscellaneous: Resided Philadelphia, PA. Son of Rear Admiral John A.B. Dahlgren.

Buried: Laurel Hill Cemetery, Philadelphia, PA (Section L, Lots 50–54)

References: John A.B. Dahlgren. *Memoir of Ulric Dahlgren*. Philadelphia, PA, 1872. Eric J. Wittenberg. *Like a Meteor Blazing Brightly: The Short but Controversial Life of Colonel Ulric Dahlgren*. El Dorado Hills, CA, 2015. Byron Sunderland. *In Memoriam Colonel Ulric Dahlgren*. Boston, MA, 1864. William H. Powell, editor. *Officers of the Army and Navy (Volunteer) Who Served in the Civil War*. Philadelphia, PA, 1893. *The National Cyclopaedia of American Biography*. Vol. 9. New York City, NY, 1899. Letters Received, Volunteer Service Branch, Adjutant General's Office, File D167(VS)1863, National Archives. Meriwether Stuart, "Colonel Ulric Dahlgren and Richmond's Union Underground, April 1864," *Virginia Magazine of History and Biography*, Vol. 72, No. 2 (April 1964). Morris Fradin, "Curious Burial for a Hero's Leg," *The Hagerstown Cracker Barrel*, Vol. 2, No. 6 (November 1972). Nels Hokanson. *Swedish Immigrants in Lincoln's Time*. New York and London, 1942.

Ulric Dahlgren (courtesy Steve Meadow).

Ulric Dahlgren (Massachusetts MOLLUS Collection, USAHEC [Vol. 70, p. 3460L]).

Joseph Darr, Jr.

Major, 1 WV Cavalry, Sept. 23, 1861. Acting AAG and Provost Marshal, Staff of Brig. Gen. William S. Rosecrans, Department of Western Virginia, Oct. 1861–March 1862. Provost Marshal General, Staff of Major Gen. John C. Fremont, Mountain Department, March–June 1862. Provost Marshal General, State of Virginia, August 1862–April 1863. Commanded Post of Wheeling (WV), 8 Army Corps, Middle Department, April–June 1863. Acting Assistant Provost Marshal General, State of West Virginia, April 1863–July 1864. Lieutenant Colonel, 1 WV Cavalry, May 17, 1863. Resigned July 31, 1864. *Colonel,* Acting Provost Marshal

General, Staff of Major Gen. William S. Rosecrans, Department of the Missouri, Oct.–Dec. 1864.

Born: Aug. 1829 Cincinnati, OH

Died: Jan. 28, 1904 Washington, D.C.

Education: Graduated St. Xavier College, Cincinnati, OH, 1847

Occupation: Bookkeeper before war. Music publisher and dealer in pianos and musical instruments, 1867–68. Hotelkeeper, 1869–76. Clerk, U.S. War Department, 1880–1904.

Offices/Honors: Deputy Collector of U.S. Internal Revenue, 1866–67

Miscellaneous: Resided Cincinnati, OH, to 1867; Leavenworth, Leavenworth Co., KS, 1867–68; Fort Scott, Bourbon Co., KS, 1869–71; Thayer, Neosho Co., KS, 1871–72; Sherman, Grayson Co, TX, 1873–76; and Washington, D.C., after 1880. Brother of Bvt. Brig. Gen. Francis Darr.

Buried: Arlington National Cemetery, Arlington, VA (Section 3, Site 1459)

References: Obituary, *Washington Evening Star*, Jan. 29, 1904. Obituary, *Cincinnati Enquirer*, Jan. 29, 1904. Pension File and Military Service File, National Archives. Letters Received, Volunteer Service Branch, Adjutant General's Office, File D741(VS)1864, National Archives. *The War of the Rebellion: A Compilation of the Official Records of the Union and Confederate Armies*. (Vol. 41, Part 4, pp. 34–35). Washington, D.C., 1893. "Gen. Darr Obeyed Orders," *Fort Scott Daily Monitor*, July 10, 1901. "Col. Joseph Darr, Jr.," *Wheeling Daily Intelligencer*, Oct. 24, 1864.

Ernest Augustus Denicke

Private, Co. A, 10 NY Infantry, April 27, 1861. Honorably discharged, May 25, 1861. 2 Lieutenant, Co. E, 68 NY Infantry, Aug. 8, 1861. Detached as Acting Signal Officer, USA, Dec. 21, 1861. 2 Lieutenant, Co. G, 68 NY Infantry, Jan. 1, 1862. 1 Lieutenant, Co. C, 68 NY Infantry, July 17, 1862. Captain, Co. E, 68 NY Infantry, Dec. 18, 1862. Commissioned as 1 Lieutenant, U.S. Signal Corps, March 3, 1863. Resigned as Captain, 68 NY Infantry, Nov. 4, 1864. Chief Signal Officer, Staff of Brig. Gen. John W. Davidson, Cavalry Forces, Military Division of West Mississippi, Nov.–Dec. 1864. Chief Signal Officer, Staff of Brig. Gen. John W. Davidson, District of Natchez, Department of Mississippi, Military Division of West Mississippi, Jan.–May 1865. *Colonel*, 3 Enrolled MS Militia, Post of Natchez (MS), Jan. 7, 1865. Honorably mustered out, Dec. 20, 1865. Bvt. Captain, USV, March 13, 1865, for

Ernest Augustus Denicke (post-war) (*The Builders of a Great City: San Francisco's Representative Men, the City, Its History and Commerce.* San Francisco, CA, 1891).

gallant and meritorious services during the operations against Mobile, Alabama. Bvt. Major, USV, March 13, 1865, for gallant and meritorious services during the war. Battle honors: Peninsular Campaign (Yorktown, Williamsburg Road, Gaines' Mill, Savage Station, Malvern Hill), Expeditions Against Lewisburg, WV (Droop Mountain), Mobile Bay, Fort Morgan.

Born: July 13, 1840 Hanover, Germany

Died: Feb. 11, 1909 Geneva, Switzerland

Occupation: Cigar manufacturer, 1868–80. Brewery owner, 1880–90. Banker and capitalist after 1890.

Offices/Honors: U.S. Customs Inspector, 1869–73. Chief Signal Officer, California National Guard, 1890.

Miscellaneous: Resided Hoboken, Hudson Co., NJ, before war; New York City, NY, 1865–67; and San Francisco, CA, after 1867

Buried: Place of burial unknown

References: *The Builders of a Great City: San Francisco's Representative Men, the City, Its History and Commerce.* San Francisco, CA, 1891. Obituary, *San Francisco Call*, Feb. 12, 1909. Obituary, *San Francisco Chronicle*, Feb. 12, 1909. Obituary Circular, Whole No. 942, California MOLLUS. Military Service File, National Archives. Letters Received, Volunteer Service Branch, Adjutant General's Office, File D324(VS)1863, National Archives. Letters Received, Commission Branch, Adjutant General's Office, File D205(CB)1868, National Archives. J. Willard Brown. *The Signal Corps, U.S.A., in the War of the Rebellion.* Boston, MA, 1896. *The War of the Rebellion: A Compilation of the Official Records of the Union and Confederate Armies.* (Vol. 48, Part 1, p. 563). Washington, D.C., 1896. www.ancestry.com.

Charles Robert Doron

Private, Co. D, 27 PA Infantry, May 5, 1861. Detailed as Assistant Hospital Steward. Discharged for disability, Sept. 29, 1861, due to disease of the heart. Failed to receive acceptance of a regiment of heavy artillery, which he offered to the Government, Nov. 29, 1861. Although authorized, Dec. 16, 1861, to raise the 2nd Regiment, Eastern Virginia Brigade (later known as the 13th Virginia Volunteers), he was ordered to stop recruiting for the regiment in July 1862 and to disband the men already recruited. Prospective Colonel of a regiment of Pennsylvania sharpshooters, accepted by Governor Curtin as the 154 PA Infantry, Aug. 22, 1862. Authority to raise the 154 PA Infantry was, however, transferred to Colonel Benjamin C. Brooker, Oct. 29, 1862.

Born: 1834? Philadelphia, PA

Died: 1873? Chicago, IL?

Education: Attended Philadelphia Central High School, 1851–53

Occupation: Druggist before war. Lawyer after war.

Miscellaneous: Resided Philadelphia, PA, to 1865; and Chicago, IL, after 1865. Describing himself as "late Brevet Major General, USA," and prominent member of the staff of General Sheridan, he filed a divorce suit against his wife, Amanda, in January 1873. His ineffectiveness in personally conducting the case was reported with amusement in the Chicago newspapers. In April 1873, before the case was settled, he was reported as being in Philadelphia, wearing the uniform of a Major General, borrowing money from citizens of the city, and claiming he was on his way to take command of the Department of the Pacific. He apparently died in 1873, because Amanda Doron is listed in the 1873 Chicago Directory as "widow of Charles R."

Buried: Place of burial unknown

References: Military Service File, National Archives. *General Catalogue of the Central High School of Philadelphia from 1838 to 1890.* Philadelphia, PA, 1890. Letters Received, Volunteer Service Branch, Adjutant General's Office, Files D85(VS)1861, U5(VS)1861, B1675(VS)1862, D108(VS)1862, D656(VS)1862, and B187(VS)1863, National Archives. "The Law Courts," *Chicago Daily Tribune*, Feb. 13, 1873. Letters Received, Appointment, Commission, and Personal Branch, Adjutant General's Office, File 1720(ACP)1873, National Archives. www.ancestry.com.

Alexander Doull

Major, 2 NY Heavy Artillery, Oct. 30, 1861. Acting Ordnance Officer, Siege Train, Army of the Potomac, April–Oct. 1862. Inspector of Artillery, Staff of Brig. Gen. Henry J. Hunt, Chief of Artillery, Army of the Potomac, Oct. 1862–May 1863. Although he was commissioned as Colonel of Light Artillery by the Governor of the State of New York and served as such on staff duty, Secretary of War Stanton would not permit him to be mustered in since there was no precedent for crediting field officers to light artillery batteries from a state. Resigned Aug. 3, 1863, since "the steady refusal of the national and state authorities to grant me promotion, ... having convinced me that the Artillery is a branch of the service where one may do good service to the country and obtain credit for one's services, but in which one must not expect to be rewarded, I do not think I can legitimately be called on to serve on these terms for longer than the period I have already served." Battle honors: Peninsular Campaign (Yorktown, Hanover Court House), Antietam, Fredericksburg, Chancellorsville.

Born: Jan. 28, 1836 England

Died: March 26, 1865 Meadville, PA (scarlet fever)

Education: Attended St. Cyr (France) Military School and University of London (England)

Alexander Doull (Royal British Artillery, 1860) (Pension File, National Archives).

Alexander Doull (courtesy Steve Meadow).

Alexander Doull (Gardner, Corner 7th & D Sts., Washington, D.C.; author's photograph).

Other Wars: Crimean War

Occupation: Lieutenant, Royal British Artillery, and Professor at the Royal Military College, Sandhurst, England, before war. Civil engineer after resigning from U.S. Army.

Miscellaneous: Resided New York City, NY

Buried: Woodland Cemetery, Cleveland, OH (Section 21, Lot 62)

References: Obituary, *New York Times*, April 8, 1865. Obituary (Alexander Doull), *Army and Navy Journal*, Vol. 2, No. 34 (April 15, 1865). Pension File and Military Service File, National Archives. Letters Received, Volunteer Service Branch, Adjutant General's Office, File D176(VS)1862, National Archives. Letters Received, Commission Branch, Adjutant General's Office, File D409(CB)1863, National Archives.

Oscar Eastmond

Private, Co. D, 83 NY Infantry, May 27, 1861. Sergeant, Co. C, 1 NY Marine Artillery, Oct. 25, 1861. 2 Lieutenant, Co. C, 1 NY Marine Artillery, May 1, 1862. Captain, Co. G, 1 NC Infantry, March 30, 1863. Taken prisoner, Plymouth, NC, April 21, 1864, while on recruiting duty. Confined Columbia, SC. Paroled Dec. 10, 1864. Rejoined regiment, April 6, 1865. Lieutenant Colonel, 1 NC Infantry, May 29, 1865. Colonel, 1 NC Infantry, June 20, 1865. Honorably mustered out, June 27, 1865.

Born: 1840? New York City, NY

Died: Aug. 7, 1909 Dayton, OH (murdered by Edward Leonard, a fellow resident of the Soldiers' Home)

Occupation: Harness maker before war. Clerk and railroad conductor after war.

Offices/Honors: Freedmen's Bureau Agent, Asheville, NC, 1867–68. Mayor, Asheville, NC, 1868.

Miscellaneous: Resided Newark, Essex Co., NJ, before war; New Bern, Craven Co., NC; Raleigh, Wake Co., NC; Asheville, Buncombe Co., NC; Washington, D.C. (1870); New York City, NY (1880), and Dayton, Montgomery Co., OH, after war

Buried: Dayton National Cemetery, Dayton, OH (Section Q, Row 24, Grave 37)

References: Pension File and Military Service File, National Archives. Letters Received, Volunteer Service Branch, Adjutant General's Office, File E50(VS)1865, National Archives. Theodore L. Eastmond. *Eastmond-Benson Genealogy & Biography*. N.p., 1979. "Murders Comrade; Shoots Two More," *Dayton Herald*, Aug. 7, 1909. Steven E. Nash. *Reconstruction's Ragged Edge: The Politics of Postwar Life in the Southern Mountains*. Chapel Hill, NC, 2016.

Charles Rivers Ellet

Medical Cadet, U.S. Army, April 26, 1862. Colonel, Mississippi Ram Fleet, Nov. 5, 1862. Colonel, 1 Infantry, Mississippi Marine Brigade, March 26, 1863. Resigned Sept. 8, 1863. Battle honors: Memphis, Arkansas Post, Passage of the Vicksburg Batteries, Duck River Island, Vicksburg Campaign, Capture of ram *Queen of the West* in Red River.

Born: June 1, 1843 Philadelphia, PA

Died: Oct. 29, 1863 Bunker Hill, IL

Education: Attended Georgetown College, Washington, D.C.

Occupation: Medical student

Miscellaneous: Resided Philadelphia, PA; and Washington, D.C. Son of Colonel Charles Ellet, Jr. (Mississippi Ram Fleet). Nephew of Brig. Gen. Alfred W. Ellet.

Buried: Laurel Hill Cemetery, Philadelphia, PA (Section C, Lot 12)

References: *The National Cyclopaedia of American Biography*. Vol. 4. New York City, NY, 1897. Warren D. Crandall and Isaac D. Newell. *History of the Ram Fleet and the Mississippi Marine Brigade in the War for the Union on the Mississippi and Its Tributaries*. St. Louis, MO, 1907. Obituary, *Memphis Bulletin*, Nov. 3, 1863. Obituary, *New York Herald*, Nov. 3, 1863. Obituary, *Chicago Daily Tribune*, Nov. 6, 1863. Obituary (Charles Rivers Ellet), *Army and Navy Journal*, Vol. 1, No. 11 (Nov. 7, 1863). John S.C. Abbott, "Heroic Deeds of Heroic Men: Charles Ellet and His Naval Steam Rams," *Harper's New Monthly Magazine*, Vol. 32, No. 189 (Feb. 1866). Chester G. Hearn. *Ellet's Brigade: The Strangest Outfit of All*. Baton Rouge, LA, 2000. Myron J. Smith, Jr. *Civil War Biographies from the Western Waters*. Jefferson, NC, 2015. Military Service File, National Archives. Letters Received, Volunteer

Charles Rivers Ellet (author's photograph).

Service Branch, Adjutant General's Office, File E268(VS)1862, National Archives. Edwin Cole Bearss. *The Vicksburg Campaign.* 3 vols. Dayton, OH, 1985–86.

Elias M. Greene

Captain, AQM, USV, Oct. 3, 1862. Assigned to duty as Lieutenant Colonel, Oct. 3, 1862–Aug. 24, 1864. Chief Quartermaster, Staff of Major Gen. Samuel P. Heintzelman, Military District of Washington, Oct. 1862–Feb. 1863. Chief Quartermaster, Department of Washington, Feb. 1863 Aug. 1864. *Colonel,* 4 Regiment, Quartermaster's Volunteers, Department of Washington, Aug. 5, 1864. Tendered his resignation as Captain, AQM, USV, Nov. 17, 1864, since "a two-year absence from my home has increased the confusion in my private affairs." After settling his quartermaster accounts, he was finally honorably mustered out, July 28, 1865.

Born: 1829? New York City, NY
Died: Dec. 8, 1899 New York City, NY
Other Wars: Mexican War
Occupation: Merchant dealing in crockery ware and clothing before war. Promoter of various business enterprises after war, serving as Vice President of the Magneto-Electric Manufacturing Co., among others.
Miscellaneous: Resided New York City, NY
Buried: Green-Wood Cemetery, Brooklyn, NY (Section K, Lot 15977, Grave 11)

Elias M. Greene (Philp & Solomons' Metropolitan Gallery, 332 Pennsylvania Avenue; author's photograph).

References: Obituary, *New York Tribune,* Dec. 9, 1899. Obituary, *New York Sun,* Dec. 9, 1899. Obituary, *New York Times,* Dec. 9, 1899. Obituary, *New York World,* Dec. 9, 1899. Letters Received, Commission Branch, Adjutant General's Office, Files G644(CB)1864 and Q47(CB)1864, National Archives. Advertisement (Bright's Kidney beans), *The Cambrian: A Monthly Magazine.* Vol. 19. Utica, NY, 1899.

William Briggs Holbrook

Captain, Co. E, 72 IL Infantry, Aug. 21, 1862. Awarded 17 Army Corps, Department of the Tennessee, Medal of Honor, April 4, 1864, inscribed "Champion's Hill, Vicksburg." Acting AIG, Staff of Colonel Frederick A. Starring, 1 Brigade, 1 Division, 17 Army Corps, Army of the Tennessee, June–Sept. 1864. Detached as *Colonel,* 1 Enrolled Militia, District of Vicksburg, Department of Mississippi, Sept. 30, 1864. Brig. Gen., Enrolled Militia, District of Vicksburg, Department of Mississippi, June–Aug. 1865. Honorably mustered out, Aug. 7, 1865. Battle honors: Champion's Hill, Vicksburg.

William Briggs Holbrook (A. Pattiani, Photographer, No. 75 Lake St., Chicago, IL; Massachusetts MOLLUS Collection, USAHEC [Vol. 130, p. 6652]).

William Briggs Holbrook (USAHEC [RG98S-CWP72.90]).

Born: Nov. 17, 1837 Whitesboro, Oneida Co., NY
Died: Feb. 7, 1875 Minneapolis, MN
Occupation: Bookkeeper for lumber company before war. Bookkeeper after war, holding the position of Secretary and Treasurer of the Minneapolis Harvester Works in his later years.
Miscellaneous: Resided Chicago, IL, before war; Memphis, Shelby Co., TN, 1865–69; and Minneapolis, Hennepin Co., MN, after 1869
Buried: Lakewood Cemetery, Minneapolis, MN (Section 5, Lot 57)
References: Obituary, *Minneapolis Daily Tribune*, Feb. 9, 1875. Obituary, *St. Paul Daily Dispatch*, Feb. 8, 1875. Pension File and Military Service File, National Archives. Obituary, *Chicago Daily Tribune*, Feb. 9, 1875. Obituary, *Chicago Times*, Feb. 9, 1875. "Organization of the Militia," *Vicksburg Herald*, Oct. 7, 1864. John S. Lawrence, compiler. *The Descendants of Moses and Sarah Kilham Porter of Pawlet, Vermont.* Grand Rapids, MI, 1910. Stanley S. Phillips. *Civil War Corps Badges and Other Related Awards, Badges, Medals of the Period.* Lanham, MD, 1982.

Charles Henry Irvin

1 Lieutenant, RQM, 9 MI Infantry, Oct. 12, 1861. Acting AQM, Staff of Colonel William W. Duffield, 23 Independent Brigade, Army of the Ohio, April–June 1862. Captain, AQM, USV, July 31, 1863. AQM, Nashville (TN) Quartermaster Depot, July 1863–July 1866. *Colonel*, 1 Regiment, (and commanding 1 Brigade), Quartermaster's

Forces, Department of the Cumberland, Sept. 3, 1864. Bvt. Colonel, USV, May 8, 1865, for distinguished and faithful services in the Quartermaster's Department. Honorably mustered out, March 6, 1867.

Born: Feb. 27, 1832 Thornton, Pickering Parish, Yorkshire, England

Died: Nov. 22, 1906 Boise, ID

Education: Attended King's College, Cambridge, England

Occupation: Civil engineer

Miscellaneous: Resided Detroit, Wayne Co., MI (1860); Lebanon, Wilson Co., TN (1870); Marshall, Harrison Co., TX (1880); and Boise, Ada Co., ID, after 1890

Buried: Pioneer Cemetery, Boise, ID (Block 4, Lot 67)

References: Pension File, National Archives. Obituary, *Idaho Daily Statesman*, Nov. 23, 1906. Reports of Examining Boards as to Qualifications of Quartermaster Officers, 1864–65, Record Group 92, Entry 418, National Archives. Letters Received, Commission Branch, Adjutant General's Office, File I22(CB)1867, National Archives. *The War of the Rebellion: A Compilation of the Official Records of the Union and Confederate Armies.* Series 1, Vol. 52, Part 1, pp. 635–638. Washington, D.C., 1898.

Charles Henry Irvin (Morse's Gallery of the Cumberland, 25 Cedar St., Opposite Commercial Hotel, Nashville, TN; USAHEC [RG98S-CWP90.28]).

George Isenstein

Private, Co. A, 2 MO Infantry (3 months), April 22, 1861. 1 Lieutenant, Co. I, 15 MO Infantry, Aug. 25, 1861. Captain, Co. E, 15 MO Infantry, Jan. 15, 1862. Acting Assistant Commissary of Subsistence, Staff of Colonel Bernard Laibold, 2 Brigade, 3 Division, 20 Army Corps, Army of the Cumberland, Jan.–May 1863. Acting AQM, Post of Cowan (TN), Aug. 1863–June 1864. AQM, Nashville (TN) Quartermaster Depot, July 1864–Feb. 1865. *Lieutenant Colonel,* 2 Regiment, Quartermaster's Forces, Department of the Cumberland, Sept. 3, 1864. *Colonel,* 5 Regiment, Quartermaster's Forces, Department of the Cumberland, Sept. 14, 1864. Captain, AQM, USV, Sept. 15, 1864. AQM, Post of Morehead City (NC), March–April 1865. AQM, Post of Clarksville (TN), June 1865–Feb. 1866. Honorably mustered out, March 13, 1866. Battle honors: Pea Ridge, Perryville, Stone's River.

Born: Dec. 25, 1830 (or 1832) Hanover, Germany

Died: Oct. 22, 1902 Milwaukee, WI

Occupation: Primarily an actor and theater manager, he was also engaged in cigar manufacturing while in Tennessee after the war

Offices/Honors: Postmaster, Clarksville, TN, 1866–67

Miscellaneous: Resided Springfield, Sangamon Co., IL; and St. Louis, MO, before war; Clarksville, Montgomery Co., TN, 1865–70; Nashville, Davidson Co., TN, 1870–73; Chicago, IL, 1873–91; and NHDVS, Milwaukee, WI, after 1891

Buried: Wood National Cemetery, Milwaukee, WI (Section 13, Grave 1)

References: Pension File and Military Service File, National Archives. Letters Received, Volunteer Service Branch, Adjutant General's Office, File 6315(VS)1872, National Archives. Death notice, *Chicago Daily News*, Oct. 25, 1902. *The War of the Rebellion: A Compilation of the Official Records of the Union and Confederate Armies.* Series 1, Vol. 52, Part 1, pp. 635–638. Washington, D.C., 1898. www.ancestry.com.

George Isenstein (Wallis Brothers, Premium Photograph Gallery, 117 Lake St., Chicago, IL; Gil Barrett Collection).

John Franklin Isom

1 Lieutenant, Co. G, 25 IL Infantry, Aug. 8, 1861. Shell wound hand, Pea Ridge, AR, March 7, 1862. Acting ADC, Staff of Colonel William E. Woodruff, 3 Brigade, 1 Division, Right Wing, 14 Army Corps, Army of the Cumberland, Dec. 1862–Jan. 1863. Captain, Co. G, 25 IL Infantry, Feb. 14, 1863. Acting AQM, Staff of Brig. Gen. Robert S. Granger, Post of Nashville (TN), Department of the Cumberland, June 1863–June 1864. Acting AQM, Staff of Brig. Gen. John F. Miller, Post of Nashville (TN), Department of the Cumberland, June–Oct. 1864. *Colonel*, 5 Regiment, Quartermaster's Forces, Department of the Cumberland, Sept. 3, 1864. *Colonel*, 8 Regiment, Quartermaster's Forces, Department of the Cumberland, Sept. 14, 1864. Honorably mustered out, Nov. 25, 1864. Battle honors: Pea Ridge, Corinth, Perryville, Stone's River.

Born: Feb. 18, 1831 London, England

Died: Sept. 25, 1898 Cleveland, OH

Education: Graduated Western Reserve Medical School, Cleveland, OH, 1877

Occupation: Physician. Engaged in wholesale millinery business for five years after war.

Miscellaneous: Resided Champaign, Champaign Co., IL, before war; and Cleveland, Cuyahoga Co., OH, after war

Buried: Lake View Cemetery, Cleveland, OH (Section 11, Lot 20)

References: Obituary, *Cleveland Plain Dealer*, Sept. 26, 1898. Obituary, *Cleveland Leader*, Sept. 26, 1898. Letters Received, Commission Branch, Adjutant General's Office, File I69(CB)1864, National Archives. Robert H. Behrens. *From Salt Fork to*

Chickamauga: Champaign County Soldiers in the Civil War. Urbana, IL, 1988. John B. Hamilton, editor. *The Journal of the American Medical Association.* Vol. 31, July–Dec. 1898. Chicago, IL, 1898. *The War of the Rebellion: A Compilation of the Official Records of the Union and Confederate Armies.* Series 1, Vol. 52, Part 1, pp. 635–638. Washington, D.C., 1898.

George Washington Kirk

Private, Co. I, 1 TN Cavalry, Aug. 1, 1862. Private, Co. G, 4 TN Infantry, June 15, 1863. Captain, Co. D, 8 TN Cavalry, June 30, 1863. Honorably mustered out, April 15, 1864. Captain, Co. A, 3 NC Mounted Infantry, June 11, 1864. GSW left arm, Yellow Mountain, NC, June 30, 1864. Lieutenant Colonel, 3 NC Mounted Infantry, Sept. 20, 1864. Colonel, 3 NC Mounted Infantry, March 14, 1865. Honorably mustered out, Aug. 8, 1865. Battle honors: Raid from Morristown (TN) into North Carolina (Yellow Mountain), Red Banks, Stoneman's Raid (March–April 1865).

John Franklin Isom (and wife) (Massachusetts MOLLUS Collection, USAHEC [Vol. 83, p. 4188]).

Born: June 25, 1837 near Greeneville, TN

Died: Feb. 15, 1905 Gilroy, CA

Occupation: Farmer and carpenter before war. Farmer, merchant, U.S. Capitol policeman, and miner after war.

Miscellaneous: Resided Greeneville, Greene Co., TN, to 1868; Jonesborough, Washington Co., TN, 1868–70; Washington, D.C., 1870–84; Allentown, Carter Co., TN; Erwin, Unicoi Co., TN; Sullivan, Moultrie Co., IL; and Gilroy, Santa Clara Co., CA, after war. In June–July 1870 he commanded a regiment of North Carolina militia engaged in combating Ku Klux Klan terrorism in Alamance and Caswell counties.

Buried: Gavilan Hills Memorial Park, Gilroy, CA (Section 1, Block 6, Lot 4, Grave 6)

References: William S. Powell, editor. *Dictionary of North Carolina Biography.* Chapel Hill, NC, 1988. Obituary, *Gilroy Advocate,* Feb. 25, 1905. Pension File and Military Service File, National Archives. Letters Received, Volunteer Service Branch, Adjutant General's Office, File P136(VS)1870, National Archives. Leroy P. Graf, editor. *The Papers of Andrew Johnson.* Vol. 7, 1864–1865. Knoxville, TN, 1986. Ron V.

George Washington Kirk (USAHEC [RG98S-CWP211.107]).

George Washington Kirk (T.M. Schleier's Fine Art Gallery, Knoxville, East Tennessee; courtesy John Sickles).

Killian. *A History of the North Carolina Third Mounted Infantry Volunteers, U.S.A., March 1864 to August 1865.* Bowie, MD, 2000. Matthew Bumgarner. *Kirk's Raiders: A Notorious Band of Scoundrels and Thieves.* Hickory, NC, 2000. Richard N. Current. *Lincoln's Loyalists: Union Soldiers from the Confederacy.* Boston, MA, 1992. www.findagrave.com. www.ancestry.com.

James Grafton Carleton Lee

Captain, AQM, USV, Nov. 26, 1862. Acting Chief Quartermaster, Staff of Major Gen. Alfred Pleasanton, Cavalry Corps, Army of the Potomac, June–Aug. 1863. AQM, Alexandria (VA) Quartermaster Depot, Dec. 1863–March 1866. Captain, AQM, USA, July 2, 1864. *Colonel*, 3 Regiment, Quartermaster's Volunteers, Department of Washington, Aug. 3, 1864. Bvt. Major, USA, July 31, 1865, for faithful and meritorious services during the war. Bvt. Lieutenant Colonel, USA, July 31, 1865, for faithful and meritorious services.

Born: Aug. 12, 1836 Hamilton, Ontario, Canada
Died: July 26, 1916 Hague, NY
Education: Attended Victoria College, Cobourg, Ontario, Canada
Other Wars: Spanish American War (Colonel, Assistant Quartermaster General)
Occupation: Civil engineer before war. Regular Army (Brigadier General, retired April 23, 1904).
Miscellaneous: Resided Cincinnati, OH, before war; Tucson, Pima Co., AZ

James Grafton Carleton Lee (Henry Ulke, 278 Pennsylvania Avenue, Washington, D.C. 1865; author's photograph).

James Grafton Carleton Lee (post-war) (Massachusetts MOLLUS Collection, USAHEC [Vol. 134, p. 6881]).

(1870); St. Paul, Ramsey Co., MN (1880); San Antonio, Bexar Co., TX (1910); and Hague, Warren Co., NY

Buried: Arlington National Cemetery, Arlington, VA (Section 1, Site 113-A)

References: Constance W. Altshuler. *Cavalry Yellow & Infantry Blue.* Tucson, AZ, 1991. *Who Was Who in America, 1897–1942.* Chicago, IL, 1942. Elisha S. Loomis. *Descendants of Joseph Loomis in America and His Antecedents in the Old World.* Berea, OH, 1908. Obituary Circular, Whole No. 1225, California MOLLUS. Obituary, *Glens Falls Post-Star,* July 28, 1916. Obituary, *Rutland Daily Herald,* July 28, 1916. Reports of Examining Boards as to Qualifications of Quartermaster Officers, 1864–65, Record Group 92, Entry 418, National Archives. Letters Received, Adjutant General's Office, L656(AGO)1862, National Archives. Letters Received, Commission Branch, Adjutant General's Office, Files Q47(CB)1864 and S1089(CB)1864, National Archives. *The War of the Rebellion: A Compilation of the Official Records of the Union and Confederate Armies.* Series 3, Vol. 4, pp. 699–700. Washington, D.C., 1900.

Absalom Hanks Markland

Nominally a Special U.S. Mail Agent reporting to the Post Office Department, he was ordered by General Grant, Feb. 6, 1862, to "take charge of all mail matter from and to the troops." He organized a system under which every regiment and isolated command had its postmaster reporting in turn to brigade and division postmasters. Although never actually commissioned as colonel, he was invested with the authority of a colonel in accomplishing his difficult and dangerous duties and bore the title of Superintendent of Mails for the Army of the United States at the end of the war.

Born: Feb. 18, 1825 Winchester, Clark Co., KY

Died: May 25, 1888 Washington, D.C.

Education: Attended Maysville (KY) Seminary and Augusta (KY) College

Occupation: Employed in U.S. Indian Bureau and U.S. Post Office Department before war. Special Agent, U.S. Post Office Department, and lawyer after war.

Miscellaneous: Resided Paducah McCracken Co., KY; and Washington, D.C., before war. Washington, D.C.; and Indianapolis, Marion Co., IN, after war

Buried: Oak Hill Cemetery, Washington, D.C. (Corcoran Section, Lot 17)

References: Allen Thorndike Rice, editor. *Reminiscences of Abraham Lincoln by Distinguished Men of His Time.* New York City, NY, 1889. Obituary, *New York Times,* May 26, 1888. Obituary, *Washington Evening Star,* May 25, 1888. Obituary, *Cincinnati Commercial Gazette,* May 26, 1888. *Report of the Proceedings of the Society of the Army of the Tennessee at the Twenty-First Meeting.* Cincinnati, OH, 1893. Obituary, *Louisville Courier-Journal,* May 26, 1888. *Appletons' Annual Cyclopaedia and Register of Important Events of the Year 1888.* New Series, Vol. 13. New York City, NY, 1889. James Grant Wilson, editor. *Appletons' Cyclopaedia of American Biography.* Vol. 7. New York City, NY, 1901. Letters Received, Adjutant General's Office, Files M1423(AGO)1861 and M82(AGO)1865, National Archives. Letters Received, Commission Branch, Adjutant General's Office, File M1627(CB)1865, National Archives.

Absalom Hanks Markland (Massachusetts MOLLUS Collection, USAHEC [Vol. 69, p. 3422]).

Joseph Miller McChesney

Private, Co. E, 13 NY State Militia (3 months), April 23, 1861. Honorably mustered out, Aug. 6, 1861. Captain, Co. M, 9 NJ Infantry, Sept. 17, 1861. GSW leg, New Berne, NC, March 14, 1862. Captain, Co. A, 9 NJ Infantry, Nov. 24, 1862. Lieutenant Colonel, 1 NC Infantry, March 27, 1863. Commanded District of the Pamlico, Department of North Carolina, June–July 1863. Colonel, 1 NC Infantry, Sept. 18, 1863. Commanded Sub-District of the Pamlico, District of North Carolina, Department

Joseph Miller McChesney (Massachusetts MOLLUS Collection, USAHEC [Vol. 130, p. 6666L]).

Joseph Miller McChesney (USAHEC [RG98S-CWP45.42]).

of Virginia and North Carolina, Nov. 1863–March 1864. Commanded Fort Macon (NC), May–Sept. 1864. Commanded Sub-District of Beaufort, District of North Carolina, Department of Virginia and North Carolina, Oct. 1864–Jan. 1865. GSW right knee, Washington, NC, Jan. 18, 1865. Resigned May 13, 1865, on account of physical disability from wounds received in action. Battle honors: New Berne, Kinston, White Hall, Siege of Washington (NC).

Born: Sept. 25, 1838 Trenton, NJ
Died: Aug. 14, 1865 Beaufort, NC
Occupation: Jeweler
Miscellaneous: Resided Brooklyn, NY
Buried: Westminster Cemetery (also known as Second Presbyterian Church Cemetery), Cranbury, Middlesex Co., NJ
References: Katherine E. Schultz. *The Descendants of Robert McChesney of Monmouth County, New Jersey.* Annville, PA, 1966. Obituary, *Brooklyn Daily Union,* Aug. 23, 1865. Obituary, *New York Evening Post,* Aug. 21, 1865. Obituary, *New York Times,* Aug. 28, 1865. Pension File and Military Service File, National Archives. Letters Received, Volunteer Service Branch, Adjutant General's Office, File M1695(VS)1865, National Archives. Edward G. Longacre. *The Sharpshooters: A History of the Ninth New Jersey Volunteer Infantry in the Civil War.* Lincoln, NE, 2016. J. Madison Drake. *The History of the Ninth New Jersey Veteran Vols.* Elizabeth, NJ, 1889.

Matthew Murray Miller

Private, Co. C, 45 IL Infantry, Jan. 10, 1862. GSW left breast, Shiloh, TN, April 6, 1862. Taken prisoner, Toone's Station, TN, Aug. 31, 1862. Bayonet wound, head, Milliken's Bend, LA, June 7, 1863. 2 Lieutenant, Co. G, 9 LA Infantry of African Descent, June 25, 1863. 1 Lieutenant, Co. G, 9 LA Infantry of African Descent, August 1, 1863. Designation of regiment changed to I MS Heavy Artillery of African Descent, Sept. 26, 1863. Captain, Co. C, 1 MS Heavy Artillery of African Descent, Nov. 30, 1863. Designation of regiment changed to 4 U.S. Colored Heavy Artillery, March 11, 1864. Designation of regiment changed to 5 U.S. Colored Heavy Artillery, April 26, 1864. Detached as *Colonel*, 1 Enrolled Militia (Freedmen), District of Vicksburg, Department of Mississippi, Nov. 5, 1864. Resigned May 29, 1865, "in order that I may be able to help support my mother and two young sisters as well as my father." Battle honors: Fort Donelson, Shiloh, Toone's Station, Milliken's Bend.

Born: Nov. 28, 1840 Galena, IL

Died: Nov. 29, 1918 Topeka, KS

Education: Attended Phillips Academy, Andover, MA. Attended Yale University, New Haven, CT.

Occupation: Merchant and miller before war. Lawyer after war.

Matthew Murray Miller (author's photograph).

Miscellaneous: Resided Galena, Jo Daviess Co., IL, to 1872; Clay Center, Clay Co., KS, 1872–94; and Topeka, Shawnee Co., KS, 1894–1918. Very active in freemasonry, being the oldest thirty-third degree Mason in Kansas at his death.

Buried: Mount Hope Cemetery, Topeka, KS

References: Obituary, *Topeka Daily Capital*, Nov. 30, 1918. Obituary Circular, Whole No. 449, Kansas MOLLUS. Obituary, *Clay Center Times*, Dec. 5, 1918. Obituary, *Topeka State Journal*, Nov. 30, 1918. Pension File and Military Service File, National Archives. Letters Received, Colored Troops Branch, Adjutant General's Office, File M127(CT)1863, National Archives. *A History of the Class of 1863, Yale College, Being the Fourth of Those Printed by Order of the Class.* New Haven, CT, 1905. *The War of the Rebellion: A Compilation of the Official Records of the Union and Confederate Armies.* Series 3, Vol. 3, pp. 452–453. Washington, D.C., 1899. John Wearmouth, editor. *The Cornwell Chronicles: Tales of an American Life on the Erie*

Canal, Building Chicago, in the Volunteer Civil War Western Army, on the Farm, in a Country Store. Bowie, MD, 1998. John M. Adair. *Historical Sketch of the Forty-Fifth Illinois Regiment.* Lanark, IL, 1869.

John Christie Peterson

Captain, 15 U.S. Infantry, Aug. 5, 1861. GSW forehead, Shiloh, TN, April 7, 1862. Acting AIG, Staff of Major Gen. William S. Rosecrans, 14 Army Corps, Department of the Cumberland, Oct. 1862–June 1863. President of Cincinnati (OH) Board of Transfer to Veteran Reserve Corps, June 1863–April 1864. Facing unproven charges of cowardice, he resigned Aug. 11, 1864, "being totally unable for field duty on account of physical disability ... and having been most outrageously insulted and traduced by my brigade commander, Brig. Gen. John H. King, U.S. Vols." *Lieutenant Colonel,* 1 Regiment, Quartermaster's Forces, Department of the Cumberland, Sept. 3, 1864. *Colonel,* 2 Regiment, Quartermaster's Forces, Department of the Cumberland, Sept. 14, 1864. Battle honors: Shiloh, Siege of Corinth, Atlanta Campaign, Forrest's Raid into West Tennessee (Johnsonville).

Born: Feb. 19, 1831 Union Springs, NY
Died: Oct. 7, 1867 Waterloo, NY (committed suicide)
Education: Attended U.S. Military Academy, West Point, NY (Class of 1852)
Occupation: Physician
Miscellaneous: Resided St. John, New Brunswick, Canada; and Union Springs, Cayuga Co., NY, before war; and Waterloo, Seneca Co., NY, after war
Buried: Chestnut Hill Cemetery, Union Springs, NY (Section 1, Lot 242)
References: Pension File, National Archives. Obituary, *Seneca Falls Reveille,* Oct. 11, 1867. Obituary, *New York Commercial Advertiser,* Oct. 10, 1867. Letters Received, Commission Branch, Adjutant General's Office, Files M1023(CB)1864 and P781(CB)1864, National Archives. Letters Received, Adjutant General's Office, Files P452(AGO)1861 and P934(AGO)1862, National Archives. Mark W. Johnson. *That Body of Brave Men: The U.S. Regular Infantry and the Civil War in the West.* Cambridge, MA, 2003. U.S. Military Academy Cadet Application Papers, 1805–1866, National Archives. *The War of the Rebellion: A Compilation of the Official Records of the Union and Confederate Armies.* Series 1, Vol. 52, Part 1, pp. 635–638 and 655–657. Washington, D.C., 1898.

George Myron Sabin

Corporal, Co. K, 1 WI Infantry (3 months), April 17, 1861. Honorably mustered out, Aug. 21, 1861. 1 Lieutenant, RQM, 11 WI Infantry, Sept. 10, 1861. Resigned Nov. 6, 1861. 1 Lieutenant, Adjutant, 16 WI Infantry, Nov. 19, 1861. Acting AIG, Staff of Brig. Gen. John McArthur, District of Vicksburg, April–July 1864. Judge Advocate, District of Vicksburg, Sept. 1864. Honorably mustered out, Dec. 20, 1864. *Colonel,* 2 Enrolled Militia, District of Vicksburg, Department of Mississippi, June–July 1865. Battle honors: Shiloh, Corinth, Vicksburg Campaign.

Born: Sept. 18, 1834 Strongsville, Cuyahoga Co., OH
Died: May 12, 1890 San Francisco, CA

George Myron Sabin (author's photograph).

George Myron Sabin (The Wisconsin Veterans Museum [WVM.0004.1094]).

Education: Graduated Western Reserve College, Hudson, OH, 1856

Occupation: Lawyer and judge

Offices/Honors: Brig. Gen., Nevada State Militia, 1878–82. Judge, U.S. District Court, District of Nevada, 1882–90

Miscellaneous: Resided Madison, Dane Co., WI, to 1868; Treasure Hill, White Pine Co., NV, 1868–72; Pioche, Lincoln Co., NV, 1872–77; Eureka, Eureka Co., NV, 1877–81; and San Francisco, CA, after 1881

Buried: Lone Mountain Cemetery, Carson City, NV (Section W1E, Row 18, Plot 12)

References: Obituary, *San Francisco Chronicle,* May 13, 1890. Obituary Circular, Whole No. 232, California MOLLUS. Obituary, *San Francisco Morning Call,* May 13, 1890. Obituary, *Sacramento Daily Record-Union,* May 13, 1890. Obituary, *Reno Evening Gazette,* May 12, 1890.

Charles B. Smith

1 Lieutenant, Co. E, 15 OH Infantry (3 months), April 27, 1861. Honorably mustered out, Aug. 27, 1861. 2 Lieutenant, Co. F, 61 IL Infantry, March 24, 1862. Acting ADC, Staff of Brig. Gen. Mason Brayman, Post of Bolivar (TN), District of Cairo (IL), and Post of Natchez (MS), Nov. 1862–Aug. 1864. 1 Lieutenant, Co. F, 61 IL Infantry, May 8, 1863. Acting AAG, Staff of Brig. Gen. Mason Brayman, Post of Natchez (MS), Aug.–Oct. 1864. Resigned Oct. 29, 1864. *Colonel,* 3 Enrolled MS Militia, Post of Natchez (MS), Nov. 1864–Jan. 1865. Manager, U.S. Military Telegraph, District of Mobile (AL), March–May 1865. Battle honors: Laurel Hill, Carrick's Ford, Shiloh, Corinth.

Born: 1842? Place of birth unknown
Died: Sept. 5, 1873 Owatonna, MN
Occupation: Telegraph operator
Miscellaneous: Resided Bloomington, McLean Co., IL
Buried: Forest Hill Cemetery, Owatonna, MN (Block 1, Soldier's Point). Cenotaph Maple Grove Cemetery, Granville, Licking Co., OH (Section 4, Lot 43).
References: Pension File, National Archives. Obituary, *Minneapolis Daily Tribune,* Sept. 6, 1873. Obituary, *Owatonna Journal,* Sept. 11, 1873. Letters Received, Commission Branch, Adjutant General's Office, File S1351(CB)1864, National Archives. *The War of the Rebellion: A Compilation of the Official Records of the Union and Confederate Armies.* Series 1, Vol. 48, Part 1, p. 563. Washington, D.C., 1896. *The War of the Rebellion: A Compilation of the Official Records of the Union and Confederate Armies.* Series 1, Vol. 49, Part 2, p. 511. Washington, D.C., 1897. "News By Telegraph: Matters at Natchez, Memphis and Vicksburg," *Chicago Tribune,* Nov. 26, 1864. William R. Plum. *The Military Telegraph during the Civil War in the United States.* Chicago, IL, 1882.

Charles B. Smith (Washington Gallery, Odd Fellows' Hall, Vicksburg, MS; author's photograph).

Sylvanus Harlow Stevens

1 Sergeant, Chicago Board of Trade Battery, IL Light Artillery. July 31, 1862. 1 Lieutenant, Chicago Board of Trade Battery, IL Light Artillery, Dec. 8, 1862. GSW Farmington, TN, Oct. 7, 1863. Acting AQM, Nashville (TN) Quartermaster Depot, Jan. 1864–June 1865. *Colonel,* 3 Regiment, Quartermaster's Forces, Department of the Cumberland, Sept. 3, 1864. *Colonel,* 6 Regiment, Quartermaster's Forces, Department of the Cumberland, Sept. 14, 1864. Honorably mustered out, June 30, 1865. Battle honors: Stone's River, Middle Tennessee Campaign, Chickamauga, Farmington, Forrest's Raid into West Tennessee.

Born: Oct. 26, 1827 Livermore, ME
Died: Dec. 19, 1902 Chicago, IL
Occupation: Grain merchant before war. Lumber merchant, 1870–82. Chief Inspector of Flax Seed for Chicago Board of Trade, 1882–1902.
Offices/Honors: Kansas House of Representatives, 1876
Miscellaneous: Resided Quincy, Adams Co., IL, 1843–54; Chicago, IL, 1854–62 and 1882–1902; Nashville, Davidson Co., TN, 1865–70; and Humboldt, Allen Co., KS, 1870–82

Buried: Graceland Cemetery, Chicago, IL (Section B, Lot 370)

References: *Memorials of Deceased Companions of the Commandery of the State of Illinois MOLLUS, from July 1, 1901, to Dec. 31, 1911.* Chicago, IL, 1912. Obituary Circular, Whole No. 451, Illinois MOLLUS. Obituary, *Chicago Daily Tribune*, Dec. 21, 1902. Obituary, *Humboldt Union*, Dec. 27, 1902. Obituary (Sylvanus H. Stevens), *Grain Dealers Journal*, Vol. 9, No. 12 (Dec. 25, 1902). Pension File, National Archives. *Historical Sketch of the Chicago Board of Trade Battery Horse Artillery Illinois Volunteers.* Chicago, IL, 1902. Letters Received, Commission Branch, Adjutant General's Office, File S2027(CB)1864, National Archives. Letters Received, Volunteer Service Branch, Adjutant General's Office, File S1728(VS)1864, National Archives. *The War of the Rebellion: A Compilation of the Official Records of the Union and Confederate Armies.* Series 1, Vol. 52, Part 1, pp. 635–638. Washington, D.C., 1898.

Sylvanus Harlow Stevens (post-war) (*Memorials of Deceased Companions of the Commandery of the State of Illinois MOLLUS, from July 1, 1901, to Dec. 31, 1911.* Chicago, IL, 1912).

William Timothy Sullivan

Private, Co. K, 17 IL Infantry, May 25, 1861. Sergeant, Co. K, 17 IL Infantry, July 2, 1862. 1 Sergeant, Co. K, 17 IL Infantry, Oct. 22, 1862. Taken prisoner and paroled, Collierville, TN, Jan. 2, 1863. Reduced to the ranks, Sept. 1, 1863. 1 Lieutenant, Adjutant, 4 MS Infantry of African Descent, Jan. 13, 1864. Designation of regiment changed to 66 U.S. Colored Infantry, March 11, 1864. Captain, Co. D, 66 U.S. Colored Infantry, Oct. 14, 1864. Judge Advocate, District of Vicksburg, Department of Mississippi, March 1865–March 1866. Detached as *Colonel*, 1 Enrolled Militia (Freedmen), District of Vicksburg, Department of Mississippi, June–July 1865. Honorably mustered out, March 20, 1866. Battle honors: Fredericktown, Fort Donelson, Shiloh, Iuka, Corinth.

Born: Dec. 27, 1842 Richland Twp., Jones Co., IA

Died: May 17, 1910 Gallatin, MO

Occupation: School teacher and farmer before war. Lawyer, newspaper editor, and U.S. Post Office inspector after war.

Miscellaneous: Resided Cascade, Dubuque Co., IA, before war; Gallatin, Daviess Co., MO; St. Louis, MO; and many other locations, after war

Buried: Greenwood Cemetery, Gallatin, MO

References: Edwin L. Hobart. *Semi-History of a Boy-Veteran of the Twenty-Eighth Regiment Illinois Infantry Volunteers in a Black Regiment.* Denver, CO, 1909. Pension File and Military Service File, National Archives. Obituary, *Chillicothe Daily Constitution,* May 18, 1910. Obituary, *St. Louis Globe-Democrat,* May 18, 1910. Letters Received, Colored Troops Branch, Adjutant General's Office, File S269(CT)1864, National Archives. Letters Received, Commission Branch, Adjutant General's Office, File S121(CB)1869, National Archives. John C. and Buel Leopard (Daviess County). *History of Daviess and Gentry Counties, Missouri.* Topeka and Indianapolis, 1922. *The History of Daviess County, Missouri.* Kansas City, MO, 1882.

William Timothy Sullivan (Abraham Lincoln Presidential Library & Museum).

Eugene von Kielmansegge

Captain, Co. C, Fremont Hussars, Sept. 4, 1861. Captain, Co. E, 4 MO Cavalry, Feb. 14, 1862. Major, 4 MO Cavalry, March 1, 1862. Being absent from his regiment without authority at the time of the special muster of Aug. 18, 1862, he was mustered out to take effect June 24, 1862. Colonel, 1 MD Cavalry, Nov. 15, 1862. Commanded 2 Brigade, 3 Division, Cavalry Corps, Army of the Potomac, Feb. 1863. Dismissed May 14, 1863, "having been discharged the service as Major of the 4 MO Cavalry ... for absence without leave, and no authority given for him to re-enter the service." *Colonel,* 1 FL Cavalry, March 29, 1864. Regiment not completing organization, he was mustered in as Major, 1 FL Cavalry, June 26, 1864. Lieutenant Colonel, 1 FL Cavalry, Aug. 23, 1864. Disability resulting from dismissal (from 1 MD Cavalry) removed, Oct. 4, 1864, and he was re-mustered as Major and Lieutenant Colonel, 1 FL Cavalry, Nov. 4, 1864. Discharged for disability, April 17, 1865, "on account of myopia contracted prior to his muster into service." Battle honors: Pea Ridge, Searcy Landing

Born: 1830 Aurich, Hanover, Germany

Died: Sept. 3, 1868 St. Andrews City, Washington Co. (now Bay Co.), FL

Occupation: Captain of Hussars in Austrian army before war. U.S. Customs inspector after war.

Offices/Honors: Postmaster, Apalachicola, FL, 1865–67

Miscellaneous: Resided Hoboken, Hudson Co., NJ; and Apalachicola, Franklin Co., FL

Buried: St. Andrews City (now part of Panama City), FL (cemetery unknown)

References: Mark Curenton, "Apalachicola's Most Prominent Carpetbagger," *The*

Apalachicola & Carrabelle Times, Aug. 9, 2018. Pension File and Military Service File, National Archives. Letters Received, Volunteer Service Branch, Adjutant General's Office, File K232(VS)1863, National Archives. Sharon D. Marsh. *The 1st Florida Union Cavalry Volunteers in the Civil War.* N.p., 2017. William S. Burns. *Recollections of the 4th Missouri Cavalry.* Edited by Frank Allen Dennis. Dayton, OH, 1988. Daniel C. Toomey and Charles A. Earp. *Marylanders in Blue: The Artillery and the Cavalry.* Baltimore, MD, 1999.

Thomas G. Whytal

Captain, Co. D, 43 MA Infantry, Sept. 12, 1862. Honorably mustered out, July 30, 1863. Captain, AQM, USV, Nov. 13, 1863. AQM, Alexandria (VA) Quartermaster Depot, Dec. 1863–Nov. 1864. *Colonel,* 7 Regiment (originally 2 Colored Regiment), Quartermaster's Volunteers, Department of Washington, Aug. 4, 1864. AQM, Augusta (ME) Quartermaster Depot, Nov. 1864–Feb. 1866. Chief Quartermaster, Military District of Fort Monroe (VA), July 1866–Sept. 1867. Honorably mustered out, Oct. 5, 1867. Bvt. Major, USV, and Bvt. Lieutenant Colonel, USV, March 13, 1865, for faithful and efficient services during the war.

Born: Aug. 6, 1825 Halifax, Nova Scotia

Thomas G. Whytal (Massachusetts MOLLUS Collection, USAHEC [Vol. 103, p. 5340L]).

Thomas G. Whytal (Silsbee, Case & Co., Photographic Artists, 299½ Washington Street, Boston, MA; Massachusetts MOLLUS Collection, USAHEC [Vol. 103, p. 5337L]).

Thomas G. Whytal (Philp & Solomons' Metropolitan Gallery, 332 Penn. Avenue, Washington, D.C.; USAHEC [RG98S-CWP90.32]).

Died: Nov. 19, 1908 Bayside, Queens Co., NY

Occupation: Tea merchant before war. Clerk in Naval Office, New York Custom House, 1871–87.

Miscellaneous: Resided Boston, MA, before war; New York City, NY, 1870–1904; and Bayside, Queens Co., NY, 1904–08

Died: Forest Hills Cemetery, Jamaica Plain, MA (Spruce Avenue, Lot 1164)

References: Pension File and Military Service File, National Archives. Obituary, *Brooklyn Daily Eagle*, Nov. 21, 1908. Obituary, *New York Times*, Nov. 21, 1908. Letters Received, Commission Branch, Adjutant General's Office, Files Q47(CB)1864 and W169(CB)1864, National Archives. Edward H. Rogers. *Reminiscences of Military Service in the Forty-Third Regiment, Massachusetts Infantry, During the Great Civil War, 1862–63*. Boston, MA, 1883. *The War of the Rebellion: A Compilation of the Official Records of the Union and Confederate Armies*. Series 3, Vol. 4, pp. 699–700. Washington, D.C., 1900.

Isaiah Churchill (aka Isaac C.) Woods

Captain, Commissary of Subsistence, USV, Sept. 9, 1861. Colonel, Chief of Transportation, Staff of Major Gen. John C. Fremont, Western Department, Sept. 20, 1861. Resigned Nov. 30, 1861

Born: Oct. 8, 1824 Saco, ME

Died: Feb. 16, 1880 Mare Island, CA

Occupation: Commission merchant and entrepreneur. Manager of the banking and express agency of Adams & Co. in San Francisco, gaining a reputation as "notorious" from his association with the demise of Adams & Co. in 1855. Later operated a short-lived Overland Mail Line from San Antonio (TX) to San Diego (CA).

Miscellaneous: Resided San Francisco, CA; and Vallejo, Solano Co., CA

Buried: Mare Island Cemetery, Vallejo, CA

References: Albert Shumate. *The Notorious I.C. Woods of the Adams Express*. Glendale, CA, 1986. Obituary, *San Francisco Bulletin*, Feb. 17, 1880. Theodore A. Barry and Benjamin A. Patten. *Men and Memories of San Francisco in the "Spring of '50."* San Francisco, CA, 1873. Pension File, National Archives. Obituary, *Sacramento Record-Union*, Feb. 18, 1880. *Report of the Joint Committee on the Conduct of the War*. Part 3-Department of the West. Washington, D.C., 1863. "The Notorious I.C. Woods," *San Francisco Bulletin*, Feb. 3, 1862.

William Woods

Captain, Co. A, 2 WI Cavalry, Nov. 19, 1861. Ordnance Officer, District of Rolla (MO), Department of the Missouri, July 30, 1863. Chief of Cavalry, District of Rolla

(MO), Department of the Missouri, Oct. 7, 1863. Major, 2 WI Cavalry, June 20, 1864. Honorably mustered out, Jan. 25, 1865. *Colonel*, 2 Enrolled Militia, District of Vicksburg, Department of Mississippi, April–June 1865.

Born: 1827? VT

Died: Oct. 13, 1897 Santa Monica, CA

Occupation: Clerk and bookkeeper

Miscellaneous: Resided Eldorado Twp., Fond du Lac Co., WI, before war; Fond du Lac, Fond du Lac Co., WI, to 1872; Bismarck, Burleigh Co., Dakota Territory, 1872–85; San Luis Obispo, San Luis Obispo Co., CA (1888); and Los Angeles, CA

Buried: Los Angeles National Cemetery, Los Angeles, CA (Section 4, Row A, Grave 16)

References: Obituary, *Los Angeles Times*, Oct. 15, 1897. Obituary, *Los Angeles Herald*, Oct. 15, 1897. Obituary, *San Francisco Examiner*, Oct. 15, 1897. Pension File, National Archives. *The War of the Rebellion: A Compilation of the Official Records of the Union and Confederate Armies.* Series 1, Vol. 48, Part 2, p. 257. Washington, D.C., 1896. *The History of Fond du Lac County, Wisconsin.* Chicago, IL, 1880. www.ancestry.com.

Juan (aka John) Napoleon Zerman

Colonel, Inspector General, Staff of Major Gen. John C. Fremont, Western Department, Aug. 7, 1861. Discharged Feb. 4, 1862. Nominated Brig. Gen., USV, March 15, 1862. Nomination confirmed, May 2, 1862. Return of confirmation requested, May 5, 1862. Nomination withdrawn, June 18, 1862, probably due to disclosure of his reputation as "a swindler and scamp of the worst and most dangerous character," blamed primarily on "the intrigues of foreign politicians."

Born: June 24, 1790 Venice, Italy

Died: Dec. 10, 1876 San Francisco, CA

Occupation: Commanded Turkish Black Sea Fleet, 1842–47. Assuming the role of an Admiral in the Mexican Navy, he led a filibustering expedition into Baja California in 1855, hoping to take advantage of the revolutionary unrest then prevalent in Mexico. However, he and his two ships were seized, and all members of the expedition were imprisoned under harsh conditions for more than two years before being released.

Juan Napoleon Zerman (E. & H.T. Anthony, 501 Broadway, New York, from photographic negative in Brady's National Portrait Gallery; Massachusetts MOLLUS Collection, USAHEC [Vol. 98, p. 5034]).

Juan Napoleon Zerman (Massachusetts MOLLUS Collection, USAHEC [Vol. 98, p. 5034L]).

Miscellaneous: Resided New York City, NY; and San Francisco, CA

Buried: Originally Mission Dolores Cemetery, San Francisco, CA. Removed (as Jean N. Zerman), April 19, 1889, to Holy Cross Catholic Cemetery, Colma, CA (Section G, Row 5, Area 11, Grave 4).

References: Correspondence Concerning Fremont's Appointments, 1861–64,

Record Group 94, Entry 164, National Archives. Letters Received, Adjutant General's Office, File Z3(AGO)1861, National Archives. Union Citizens File, Admiral Zerman, National Archives. Roy P. Basler, editor. *The Collected Works of Abraham Lincoln.* Vol. 5. New Brunswick, NJ, 1953. Death notice, *San Francisco Bulletin,* Dec. 11, 1876. "The Confirmation of Zerman," *New York Times,* May 7, 1862. "Gen. Zerman," *New York Tribune,* June 5, 1862. "Distinguished Visitor," *Altoona Tribune,* July 6, 1871. Abraham Lincoln Papers: Series 1. General Correspondence. 1833–1916: Zerman, J. Napoleon, to Senate, Monday, June 02, 1862, Library of Congress. Joseph A. Stout, Jr. *Schemers and Dreamers: Filibustering in Mexico, 1848–1921.* Fort Worth, TX, 2002. Eugene K. Chamberlin, "Baja California After Walker: The Zerman Expedition," *The Hispanic American Historical Review,* Vol. 34, No. 2 (May 1954). www.ancestry.com.

Bibliography

Books

Adair, John M. *Historical Sketch of the Forty-Fifth Illinois Regiment.* Lanark, IL: Carroll County Gazette Print, 1869.

Adams, Andrew N., ed. *A Genealogical History of Robert Adams of Newbury, Mass., and His Descendants, 1635–1900.* Rutland, VT: Tuttle Co., 1900.

Adams, William, ed. *Historical Gazetteer and Biographical Memorial of Cattaraugus County, N.Y.* Syracuse, NY: Lyman, Horton & Co., 1893.

Album of Genealogy and Biography Cook County, Illinois. Chicago: Calumet Book & Engraving Co., 1897.

Alexander, W.E. *History of Winneshiek and Allamakee Counties, Iowa.* Sioux City, IA: Western Publishing Co., 1882.

Altshuler, Constance W. *Cavalry Yellow & Infantry Blue.* Tucson, AZ: Arizona Historical Society, 1991.

Alumni Record of Wesleyan University, Middletown, Connecticut. Third Edition, 1881–83. Hartford, CT: Case, Lockwood & Brainard Co., 1883.

American Biographical History of Eminent and Self-Made Men. Michigan Volume. Cincinnati: Western Biographical Publishing Co., 1878.

American Biography: A New Cyclopedia. Vol. 3. New York: American Historical Society, 1918.

Anderson, Joseph, ed. *The Town and City of Waterbury, Connecticut, from the Aboriginal Period to the Year Eighteen Hundred and Ninety-Five.* New Haven, CT: Price & Lee Co., 1896.

Andreas, Alfred T. *History of Chicago from the Earliest Period to the Present Time.* Chicago: A.T. Andreas Co., 1884.

———. *History of Northern Wisconsin.* Chicago: Western Historical Co., 1881.

———. *History of the State of Kansas.* Chicago: A.T. Andreas, 1883.

Andrews, Christopher C., ed. *History of St. Paul, Minnesota.* Syracuse, NY: D. Mason & Co., 1890.

Appletons' Annual Cyclopaedia and Register of Important Events of the Year 1888. New Series, Vol. 13. New York: D. Appleton & Co., 1889.

Atkinson, Joseph. *The History of Newark, New Jersey.* Newark, NJ: William B. Guild, 1878.

Aubin, J. Harris, comp. *Register of the Military Order of the Loyal Legion of the United States.* Boston: Massachusetts Commandery, 1906.

Backus, Reno W. *The Backus Families of Early New England.* N.p.: Reno W. Backus, 1966.

Baird, William Raimond. *Betas of Achievement.* New York: Beta, 1914.

Baldwin, Elmer. *History of LaSalle County, Illinois.* Chicago: Rand, McNally & Co., 1877.

Bangs, Isaac S., "The Ullman Brigade," *War Papers Read Before the Commandery of the State of Maine, MOLLUS.* Vol. 2. Portland, ME: Lefavor-Tower Co., 1902.

Banquet Given by the Members of the Union League Club of 1863 and 1864, to Commemorate the Departure for the Seat of War of the Twentieth Regiment of United States Colored Troops Raised by the Club. New York: George F. Nesbitt & Co., 1886.

Banta, Theodore M. *A Frisian Family: The Banta Genealogy, Descendants of Epke Jacobse, Who Came from Friesland, Netherlands, to New Amsterdam, February 1659.* New York: T.M. Banta, 1893.

Barnes, William Horatio. *History of Congress. The Forty-First Congress of the United States, 1869–1871.* New York: W.H. Barnes & Co., 1872.

Barnet, James, ed. *The Martyrs and Heroes of Illinois in the Great Rebellion.* Second Edition. Chicago: Press of J. Barnet, 1866.

Barriger, John W. *Legislative History of the Subsistence Department of the United States Army from June 16, 1775 to August 15, 1876.* Washington, D.C.: Government Printing Office, 1877.

Barry, Joseph. *The Strange Story of Harper's Ferry with Legends of the Surrounding Country.* Martinsburg, WV: Thompson Brothers, 1903.

Barry, Theodore A., and Benjamin A. Patten. *Men and Memories of San Francisco in the "Spring of '50."* San Francisco: A.L. Bancroft & Co., 1873.

Basler, Roy P., ed. *The Collected Works of Abraham Lincoln.* Vol. 5. New Brunswick, NJ: Rutgers University Press, 1953.

Bateman, Newton, and Paul Selby, eds. *Historical Encyclopedia of Illinois and History of*

Sangamon County. Chicago: Munsell Publishing Co., 1912.

Bates, Joseph C., editor. *History of the Bench and Bar of California.* San Francisco: Bench and Bar Publishing Co., 1912.

Bausman, Joseph H. *History of Beaver County, Pennsylvania, and Its Centennial Celebration.* New York: Knickerbocker Press, 1904.

Baxter, Albert. *History of the City of Grand Rapids, Michigan.* New York: Munsell & Co., 1891.

The Bay of San Francisco, the Metropolis of the Pacific Coast and Its Suburban Cities: A History. Chicago: Lewis Publishing Co., 1892.

Baylor, Orval Walker, and Henry Bedinger Baylor, eds. *Baylor's History of the Baylors: A Collection of Records and Important Family Data.* LeRoy, IL: LeRoy Journal Printing Co., 1914.

Beall, Fielder M.M., ed. *Colonial Families of the United States Descended from the Immigrants Who Arrived Before 1700, Mostly from England and Scotland, and Who are Now Represented by Citizens of the Following Names: Bell, Beal, Bale, Beale, Beall.* Washington, D.C.: Charles H. Potter & Co., 1929.

Bearss, Edwin Cole. *The Vicksburg Campaign.* 3 vols. Dayton, OH: Morningside House, 1985–86.

Beauchamp, William M. *Past and Present of Syracuse and Onondaga County, New York, From Prehistoric Times to the Beginning of 1908.* New York: S.J. Clarke Publishing Co., 1908.

Beckwith, Hiram W. *History of Vigo and Parke Counties, Together with Historic Notes on the Wabash Valley.* Chicago: H.H. Hill and N. Iddings, 1880.

Beecher, Herbert W. *History of the First Light Battery Connecticut Volunteers, 1861–1865.* New York: A.T. De La Mare Printing & Publishing, 1901.

Behrens, Robert H. *From Salt Fork to Chickamauga: Champaign County Soldiers in the Civil War.* Urbana, IL: Urbana Free Library, 1988.

Benedict, George G. *Vermont in the Civil War: A History of the Part Taken by the Vermont Soldiers and Sailors in the War for the Union, 1861–65.* Burlington, VT: Free Press Association, 1886.

Benedict, Henry M. *A Contribution to the Genealogy of the Stafford Family in America; Containing an Account of Col. Joab Stafford and a Complete Record of His Descendants in the Male Lines.* New York: Styles & Cash, 1895.

Benson, Al, Jr., and Walter D. Kennedy. *Lincoln's Marxists.* Gretna, LA: Pelican Publishing Co., 2011.

Benson, Gunnar A. *Centennial Anniversary of Whiteside County Education Association, 1856–1956.* Sterling, IL: Whiteside County Education Association, 1956.

Beyer, Walter F., and Oscar F. Keydel, eds. *Deeds of Valor: How America's Heroes Won the Medal of Honor.* Detroit, MI: Perrien-Keydel Co., 1903.

Bidwell, Frederick D., comp. *History of the Forty-Ninth New York Volunteers.* Albany, NY: J.B. Lyon Co., 1916.

Bierbower, James C., and Charles W. Beerbower, comp. *House of Bierbauer: Two Hundred Years of Family History, 1742–1942.* New Wilmington, PA: Globe Printing Co., 1942.

Bierman, E. Benjamin. *Lebanon County in Our State Legislature. A Paper Read Before the Lebanon County Historical Society, February 19, 1904.* Lebanon, PA: Lebanon County Historical Society, 1904.

Bigelow, Samuel F., and George J. Hagar, eds. *The Biographical Cyclopedia of New Jersey.* New York: National Americana Society, 1908.

Biographical and Historical Record of Ringgold and Decatur Counties, Iowa. Chicago: Lewis Publishing Co., 1887.

Biographical and Historical Souvenir for the Counties of Clark, Crawford, Harrison, Floyd, Jefferson, Jennings, Scott and Washington, Indiana. Chicago: John M. Gresham & Co., 1889.

A Biographical Album of Prominent Pennsylvanians. First Series. Philadelphia: American Biographical Publishing Co., 1888.

Biographical Annals of Lancaster County, Pennsylvania. Chicago: J.H. Beers & Co., 1903.

The Biographical Cyclopedia and Portrait Gallery with an Historical Sketch of the State of Ohio. Vol. 3. Cincinnati: Western Biographical Publishing Co., 1884.

The Biographical Cyclopedia and Portrait Gallery with an Historical Sketch of the State of Ohio. Vol. 4. Cincinnati: Western Biographical Publishing Co., 1887.

The Biographical Encyclopaedia of Illinois of the Nineteenth Century. Philadelphia: Galaxy Publishing Co., 1875.

The Biographical Encyclopaedia of Ohio of the Nineteenth Century. Cincinnati and Philadelphia: Galaxy Publishing Co., 1876.

A Biographical History of Eminent and Self-Made Men of the State of Indiana. Cincinnati: Western Biographical Publishing Co., 1880.

The Biographical Record of Bureau, Marshall and Putnam Counties, Illinois. Chicago: S.J. Clarke Publishing Co., 1896.

The Biographical Record of Knox County, Ohio. Chicago: Lewis Publishing Co., 1902.

Biographical Review (Volume XXI) Containing Life Sketches of Leading Citizens of Strafford and Belknap Counties, New Hampshire. Boston: Biographical Review Publishing Co., 1897.

Biographical Review Cumberland County, Maine. Boston: Biographical Review Publishing Co., 1896.

Blackburn, John. *A Hundred Miles A Hundred Heartbreaks.* Owensboro, KY: John Blackburn, 1972.

Blackmar, Frank William, ed. *Kansas: A Cyclopedia of State History.* Chicago: Standard Publishing Co., 1912.

Bliss, Aaron T. *Genealogy of the Bliss Family in America*. Midland, MI: A.T. Bliss, 1982.

Bliss, John Homer, comp. *Genealogy of the Bliss Family in America from About the Year 1550 to 1880*. Boston: J.H. Bliss, 1881.

Boase, Frederic. *Modern English Biography*. London, England: Frank Cass & Co., 1965.

Bodley, Temple. *History of Kentucky: The Blue Grass State*. Chicago and Louisville: S.J. Clarke Publishing Co., 1928.

Boltwood, Lucius M., comp. *History and Genealogy of the Family of Thomas Noble of Westfield, Massachusetts*. Hartford, CT: Case, Lockwood & Brainard Co., 1878.

Book of Biographies: Biographical Sketches of Leading Citizens of Chenango County, New York. Buffalo, NY: Biographical Publishing Co., 1898.

Bostwick, Henry A., comp. *Genealogy of the Bostwick Family in America: The Descendants of Arthur Bostwick of Stratford, Conn*. Hudson, NY: Bryan Printing Co., 1901.

Botsford Family Genealogy: The Line of Joseph, 1.1.12; Youngest Son of Elnathan, 1.1; Grandson of Henry, 1. Baltimore, MD: Gateway Press, 1983.

Bowen, James L. *Massachusetts in the War, 1861–1865*. Springfield, MA: Clark W. Bryan & Co., 1889.

Bradsby, Henry C., ed. *History of Bureau County, Illinois*. Chicago: World Publishing Co., 1885.

———. *History of Luzerne County, Pennsylvania, with Biographical Selections*. Chicago: S.B. Nelson & Co., 1893.

Brennan, J. Fletcher, ed. *The Biographical Cyclopedia and Portrait Gallery of Distinguished Men, with an Historical Sketch of the State of Ohio*. Cincinnati: John C. Yorston & Co., 1879.

Bridgman, Burt N., and Joseph C. Bridgman, comps. *Genealogy of the Bridgman Family: Descendants of James Bridgman, 1636–1894*. Hyde Park, MA: C.W. Bryan Co., 1894.

Brown, Dee. *The Galvanized Yankees*. Urbana, IL: University of Illinois Press, 1963.

Brown, Francis H. *Harvard University in the War of 1861–1865*. Boston: Cupples, Upham, and Co., 1886.

———. *Roll of Students of Harvard University Who Served in the Army or Navy of the United States During the War of the Rebellion*. Cambridge, MA: Welch, Bigelow & Co., 1866.

Brown, Fred R. *History of the Ninth U.S. Infantry, 1799–1909*. Chicago: R.R. Donnelley & Sons Co., 1909.

Brown, J. Willard. *The Signal Corps, U.S.A., in the War of the Rebellion*. Boston: U.S. Veteran Signal Corps Association, 1896.

Brown, Leonard. *American Patriotism; or, Memoirs of "Common Men."* Des Moines, IA: Redhead and Wellslager, 1869.

Bryant, Benjamin F., ed. *Memoirs of La Crosse County*. Madison, WI: Western Historical Association, 1907.

Buffum, Francis H. *A Memorial of the Great Rebellion: Being a History of the Fourteenth Regiment New Hampshire Volunteers, Covering Its Three Years of Service, with Original Sketches of Army Life, 1862–1865*. Boston: Franklin Press, 1882.

The Builders of a Great City: San Francisco's Representative Men, the City, Its History and Commerce. San Francisco: San Francisco Journal of Commerce Publishing Co., 1891.

Bumgarner, Matthew. *Kirk's Raiders: A Notorious Band of Scoundrels and Thieves*. Hickory, NC: Piedmont Press, 2000.

Buresh, Lumir F. *October 25th and the Battle of Mine Creek*. Kansas City, MO: Lowell Press, 1977.

Burgess, Ebenezer. *Burgess Genealogy: Memorial of the Family of Thomas and Dorothy Burgess, Who Were Settled at Sandwich, in the Plymouth Colony in 1637*. Boston: T.R. Marvin & Son, 1865.

Burns, William S. *Recollections of the 4th Missouri Cavalry*. Edited by Frank Allen Dennis. Dayton, OH: Morningside House, 1988.

Butler, Benjamin F. *Autobiography and Personal Reminiscences of Major General Benjamin F. Butler: Butler's Book*. Boston: A.M. Thayer & Co., 1892.

Callahan, Edward W., ed. *List of Officers of the Navy of the United States and of the Marine Corps from 1775 to 1900*. New York: L.R. Hamersly & Co., 1901.

Cannon, Le Grand B. *Personal Reminiscences of the Rebellion, 1861–1866*. New York: Burr Printing House, 1895.

Card, Eva G., and Howard A. Guernsey, comps. *The Garnsey-Guernsey Genealogy*. Urbana, IL: Eva G. Card, 1963.

Carleton, Hiram, ed. *Genealogical and Family History of the State of Vermont*. New York and Chicago: Lewis Publishing Co., 1903.

Carpenter, Edward, and Louis Henry Carpenter, comps. *Samuel Carpenter and His Descendants*. Philadelphia: J.B. Lippincott Co., 1912.

Carr, Arthur A. *The Carr Book: Sketches of the Lives of Many of the Descendants of Robert and Caleb Carr, Whose Arrival on This Continent in 1635 Began the American Story of Our Family*. Ticonderoga, NY: Arthur A. Carr, 1947.

Carr, Edson I. *The Carr Family Records*. Rockton, IL: Herald Printing House, 1894.

Carter, William H. *From Yorktown to Santiago with the Sixth U.S. Cavalry*. Baltimore, MD: Lord Baltimore Press, 1900.

Case, Lafayette W., ed. *The Goodrich Family in America: A Genealogy of the Descendants of John and William Goodrich of Wethersfield, Conn., Richard Goodrich of Guilford, Conn., and William Goodridge of Watertown, Mass*. Chicago: Fergus Printing Co., 1889.

Catalogue of Alpha Delta Phi. New York: Alpha Delta Phi Fraternity, 1899.

Catalogue of Phi Alpha Society, Illinois College, 1845–1890. Jacksonville, IL: Tuttle, Morehouse & Taylor, 1890.

Catalogue of the Officers and Students of Hamilton College, with Societies, 1865–66. Clinton, NY: Roberts, Book and Job Printer, 1866.

Catalogue of the Sigma Phi with the Thesaurus. Boston: Sigma Phi Society, 1891.

Chamberlain, Portia, ed. *Bardwell/Bordwell Descendants.* Book 2. Los Altos, CA: Robert Bardwell Ancestry Association, 1974.

Chapman, George T. *Sketches of the Alumni of Dartmouth College.* Cambridge, MA: Riverside Press, 1867.

Chase, Theodore R. *The Michigan University Book, 1844–1880.* Detroit, MI: Richmond, Backus & Co., 1880.

Chittenden, Lucius E. *Personal Reminiscences, 1840–1890, Including Some Not Hitherto Published of Lincoln and the War.* New York: Richmond, Croscup & Co., 1893.

Christoph, Florence A. *Schuyler Genealogy: The Schuyler Families in America Prior to 1900.* Albany, NY: Friends of Schuyler Mansion, 1992.

Churchill, Franklin Hunter. *Sketch of the Life of Bvt. Brig. Gen. Sylvester Churchill, Inspector General, U.S. Army, with Notes and Appendices.* New York: Willis McDonald & Co., 1888.

Churchill, Gardner A. and Nathaniel W., comps. *The Churchill Family in America.* Boston: Family of Gardner A. Churchill, 1904.

Clark, Orton S. *One Hundred and Sixteenth Regiment of New York State Volunteers.* Buffalo, NY: Matthews & Warren, 1868.

Cleaveland, Nehemiah, and Alpheus S. Packard. *History of Bowdoin College with Biographical Sketches of Its Graduates from 1806 to 1879, Inclusive.* Boston: James Ripley Osgood & Co., 1882.

Cleveland, Edmund J., and Horace G. Cleveland, comps. *The Genealogy of the Cleveland and Cleaveland Families.* Hartford, CT: Case, Lockwood & Brainard Co., 1899.

Cobb, John C., "One Year of My More Than Three Years' Service with the Army of the Gulf," *War Papers Read Before the Commandery of the State of Maine MOLLUS.* Vol. 3. Portland, ME: Lefavor-Tower Co., 1908.

Coleman, Lyman. *Genealogy of the Lyman Family in Great Britain and America.* Albany, NY: J. Munsell, 1872.

Collins, Emerson, and John W. Jordan, eds. *Genealogical and Personal History of Lycoming County, Pennsylvania.* New York and Chicago: Lewis Publishing Co., 1906.

Commemorative Biographical Record of the Upper Lake Region. Chicago: J.H. Beers & Co., 1905.

Commemorative Historical and Biographical Record of Wood County, Ohio: Its Past and Present. Chicago: J.H. Beers & Co., 1897.

Companions of the Military Order of the Loyal Legion of the United States. New York: L.R. Hamersly Co., 1901.

Cone, William Whitney, comp. *Some Account of the Cone Family in America, Principally of the Descendants of Daniel Cone, Who Settled in Haddam, Connecticut, in 1662.* Topeka, KS: Crane & Co., 1903.

Connelley, William E. *A Standard History of Kansas and Kansans.* Chicago and New York: Lewis Publishing Co., 1918.

Conyngham, David P. *The Irish Brigade and Its Campaigns.* Boston: Patrick Donahoe, 1869.

Cooper, W. *Sketches of the Senators and Representatives in the Fifty-Fourth General Assembly of the State of Ohio.* Columbus, OH: W. Cooper, 1861.

Cornell, John. *Genealogy of the Cornell Family, Being an Account of the Descendants of Thomas Cornell of Portsmouth, R.I.* New York: Press of T.A. Wright, 1902.

Corson, Hiram. *The Corson Family: A History of the Descendants of Benjamin Corson.* Philadelphia: Henry Lawrence Everett, 1896.

Counties of LaGrange and Noble, Indiana. Historical and Biographical. Chicago: F.A. Battey & Co., 1882.

Cox, Dale. *The Battle of Marianna, Florida: Expanded Edition.* Bascom, FL: Dale Cox, 2011.

Cox, William Van Zandt, and Milton Harlow Northrup. *Life of Samuel Sullivan Cox.* Syracuse, NY: M.H. Northrup, 1899.

Crandall, Warren D., and Isaac D. Newell. *History of the Ram Fleet and the Mississippi Marine Brigade in the War for the Union on the Mississippi and Its Tributaries.* St. Louis: Press of Buschart Brothers, 1907.

Crofts, Thomas, comp. *History of the Service of the Third Ohio Veteran Volunteer Cavalry in the War for the Preservation of the Union from 1861–1865.* Toledo, OH: Stoneman Press, 1910.

Cullum, George W. *Biographical Register of the Officers and Graduates of the U.S. Military Academy at West Point, N.Y.* Third Edition. Boston and New York: Houghton, Mifflin & Co., 1891.

Cummings, Horace S. *Dartmouth College. Sketches of the Class of 1862.* Washington, D.C.: H. I. Rothrock, 1884.

Current, Richard N. *Lincoln's Loyalists: Union Soldiers from the Confederacy.* Boston: Northeastern University Press, 1992.

Cutter, William R., ed. *Genealogical and Family History of Western New York.* New York: Lewis Historical Publishing Co., 1912.

Dahlgren, John A.B. *Memoir of Ulric Dahlgren.* Philadelphia: J.B. Lippincott & Co., 1872.

Darby, John F. *Personal Recollections of Many Prominent People Whom I Have Known, and of Events, Especially of Those Relating to the History of St. Louis, During the First Half of the Present Century.* St. Louis: G.I. Jones & Co., 1880.

Davis, William W. *History of Whiteside County, Illinois, from Its Earliest Settlement to 1908.* Chicago: Pioneer Publishing Co., 1908.
Dean, Benjamin D. *Recollections of the 26th Missouri Infantry in the War for the Union.* Lamar, MO: Southwest Missourian Office, 1892.
Dictionary of American Biography. Supplement 1. New York: Charles Scribner's Sons, 1944.
Directory of Knox People. Galesburg, IL: Knox College, 1923.
Dobak, William A. *Freedom by the Sword: The U.S. Colored Troops, 1862–1867.* Washington, D.C.: Center of Military History, United States Army, 2011.
Dole, Samuel T. *Windham in the Past.* Auburn, ME: Merrill & Webber Co., 1916.
Dorsey, Jean M., and Maxwell J. Dorsey. *Christopher Gist of Maryland and Some of His Descendants, 1679–1957.* Chicago: John S. Swift Co., 1958.
Drake, Francis S. *Dictionary of American Biography Including Men of the Time.* Boston: James R. Osgood & Co., 1872.
Drake, J. Madison. *The History of the Ninth New Jersey Veteran Vols.* Elizabeth, NJ: Journal Printing House, 1889.
Drury, Augustus W. *History of the City of Dayton and Montgomery County, Ohio.* Chicago and Dayton: S.J. Clarke Publishing Co., 1909.
Duis, Dr. E. *The Good Old Times in McLean County, Illinois.* Bloomington, IL: Leader Publishing & Printing House, 1874.
Duncan, L. Wallace, and Charles F. Scott, eds. *History of Allen and Woodson Counties, Kansas.* Iola, KS: Iola Register, 1901.
Duncan, Russell, ed. *Blue-Eyed Child of Fortune: The Civil War Letters of Colonel Robert Gould Shaw.* Athens, GA: University of Georgia Press, 1992.
Dungan, J. Irvine. *History of the Nineteenth Regiment Iowa Volunteer Infantry.* Davenport, IA: Luse & Griggs, 1865.
Durham, Walter T. *Rebellion Revisited: A History of Sumner County, Tennessee, from 1861 to 1870.* Franklin, TN: Hillsboro Press, 1999.
Dwight, Melatiah Everett. *The Kirbys of New England.* New York: The Trow Print, 1898.
Eagleburger, Len. *The Fighting 10th: The History of the 10th Missouri Cavalry, U.S.* Bloomington, IN: 1stBooks, 2004.
Earle, Pliny, comp. *Ralph Earle and His Descendants.* Worcester, MA: C. Hamilton, 1888.
Early, Ruth H. *Campbell Chronicles and Family Sketches Embracing the History of Campbell County, Virginia, 1782–1926.* Lynchburg, VA: J.P. Bell Co., 1927.
Eastmond, Theodore L. *Eastmond-Benson Genealogy & Biography.* N.p.: T.L. Eastmond, 1979.
Eddy, Thomas M. *The Patriotism of Illinois.* Chicago: Clarke & Co., 1865.
Edgar, John F. *Pioneer Life in Dayton and Vicinity, 1796–1840.* Dayton, OH: W.J. Shuey, 1896.
Edmonds, David C. *The Guns of Port Hudson: The Investment, Siege and Reduction.* Lafayette, LA: Acadiana Press, 1984.
Eleventh Annual Reunion of the Association of the Graduates of the U.S. Military Academy at West Point, NY. East Saginaw, MI: E.W. Lyon, 1880.
Ellis, Franklin. *History of Cattaraugus County, New York.* Philadelphia: L.H. Everts, 1879.
Eminent and Representative Men of Virginia and the District of Columbia of the Nineteenth Century. Madison, WI: Brant & Fuller, 1893.
Evans, Nelson W. *A History of Scioto County, Ohio, Together with A Pioneer Record of Southern Ohio.* Portsmouth, OH: Nelson W. Evans, 1903.
Fairbanks, Edward T. *Yale College Class of 1859, Decennial Record.* New Haven, CT: The College Courant Print, 1870.
Farnam, Charles H. *History of the Descendants of John Whitman of Weymouth, Mass.* New Haven, CT: Tuttle, Morehouse & Taylor, 1889.
Farnsworth, Claudius B. *Matthias Farnsworth and his Descendants in America.* Pawtucket, RI: C.B. Farnsworth, 1891.
Field Record of Officers of the Veteran Reserve Corps from the Commencement to the Close of the Rebellion. Washington, D.C.: Scriver & Swing, 1865.
Fitch, John. *Annals of the Army of the Cumberland.* Philadelphia: J.B. Lippincott Co., 1863.
Foote, Horace S., ed. *Pen Pictures from the Garden of the World, or Santa Clara County, California.* Chicago: Lewis Publishing Co., 1888.
Forty-Fourth Annual Reunion of the Association of the Graduates of the United States Military Academy at West Point, New York, June 11, 1913. Saginaw, MI: Seemann & Peters, 1913.
Fourth Annual Report of the Bureau of Military Statistics, State of New York. Albany, NY: C. Van Benthuysen & Sons, 1867.
Fout, Frederick W. *The Dark Days of the Civil War, 1861 to 1865.* St. Louis: F. A. Wagenfuehr, 1904.
Franklin and Marshall College Obituary Record. Nos. 12–13 (Vol. 2-Parts 8–9). Lancaster, PA: Franklin and Marshall College Alumni Association, 1909.
Fremont, Jessie Benton. *The Story of the Guard: A Chronicle of the War.* Boston: Ticknor & Fields, 1863.
Fuller, George W. *Descendants of Thomas Stoughton (1600–1661) of Dorchester, Mass.* Potsdam, NY: Herald-Recorder Press, 1929.
Furnish, Mark A., ed. *The Civil War Letters of Col. Michael C. Garber.* Madison, IN: Jefferson County Historical Society, 2009.
Gaffney, Wilbur G. *The Fillmore County Story.* Geneva, NE: Geneva Community Grange No. 403, 1968.
A Genealogy of the King Family. Buffalo, NY: American Heraldic Society, 1930.
General Catalogue of Bowdoin College and the Medical School of Maine: A Biographical

Record of Alumni and Officers, 1794–1950. Brunswick, ME: Bowdoin College, 1950.

General Catalogue of the Central High School of Philadelphia from 1838 to 1890. Philadelphia: Board of Public Education, 1890.

General Catalogue of the Non-Graduates of Bowdoin College, 1794–1915. Brunswick, ME: Bowdoin College, 1916.

Gerhart, Ross G. *The Johann Peter and Elisabeth (Schmidt) Gerhart Family of Earlington, Franconia Township, Montgomery County, Pennsylvania, 1739–1989.* Baltimore, MD: Gateway Press, 1990.

Gillett, Mary C. *The Army Medical Department, 1818–1865.* Washington, D.C.: Center of Military History, United States Army, 1987.

Gracey, Samuel L. *Annals of the Sixth Pennsylvania Cavalry.* Philadelphia: E.H. Butler & Co., 1868.

Graf, Leroy P., ed. *The Papers of Andrew Johnson.* Vol. 7, 1864–1865. Knoxville, TN: University of Tennessee Press, 1986.

_____, and Ralph W. Haskins, eds. *The Papers of Andrew Johnson.* Volume 6, 1862–1864. Knoxville, TN: University of Tennessee Press, 1983.

Griswold, Glenn E., comp. *The Griswold Family, England-America: Edward of Windsor, Connecticut; Matthew of Lyme, Connecticut; Michael of Wethersfield, Connecticut.* Rutland, VT: Tuttle Publishing Co., 1943.

Groce, George C., and David H. Wallace. *The New-York Historical Society's Dictionary of Artists in America, 1564–1860.* New Haven, CT: Yale University Press, 1957.

Gue, Benjamin F. *Biographies and Portraits of the Progressive Men of Iowa.* Des Moines, IA: Conaway & Shaw, 1899.

Guinn, James M. *Historical and Biographical Record of Southern California.* Chicago: Chapman Publishing Co., 1902.

Gurley, Albert E. *The History and Genealogy of the Gurley Family.* Hartford, CT: Case, Lockwood & Brainard Co., 1897.

Haight, Theron W., ed. *Memoirs of Waukesha County.* Madison, WI: Western Historical Association, 1907.

Hain, Harry Harrison. *History of Perry County, Pennsylvania.* Harrisburg, PA: Hain-Moore Co., 1922.

Hall, Henry, and James Hall. *Cayuga in the Field: A Record of the 19th New York Volunteers, All the Batteries of the 3rd New York Artillery, and 75th New York Volunteers.* Auburn, NY: Truair, Smith & Co., 1873.

Hamilton, John B., ed. *The Journal of the American Medical Association.* Vol. 31, July-Dec. 1898. Chicago: American Medical Association Press, 1898.

Hammer, Kenneth. *Men With Custer: Biographies of the 7th Cavalry, 25 June, 1876.* Fort Collins, CO: Old Army Press, 1972.

Hanaburgh, David H. *History of the One Hundred and Twenty-Eighth Regiment, New York Volunteers in the Late Civil War.* Poughkeepsie, NY: Enterprise Publishing Co., 1894.

Hancock, Ellery M. *Past and Present of Allamakee County, Iowa: A Record of Settlement, Organization, Progress and Achievement.* Chicago: S.J. Clarke Publishing Co., 1913.

Harbaugh, Elizabeth D. *The Davidson Genealogy.* Ironton, OH: Edwards Bros., 1948.

Harrington, George B. *Past and Present of Bureau County, Illinois.* Chicago: Pioneer Publishing Co., 1906.

Harris, Alexander. *A Biographical History of Lancaster County.* Lancaster, PA: Elias Barr & Co., 1872.

Harris, Joseph S. *Notes on the Ancestry of the Children of Joseph Smith Harris and Delia Silliman Brodhead.* Philadelphia: Allen, Lane & Scott, 1898.

_____. *Record of the Harris Family Descended from John Harris, Born 1680 in Wiltshire, England.* Philadelphia: George F. Lasher, 1903.

Harrison, James L., comp. *Biographical Directory of the American Congress, 1774–1949.* Washington, D.C.: Government Printing Office, 1950.

Hart, H.G. *The New Annual Army List for 1852.* London, England: John Murray, 1852.

Harvey, Oscar J. *A History of Lodge No. 61, F. and A. M., Wilkes-Barre, PA.* Wilkes-Barre, PA: O.J. Harvey, 1897.

Haskin, William L., comp. *The History of the First Regiment of Artillery from Its Organization in 1821, to January 1st, 1876.* Portland, ME: B. Thurston & Co., 1879.

Haupt, Herman. *Reminiscences of General Herman Haupt.* Milwaukee, WI: Wright & Joys Co., 1901.

Hayden, Horace E., Alfred Hand and John W. Jordan, eds. *Genealogical and Family History of the Wyoming and Lackawanna Valleys, Pennsylvania.* New York and Chicago: Lewis Publishing Co., 1906.

Headley, Katy McCaleb. *McCaleb (McKillop) Clan of Scotland and the United States.* Chillicothe, MO: Elizabeth Prather Ellsberry, 1964.

Hearn, Chester G. *Ellet's Brigade: The Strangest Outfit of All.* Baton Rouge, LA: Louisiana State University Press, 2000.

Heidgerd, William. *The American Descendants of Chretien Du Bois of Wicres, France.* Part 7. New Paltz, NY: Huguenot Historical Society, 1973.

Heitman, Francis B. *Historical Register and Dictionary of the United States Army.* Washington, D.C.: Government Printing Office, 1903.

Hemenway, Abby Maria. *The History of Washington County in the Vermont Historical Gazetteer.* Montpelier, VT: Vermont Watchman & State Journal Press, 1882.

Henry, Guy V. *Military Record of Civilian Appointments in the United States Army.* Vol. 1. New York: Carleton, 1869.

Herr, Pamela, and Mary Lee Spence, eds. *The*

Letters of Jessie Benton Fremont. Urbana, IL: University of Illinois Press, 1993.

Higginson, Mary Thacher. *Thomas Wentworth Higginson: The Story of His Life*. Boston: Houghton Mifflin Co., 1914.

Higginson, Thomas W. *Army Life in a Black Regiment: A New Edition with Notes and a Supplementary Chapter*. Boston: Houghton, Mifflin & Co., 1900.

———. *Cheerful Yesterdays*. Boston: Houghton, Mifflin & Co., 1900.

———. *Descendants of the Reverend Francis Higginson*. N.p.: T.W. Higginson, 1910.

High, Edwin W. *History of the Sixty-Eighth Regiment Indiana Volunteer Infantry, 1862–1865*. N.p.: Sixty-Eighth Indiana Infantry Association, 1902.

Hill, Luther B. *A History of the State of Oklahoma*. Chicago and New York: Lewis Publishing Co., 1909.

Hill, Norman N., Jr., comp. *History of Knox County, Ohio, Its Past and Present*. Mount Vernon, OH: A.A. Graham & Co., 1881.

Hinman, Wilbur F. *The Story of the Sherman Brigade*. Alliance, OH: Wilbur F. Hinman, 1897.

Historical Catalogue of Brown University, 1764–1904. Providence, RI: Brown University, 1905.

Historical Sketch of the Chicago Board of Trade Battery Horse Artillery Illinois Volunteers. Chicago: Henneberry Co., 1902.

A History and Biographical Cyclopaedia of Butler County, Ohio. Cincinnati: Western Biographical Publishing Co., 1882.

The History of Buchanan County, Missouri. St. Joseph, MO: Union Historical Co., 1881.

The History of Cedar County, Iowa. Chicago: Western Historical Co., 1878.

History of Champaign County, Illinois. Philadelphia: Brink, McDonough & Co., 1878.

History of Cincinnati and Hamilton County, Ohio: Their Past and Present. Cincinnati: S.B. Nelson & Co., 1894.

History of Columbiana County, Ohio, with Illustrations and Biographical Sketches of Some of Its Prominent Men and Pioneers. Philadelphia: D.W. Ensign & Co., 1879.

The History of Daviess County, Missouri. Kansas City, MO: Birdsall & Dean, 1882.

History of Des Moines County, Iowa. Chicago: Western Historical Co., 1879.

The History of Fond du Lac County, Wisconsin. Chicago: Western Historical Co., 1880.

History of Gallatin, Saline, Hamilton, Franklin, and Williamson Counties, Illinois, from the Earliest Time to the Present. Chicago: Goodspeed Publishing Co., 1887.

History of Jefferson County, Iowa. Chicago: Western Historical Co., 1879.

The History of Jo Daviess County, Illinois. Chicago: H.F. Kett & Co., 1878.

The History of Jones County, Iowa. Chicago: Western Historical Co., 1879.

History of Kent County, Michigan. Chicago: Charles C. Chapman & Co., 1881.

History of La Crosse County, Wisconsin. Chicago: Western Historical Co., 1881.

History of Lafayette County, Wisconsin. Chicago: Western Historical Co., 1881.

History of Lee County. Chicago: H.H. Hill & Co., 1881.

History of Litchfield County, Connecticut, With Illustrations and Biographical Sketches of the Prominent Men and Pioneers. Philadelphia: J.W. Lewis & Co., 1881.

The History of McLean County, Illinois. Chicago: William Le Baron, Jr., & Co., 1879.

History of Medina County and Ohio. Chicago: Baskin & Battey, 1881.

The History of Pettis County, Missouri. N.p., 1882.

The History of Polk County, Iowa. Des Moines, IA: Union Historical Co., 1880.

History of Porter County, Indiana. Chicago and New York: Lewis Publishing Co., 1912.

History of Sangamon County, Illinois. Chicago: Inter-State Publishing Co., 1881.

History of Seneca County, Ohio. Chicago: Warner, Beers & Co., 1886.

History of St. Joseph County, Michigan. Philadelphia: L.H. Everts & Co., 1877.

History of Tennessee from *the Earliest Time to the Present, Together with an Historical and a Biographical Sketch of the County of Shelby and the City of Memphis*. Nashville, TN: Goodspeed Publishing Co., 1887.

History of the City of Denver, Arapahoe County, and Colorado. Chicago: O.L. Baskin & Co., 1880.

A History of the Class of 1863, Yale College, Being the Fourth of Those Printed by Order of the Class. New Haven, CT: Tuttle, Morehouse & Taylor Co., 1905.

History of the Ninth U.S.C. Troops from Its Organization Till Muster Out. Philadelphia: King & Baird, 1866.

History of the Upper Mississippi Valley. Minneapolis, MN: Minnesota Historical Co., 1881.

History of Warrick, Spencer and Perry Counties, Indiana. Chicago: Goodspeed Brothers & Co., 1885.

History of Washington, New Hampshire, from the First Settlement to the Present Time, 1768–1886. Claremont, NH: Claremont Manufacturing Co., 1886.

History of Washtenaw County, Michigan. Chicago: Charles C. Chapman & Co., 1881.

History of Western Iowa: Its Settlement and Growth. Sioux City, IA: Western Publishing Co., 1882.

Hitchcock, Frederick L. *History of Scranton and Its People*. New York: Lewis Historical Publishing Co., 1914.

———. *War From the Inside: The Story of the 132nd Regiment Pennsylvania Volunteer Infantry in the War for the Suppression of the Rebellion, 1862–1863*. Philadelphia: J.B. Lippincott Co., 1904.

Hitchcock, Mary L., comp. *The Genealogy of the Hitchcock Family Who Are Descended from Matthias Hitchcock of East Haven, Conn., and Luke Hitchcock of Wethersfield, Conn.* Amherst, MA: Carpenter & Morehouse, 1894.

Hoagland, Edward C. *The Coolbaugh Family in America.* Towanda, PA: Edward C. Hoagland, 1938.

Hobart, Edwin L. *Semi-History of a Boy-Veteran of the Twenty-Eighth Regiment Illinois Infantry Volunteers in a Black Regiment.* Denver, CO: E.L. Hobart, 1909.

Hodge, Orlando John, comp. *Hodge Genealogy from the First of the Name in This Country to the Present Time.* Boston: Rockwell and Churchill Press, 1900.

Hodges, Lawrence K., ed. *Mining in the Pacific Northwest.* Seattle, WA: The Post-Intelligencer, 1897.

Hokanson, Nels. *Swedish Immigrants in Lincoln's Time.* New York and London: Harper & Brothers, 1942.

Hollandsworth, James G., Jr. *The Louisiana Native Guards: The Black Military Experience During the Civil War.* Baton Rouge, LA: Louisiana State University Press, 1995.

Holmes, Richard. *A View from Meeting House Hill: A History of Sandown, New Hampshire.* Portsmouth, NH: P. E. Randall, 1988.

Horton, Joshua H., and Solomon Teverbaugh, comps. *A History of the Eleventh Regiment (Ohio Volunteer Infantry).* Dayton, OH: W.J. Shuey, 1866.

Howe, Daniel W. *Howe Genealogies.* Boston: New England Historic Genealogical Society, 1929.

Howe, Mrs. Lucien. *Frontiersmen.* Cambridge, MA: Harvard University Press, 1931.

Huntington, Elijah B. *A Genealogical Memoir of the Lo-Lathrop Family in this Country.* Ridgefield, CT: Julia M. Huntington, 1884.

Hyde, William, and Howard L. Conard, eds. *Encyclopedia of the History of St. Louis.* New York, Louisville, and St. Louis: Southern History Co., 1899.

An Illustrated History of Los Angeles County, California. Chicago: Lewis Publishing Co., 1889.

Indiana at Chickamauga, 1863–1900. Report of Indiana Commissioners Chickamauga National Military Park. Indianapolis, IN: William B. Burford, 1901.

Indiana in the War of the Rebellion: Official Report of W.H.H. Terrell, Adjutant General. Indianapolis, IN: Douglass & Conner, 1869.

Irwin, Richard B. *History of the Nineteenth Army Corps.* New York and London: Knickerbocker Press, 1893.

Johnson, Allen, and Dumas Malone, editors. *Dictionary of American Biography.* New York: Charles Scribner's Sons, 1964.

Johnson, E. Polk. *A History of Kentucky and Kentuckians.* Chicago and New York: Lewis Publishing Co., 1912.

Johnson, Henry C., ed. *Tenth General Catalogue of the Psi Upsilon Fraternity.* Bethlehem, PA: Psi Upsilon Fraternity, 1888.

Johnson, Leland R. *The Falls City Engineers: A History of the Louisville District Corps of Engineers, United States Army.* Louisville, KY: U.S. Army Corps of Engineers, 1974.

Johnson, Mark W. *That Body of Brave Men: The U.S. Regular Infantry and the Civil War in the West.* Cambridge, MA: Da Capo Press, 2003.

Jordan, Ewing, comp. *University of Pennsylvania Men Who Served in the Civil War, 1861–1865: Department of Medicine, Classes 1816–1862.* Philadelphia: University of Pennsylvania, 1915.

Kaufmann, Wilhelm. *The Germans in the American Civil War.* Translated by Steven Rowan and edited by Don Heinrich Tolzmann with Werner D. Mueller and Robert E. Ward. Carlisle, PA: John Kallmann, 1999.

Kelly, Howard A. *A Cyclopedia of American Medical Biography.* Philadelphia and London: W.B. Saunders Co., 1912.

Killian, Ron V. *A History of the North Carolina Third Mounted Infantry Volunteers, U.S.A., March 1864 to August 1865.* Bowie, MD: Heritage Books, 2000.

King, Cameron H., comp. *The King Family of Suffield, Connecticut.* San Francisco: Walter N. Brunt Co., 1908.

King, Moses. *Notable New Yorkers, 1896–1899.* New York: Moses King, 1899.

Kingman Brothers, comps. *Combination Atlas Map of Howard County, Indiana.* Chicago, Kingman Brothers, 1877.

Kingsbury, George W. *History of Dakota Territory.* Chicago: S. J. Clarke Publishing Co., 1915.

Kirkland, Joseph. *The Chicago Massacre of 1812 with Illustrations and Historical Documents.* Chicago: Dibble Publishing Co., 1893.

_____. *The Story of Chicago.* Chicago: Dibble Publishing Co., 1892.

Klement, Frank L. *The Copperheads in the Middle West.* Chicago: University of Chicago Press, 1960.

_____. *Dark Lanterns: Secret Political Societies, Conspiracies, and Treason Trials in the Civil War.* Baton Rouge, LA: Louisiana State University Press, 1984.

Klokner, James B. *The Officer Corps of Custer's Seventh Cavalry, 1866–1876.* Atglen, PA: Schiffer Publishing, 2007.

Lang, George, Raymond L. Collins, and Gerard F. White, comps. *Medal of Honor Recipients, 1863–1994.* New York: Facts on File, 1995.

Langkau, David A. *Civil War Veterans of Winnebago County, Wisconsin.* Bowie, MD: Heritage Books, 1993.

Larned, Johney. *Though Silent They Speak: The Larned Family History.* Bloomington, IN: Xlibris Corporation, 2006.

Lawrence, John S., comp. *The Descendants of Moses and Sarah Kilham Porter of Pawlet, Vermont.* Grand Rapids, MI: F.A. Onderdonk, 1910.

Learned, William L., comp. *The Learned Family (Learned, Larned, Learnard, Larnard and Lerned) Being Descendants of William Learned, Who Was of Charlestown, Massachusetts, in 1632.* Albany, NY: Weed-Parsons Printing Co., 1898.

Lee, Francis Bazley, ed. *Genealogical and Memorial History of the State of New Jersey.* New York: Lewis Historical Publishing Co., 1910.

Lee, William Wallace, comp. *A Catalogue of Barkhamsted Men Who Served in the Various Wars, 1775 to 1865.* Meriden, CT: Republican Publishing Co., 1897.

Lengyel, Emil. *Americans From Hungary.* Philadelphia and New York: J.B. Lippincott Co., 1948.

Leopard, John C. and Buel (Daviess County). *History of Daviess and Gentry Counties, Missouri.* Topeka and Indianapolis: Historical Publishing Co., 1922.

Lewis, Gene D. *Charles Ellet, Jr., The Engineer as Individualist, 1810–1862.* Urbana, IL: University of Illinois Press, 1968.

L'Hommedieu, Arthur W. *L'Hommedieu Genealogy.* Chicago: A.W. L'Hommedieu, 1951.

Life of Edward Herrick Castle. Chicago: Millard G. Peck, 1893.

Longacre, Edward G. *The Sharpshooters: A History of the Ninth New Jersey Volunteer Infantry in the Civil War.* Lincoln, NE: University of Nebraska Press, 2016.

Lonn, Ella. *Foreigners in the Union Army and Navy.* Baton Rouge, LA: Louisiana State University Press, 1951.

Loomis, Elisha S. *Descendants of Joseph Loomis in America and His Antecedents in the Old World.* Berea, OH: Elisha S. Loomis, 1908.

Lord, Charles C. *Life and Times in Hopkinton, New Hampshire.* Concord, NH: Republican Press Association, 1890.

Lothrop, Charles H. *A History of the First Regiment Iowa Cavalry Veteran Volunteers.* Lyons, IA: Beers & Eaton, 1890.

Lovejoy, Clarence E. *The Lovejoy Genealogy With Biographies and History, 1460–1930.* New York: Clarence E. Lovejoy, 1930.

Lovejoy, Evelyn M. Wood. *History of Royalton, Vermont, with Family Genealogies, 1769–1911.* Burlington, VT: Free Press Printing Co., 1911.

Lowry, Thomas P. *Tarnished Eagles: The Courts-Martial of Fifty Union Colonels and Lieutenant Colonels.* Mechanicsburg, PA: Stackpole Books, 1997.

Maclean, Paul. *History of Carroll County, Iowa.* Chicago: S.J. Clarke Publishing Co., 1912.

Macomb, Henry A., comp. *Macomb Family Record: Being an Account of the Family Since the Settlement in America.* Camden, NJ: Sinnickson Chew & Sons, 1917.

Magdol, Edward. *Owen Lovejoy: Abolitionist in Congress.* New Brunswick, NJ: Rutgers University Press, 1967.

Marsh, Sharon D. *The 1st Florida Union Cavalry Volunteers in the Civil War.* N.p.: Sharon D. Marsh, 2017.

Martin, Charles A., ed. *DePauw University: Alumnal Register of Officers, Faculties and Graduates, 1837–1900.* Greencastle, IN: DePauw University, 1901.

Martin, David G. *Carl Bornemann's Regiment: The Forty-First New York Infantry (DeKalb Regiment) in the Civil War.* Hightstown, NJ: Longstreet House, 1987.

Martin, George W., ed. *Transactions of the Kansas State Historical Society, 1897–1900.* Topeka, KS: W.Y. Morgan, State Printer, 1900.

_____, ed. *Transactions of the Kansas State Historical Society, 1901–1902.* Topeka, KS: W.Y. Morgan, State Printer, 1902.

Marvin, George F. and William T.R. *Descendants of Reinold and Matthew Marvin of Hartford, CT, 1638 and 1635, Sons of Edward Marvin, of Great Bentley, England.* Boston: T.R. Marvin & Son, 1904.

Mathews, Barbara Jean. *Philo Hodge (1756–1842) of Roxbury, Connecticut.* Baltimore, MD: Gateway Press, 1992.

Mattox, Absalom H. *A History of the Cincinnati Society of Ex-Army and Navy Officers.* Cincinnati: Peter G. Thomson, 1880.

McAdam, David, et al., eds. *History of the Bench and Bar of New York.* New York: New York History Co., 1897.

McAdams, Benton. *Rebels at Rock Island: The Story of a Civil War Prison.* DeKalb, IL: Northern Illinois University Press, 2000.

McAdams, Francis M. *Every-Day Soldier Life, or A History of the One Hundred and Thirteenth Ohio Volunteer Infantry.* Columbus, OH: Chas. M. Cott & Co., 1884.

McBride, Robert M., and Dan M. Robison. *Biographical Directory of the Tennessee General Assembly.* Vol. 2, 1861–1901. Nashville, TN: Tennessee Historical Commission, 1979.

McCormack, Thomas J., ed. *Memoirs of Gustave Koerner, 1809–1896.* Cedar Rapids, IA: Torch Press, 1909.

McMullin, Thomas A., and David Walker. *Biographical Directory of American Territorial Governors.* Westport, CT: Meckler, 1984.

McMurray, John. *Recollections of a Colored Troop.* Brookville, PA: McMurray Co., 1994.

McRae, Bennie J., Jr., Curtis M. Miller, and Cheryl Trowbridge-Miller. *Nineteenth Century Freedom Fighters: The 1st South Carolina Volunteers.* Charleston, SC: Arcadia Publishing, 2007.

McRae, Norman. *Negroes in Michigan During the Civil War.* Lansing, MI: Michigan Civil War Centennial Observance Commission, 1966.

A Memorial and Biographical Record of Iowa. Chicago: Lewis Publishing Co., 1896.

Memorial and Family History of Erie County, New York. New York and Buffalo: Genealogical Publishing Co., 1906–08.

Memorial Record of Alabama. Madison, WI: Brant & Fuller, 1893.

Memorials of Deceased Companions of the Commandery of the State of Illinois MOLLUS, from July 1, 1901 to Dec. 31, 1911. Chicago: Illinois Commandery MOLLUS, 1912.

The Men of New York. Buffalo, NY: George E. Matthews & Co., 1898.

Merritt, Douglas, comp. *Revised Merritt Records.* New York: Tobias A. Wright, 1916.

Michigan: A Centennial History of the State and Its People. Vol. 5. Chicago: Lewis Publishing Co., 1939.

Michigan Biographies. Lansing, MI: Michigan Historical Commission, 1924.

Michno, Gregory. *The Deadliest Indian War in the West: The Snake Conflict, 1864–1868.* Caldwell, ID: Caxton Press, 2007.

A Military Album Containing Over One Thousand Portraits of Commissioned Officers Who Served in the Spanish-American War. New York: L.R. Hamersly Co., 1902.

Military History and Reminiscences of the Thirteenth Regiment of Illinois Volunteer Infantry in the Civil War in the United States, 1861–1865. Chicago: Woman's Temperance Publishing Association, 1892.

Miller, Edward A., Jr. *The Black Civil War Soldiers of Illinois: The Story of the Twenty-Ninth U.S. Colored Infantry.* Columbia, SC: University of South Carolina Press, 1998.

Millett, Allan R., and Jack Shulimson. *Commandants of the Marine Corps.* Annapolis, MD: Naval Institute Press, 2004.

Mills, Charles K. *Harvest of Barren Regrets: The Army Career of Frederick William Benteen, 1834–98.* Glendale, CA: Arthur H. Clark Co., 1985.

Mitchell, William Ansel. *Linn County, Kansas: A History.* Kansas City, MO: Campbell-Gates, 1928.

Mitchell, William Bell. *History of Stearns County, Minnesota.* Chicago: H.C. Cooper, Jr., & Co., 1915.

Molyneux, Nellie Zada Rice, comp. *History Genealogical and Biographical of the Eaton Families.* Syracuse, NY: C.W. Bardeen, 1911.

Morgan, Appleton. *A History of the Family of Morgan from the Year 1089 to Present Times.* New York: Appleton Morgan, 1902.

Morris, Charles, ed. *Makers of Philadelphia.* Philadelphia: L.R. Hamersly & Co., 1894.

Moses, John, ed. *Biographical Dictionary and Portrait Gallery of the Representative Men of the United States.* Illinois Volume. Chicago: Lewis Publishing Co., 1896.

Moulton, Henry W. *Moulton Annals.* Chicago: Edward A. Claypool, 1906.

Mulholland, St. Clair A. *Military Order Congress Medal of Honor Legion of the United States.* Philadelphia: Town Printing Co., 1905.

Murray, Stuart. *A Time of War: A Northern Chronicle of the Civil War.* Lee, MA: Berkshire House, 2001.

Nash, Eugene A. *A History of the Forty-Fourth Regiment New York Volunteer Infantry.* Chicago: R.R. Donnelley & Sons, 1911.

Nash, Steven E. *Reconstruction's Ragged Edge: The Politics of Postwar Life in the Southern Mountains.* Chapel Hill, NC: University of North Carolina Press, 2016.

Nason, Henry B., ed. *Biographical Record of the Officers and Graduates of the Rensselaer Polytechnic Institute, 1824–1886.* Troy, NY: William H. Young, 1887.

The National Cyclopaedia of American Biography. New York: James T. White, 1898–1926.

Neal, William A. *An Illustrated History of the Missouri Engineer and the 25th Infantry Regiments.* Chicago: Donohue and Henneberry, 1889.

Nebelsick, Alvin L. *A History of Belleville.* Belleville, IL: Township High School and Junior College, 1951.

Nelke, David I. *The Columbian Biographical Dictionary and Portrait Gallery of the Representative Men of the United States.* Wisconsin Volume. Chicago: Lewis Publishing Co., 1895.

Newson, Thomas M. *Pen Pictures of St. Paul, Minnesota, and Biographical Sketches of Old Settlers.* St. Paul, MN: T.M. Newson, 1886.

Norton, Wilbur T., ed. *Centennial History of Madison County, Illinois, and Its People, 1812–1912.* Chicago and New York: Lewis Publishing Co., 1912.

Noyes, Henry E. and Harriette E., comps. *Genealogical Record of Some of the Noyes Descendants of James, Nicholas and Peter Noyes.* Boston: Henry E. Noyes, 1904.

Obituary Record of Alumni of Wesleyan University, for the Academic Year Ending June 28, 1888. Middletown, CT: Wesleyan University, 1888.

Obituary Record of Graduates of Yale College Deceased during the Academical Year Ending in July 1869. New Haven, CT: Yale College, 1869.

Obituary Record of Graduates of Yale College Deceased during the Academical Year Ending in June 1879. New Haven, CT: Tuttle, Morehouse & Taylor Co., 1880.

Obituary Record of Graduates of Yale University Deceased during the Year Ending July, 1, 1918. New Haven, CT: Yale University, 1919.

Obituary Record of Graduates of Yale University Deceased from June 1900 to June 1910. New Haven, CT: Tuttle, Morehouse & Taylor Co., 1910.

O'Brien, Lyster M., comp. *The Class of "Fifty Eight," University of Michigan, 1858 to 1913.* Cleveland, OH: L.E. Holden, 1913.

Ochs, Stephen J. *A Black Patriot and a White Priest: Andre Cailloux and Claude Paschal Maistre in Civil War New Orleans.* Baton Rouge, LA: Louisiana State University Press, 2000.

Ofele, Martin W. *German-Speaking Officers in the U.S. Colored Troops, 1863–1867.* Gainesville, FL: University Press of Florida, 2004.

Official Army Register of the Volunteer Force of the United States Army for the Years 1861, '62, '63, '64, '65. 8 Vol. Washington, D.C.: Government Printing Office, 1865–1867.

Old Woodward: A Memorial Relating to Woodward High School, 1831–36, and Woodward College, 1836–51. Cincinnati: Robert Clarke & Co., 1884.

Olson, Ernst W., ed. *History of the Swedes of Illinois.* Chicago: Engberg-Holmberg Publishing Co., 1908.

Owen, Thomas M. *History of Alabama and Dictionary of Alabama Biography.* Chicago: S.J. Clarke Publishing Co., 1921.

Parker, Amasa J., ed. *Landmarks of Albany County, New York.* Syracuse, NY: D. Mason & Co., 1897.

Parker, Harvey M. *Proceedings of the First Reunion of the Eleventh Regiment Illinois Volunteer Infantry.* Ottawa, IL: Osman & Hapeman, 1875.

Parker, Thomas H. *History of the 51st Regiment of P.V. and V.V.* Philadelphia: King & Baird, 1869.

Parsons, Eben B. *1855–1859–1884. Class of Fifty-Nine, Williams College—Four Years in College and Twenty-Five Years Out of College.* Syracuse, NY: Smith & Bruce, 1884.

The Past and Present of LaSalle County, Illinois. Chicago: H.F. Kett & Co., 1877.

Paxton, William M. *The Marshall Family.* Cincinnati: Robert Clarke & Co., 1885.

Pelka, Fred, ed. *The Civil War Letters of Colonel Charles F. Johnson, Invalid Corps.* Amherst and Boston: University of Massachusetts Press, 2004.

Perley, Martin Van Buren, comp. *History and Genealogy of the Perley Family.* Salem, MA: M.V.B. Perley, 1906.

Phillips, Stanley S. *Civil War Corps Badges and Other Related Awards, Badges, Medals of the Period.* Lanham, MD: Stanley S. Phillips, 1982.

Pierce, Frederick Clifton. *Field Genealogy.* Chicago: W.B. Conkey Co., 1901.

_____. *Foster Genealogy, Being the Record of the Posterity of Reginald Foster, an Early Inhabitant of Ipswich, in New England.* Chicago: W.B. Conkey Co., 1899.

Pierce, Lyman B. *History of the Second Iowa Cavalry.* Burlington, IA: Hawk-Eye Steam Book and Job Printing, 1865.

Pilcher, James E. *The Surgeon Generals of the Army of the United States of America.* Carlisle, PA: Association of Military Surgeons, 1905.

Pitkin, Albert P. *Pitkin Family of America: A Genealogy of the Descendants of William Pitkin.* Hartford, CT: Case, Lockwood & Brainard Co., 1887.

Pivany, Eugene. *Hungarians in the American Civil War.* Cleveland, OH: E. Pivany, 1913.

Plum, William R. *The Military Telegraph during the Civil War in the United States.* Chicago: Jansen, McClurg & Co., 1882.

Pomeroy, Albert A. *History and Genealogy of the Pomeroy Family.* Toledo, OH: Franklin Printing & Engraving Co., 1912.

Portrait and Biographical Album of Ingham and Livingston Counties, Michigan. Chicago: Chapman Brothers, 1891.

Portrait and Biographical Album of Lee County, Iowa. Chicago: Chapman Brothers, 1887.

Portrait and Biographical Album of Polk County, Iowa. Chicago: Lake City Publishing Co., 1890.

Portrait and Biographical Album of St. Joseph County, Michigan. Chicago: Chapman Brothers, 1889.

Portrait and Biographical Record of Lancaster County, Pennsylvania. Chicago: Chapman Publishing Co., 1894.

Portrait and Biographical Record of Leavenworth, Douglas, and Franklin Counties, Kansas. Chicago: Chapman Publishing Co., 1899.

Portrait and Biographical Record of Lee County, Illinois. Chicago: Biographical Publishing Co., 1892.

Portrait and Biographical Record of St. Clair County, Illinois. Chicago: Chapman Brothers, 1892.

Portrait and Biographical Record of Waukesha County, Wisconsin. Chicago: Excelsior Publishing Co., 1894.

Post, Marie Caroline De Trobriand. *The Post Family.* New York: Sterling Potter, 1905.

Powell, William H. *A History of the Organization and Movements of the Fourth Regiment of Infantry, United States Army.* Washington, D.C.: McGill & Witherow, 1871.

_____, and Edward Shippen, eds. *Officers of the Army and Navy (Regular) Who Served in the Civil War.* Philadelphia: L.R. Hamersly & Co., 1892.

_____, ed. *Officers of the Army and Navy (Volunteer) Who Served in the Civil War.* Philadelphia: L.R. Hamersly & Co., 1893.

_____. *Powell's Records of Living Officers of the United States Army.* Philadelphia: L.R. Hamersly & Co., 1890.

Powell, William S., ed. *Dictionary of North Carolina Biography.* Chapel Hill, NC: University of North Carolina Press, 1988.

Power, John C. *History of the Early Settlers of Sangamon County, Illinois.* Springfield, IL: Edwin A. Wilson & Co., 1876.

Proceedings of the American Society of Civil Engineers. Vol. 8 (January to December 1882). New York: American Society of Civil Engineers, 1882.

Pyne, Frederick W. *Descendants of the Signers of the Declaration of Independence.* Camden, ME: Picton Press, 1998.

Rankin, David C., ed. *Diary of a Christian Soldier: Rufus Kinsley and the Civil War.* Cambridge, UK: Cambridge University Press, 2004.

Record of the Class of 1845 of Yale College. New York: Jenkins & Thomas, 1881.

Records of the Class of 1859, Harvard College. Cambridge, MA: Edward W. Wheeler, 1896.

Redington, Edward D., comp. *Military Record of the Sons of Dartmouth in the Union Army and Navy, 1861–1865.* Cambridge, MA: Dartmouth College, 1907.

Reed, David W. *Campaigns and Battles of the Twelfth Regiment Iowa Veteran Volunteer Infantry from Organization, September, 1861, to Muster-Out, January 20, 1866.* Evanston, IL: David W. Reed, 1903.

Reed, George Irving, ed. *Encyclopedia of Biography of Indiana.* Chicago: Century Publishing & Engraving Co., 1895.

Reed, I. Richard. *One Hundred Years Ago Today: Niagara County in the Civil War As Reported in the Pages of the Niagara Falls Gazette.* Lockport, NY: Niagara County Historical Society, 1966.

Reid, Harvey. *Biographical Sketch of Enoch Long, an Illinois Pioneer.* Chicago: Fergus Printing Co., 1884.

Report Annual Reunion and Dinner of the Old Guard Association, 12th Regiment, N. G. S. N. Y. New York: Old Guard Association, Twelfth Regiment, N.G.S.N.Y., 1894.

Report of the Joint Committee on the Conduct of the War. Part 3-Department of the West. Washington, D.C.: Government Printing Office, 1863.

Report of the Proceedings of the Society of the Army of the Tennessee at the Fifteenth Annual Meeting. Cincinnati: Society of the Army of the Tennessee, 1885.

Report of the Proceedings of the Society of the Army of the Tennessee at the Thirty-Third Meeting. Cincinnati: Press of F.W. Freeman, 1902.

Report of the Proceedings of the Society of the Army of the Tennessee at the Twenty-First Meeting. Cincinnati: Society of the Army of the Tennessee, 1893.

Report of the Proceedings of the Society of the Army of the Tennessee at the Twenty-Third Meeting. Cincinnati: Society of the Army of the Tennessee, 1893.

Reynolds, Cuyler, ed. *Genealogical and Family History of Southern New York and the Hudson River Valley.* New York: Lewis Historical Publishing Co., 1914.

Rice, Allen Thorndike, ed. *Reminiscences of Abraham Lincoln by Distinguished Men of His Time.* New York: North American Review, 1889.

Richards, David L. *Priceless Treasures: A History of the Muncy Soldiers' Memorial and the Patriots It Commemorates.* Muncy, PA: Muncy Historical Society, 2001.

Richardson, James D. *Tennessee Templars: A Register of Names with Biographical Sketches of the Knights Templar of Tennessee.* Nashville, TN: Robert H. Howell & Co., 1883.

Richmond, Joshua B. *The Richmond Family, 1594–1896.* Boston: Joshua B. Richmond, 1897.

Roberts, Thomas P. *Memoirs of John Bannister Gibson, Late Chief Justice of Pennsylvania.* Pittsburgh, PA: Joseph Eichbaum & Co., 1890.

Robinson, Fayette. *An Account of the Organization of the Army of the United States With Biographies of Distinguished Officers of All Grades.* Philadelphia: E.H. Butler & Co., 1848.

Rodenbough, Theophilus F, comp., and William L. Haskin, eds. *The Army of the United States: Historical Sketches of Staff and Line with Portraits of Generals-in-Chief.* New York: Maynard, Merrill & Co., 1896.

———. *The Bravest Five Hundred of '61.* New York: G.W. Dillingham, 1891.

———. *From Everglade to Canyon with the Second Dragoons (Second United States Cavalry).* New York: D. Van Nostrand, 1875.

Rogers, Edward H. *Reminiscences of Military Service in the Forty-Third Regiment, Massachusetts Infantry, During the Great Civil War, 1862–63.* Boston: Franklin Press, 1883.

Rombauer, Robert J. *The Union Cause in St. Louis in 1861: An Historical Sketch.* St. Louis: Nixon-Jones Printing Co., 1909.

Ruttenber, Edward M., and Lewis H. Clark, comps. *History of Orange County, New York.* Philadelphia: Everts & Peck, 1881.

Sanford, Carlton E. *Thomas Sanford, the Emigrant to New England: Ancestry, Life and Descendants, 1634–1910.* Rutland, VT: Tuttle Co., 1911.

Scharf, J. Thomas. *History of Saint Louis City and County.* Philadelphia: Louis H. Everts & Co., 1883.

———. *History of Westchester County, New York.* Philadelphia: L.E. Preston & Co., 1886.

Schultz, Katherine E. *The Descendants of Robert McChesney of Monmouth County, New Jersey.* Annville, PA; Katherine E. Schultz, 1966.

Scott, William Forse. *Roster of the Fourth Iowa Cavalry Veteran Volunteers, 1861–1865.* New York: J.J. Little & Co., 1902.

———. *The Story of a Cavalry Regiment: The Career of the Fourth Iowa Veteran Volunteers from Kansas to Georgia, 1861–1865.* New York: G.P. Putnam's Sons, 1893.

Scull, William Ellis. *The Family of Scull.* Philadelphia: John C. Winston Co., 1930.

Sears, Cyrus. *The Battle of Milliken's Bend and Some Reflections Concerning the Colored Troops, the Debt We Owe Them, and How We Paid It.* Columbus, OH: F.J. Heer Printing Co., 1909.

Sears, Richard D. *Camp Nelson, Kentucky: A Civil War History.* Lexington, KY: University Press of Kentucky, 2002.

Shaw, William H., comp. *History of Essex and Hudson Counties, New Jersey.* Philadelphia: Everts & Peck, 1884.

Shepherd, Rebecca A., Charles W. Calhoun, Elizabeth Shanahan-Shoemaker, and Alan F. January, editors. *A Biographical Directory of the Indiana General Assembly.* Vol. 1, 1816–1899. Indianapolis, IN: Indiana Historical Bureau, 1980.

Shumate, Albert. *The Notorious I.C. Woods of the Adams Express*. Glendale, CA: Arthur H. Clark Co., 1986.

Siegel, Alan A. *For the Glory of the Union: Myth, Reality, and the Media in Civil War New Jersey*. Rutherford, NJ: Fairleigh Dickinson University Press, 1984.

Signor, Isaac S., ed. *Landmarks of Orleans County, New York*. Syracuse, NY: D. Mason & Co., 1894.

Silinonte, Joseph M. *Tombstones of the Irish Born: Cemetery of the Holy Cross, Flatbush, Brooklyn*. Westminster, MD: Heritage Books, 2006.

Simon, John Y., ed. *The Papers of Ulysses S. Grant*. Vol. 6: September 1-December 8, 1862. Carbondale, IL: Southern Illinois University Press, 1977.

―――, ed. *The Papers of Ulysses S. Grant*. Vol. 7: December 9, 1862-March 31, 1863. Carbondale, IL: Southern Illinois University Press, 1979.

―――, ed. *The Papers of Ulysses S. Grant*. Vol. 8: April 1-July 6, 1863. Carbondale, IL: Southern Illinois University Press, 1979.

―――, ed. *The Papers of Ulysses S. Grant*. Vol. 10: January 1-May 31, 1864. Carbondale, IL: Southern Illinois University Press, 1982.

―――, ed. *The Papers of Ulysses S. Grant*. Vol. 15: May 1-December 31, 1865. Carbondale, IL: Southern Illinois University Press, 1988.

―――, ed. *The Papers of Ulysses S. Grant*. Vol. 26: 1875. Carbondale, IL: Southern Illinois University Press, 2003.

Simons, Ezra D. *A Regimental History: The One Hundred and Twenty-Fifth New York State Volunteers*. New York: Ezra D. Simons, 1888.

Slifer, H. Seger, ed. *Catalogue of Chi Psi Fraternity, 1841–1932*. Ann Arbor, MI: Chi Psi Fraternity, 1929.

Slocum, Charles E. *History of the Slocums, Slocumbs, and Slocombs of America: Genealogical and Biographical*. Defiance, OH: Charles E. Slocum, 1908.

―――. *The Life and Services of Major General Henry Warner Slocum*. Toledo, OH: Slocum Publishing Co., 1913.

Smith, Charles H. *The History of Fuller's Ohio Brigade, 1861–1865*. Cleveland, OH: Press of A.J. Watt, 1909.

Smith, Charles Perrin. *Lineage of the Lloyd and Carpenter Family*. Camden, NJ: S. Chew, 1870.

Smith, H. Perry, ed. *History of the City of Buffalo and Erie County*. Syracuse, NY: D. Mason & Co., 1884.

Smith, Henry I. *History of the Seventh Iowa Veteran Volunteer Infantry During the Civil War*. Mason City, IA: E. Hitchcock, 1903.

Smith, Myron J., Jr. *Civil War Biographies from the Western Waters*. Jefferson, NC: McFarland & Co., 2015.

Smith, Ned. *The 2nd Maine Cavalry in the Civil War: A History and Roster*. Jefferson, NC: McFarland & Co., 2014.

Society of the Army of the Cumberland. *Thirty-Second Reunion, Indianapolis, Indiana*. Cincinnati: Robert Clarke Co., 1905.

Society of the Army of the Cumberland. *Twenty-first Reunion, Toledo, Ohio*. Cincinnati: Robert Clarke & Co., 1891.

Society of the Army of the Cumberland. *Twenty-Fourth Reunion, Cleveland, Ohio*. Cincinnati: Robert Clarke & Co., 1894.

Society of the Army of the Cumberland. *Twenty-Third Reunion, Chickamauga, Georgia*. Cincinnati: Robert Clarke & Co., 1892.

Speed, Thomas, Robert M. Kelly, and Alfred Pirtle. *The Union Regiments of Kentucky*. Louisville, KY: Courier-Journal Job Printing Co., 1897.

Sperry, Andrew F. *History of the 33d Iowa Infantry Volunteer Regiment, 1863–6*. Des Moines, IA: Mills & Co., 1866.

Sprague, Augustus B.R. *Genealogy (in Part) of the Sprague Families in America*. Worcester, MA: Augustus B.R. Sprague, 1902.

Sprague, Homer B. *History of the 13th Infantry Regiment of Connecticut Volunteers during the Great Rebellion*. Hartford, CT: Case, Lockwood & Co., 1867.

―――. *Lights and Shadows in Confederate Prisons: A Personal Experience, 1864–5*. New York: G.P. Putnam's Sons, 1915.

Steiner, Paul E. *Medical History of a Civil War Regiment: Disease in the Sixty-Fifth United States Colored Infantry*. Clayton, MO: Institute of Civil War Studies, 1977.

Sterling, Wilson, ed. *Quarter-Centennial History of the University of Kansas, 1866–1891*. Topeka, KS: George W. Crane & Co., 1891.

Stevens, Charles A. *Berdan's United States Sharpshooters in the Army of the Potomac, 1861–1865*. St. Paul, MN: Price-McGill Co., 1892.

Stewart, A.J.D., ed. *The History of the Bench and Bar of Missouri*. St. Louis: Legal Publishing Co., 1898.

Stickney, Matthew A. *The Stickney Family: A Genealogical Memoir of the Descendants of William and Elizabeth Stickney from 1637 to 1869*. Salem, MA: Essex Institute Press, 1869.

The Story of the Fifty-Fifth Regiment Illinois Volunteer Infantry in the Civil War, 1861–1865. Huntington, WV: Blue Acorn Press, 1993.

Stout, Joseph A., Jr. *Schemers and Dreamers: Filibustering in Mexico, 1848–1921*. Fort Worth, TX: Texas Christian University Press, 2002.

Stover, Clyde B., and Charles W. Beachem. *The Alumni Record of Gettysburg College, 1832–1932*. Gettysburg, PA: Gettysburg College, 1932.

Stowits, George H. *History of the 100th Regiment of New York State Volunteers*. Buffalo, NY: Matthews & Warren, 1870.

Stuart, Addison A. *Iowa Colonels and Regiments*. Des Moines, IA: Mills & Co., 1865.

Stuart, Charles B. *Lives and Works of Civil and*

Military Engineers of America. New York: D. Van Nostrand, 1871.

Styple, William B. *McClellan's Other Story: The Political Intrigue of Colonel Thomas M. Key, Confidential Aide to General George B. McClellan*. Kearny, NJ: Belle Grove Publishing Co., 2012.

Sullivan, David M. *The United States Marine Corps in the Civil War*. 4 vols. Shippensburg, PA: White Mane Publishing Co., 1997–2000.

Sunderland, Byron. *In Memoriam Colonel Ulric Dahlgren*. Boston: Young Men's Christian Association, 1864.

Sutor, J. Hope. *Past and Present of the City of Zanesville and Muskingum County, Ohio, Together with Biographical Sketches of Many of Its Leading and Prominent Citizens and Illustrious Dead*. Chicago: S.J. Clarke Publishing Co., 1905.

Swope, Belle McKinney Hays. *History of the Families of McKinney-Brady-Quigley*. Chambersburg, PA: Franklin Repository Printery, 1905.

Sypher, Josiah R. *History of the Pennsylvania Reserve Corps*. Lancaster, PA: Elias Barr & Co., 1865.

Taylor, John C., and Samuel P. Hatfield, comps. *History of the First Connecticut Artillery and of the Siege Trains of the Armies Operating Against Richmond, 1862–1865*. Hartford, CT: Case, Lockwood & Brainard Co., 1893.

Teetor, Paul R. *A Matter of Hours: Treason at Harper's Ferry*. Rutherford, NJ: Fairleigh Dickinson University Press, 1982.

Tenney, William J. *The Military and Naval History of the Rebellion in the United States*. New York: D. Appleton & Co., 1865.

Tevis, C.V., and D.R. Marquis, comps. *The History of the Fighting Fourteenth*. Brooklyn, NY: Brooklyn Eagle Press, 1911.

Thompson, Jerry D. *A Civil War History of the New Mexico Volunteers & Militia*. Albuquerque: University of New Mexico Press, 2015.

Thrapp, Dan L. *Encyclopedia of Frontier Biography*. Glendale, CA: Arthur H. Clark Co., 1988.

Todd, Charles B. *A General History of the Burr Family*. New York: Knickerbocker Press, 1902.

Tompkins, Robert A. and Clare F., comps. *The Tomkins-Tompkins Genealogy*. Los Angeles: Robert A. Tompkins, 1942.

Toomey, Daniel C., and Charles A. Earp. *Marylanders in Blue: The Artillery and the Cavalry*. Baltimore, MD: Toomey Press, 1999.

Transactions of the McLean County Historical Society, Bloomington, Ill. Vol. 1 (War Record of McLean County with Other Papers). Bloomington, IL: Pantagraph Printing & Stationery Co., 1899.

Treat, John Harvey. *The Treat Family: A Genealogy of Trott, Tratt, and Treat for Fifteen Generations, and Four Hundred and Fifty Years in England and America*. Salem, MA: Salem Press Publishing & Printing Co., 1893.

Tucker, Spencer C., ed. *The Encyclopedia of the Mexican-American War: A Political, Social, and Military History*. Santa Barbara, CA: ABC-CLIO, 2013.

Tuley, William F. *The Tuley Family Memoirs*. New Albany, IN: W.J. Hedden, 1906.

Twentieth Annual Reunion of the Association of the Graduates of the U.S. Military Academy at West Point, NY. East Saginaw, MI: Evening News Printing & Binding House, 1889.

Twenty-Fifth Annual Reunion of the Association of the Graduates of the United States Military Academy at West Point, New York. Saginaw, MI: Seemann & Peters, 1894.

Twenty-Third Annual Reunion of the Association of the Graduates of the United States Military Academy at West Point, New York. Saginaw, MI: Seemann & Peters, 1892.

Tyler, Lyon G., ed. *Encyclopedia of Virginia Biography*. New York: Lewis Historical Publishing Co., 1915.

Ullery, Jacob G., comp. *Men of Vermont: An Illustrated Biographical History of Vermonters and Sons of Vermont*. Brattleboro, VT: Transcript Publishing Co., 1894.

The Union Army. New York Edition. Vol. 8. Madison, WI: Federal Publishing Co., 1908.

———. Ohio Edition. Vol. 8. Madison, WI: Federal Publishing Co., 1908.

The United States Biographical Dictionary. Kansas Volume. Chicago and Kansas City: S. Lewis & Co., 1879.

The United States Biographical Dictionary and Portrait Gallery of Eminent and Self-Made Men. Minnesota Volume. New York and Chicago: American Biographical Publishing Co., 1879.

———. Illinois Volume. Chicago, Cincinnati, and New York: American Biographical Publishing Co., 1876.

———. Iowa Volume. Chicago and New York: American Biographical Publishing Co., 1878.

University of Pennsylvania: Biographical Catalogue of the Matriculates of the College, 1749–1893. Philadelphia: Avil Printing Co., 1894.

Upham, Warren, and Rose B. Dunlap, comps. *Collections of the Minnesota Historical Society, Volume 14. Minnesota Biographies, 1655–1912*. St. Paul, MN: Minnesota Historical Society, 1912.

Utley, Robert M., ed. *Life in Custer's Cavalry: Diaries and Letters of Albert and Jennie Barnitz, 1867–1868*. New Haven, CT: Yale University Press, 1977.

Van Rensselaer, Florence, comp. *The Livingston Family in America and Its Scottish Origins*. New York: F. Van Rensselaer, 1949.

Van Wagenen, Avis Stearns. *Genealogy and Memoirs of Charles and Nathaniel Stearns and Their Descendants*. Syracuse, NY: Courier Printing Co., 1901.

Vasvary, Edmund. *Lincoln's Hungarian Heroes: The Participation of Hungarians in the Civil War, 1861–1865*. Washington, D.C.: Hungarian Reformed Federation of America, 1939.

Vedder, O. F. *History of the City of Memphis and Shelby County, Tennessee.* Syracuse, NY: D. Mason & Co., 1888.

Vida, Istvan Kornel. *Hungarian Emigres in the American Civil War: A History and Biographical Dictionary.* Jefferson, NC: McFarland, 2012.

Virkus, Frederick A., ed. *The Abridged Compendium of American Genealogy.* Vol. 3. Chicago: F.A. Virkus & Co., 1928.

Waggoner, Clark, ed. *History of the City of Toledo and Lucas County, Ohio.* New York and Toledo: Munsell & Co., 1888.

The War of the Rebellion: A Compilation of the Official Records of the Union and Confederate Armies. 128 vol. Washington, D.C.: Government Printing Office, 1880–1901.

Ward, William H., ed. *Records of Members of the Grand Army of the Republic with a Complete Account of the Twentieth National Encampment.* San Francisco: H.S. Crocker & Co., 1886.

Ware, Eugene F. *The Lyon Campaign in Missouri: Being a History of the First Iowa Infantry.* Topeka, KS: Crane & Co., 1907.

Washington, Versalle F. *Eagles on Their Buttons: A Black Infantry Regiment in the Civil War.* Columbia: University of Missouri Press, 1999.

Way, Virgil G., comp. *History of the Thirty-Third Regiment Illinois Veteran Volunteer Infantry in the Civil War.* Gibson City, IL: Press of the Gibson Courier, 1902.

Wearmouth, John, ed. *The Cornwell Chronicles: Tales of an American Life on the Erie Canal, Building Chicago, in the Volunteer Civil War Western Army, on the Farm, in a Country Store.* Bowie, MD: Heritage Books, 1998.

Weaver, Clare P., ed. *Thank God My Regiment an African One: The Civil War Diary of Colonel Nathan W. Daniels.* Baton Rouge, LA: Louisiana State University Press, 1998.

Webb, Walter P., ed. *The Handbook of Texas.* Austin: Texas State Historical Association, 1952.

Weber, John B. *Autobiography of John B. Weber.* Buffalo, NY: John B. Weber, 1924.

Weber, Thomas. *The Northern Railroads in the Civil War, 1861–1865.* New York: King's Crown Press, 1952.

Webster, Dan, and Don C. Cameron. *History of the First Wisconsin Battery Light Artillery.* Washington, D.C.: National Tribune Co., 1907.

Weygant, Charles H. *History of the One Hundred and Twenty-Fourth Regiment N.Y.S.V.* Newburgh, NY: Journal Printing House, 1877.

Wharton, Clarence R. *History of Fort Bend County.* Houston, TX: Anson Jones Press, 1950.

White, Almira L. *Genealogy of the Descendants of John White of Wenham and Lancaster, Massachusetts, 1638–1900.* Haverhill, MA: Chase Brothers, 1900.

Whittemore, Henry. *History of the Sage and Slocum Families of England and America.* New York: Henry Whittemore, 1908.

Who Was Who in America, 1897–1942. Chicago: A.N. Marquis Co., 1942.

Wickman, Don. *"We Are Coming Father Abra'am," The History of the 9th Vermont Volunteer Infantry, 1862–1865.* Lynchburg, VA: Schroeder Publications, 2005.

Williams, Edward T. *Niagara County, New York: A Concise Record of Her Progress and People, 1821–1921.* Chicago: J. H. Beers & Co., 1921.

_____. *Official Record of the Niagara Falls Memorial Commission, In Succession to the William B. Rankine Memorial Commission.* Niagara Falls, NY: Niagara Falls Memorial Commission, 1924.

Williams, J. Fletcher. *A History of the City of Saint Paul and of the County of Ramsey, Minnesota.* Saint Paul: Minnesota Historical Society, 1876.

Wilson, Ephraim A. *Memoirs of the War.* Cleveland, OH: N.p., 1893.

Wilson, James Grant, ed. *Appletons' Cyclopaedia of American Biography.* Vol. 7. New York: D. Appleton & Co., 1901.

_____, and John Fiske, eds. *Appletons' Cyclopedia of American Biography.* New York: D. Appleton & Co., 1888.

Wilson, James Harrison. *Under the Old Flag.* New York: D. Appleton & Co., 1912.

Wilson, Joseph T. *The Black Phalanx: A History of the Negro Soldiers of the United States in the Wars of 1775–1812, 1861–65.* Hartford, CT: American Publishing Co., 1888.

Wittenberg, Eric J. *Like a Meteor Blazing Brightly: The Short but Controversial Life of Colonel Ulric Dahlgren.* El Dorado Hills, CA: Savas Beatie, 2015.

Wood, David W., comp. *History of the 20th O.V.V.I. Regiment and Proceedings of the First Reunion.* Columbus, OH: Paul & Thrall, 1876.

Wood, Richard G. *Stephen Harriman Long, 1784–1864, Army Engineer, Explorer, Inventor.* Glendale, CA: Arthur H. Clark Co., 1966.

Woodbridge, Dwight E., and John S. Pardee, eds. *History of Duluth and St. Louis County Past and Present.* Chicago: C.F. Cooper & Co., 1910.

Woodward, Evan M. *Our Campaigns; or, the Marches, Bivouacs, Battles, Incidents of Camp Life and History of Our Regiment During Its Three Years Term of Service.* Philadelphia: John E. Potter & Co., 1865.

Woodward, Norma S. *Descendants of Richard Woodward, New England, 1589–1982.* Baltimore, MD: Gateway Press, 1982.

Woollen, William W. *Biographical and Historical Sketches of Early Indiana.* Indianapolis: Hammond & Co., 1883.

Wright, Arthur W. *History of the Class of 1859, Yale College: A Record of Fifty-Nine Years.* New Haven, CT: Tuttle, Morehouse & Taylor Co., 1914.

Wynar, Bohdan S., ed. *Dictionary of American Library Biography.* Littleton, CO: Libraries Unlimited, 1978.

Yancey, Rosa F. *Lynchburg and Its Neighbors*. Richmond, VA: J.W. Fergusson & Sons, 1935.

Zeller, Paul G. *The Second Vermont Volunteer Infantry Regiment, 1861–1865*. Jefferson, NC: McFarland & Co., 2002.

Zeta Psi Fraternity of North America: Semicentennial Biographical Catalogue. New York: John C. Rankin Co., 1899.

Periodical and Newspaper Articles

Abbott, John S.C., "Heroic Deeds of Heroic Men: Charles Ellet and His Naval Steam Rams," *Harper's New Monthly Magazine*, Vol. 32, No. 189 (Feb. 1866).

Advertisement (Bright's Kidney Beans). *The Cambrian: A Monthly Magazine*. Vol. 19. Utica, NY, 1899.

Alter, J. Cecil, and Robert J. Dwyer, eds. "The Utah War: Journal of Captain Albert Tracy, 1858–1860," *Utah Historical Quarterly*, Vol. 13 (1945).

Angellotti, Mrs. Frank M., "John Devereux of Marblehead, Mass., and Some of His Descendants," *New England Historical and Genealogical Register*, Vol. 74, No. 4 (Oct. 1920).

"Appointment to Texas," *New Orleans Daily Picayune*, Dec. 31, 1868.

"Arrest of General Coolbaugh," *Daily Missouri Democrat*, Feb. 3, 1866.

"Arrest of General Coolbaugh," *New York Daily Herald*, Feb. 16, 1866.

Bash, Frank S. "Memories of Col. George G. Pride Are Related by Bash in Reviewing City History," *Huntington Herald*, Jan. 6, 1923.

Berfield, Karen. "Julian Bryant: Martyr for Equality," *Civil War Times Illustrated*, Vol. 22, Issue 2 (April 1983).

Beszedits, Stephen. "Hungarian Companions of the First Class in the Military Order of the Loyal Legion of the United States," *Vasvary Collection Newsletter* (2015, No. 2).

Beszedits, Stephen. "Hungarians with General John C. Fremont in the American Civil War," *Vasvary Collection Newsletter* (2003, No. 2).

Beszedits, Stephen. "Ignatz Kappner: A Hungarian Officer in the United States Colored Troops during the Civil War," *Vasvary Collection Newsletter* (2015, No. 2).

Beszedits, Stephen. "The Life and Times of Philip Figyelmessy (1822–1907)," *Vasvary Collection Newsletter* (2006, No. 2).

Blanchard, James A. "An Eloquent Memorial Tribute," *Grand Army Review*, Vol. 3, No. 10 (March 1888).

"A Bogus Special Mail Agent in Colorado," *Wilmington Morning Star*, May 14, 1868.

Brown, Russell K. "The Last Civil War Volunteers: The 125th U.S. Colored Infantry in New Mexico, 1866–1867," *Army History*, No. 92 (Summer 2014).

Browne, Junius Henri. "Letter from Hungary," *Cincinnati Daily Enquirer*, Aug. 22, 1869.

Butterfield, Consul Willshire. "The Bench and Bar of Duluth," *Magazine of Western History*, Vol. 9, No. 5 (March 1889).

"Capt. Castle's Four Score Years." *Chicago Daily Tribune*, Aug. 5, 1891.

Carter. Constance. "John Gould Stephenson: Largely Known and Much Liked," *Quarterly Journal of the Library of Congress*, Vol. 33 (April 1976).

Chamberlin, Eugene K. "Baja California After Walker: The Zerman Expedition," *The Hispanic American Historical Review*, Vol. 34, No. 2 (May 1954).

Christ, Mark K. "They Will Be Armed: Lorenzo Thomas Recruits Black Troops in Helena, April 6, 1863," *Arkansas Historical Quarterly*, Vol. 72, No. 4 (Winter 2013).

"Col. Ernest Holmstedt, Gravier Street," *New Orleans Times*, Dec. 21, 1865.

"Col. John G. Klinck and the Colored Regiments," *Cazenovia Republican*, May 13, 1863.

"Col. Joseph Darr, Jr.," *Wheeling Daily Intelligencer*, Oct. 24, 1864.

"Colonel Christopher A. Morgan," *Fort Morgan Times*, Dec. 6, 1889.

"Colonel Simon Jones," *New Orleans Republican*, March 24, 1868.

"The Colonels Ellet," *Army and Navy Journal*, Vol. 1, No. 14 (Nov. 28, 1863).

"The Confirmation of Zerman," *New York Times*, May 7, 1862.

"Court Martial of Col. Scroggs," *Buffalo Courier*, May 7, 1864.

Curenton, Mark. "Apalachicola's Most Prominent Carpetbagger," *The Apalachicola & Carrabelle Times*, Aug. 9, 2018.

Davis, Robert S., Jr. "Forgotten Union Guerrillas of the North Georgia Mountains," *A North Georgia Journal of History*, Vol. 1 (1989).

"De Kalb Regiment United States Volunteers," *New York Herald*, June 17, 1861.

Dirck, Brian R. "By the Hand of God: James Montgomery and Redemptive Violence," *Kansas History: A Journal of the Central Plains*, Vol. 27, No. 1–2 (Spring-Summer 2004).

"Distinguished Visitor." *Altoona Tribune*, July 6, 1871.

"A Distinguished Visitor." *Harrisburg Telegraph*, Aug. 25, 1866.

Doolittle, Rolla. "Colonel Michael C. Garber." *The Indianian: An Illustrated Monthly Magazine*, Vol. 5, No. 2 (Feb. 1900).

Eisenschiml, Otto. "The 55th Illinois at Shiloh," *Journal of the Illinois State Historical Society*, Vol. 56, No. 2 (Summer 1963).

"An Episode of the Late War." *Lebanon Courier*, Oct. 31, 1872.

"Extraordinary Case of Swindling." *New York World*, May 27, 1865.

"Fighting Them Over, What Our Veterans Have to Say About Their Old Campaigns. Port Republic, Capt. Huntington Replies to Dr. Capehart." *Washington National Tribune*, Dec. 5, 1889.

"The First and Second Kentucky Regiments in the Pittsburg Battle." *Cincinnati Enquirer,* April 16, 1862.

Folkedahl, Beulah. "The Reorganized Church of Jesus Christ of Latter Day Saints in Southwestern Wisconsin." *Wisconsin Magazine of History,* Vol. 36, No. 2 (Winter 1952–53).

Foreman, Carolyn Thomas. "Colonel William Whistler." *The Chronicles of Oklahoma,* Vol. 18, No. 4 (December 1940).

Fradin, Morris. "Curious Burial for a Hero's Leg." *The Hagerstown Cracker Barrel,* Vol. 2, No. 6 (November 1972).

Fraser, Walter J., Jr. "Lucien Bonaparte Eaton: Politics and the Memphis Post, 1867–1869." *West Tennessee Historical Society Papers,* Vol. 20 (1966).

"From North West Georgia: Capture of the Notorious Ashworth and His Command." *Augusta Chronicle,* Dec. 4, 1864.

Frye, Dennis E. "Stonewall Attacks!—The Siege of Harpers Ferry." *Blue & Gray Magazine,* Vol. 5, Issue 1 (September 1987).

"Funeral of Col. DeWitt C. Brown." *Dayton Daily Journal,* Feb. 26, 1875.

"Funeral of Col. Wallace Campbell." *Chicago Daily Tribune,* Feb. 14, 1893.

"The Funeral of Colonel Lathrop." *Cincinnati Commercial Tribune,* March 14, 1865.

"Gen. Darr Obeyed Orders." *Fort Scott Daily Monitor,* July 10, 1901.

"Gen. Lane's Staff Appointed by the President." *Leavenworth Times,* Jan. 31, 1862.

"Gen. Zerman." *New York Tribune,* June 5, 1862.

"General Coolbaugh, the Mexican Filibustero." *Daily Missouri Democrat,* Sept. 22, 1864.

"General Devereux." *Cleveland Leader and Morning Herald,* March 24, 1886.

Gillett, Mary C. "Thomas Lawson, Second Surgeon General of the U.S. Army: A Character Sketch." *Prologue: Quarterly of the National Archives and Records Administration,* Vol. 14, No. 1 (Spring 1982).

"A Good Nomination." *Wisconsin State Journal,* Oct. 22, 1866.

Gorenfeld, Will, and George Stammerjohn, eds. "A Death in the Family: The Letters of Maj. Lloyd J. Beall to His Brother Bvt. Maj. Benjamin L. Beall." *Military Collector and Historian,* Vol. 60, No. 2 (Summer 2008).

"A Great Gathering of Negroes—Incipient Movements Toward Their Organization into Regiments—A Biographical Sketch of Colonel John G. Klinck." *Philadelphia Inquirer,* April 25, 1863.

Halliday, John. "Stephen Long, a Famed Explorer." *Military Images,* Vol. 23, No. 4 (Jan.-Feb. 2002).

"Henry Barns. The True Story of the Founder of the Detroit Tribune." *Detroit News-Tribune,* Jan. 6, 1901.

Holmberg, James J. "Browsing in Our Archives: Louisville Fire Fighting." *The Filson,* Vol. 11, No. 2 (Summer 2011).

"Hon. Frank P. Blair, Jr., and Col. J.T. Fiala." *Daily Missouri Democrat,* Oct. 16, 1862.

"Hon. J.C. McKibbin." *Philadelphia Press,* Sept. 23, 1864.

"Incidents of the Great Fight." *Daily Illinois State Journal,* April 16, 1862.

"Indian Troubles on the Yellowstone." *Montana Post,* June 24, 1865.

Irwin, Ray W., ed. "Missouri in Crisis: The Journal of Captain Albert Tracy, 1861." *Missouri Historical Review,* Vol. 51, No. 1–3 (Oct. 1956, Jan. 1957, April 1957).

"James Trimble, of Tennessee: An Eccentric Fellow—Soldier, Lecturer, Philosopher, and Lunatic." *Rome Sentinel,* May 21, 1878.

Kaufman, A. Fred. "The Fifty-Fourth U.S. Colored Infantry: The Forgotten Regiment." *Ozark Historical Review,* Vol. 16, No.1 (Spring 1987).

Kennedy, J.H. "General J.H. Devereux." *Magazine of Western History,* Vol. 4, No. 2 (June 1886).

"Lamar House Change of Management." *Knoxville Daily Chronicle,* Feb. 19, 1882.

"The Law Courts." *Chicago Daily Tribune,* Feb. 13, 1873.

"Letter from Nashville." *Cleveland Morning Leader,* Oct. 4, 1864.

Lindberg, Kip, and Jeff Patrick. "In the Shadow of the Light Brigade: The Charge of Fremont's Body Guard." *North & South,* Vol. 7, No. 3 (May 2004).

Lobdell, Jared C., ed. "The Civil War Journal and Letters of Colonel John Van Deusen Du Bois, April 12, 1861 to October 16, 1862." *Missouri Historical Review,* Vol. 60, No. 4 (July 1966) and Vol. 61, No. 1 (Oct. 1966).

"Major Simon B. Brown: In Memoriam." *Chicago Inter Ocean,* May 20, 1889.

McCormick, Mike. "Wabash Valley Profiles: Robert N. Hudson." *Terre Haute Tribune-Star,* Sept. 18, 1999.

Meszaros, Rosemary. "From the Archives: In the Matter of Charles Frederick Havelock." *North & South,* Vol. 13, No. 4 (Nov. 2011).

Miller, Robert E. "Zagonyi." *Missouri Historical Review,* Vol. 76, No. 2 (Jan. 1982).

"More About Gen. Coolbaugh." *Daily Missouri Democrat,* Feb. 5, 1866.

Moyer, Henry C. "Col. Charles W. Fribley." *The Now and Then,* Vol. 2, No. 11 (March-April 1890).

"Murders Comrade; Shoots Two More." *Dayton Herald,* Aug. 7, 1909.

Murray, Donald M., and Robert M. Rodney. "Colonel Julian E. Bryant: Champion of the Negro Soldier." *Journal of the Illinois State Historical Society,* Vol. 56, No. 2 (Summer 1963).

Necrology (James Duncan Graham), *The New England Historical & Genealogical Register,* Vol. 21, No. 2 (April 1867).

"Nelsonville Church Re-Dedicated." *Athens Sunday Messenger,* Oct. 17, 1926.

"The New Hampshire Sharpshooters." *Harper's Weekly,* Vol. 5, No. 249 (Oct. 5, 1861).

"News By Telegraph: Matters at Natchez, Memphis and Vicksburg." *Chicago Tribune*, Nov. 26, 1864.
Nofi, Albert A. "Colonel Whistler Retires." *North & South Magazine*, Vol. 10, No. 6 (June 2008).
"The Notorious I.C. Woods." *San Francisco Bulletin*, Feb. 3, 1862.
Obituary (Jacob Zeilin), *Army and Navy Journal*, Vol. 18, No. 16 (Nov. 20, 1880).
Obituary (Marshall S. Howe), *Army and Navy Journal*, Vol. 16, No. 20 (Dec. 21, 1878).
Obituary (George L. Schuyler), *The Illustrated American*, Vol. 3, No. 26 (Aug. 16, 1890).
Obituary (George Nauman), *Army and Navy Journal*, Vol. 1, No. 4 (Sept. 19, 1863).
Obituary (Charles Rivers Ellet), *Army and Navy Journal*, Vol. 1, No. 11 (Nov. 7, 1863).
Obituary (William E. Merrill), *Army and Navy Journal*, Vol. 29, No. 17 (Dec. 19, 1891).
Obituary (Alexander Doull), *Army and Navy Journal*, Vol. 2, No. 34 (April 15, 1865).
Obituary (Andrew P. Caraher), *Army and Navy Journal*, Vol. 22, No. 38 (April 18, 1885).
Obituary (John N. Macomb), *Army and Navy Journal*, Vol. 26, No. 30 (March 23, 1889).
Obituary (John P. Sanderson), *Army and Navy Journal*, Vol. 2, No. 9 (Oct. 22, 1864).
Obituary (Sylvanus H. Stevens), *Grain Dealers Journal*, Vol. 9, No. 12 (Dec. 25, 1902).
"Obituary of Gallant Officers Recently Deceased." *New York Daily Tribune*, Dec. 9, 1862.
"Octogenarian Castle." *Chicago Inter Ocean*, Aug. 6, 1891.
"Organization of the Militia." *Vicksburg Herald*, Oct. 7, 1864.
"Our Lake Providence Correspondence." *New York Herald*, April 23, 1863.
Pahlas, Clark J. "Gilbert A. Pierce: Eighth Territorial Governor." *The WI-IYOHI, Monthly Bulletin of the South Dakota Historical Society*, Vol. 12, No. 5 (August 1958).
"Parade of the Quartermaster's Brigade." *Washington Evening Star*, Aug. 2, 1864.
"Particulars of the Coolbaugh Suicide: The Skeleton in the Closet." *Decatur Weekly Republican*, Nov. 22. 1877.
Piston, William Garrett. "The 1st Iowa Volunteers: Honor and Community in a Ninety-Day Regiment." *Civil War History*, Vol. 44, No. 1 (March 1998).
Reed, David C. "Sabers and Saddles: The Second Regiment of United States Dragoons at Fort Washita, 1842–1845." Master's thesis, Oklahoma State University, 2013.
"Resignation of the Medical Inspector of the Army." *New York Herald*, Aug. 14, 1863.
Richards, David L. *"Recollections of Col. Charles W. Fribley." From the October 25, 1870 and November 1, 1870 Issues of the Muncy Luminary*. Gettysburg, PA, 1994.
Richter, William L. "'The Revolver Rules the Day!': Colonel DeWitt C. Brown and the Freedmen's Bureau in Paris, Texas, 1867–1868." *Southwestern Historical Quarterly*, Vol. 93, No. 3 (January 1990).
"A Sad Case: A Former Cotton Buyer in Augusta Becomes Hopelessly Insane." *Augusta Chronicle*, Nov. 8, 1883.
"The Senate of North Carolina." *Raleigh Daily Standard*, Dec. 18, 1868.
Shirk, George H. "The Lost Colonel." *Chronicles of Oklahoma*, Vol. 35, No. 2 (Summer 1957).
Smith, Joseph. "The Whistlers—A Family Illustrious in War and Peace." *The Journal of the American-Irish Historical Society*, Vol. 2, 1899.
Smith, Wilson A., and Wesley A. Dunn, eds., *The Medical Current*, Vol. 11, No. 6 (June 1895).
"The Sole Survivor of General Grant's Staff Lives as a Hermit." *Indianapolis Star*, Jan. 29, 1905.
"Some Light Is Thrown on Romantic Life of Col. Pride." *Fort Wayne Evening Sentinel*, Dec. 13, 1906.
"The State Senate—Col. Frank Cahill." *Nashville Daily American*, Sept. 16, 1876.
Stuart, Meriwether. "Colonel Ulric Dahlgren and Richmond's Union Underground, April 1864." *Virginia Magazine of History and Biography*, Vol. 72, No. 2 (April 1964).
Townsend, George Alfred. "Colonel C.W. Moulton and His Habits." *Cincinnati Enquirer*, Jan. 28, 1888.
"A Tramp's Diary: Some of His Amusing Adventures." *Geneva Courier*, April 7, 1880.
"Under Four Flags." *Lancaster Inquirer*, Aug. 3, 1907.
"A Veteran Officer." *Atlanta Constitution*, June 19, 1884.
"War Matters." *Cincinnati Daily Press*, May 15, 1861.
"A War Relic: E.H. Gurley Receives a Memento of the Rebellion." *Ukiah Republican Press*, Jan. 25, 1901.
"Washington Letter: Col. Tom M. Key." *Cincinnati Commercial*, Jan. 20, 1869.
Wayland, Francis F., editor. "Fremont's Pursuit of Jackson in the Shenandoah Valley: The Journal of Colonel Albert Tracy, March-July 1862." *Virginia Magazine of History and Biography*, Vol. 70, No. 2–3 (April-July 1962).
"A Well Deserved Appointment." *Wheeling Daily Intelligencer*, Feb. 4, 1862.
Whitehorne, Joseph W.A. "Inspector General Sylvester Churchill's Efforts to Produce a New Army Drill Manual, 1850–1862." *Civil War History*, Vol. 32, No. 2 (June 1986).
"Wiley Sword's War Letters Series." *Blue & Gray Magazine*, Vol. 24, Issue 3 (Fall 2007).
Wood, Richard G. "Librarian-in-Arms: The Career of John G. Stephenson." *Library Quarterly*, Vol. 19 (Oct. 1949).
Yockelson, Mitchell. "Their Memory Will Not Perish: Commemorating the 56th United States Colored Troops." *Gateway Heritage*, Vol. 22, No. 3 (Winter 2001–02).

Internet Sources

www.ancestry.com.
www.annefield.net/shuttleworthlinks.htm.
http://www.arlingtoncemetery.net/jnmacomb.htm.
www.crossedsabers.blogspot.com/2012/05/fiddlers-green-christopher-h-mcnally.html.
Davidson, Earnest H., "The Life of Colonel James H. Davidson," www.minnesotalegalhistoryproject.org/assets/Col.%20James%20Davidson.pdf.
Erwin, James W., "The Teacher, the Preacher and the Prussian: Officers of the 56th United States Colored Infantry," http://www.jameswerwin.com/the-t.html.
www.findagrave.com.
https://history.amedd.army.mil/surgeongenerals/T_Lawson.html.
https://www.leg.state.mn.us/legdb/fulldetail?ID=11719.
https://www.loc.gov/item/n96035157/john-g-stephenson-1828-1883/.
"Nathan W. Daniels Diary and Scrapbook," https://www.loc.gov/collections/nathan-w-daniels-diary-and-scrapbook/.
https://quartermaster.army.mil/bios/previous-qm-generals/quartermaster_general_bio-gibson.html.
http://sedgwick.org/na/families/barnabas1810/sedgwick-thomas1837.html.
"26th USCT's Other Commanding Officer," www.correctionhistory.org/html/chronicl/cw-usct/26th-usct-on-parade.html.

Manuscripts and Collections

Georgetown (DC) University. William W. Wright Collection, Special Collections Division.
Historical Society of Washington, D.C. Robert Barnard Family Papers, 1658–1917 (MS 541).
Library of Congress. Abraham Lincoln Papers: Series 1. General Correspondence. 1833–1916: Zerman, J. Napoleon, to Senate, Monday, June 02, 1862.
William W. Wright Papers, 1863–1870, Manuscript Division.
Military Order of the Loyal Legion of the United States (MOLLUS). Obituary Circulars of various State Commanderies
National Archives. Carded Records Relating to Staff Officers (Record Group 94).

Correspondence Concerning Fremont's Appointments, 1861–64 (Record Group 94, Entry 164).
Court-martial Case Files, 1809–1894 (Record Group 153).
Letters Received, Adjutant General's Office (Record Group 94).
Letters Received, Appointment, Commission and Personal Branch, Adjutant General's Office (Record Group 94).
Letters Received, Colored Troops Branch, Adjutant General's Office (Record Group 94).
Letters Received, Commission Branch, Adjutant General's Office (Record Group 94).
Letters Received, Volunteer Service Branch, Adjutant General's Office (Record Group 94).
Military Service Files (Record Group 94).
Pension Files (Record Group 15).
Personal Histories of Volunteer Officers in the Quartermaster Department, 1861–1865 (Record Group 92).
Register of Army Commissions in Hancock's First Army Corps, 1864–65 (Record Group 94).
Reports of Examining Boards as to Qualifications of Quartermaster Officers, 1864–65 (Record Group 92).
Union Citizens File (Record Group 109).
U.S. Military Academy Cadet Application Papers, 1805–1866 (Record Group 94).

National Daughters of the American Revolution. Iowa DAR, Log Cabin Chapter. Jefferson County Records, 1960–1961.
Ohio Historical Society. J. P. Sanderson Papers, 1846–1865 (MSS 209).
University of Michigan, William L. Clements Library. Eaton-Shirley Family Papers (1790–1939).
U.S. Army Heritage & Education Center. Charles F. Johnson Papers.

Newspapers

Albany (NY) Evening Journal
Alton (IL) Telegraph
Anamosa (IA) Eureka
Anamosa (IA) Journal
Arkansas Gazette (Little Rock, AR)
Army and Navy Journal
Atchison (KS) Daily Globe
Atlanta (GA) Constitution
Austin (TX) Daily Statesman
Baltimore (MD) Sun
Barre (VT) Evening Telegram
Bedford (PA) Inquirer
Bennington (VT) Banner
Berkshire County (MA) Eagle
Boston (MA) Daily Advertiser
Boston (MA) Evening Transcript
Boston (MA) Globe
Boston (MA) Herald
Boston (MA) Journal
Boston (MA) Morning Journal
Brooklyn (NY) Daily Eagle
Brooklyn (NY) Daily Union
Buffalo (NY) Commercial
Buffalo (NY) Courier
Buffalo (NY) Courier Express
Buffalo (NY) Daily Courier

Buffalo (NY) Enquirer
Buffalo (NY) Evening News
Buffalo (NY) Evening Times
Buffalo (NY) Morning Express
Buffalo (NY) Times
Buffalo (NY) Weekly Express
Bureau County (IL) Republican
Burlington (VT) Free Press
Cambridge (MA) Chronicle
Carroll (IA) Sentinel
Cedar Rapids (IA) Evening Gazette
Champaign (IL) Daily Gazette
Charleston (WV) Daily Mail
Chattanooga (TN) Daily Times
Chenango (NY) Semi-Weekly Telegraph
Chicago (IL) Daily Inter Ocean
Chicago (IL) Daily News
Chicago (IL) Daily Tribune
Chicago (IL) Inter Ocean
Chicago (IL) Record
Chicago (IL) Times
Chicago (IL) Tribune
Chillicothe (MO) Daily Constitution
Cincinnati (OH) Commercial
Cincinnati (OH) Commercial Gazette
Cincinnati (OH) Daily Commercial
Cincinnati (OH) Daily Enquirer
Cincinnati (OH) Daily Gazette
Cincinnati (OH) Enquirer
Clay Center (KS) Times
Cleveland (OH) Leader
Cleveland (OH) Leader and Morning Herald
Cleveland (OH) Plain Dealer
Colorado Daily Chieftain (Pueblo, CO)
Columbia (SC) Daily Phoenix
Connecticut Western News (North Canaan, CT)
Council Bluffs (IA) Daily Nonpareil
Daily Arkansas Gazette (Little Rock, AR)
Daily Davenport (IA) Democrat
Daily Illinois State Journal (Springfield, IL)
Daily Illinois State Register (Springfield, IL)
Daily Missouri Democrat (St. Louis, MO)
Daily Missouri Republican (St. Louis, MO)
Daily National Intelligencer (Washington, D.C.)
Daily Ohio Statesman (Columbus, OH)
Daily Yellowstone (MT) Journal
Davenport (IA) Daily Gazette
Davenport (IA) Morning Democrat
Dayton (OH) Daily Journal
Deadwood (SD) Daily Pioneer-Times
Denver (CO) Post
Des Moines (IA) Register and Leader
Detroit (MI) Advertiser and Tribune
Detroit (MI) Evening News
Detroit (MI) Free Press
Dixon (IL) Telegraph
Duluth (MN) Evening Herald
Duluth (MN) Herald
Duluth (MN) News Tribune
East St. Louis (IL) Journal
Eureka (KS) Herald
Exeter (NH) News-Letter and Rockingham Advertiser

Fairbury (IL) Blade
Florida Times-Union (Jacksonville, FL)
Fort Scott (KS) Daily Monitor
Fort Wayne (IN) Evening Sentinel
Frederick (MD) News
Gettysburg (PA) Compiler
Gettysburg (PA) Star and Sentinel
Gilroy (CA) Advocate
Girard (KS) Herald
Glens Falls (NY) Post-Star
Grand Forks (ND) Herald
Grand Rapids (MI) Evening Press
Grand Rapids (MI) Herald
Grand Rapids (MI) Press
Hartford (CT) Courant
Humboldt (KS) Union
Huntington (IN) Daily News-Democrat
Huntington (IN) Evening Herald
Hutchinson (KS) Weekly World
Idaho Daily Statesman (Boise, ID)
Illinois State Journal (Springfield, IL)
Illinois State Register (Springfield, IL)
Indianapolis (IN) Daily Sentinel
Indianapolis (IN) Journal
Indianapolis (IN) News
Iowa State Register (Des Moines, IA)
Jackson (OH) Standard
Jeffersonville (IN) Evening News
Jersey Journal (Jersey City, NJ)
Kansas Newspaper Union (Topeka, KS)
Knoxville (TN) Daily Chronicle
Kokomo (IN) Daily Tribune
La Crosse (WI) Tribune
Lancaster (PA) Daily Evening Express
Lancaster (PA) Daily Intelligencer
Lancaster (PA) Daily New Era
Lancaster (PA) Intelligencer
Lancaster (PA) New Era
Lancaster (PA) Semi-Weekly New Era
Lawrence (KS) Daily Journal
Lawrence (KS) Republican Daily Journal
Lawrence (KS) Standard
Leavenworth (KS) Standard
Lebanon (OH) Western Star
Little Falls (MN) Herald
Los Angeles (CA) Herald
Los Angeles (CA) Times
Louisville (KY) Courier-Journal
Louisville (KY) Daily Journal
Luzerne Union (Wilkes-Barre, PA)
Madison (IN) Daily Courier
Manchester (VT) Journal
Maysville (KY) Daily Public Ledger
Medina County (OH) Gazette
Memphis (TN) Bulletin
Michigan Argus (Ann Arbor, MI)
Milwaukee (WI) Journal
Minneapolis (MN) Daily Tribune
Minneapolis (MN) Journal
Minneapolis (MN) Morning Tribune
Minneapolis (MN) Tribune
Mobile (AL) Register
Montgomery (AL) Advertiser

Montpelier (VT) Argus and Patriot
Montpelier (VT) Daily Journal
Mount Pleasant (IA) Journal
Muscatine (IA) Journal
Muscatine (IA) News-Tribune
Napa (CA) Weekly Journal
Nashville (TN) Daily American
Nashville (TN) Tennessean
New Albany (IN) Ledger-Standard
New Haven (CT) Evening Register
New Haven (CT) Register
New Lisbon (OH) Journal
New Orleans (LA) Daily Picayune
New York (NY) Commercial Advertiser
New York (NY) Daily Tribune
New York (NY) Evening Post
New York (NY) Herald
New York (NY) Sun
New York (NY) Times
New York (NY) Tribune
New York (NY) World
New-York Daily Reformer (Watertown, NY)
Newark (NJ) Daily Advertiser
Niagara Falls (NY) Gazette
Norwich (CT) Bulletin
Oakland (CA) Evening Tribune
Oakland (CA) Tribune
Ohio State Journal (Columbus, OH)
Olean (NY) Daily Herald
Olean (NY) Democrat
Ottawa (IL) Free Trader
Ottawa (IL) Republican
Owatonna (MN) Journal
Owosso (MI) Times
Patterson (NJ) Morning Call
Perrysburg (OH) Journal
Philadelphia (PA) Evening Public Ledger
Philadelphia (PA) Inquirer
Philadelphia (PA) North American
Philadelphia (PA) Press
Philadelphia (PA) Public Ledger
Philadelphia (PA) Times
Pittsburgh (PA) Daily Post
Pittsfield (MA) Sun
Portland (ME) Daily Eastern Argus
Portland (ME) Daily Press
Poughkeepsie (NY) Daily Eagle
Providence (RI) Daily Post
Providence (RI) Evening Press
Randolph (VT) Herald and News
Reading (PA) Daily Times
Red Oak (IA) Express
Reno (NV) Evening Gazette
Rochester (NY) Democrat and Chronicle
Rocky Mountain News (Denver, CO)
Rutland (VT) Daily Herald
Rutland (VT) Daily Herald & Globe
Sacramento (CA) Daily Record-Union
Sacramento (CA) Record-Union
Saginaw (MI) Herald
St. Helena (CA) Star
St. Joseph (MO) Herald
St. Louis (MO) Globe-Democrat

St. Louis (MO) Post-Dispatch
St. Louis (MO) Republic
St. Paul (MN) Daily Dispatch
St. Paul (MN) Globe
Salt Lake (UT) Tribune
San Antonio (TX) Daily Express
San Antonio (TX) Evening Light
San Diego (CA) Union
San Francisco (CA) Bulletin
San Francisco (CA) Call
San Francisco (CA) Chronicle
San Francisco (CA) Examiner
San Francisco (CA) Morning Call
Sandusky (OH) Daily Register
Sandusky (OH) Star-Journal
Sauk Centre (MN) Herald
Scranton (PA) Republican
Scranton (PA) Times
Seattle (WA) Daily Times
Sedalia (MO) Daily Capital
Sedalia (MO) Democrat
Seneca Falls (NY) Reveille
Sonoma (CA) Democrat
Sunbury (PA) American
Syracuse (NY) Morning Standard
Syracuse (NY) Post-Standard
Tacoma (WA) Daily Ledger
Terre Haute (IN) Express
Three Rivers (MI) Tribune
Topeka (KS) Daily Capital
Topeka (KS) State Journal
Toronto (KS) Topic
Troy (NY) Daily Times
Troy (NY) Daily Whig
Troy (NY) Times
Tulsa (OK) Daily World
Utica (NY) Daily Observer
Utica (NY) Morning Herald
Vermont Watchman & State Journal (Montpelier, VT)
Washington (DC) Daily National Republican
Washington (DC) Evening Star
Washington (DC) Evening Times
Washington (DC) National Republican
Washington (DC) National Tribune
Washington (DC) Post
Waterloo (IA) Courier
Watertown (WI) Gazette
Watertown (WI) Weekly Leader
Waukon (IA) Standard
Wayne County (IL) Press
The Weekly Knight and Soldier (Topeka, KS)
West Chester (PA) Daily Local News
Wichita (KS) Beacon
Wichita (KS) Daily Eagle
Wilkes-Barre (PA) Evening Leader
Wilkes-Barre (PA) Record
Wilmington (DE) Evening Journal
Wilmington (DE) Morning News
Winsted (CT) Herald
Wyandot County (OH) Republican
Ypsilanti (MI) Commercial

Index

Numbers in ***bold italics*** indicate pages with illustrations

Abercrombie, John J. 124
Abert, John James 126, ***127, 128***
Abert, William S. 127
Abry, John David 4, 11
Adams, Charles Henry 3, 12
Albert, Anselme Ignacz 180, ***181***
Albrecht, J.A. 63
Alexander, Edmund B. 125
Alexander, James Madison 7, 12, ***13***
Alger, Russell A. 230
Ames, Adelbert 90
Ames, John W. 4, 92
Andrews, George L. 56
Andrews, Norman S. 4, 13, ***14***
Andrews, Timothy P. 126
Appleton, John F. 9
Archer, Martin Robert 11, 14
Armstrong, Charles Dorsey 11, 15
Armstrong, Samuel C. 4
Asboth, Alexander 67
Ashworth, John H. 248, 249
Augur, Christopher C. 68

Babcock, Orville E. 241
Backus, Electus 124, 129
Baird, Absalom 238
Baird, George William 5, ***15, 16***
Baker, Conrad 115
Ballinger, Richard Henry 7, ***17***
Bancroft, George 214
Banks, Nathaniel P. 53, 187
Bardwell, Frederick William 4, ***18***
Barlow, Francis C. 158
Barnard, Robert William 10, ***19, 20***
Barnes, Joseph K. 126
Barns, Henry 10, 20
Barrett, Theodore H. 7
Barry, Henry W. 3
Barry, William F. 123
Bartholomew, Orion A. 10
Bartlett, Charles G. 10
Bartram, Nelson Burr 5, 7, ***21, 22***
Bassett, Chauncey J. 8, 22, ***23***
Bates, Delevan 5
Batterton, Ira Abbott 248, 250
Bayley, Thomas 4, ***24***
Baylor, George Wythe 182

Baylor, John Robert 182
Beall, Benjamin Lloyd 123, 129, ***130***
Beall, Lloyd J. 129
Beatty, Samuel 159
Beecher, James C. 6
Belger, James 180, 182
Belknap, William W. 61
Belton, Francis Smith 123, ***130***
Benedict, Lewis 104
Bennett, William T. 6
Benteen, Frederick William 11, 25
Benton, William P. 224
Bentzoni, Charles 7, ***26, 27***
Berdan, Hiram 154
Bierbower, Frederick Huber 11, 27
Bird, Charles 157, ***158***
Birge, Henry W. 89
Birney, David B. 232
Bishop, John Soast 10, ***28, 29***
Blackman, Albert M. 5
Blake, George A.H. 123
Bliss, Alexander 213, ***214***
Bloodgood, Edward 149
Boggs, William R. 147
Bomford, James V. 125
Bonneville, Benjamin L.E. 124
Bostwick, Charles Edward 9, 29
Bostwick, Solomon 248, ***250, 251***
Botsford, Alban Bates 8, 30
Bouton, Edward 7
Bowman, Alexander Hamilton 127, ***131, 132***
Bowman, Samuel M. 54
Bradley, George Willett 213, 214, ***215***
Brady, Hugh 129
Brayman, Mason 274
Brazee, Andrew W. 11, 30
Brice, Benjamin W. 126
Bridgman, Eliot 9, ***31***
Brisbin, James S. 3
Brooker, Benjamin C. 259
Brooks, Horace 123
Brooks, William Sanford 7, ***32***
Brough, John 223
Brown, DeWitt Clinton 7, 32
Brown, Harvey 123
Brown, Lewis G. 10

Brown, Orlando 5
Brown, Philip P., Jr. 157
Brown, Simon Benjamin 249, 251, ***252***
Brown, William H. ***20***
Browne, Junius Henri 210
Browne, William H. 172
Browning, Orville 182
Bryant, Julian Edward 6, ***33, 34***
Bryant, William Cullen 34
Buchanan, Robert C. 124
Burbank, Sidney 124
Burbridge, Stephen G. 13, 27
Burges, Tristam 180, 182, ***183***
Burr, Raymond 213, ***215***
Burton, Henry S. 123
Butler, Benjamin F. 88, 104, 237
Butler, Speed 180, 183
Butterfield, Daniel 21, 124

Cadwalader, George 228
Cady, Albemarle 125
Cahill, Frank Patrick 172, ***173***
Camp, Elisha Ely 249, 252, ***253***
Campbell, Anna Elizabeth 241
Campbell, Cleaveland J. 5
Campbell, George Whitaker 35, 241
Campbell, Henry ***20***
Campbell, Wallace 10, 34, ***35***, 241
Canby, Edward R.S. 126
Cannon, Le Grand Bouton 180, ***184, 185***
Caraher, Andrew Patrick 168, ***169***
Carpenter, Louis Henry 3, ***36, 37***
Carr, Byron Oscar 213, ***216, 217***
Carr, Eugene A. 217
Carrington, Henry B. 125
Casey, Silas 124
Castle, Edward Herrick 248, 253, ***254***
Castle, Ephraim ***254***
Chamberlain, Edwin W. 6, 37, ***38***
Chapin, Edward P. 112
Chetlain, Augustus L. 12
Chipman, Henry L. 10
Churchill, Sylvester 126. ***132***
Churchill, Winston 132

Index

Clark, George F. 213, 217, *218*
Clark, James Cushman 8, 38, *39*
Cobb, John Clifford 9, 39, *40*
Cole, George W. 3
Cone, John E. 7, 40, *41*
Conine, James William 4, *41*, *42*
Cook, John Benajah 4, 42, *43*
Cooke, Philip St. George 123
Coolbaugh, George W. 180, *185*, *186*
Coolbaugh, William F. 186
Cooper, George E. 126, *133*
Corbin, Henry C. 5
Couch, Darius N. 228
Cox, Jacob D. 41, 247
Cox, Samuel Sullivan 255
Cox, Thomas Jefferson 249, *255*, *256*
Crandal, Frederick M. 6
Crane, John C. 213, 218, *219*, 249
Crawford, Frank M. *20*
Crawford, Samuel J. 9
Cruttenden, Joel Douglas 213, *220*
Cummings, Alexander 65
Curtin, Andrew G. 259
Curtis, Samuel R. 62, 216

Dahlgren, John A.B. 257
Dahlgren, Ulric 248, *256*, *257*
Dana, Charles A. 202
Dana, Napoleon J.T. 119
Daniels, Nathan W. 8, *43*, *44*
Darr, Francis 258
Darr, Joseph, Jr. 248, 257
Daum, Philip 180, 187
Davidson, James Hamilton 11, *45*, *46*
Davidson, John W. 48, 79, 216, 258
Davis, Henry G. *20*
Day, Hannibal 124
Dayton, Oscar V. 172
Delafield, Richard 126
Denicke, Ernest Augustus 248, *258*
Dennis, Elias S. 250
Devereux, John Henry 180, 187, *188*
Dewey, Joel A. 10
DeWitt, David P. 171
Dickey, William H. 9
Dimick, Justin 123
Dimon, Charles A.R. 168
Dodge, Grenville M. 72, 189, 244
Doron, Charles Robert 249, 259
Doubleday, Ulysses 6
Doull, Alexander 248, *260*, *261*
Downey, Thomas Jefferson 5, *46*, *47*
Draper, Alonzo G. 6
Drew, Charles W. 8
DuBois, John V.D. 180, 188, *189*
Duffield, William W. 264
Dulany, William 150
Dumont, Ebenezer 223

Duncan, Alexander 8, *47*
Duncan, Samuel A. 4, 197
Dyer, Alexander B. 127

Earle, Willard Chauncey 8, *48*, *49*
Earnest, Robert Helm 10, *50*
Eastmond, Oscar 248, 261
Easton, Langdon C. 129
Eaton, Amos B. 126
Eaton, John, Jr. 7, 52
Eaton, Lucien Bonaparte 8, *51*
Edgerton, Alonzo J. 7, 8
Ekin, James A. 249
Elison, John A. 213, 220, *221*, 249
Ellet, Alfred W. 190, 262
Ellet, Charles, Jr. 180, 189, *190*, 262
Ellet, Charles Rivers 190, 248, *262*
Elliott, Isaac H. 200
Ely, John 172
Emory, William H. 109, 124
Enos, Herbert Merton 213, 221
Enyart, David A. *98*
Erving, John 123, 134
Ewell, Richard S. 193

Fairleigh, Thomas B. 15
Farnsworth, Addison 171
Farnsworth, John Gosman 213, *222*
Farnum, John Egbert 171
Farrar, Bernard G. 3
Fellows, Stark 4, *52*
Ferry, John Hardin 213, 223
Fiala, John Thomas 180, *191*
Figyelmesy, Philip 180, *192*
Finley, Clement A. 126
Fisher, Benjamin F. 127
Foley, John 7, 53
Fontaine, Charles 250
Foster, Jacob Thomas 4, 53, *54*
Franklin, William B. 125, 245
Frazar, Douglas 10
Fremont, John C. 57, 74, 181, 191, 192, 193, 195, 196, 198, 199, 208, 210, 253, 257, 279, 280
French, William H. 225
Fribley, Charles Wesley 4, 54, *55*
Frisbie, Henry N. 9
Frohock, William T. 8
Fry, Speed S. 116
Fuller, Henry W. 8
Fuller, John W. 78
Fyffe, Edward P. 171

Gable, William *20*
Gantt, Thomas Tasker 180, *193*
Garber, Michael Christian 213, 223, *224*
Gardner, John L. 123
Garibaldi, Giuseppe 192
Garland, John 125, *134*
Garrard, Jeptha 3

Gaskill, Charles Byron 9, *56*
Gates, William 123
Gaw, William Burr 5, *57*
Gerhart, William Rickenbaugh 11, *58*
Getty, George W. 30
Gibbon, John 225
Gibson, George 126, *135*
Gilchrist, Charles A. 7
Gile, George W. 171
Gist, George Washington 157, *159*
Gist, Mordecai 159
Goff, Nathan, Jr. 6
Goodrich, Luther 9, *59*
Gordon, George H. 80
Gorman, Willis A. 231
Graham, James Duncan 127, 136, *137*
Graham, Lawrence P. 124, 136
Graham, William M. 136
Granger, Gordon 163
Granger, Robert S. 266
Grant, Ulysses S. 112, 205, 269
Greene, Elias M. 249, *263*
Greene, James D. 124
Greer, Benjamin A. F. 157, *160*
Gregory, David E. 104
Gresham, Walter Q. 61
Griffin, Charles 213
Grim, Lycurgus *20*
Grosvenor, William Mason 8, *60*
Guernsey, William Bellamy 5, *61*
Gurley, John Addison 180, 193, *194*
Gurley, John Edgar 11, 61, *62*
Guylee, John 7, 62, *63*

Hall, James A. 157
Hall, Robert M. 6
Halleck, Henry W. 74, 188, 202, 253
Hambright, Henry A. 238
Hamilton, Alexander 194
Hamilton, Alexander, Jr. 180, 194, 206
Hamilton, Schuyler 57
Hamlin, Cyrus 8
Hammond, William A. 126
Hancock, Winfield S. 196
Hanks, George H. 10, 63, *64*
Haren, Edward 191
Harker, Charles G. 51
Harrington, George Dana 241, *242*
Harris, John 150, *151*
Hartwell, Charles A. 4, 8
Harwood, Paul 7, 65
Hascall, Milo S. 97
Haskell, Llewellyn F. 6
Haskin, George 12
Hatch, Cora L.V. 45
Hatch, John P. 234
Havelock, Charles Frederick 180, *195*
Havelock, Sir Henry 195

Hazard, John G. 157
Heintzelman, Samuel P. 125, 263
Hendrickson, John 172
Herndon, William H. 17
Herron, Francis J. 75
Higginson, Thomas Wentworth 6, *66*, *67*
Hitchcock, Frederick Lyman 5, 67, *68*
Hobson, Edward H. 116
Hodge, Justin 9, 68, *69*
Hoffman, William 124
Holbrook, William Briggs 248, 263, *264*
Holman, John H. 4
Holmstedt, Ernest W. 8, *69*
Holt, Joseph 13, 43, 48, 101, 104, 126
Hooker, Joseph 256
Hottenstein, John A. 4, *70*
Hovey, Charles E. 33
Howard, Charles H. 11
Howard, John Brainard 213, 224, *225*
Howard, Oliver O. 224, 233
Howe, Albion P. 30, 138
Howe, Marshall Spring 124, 137, *138*
Howland, Henry 213, *226*, *227*
Hudson, John G. 7
Hudson, Robert N. 180, 195, *196*
Humphreys, Andrew A. 218
Hunt, Henry J. 260
Hunter, David 124, 133
Hurlbut, Stephen A. 12, 63

Inness, William 5, *71*, *72*
Irvin, Charles Henry 249, 264, *265*
Irvin, James Meikle 7, *72*, *73*
Irwin, William H. 79
Isenstein, George 249, 265, *266*
Isom, John Franklin 249, 266, *267*

Jeffries, Noah L. 172
Jenkins, George N. *20*
Jessup, Huntington C. *20*
Johnson, Absalom Yarborough 171, 173
Johnson, Adolphus James 171, *174*
Johnson, Andrew 65, 182, 218
Johnson, Charles Francis 172, *175*
Johnson, James Gould 213, *228*
Johnson, Lewis 6
Jones, Amos Balfour 180, 196, *197*
Jones, Joseph Blackburn 8
Jones, Samuel B. 8
Jones, Simon 9, 73

Kappner, Ignatz G. 3, *74*, *75*
Kempsey, Matthew Chapman 9, 75
Kendrick, Frank Asbury 7, *76*

Kennedy, Evan D. 116
Ketchum, William S. 125
Key, Thomas Marshall 180, 198
Keyes, Erasmus D. 68, 125
Kiddoo, Joseph B. 5
King, Edward Augustine 124, 138, *139*
King, John H. 125, 273
Kirby, Edmund 130
Kirk, George Washington 249, 267, *268*
Klinck, John Graham 6, *77*, *78*
Knefler, Frederick 159
Koerner, Gustavus 180, *198*
Kossuth, Louis 121

Laibold, Bernard 265
La Motte, Charles E. 157
Lane, James H. 203
Larned, Benjamin F. 126, 139, *140*
Lathrop, William Hopkins 10, *78*
Lawson, Thomas 126, *140*
Lee, George Washington 213, 228, *229*
Lee, James Grafton Carleton 249, 268, *269*
Lee, Robert E. 201
Leonard, Edward 261
Lewis, James T. 101
Lewis, John R. 171
Lieb, Herman 3
Lincoln, Abraham 12, 17, 60, 88, 101, 104, 255
Lister, Frederick W. 6
Littlefield, Milton S. 5
Long, Stephen Harriman 127, 140, *141*
Longbotham, James H. 226
Longstreet, James 135
Loomis, Gustavus 124
Lovejoy, Elijah P. 200
Lovejoy, Owen 180, *199*
Lovell, Charles S. 125

Macauley, Daniel 157
Macomb, Alexander 200
Macomb, John Navarre 180, *200*
Malmborg, Oscar 157, 160, *161*, *162*
Mansfield, John 171
Marcy, Randolph B. 126
Markland, Absalom Hanks 248, 269, *270*
Marple, William W. 6
Marshall, Louis Henry 180, *201*
Martindale, Edward 9, *79*
Martindale, John H. 80, 90
Maynadier, Henry E. 168
McAlester, Miles D. 131
McArthur, James Neilson 3, 80, *81*
McArthur, John 80, *81*, 82, 234, 273
McCaleb, Hubert Anville 3, 11, *82*, *83*

McCalla, Nathaniel 6, *84*
McChesney, Joseph Miller 248, 270, *271*
McClellan, George B. 190, 193, 195, 198, 200, 209
McClernand, John A. 85, 223, 224, 234
McCoy, Lewis 4, 85
McDowell, Irvin 200
McGowan, John E. 3
McKean, Thomas J. 77
McKibbin, David B. 202
McKibbin, Joseph Chambers 180, *202*
McKim, William Walker 213, 229, *230*
McLean, Nathaniel C. 155
McNally, Christopher Hely 168, 169
McNeill, Quincy *108*
McPherson, James B. 57, 77, 161, 185, 186
Meade, George G. 136
Meigs, Montgomery C. 126, 200
Merchant, Charles S. 123
Meredith, Solomon 206
Merrill, William Emery 157, 163, *164*
Merritt, William Hilton 180, *203*
Miles, Dixon Stansbury 124, *142*, *143*
Miller, John F. 266
Miller, Matthew Murray 248, *272*
Miller, Stephen 106
Millington, Augustus O. 5, 85
Mitchel, Ormsby M. 244, 245
Montgomery, James 6, *86*, *87*
Moon, John C. 10
Morgan, Christopher Anthony 180, *204*
Morgan, George N. 171
Morgan, George W. 53, 223
Morgan, James D. 226
Morgan, Thomas J. 5
Morgan, William H. 157
Morris, William W. 123
Morrison, Andrew Brown 7, 87, *88*
Morrison, Pitcairn 125
Moulton, Charles William 213, *230*
Mudgett, William S. 8
Mussey, Reuben D. 10, 111
Myer, Albert J. 127

Nauman, George 123, 143
Nelson, John A. 4, 8, 88
Nichols, Thomas V. *20*
Noble, Henry Theophilus 213, *231*
Noble, Silas 232
Norton, Charles Ledyard 8, 9, *89*
Noyes, Henry Taylor 6, *90*

Oliphant, Samuel D. 172

Index

Ord, Edward O.C. 53, 225, 232, 237
Organ, James Turner 8, 91
Osband, Embury D. 3
Osterhaus, Peter J. 53, 231
Owen, William Henry 213, *232, 233*

Paine, Eleazer A. 226
Palmer, Innis N. 214, 237
Palmer, John M. 226
Parsons, Lewis B. 253
Paul, Gabriel R. 125, 149
Payne, Matthew Mountjoy 123, *144*
Peck, John J. 95, 237
Perkins, Joseph Griswold 5, 91, *92*
Perley, Thomas Fitch 126, 144, *145*
Peterson, John Christie 249, 273
Pickett, George E. 147
Pierce, Francis E. 157
Pierce, Gilbert Ashville 213, *234*
Pitkin, Perley Peabody 213, *235, 236*
Pleasanton, Alfred 268
Plumly, Mardon Wilson 9, 92
Pomeroy, James M. 157, 165
Pomutz, George *81*
Pope, John 183, 189, 200, 201, 202, 204, 209, 244
Porter, Andrew 125, 224, 225
Porter, Benjamin Sabin 171, *176*
Porter, Fitz John 125
Porter, Samuel A. 11
Post, Henry Albertson Van Zo *154, 155*
Potter, Carroll H. 168
Preston, Simon M. 7
Prevost, Charles M. 172
Pride, George Greenwood 180, *205*
Pringle, William W. *20*

Quincy, Samuel M. 8, 9

Ramsay, George D. 127
Read, Joseph Corson 241, 242, *243*
Reeve, Isaac V.D. 125
Reno, Jesse L. 242
Revere, William H., Jr. 10
Reynolds, John F. 124
Reynolds, Joseph J. 232
Rice, Samuel A. 113
Richmond, Nathaniel P. 157, 165, *166*
Ripley, James W. 127
Risdon, Orlando C. 7
Robinson, George D. 9
Rodgers, John 200
Rombauer, Robert J. 191
Root, Richard 11, *93*
Rosecrans, William S. 57, 146, 163, 165, 189, 202, 244, 257, 258, 273

Ross, Leonard F. 231
Rousseau, Lovell H. 15, 236, 238
Royce, Clark Esek King 5, 93, *94*
Ruger, Thomas H. 224
Ruggles, George D. 245
Rush, Benjamin 177
Rush, Richard Henry 171, *177, 178*
Rusling, James F. 249
Russell, Charles S. 5

Sabin, George Myron 248, 273, *274*
Sage, Russell 245
Salomon, Frederick 231
Sanderson, John Phillip 125, 145, *146*
Saxton, Rufus 256
Scammon, Eliakim P. 196
Schenck, Egbert Tangier Smith 241, *243*
Schenck, Robert C. 196, 244
Schoepf, Albin 237
Schofield, John M. 11, 189, 216, 247
Schuyler, George Lee 180, 194, *206*
Schuyler, Philip 206
Scofield, Hiram 6
Scott, Winfield 209
Scroggs, Gustavus Adolphus 5, 94, *95*
Scull, Gideon, Jr. 241, *244*
Seawell, Thomas D. 7
Seawell, Washington 124
Sedgewick, Thomas Duncan 10, 95, *96, 97, 98*
Sedgwick, John 124
Sewall, Frederick D. 171
Seymour, Truman 38
Shafter, William R. 5
Shannon, John Andrew 3, 97, *99*
Shaw, James, Jr. 4
Sheley, Charles S. 7, 99, *100*
Shepard, Isaac F. 7, 17
Shepherd, Oliver L. 125
Sheridan, Philip H. 36, 225, 259
Sherman, Thomas W. 77, 123
Sherman, William T. 74, 125, 224, 230
Shields, James 187
Shurtleff, Giles W. 4
Shuttleworth, John G. 152
Shuttleworth, William Louis 150, 151, *152*
Sibley, Caleb C. 125
Sigel, Franz 181, 196, 256
Silliman, William 5, 100, *101*
Simonson, John S. 124
Sloan, William J. 148
Slocum, Henry W. 68, 245, 246
Slocum, Joseph Jermain 241, *245*
Smith, Absalom S. 7, 101
Smith, Charles B. 248, 274, *275*
Smith, Charles F. 124
Smith, Charles Kilgore, Jr. 213, *236, 237*

Smith, Edmund Kirby 130
Smith, Giles A. 61
Smith, Joseph L. Kirby 130
Smith, Michael William 8, *102*
Spencer, George E. 248
Sprague, Augustus B.R. 103
Sprague, Homer Baxter 9, *103*
Sprague, John T. 125
Stafford, Spencer Hallenbake 8, 104, *105*
Stahel, Julius 192
Stanley, David S. 226
Stanton, Edward M. 182, 218, 260
Starring, Frederick A. 263
Stearns, Ozora Pierson 6, 106, *107, 108*
Steedman, James B. 237
Steele, Frederick 216
Stephenson, John Gould 180, 206, *207*
Stevens, Ambrose A. 171
Stevens, Sylvanus Harlow 249, 275, *276*
Stickney, Albert 9, *109*
Stocktom, Richard 178
Stone, Charles P. 125
Stoneman, George 133, 247
Stoughton, Homer Richard 154, *155*
Strong, James C. 172
Strong, William E. 185
Sturdevant, Samuel Henry 241, 245, *246*
Sullivan, William Timothy 248, 276, *277*
Sweet, Benjamin J. 171
Symington, Elizabeth McCaw 147
Symington, John 127, *147*
Symington, William Newton 147
Sypher, Jay Hale 4

Taylor, Joseph P. 126
Thomas, George H. 57, 98, 116, 124, 133, 163, 202, 238, 239, 242
Thomas, Henry G. 5, 8
Thomas, Lorenzo 111, 126
Thomas, Samuel 7
Thompson, Charles R. 4
Tilghman, Benjamin C.
Tod, David 85
Tompkins, Charles H. 148, 249
Tompkins, Daniel D. 126, *148*
Totten, Joseph G. 126
Townsend, Benjamin Roach 4, *110*
Townsend, Nathaniel 110
Tracy, Albert 180, *208*
Tracy, Albert H. 208
Tracy, Benjamin F. 11
Treat, Richard Bryan 241, 246
Trimble, James 5, 111
True, James M. 114
Tuley, William W. 97
Turner, Joanna W. 112

Index

Turner, William Dutton 3, 4, 111, *112*

Ullmann, Daniel 32

Veatch, James C. 53
Vogdes, Israel 123
Von Kielmansegge, Eugene 248, 277

Wade, James F. 3
Wadsworth, James S. 195
Waite, Carlos A. 124
Ward, Henry C. 5
Warner, Adoniram J. 172
Warren, Fitz-Henry 37
Warren, Gouverneur K. 110
Webber, Alonzo Watson 7
Weber, John Baptiste 9, 112, *113*
Webster, Ralph Cushing 213, 237, *238*
Welch, Benjamin, Jr. 180, 209
Wessells, Henry W. 237
Whipple, Lauriston Washington 10, 113, *114*
Whistler, James McNeill 149

Whistler, Joseph N.G. 149
Whistler, William 124, 148, *149*
Whittlesey, Eliphalet 6
Whytal, Thomas G. 249, *278*, *279*
Wickersham, Dudley 157, 166, *167*
Wickersham, James P. 239
Wickersham, Morris Dickenson 213, 238, *239*
Wilde, Ferdinand A. *20*
Wiley, Edmund Roberts, Jr. 9, 114, *115*
Williams, James M. 8
Wilson, James Grant 3
Wilson, James H. 242
Wisewell, Moses N. 171
Wood, Oliver 157
Wood, Thomas J. 123, 139
Wood, William Francis 6, 115, *116*
Woodford, Stewart L. 10
Woodruff, William E. 266
Woods, Charles R. 239
Woods, Isaiah Churchill (alias Isaac C.) 248, 279
Woods, William 248, 279

Woodward, George Abisha 172, 178, *179*
Woodward, William Washington 10, 116, *117*
Wool, John E. 184, 194, 206
Wright, Charles J. *108*
Wright, Edward Henry 180, 209, *210*
Wright, Elias 4
Wright, George 125
Wright, William Wierman 6, *117*, *118*
Wyman, John B. 231

Yeoman, Stephen B. 6
Young, Van Eps 6, *119*, *120*

Zagonyi, Charles 180, 210, *211*, *212*
Zeilin, Jacob 150, 152, *153*
Zerman, Juan Napoleon 248, *280*, *281*
Ziegler, George M. 7
Zulavsky, Ladislas Louis 9, *120*, *121*

www.ingramcontent.com/pod-product-compliance
Lightning Source LLC
Chambersburg PA
CBHW060336010526
44117CB00017B/2843